HATS IN THE RING

JUDAISM AND JEWISH LIFE

Series Editor: Simcha Fishbane, Touro College, New York

Editorial Board:
Geoffrey Alderman (University of Buckingham, Buckingham)
Meir Bar-Ilan (Bar-Ilan University, Ramat Gan)
Herbert Basser (Queen's University, Kingston, Ontario)
Donatella Ester Di Cesare (Universita La Sapienza, Rome)
Roberta Rosenberg Farber (Yeshiva University, New York)
Andreas Nachama (Touro College, Berlin)
Ira Robinson (Concordia University, Montreal)
Nissan Rubin (Bar-Ilan University, Ramat Gan)
Susan Starr Sered (Suffolk University, Boston)
Reeva Spector Simon (Yeshiva University, New York)

HATS IN THE RING

Choosing Britain's Chief Rabbis
from *Adler* to *Sacks*

MEIR PERSOFF

ACADEMIC STUDIES PRESS
Boston 2013

First published in 2013 by Academic Studies Press

28 Montfern Avenue
Brighton, MA 02135
United States of America

press@academicstudiespress.com
www.academicstudiespress.com

Copyright © 2013 Meir Persoff
Meir Persoff has asserted his right under the Copyright, Designs and
Patents Act 1988 to be identified as the author of this work.

Library of Congress Cataloging-in-Publication Data:

Persoff, Meir.
Hats in the Ring: Choosing Britain's chief rabbis from Adler to Sacks / Meir Persoff.
    pages cm. — (Judaism and Jewish life)
Includes bibliographical references and index.
ISBN 978-1-61811-177-7 (cloth)
ISBN 978-1-61811-269-9 (paper)
ISBN 978-1-61811-199-9 (ebook)
1. British Chief Rabbinate—Selection and appointment—History.
2. Rabbis—Selection and appointment—England. I. Title.
BM292.P46 2013
296.6'7—dc23
                              2013000178

All rights reserved. No part of this publication may be reproduced, stored in or introduced into a retrieval system, or transmitted, in any form or by any means, electronic, mechanical, photocopying, recording, or otherwise without the prior written permission of the publisher of this book.

Book design by Adell Medovoy
Typeset in Joanna MT 11/13

Dedicated to the
revered and blessed memory of
Emeritus Chief Rabbi Lord Jakobovits
and Lady Amélie Jakobovits

'Rabbi Yitzchak said: "Do not appoint a leader before consulting the community."'

Talmud, tractate Berachot 55a

Contents

Foreword, by Stefan C. Reif	x
Preface	xv
Chapter One: Out of the Ruins	1
From the Pulpit – I: Guardian of the Law	29
Chapter Two: Between Old and New	40
From the Pulpit – II: The Ideal Jewish Pastor	59
Chapter Three: Who Pays the Piper	66
From the Pulpit – III: Moderation in Judgment	99
Chapter Four: No Imaginary Man	106
Chapter Five: Fateful Days	129
From the Pulpit – IV: Out of the Darkness	153
Chapter Six: A Blank Cheque	160
Chapter Seven: 'When I Return …'	180
From the Pulpit –V: Prophet, Priest and King	207
Chapter Eight: Natural Selection	219
From the Pulpit –VI: A Decade of Jewish Renewal	247
Notes	260
Bibliography	303
Index	326

Foreword

SOME FORTY-FOUR years ago, I was a budding young scholar, about to complete my doctoral dissertation at the University of London. I was anxious to secure a post teaching some aspects of Hebrew and Jewish studies at a university—any university would do—and I was aware that the gift of such preferment lay with the relevant academic committees.

I believed that those charged with making a decision about whom to appoint would be appropriately chosen to serve and would undertake their task in a wholly disinterested fashion. They would use totally objective criteria for judging the candidates, and would simply opt for the applicant who created the best impression.

I had no reason to assume that the situation would be any different in other areas of professional activity. Those pursuing careers or promotions in medical, legal, scientific and financial contexts would also be judged according to their merits by the most apt and qualified team available, as would those who were keen to offer their services as spiritual leaders of a religious community.

Given my years of experience, it is hardly surprising that I am these days often approached by those at the threshold of their careers who are about to undergo a similar trial by ordeal and who are keen to understand how the system operates. Will those with the best qualifications, abilities and experience, who have the finest references and perform best at the interviews, win the victor's garland and be encouraged to go on to do great work? If one is not successful, is this an indication that one lacks the necessary talents? Are those who are finally chosen by the selectors entitled to believe that they belong among the best players in the game?

Alas, I have to disabuse them of any such presuppositions. In my more mature years, I have come to realise that committees, whether academic or of any other variety, are composed of humans with the usual strengths and weaknesses. Those deciding on the composition of the committee, and those making the appointments, are individuals who may at times have their own agendas, biases or political preferences, and who are as often as not unaware that such subjective elements lie behind their views and votes.

In response to their inquiries, I warn those with pretensions to academic recognition not to conclude that the result of their applications is always a fair judge of their capacity and potential. Failure to be chosen for a post, preferment or promotion of one sort or another should not inevitably be seen as a true reflection of who is best, or who may turn out best in the long term. It often tells us more about the members of the body selecting than it does about the candidates.

But, of course, the dark and sometimes heated deliberations of such mandarins take time to emerge into the cold light of history. *Soi-disant* confidentiality, the failure of minutes to reveal more than superficial generalities, and even the conspiratorial tendency, all play a part in denying the current generation any accurate picture of what lies behind the choices made by self-selecting prima donnas performing in the operas of professional life. Are we then forever to be denied the knowledge of what motivated whom, and how this affected major as well as minor appointments?

Fortunately, those with ambitions to uncover history *wie es eigentlich gewesen ist*, as the nineteenth-century German historian Leopold von Ranke put it, or at least as near as we can realistically ever get to the truth of what occurred and why, are in a much more advantageous position today than they were in previous generations. Secret discussions are released after a reasonable amount of time; a wealth of media evidence is available; memoirs, biographies and autobiographies clutter the literary environment; and people in the know seem so much more open to being honestly interviewed than they once were—always assuming that they have reached a degree of seniority that permits them to be frank without giving the proverbial damn.

And so it is that those writing the history of Anglo-Jewry have many dusty archives, dull recollections, and individuals with long memories to consult. But before saying more about the pursuit of such historical knowledge, one is entitled to ask whether it is worth the effort. Is the Jewish community of the British Isles of any special significance in the wider context of the emergence of the modern Jewish world? Does it have special institutions that are worthy of the historian's close attention and, to cite a common view that is often anathema to the more purist of academics, is its history *relevant* to the contemporary situation?

It is well recognised that Jewish populations more often than not reflect the larger communities in which they have settled and flourished. As the Yiddish saying has it, *wie es christelt sich, so es yudelt sich* ('As it goes with Christians, so it goes with Jews'). The United Kingdom became a major, if not the major, imperial force in the course of the second half of the nineteenth century. It wielded great political, military, and cultural power across the globe, and its example was often followed by other nations. It enjoyed an arrogant degree of confidence in its leaders, institutions, and ideologies.

This situation obtained for well-nigh a century, until the exhausting efforts of two world wars and the gradual metamorphosis of an empire into a commonwealth robbed the British of their pre-eminence, as well as their financial security. They were economically and politically overtaken by third-world powers, and culturally modified by the influx of some of the latter's emigrating populations. Depressing decisions then had to be made about what could still be afforded and what remained appropriate for a society that had changed, not only ethnically, but also in its values, interests, and commitments.

By the end of the nineteenth century, the Jewish community of Britain had reached unprecedented levels of population and influence and had become committed to forming itself into a microcosm of the larger British entity. In the realms of welfare, education and spirituality, it took its lead from the dominant population. Appropriate charities, schools and synagogues were formed and managed, and long-established Anglo-Jewish families set the tone in chairing committees, presiding over events, and representing their fellow Jews in fashions that were familiar to them from their wider experiences. Anglicisation, institutionalisation and centralisation were among the key trends and led to the emergence of numerous organisations.

Among the latter was the Chief Rabbinate. Although the Chief Rabbi was primarily the leading rabbi of the centrally Orthodox communities of London, he also functioned as the spiritual head of all religiously similar congregations throughout the British Empire, and there was a limited degree of representation on the part of such congregations on the committees electing the individual who was to occupy this post.

The committees that were given—or gave themselves—the task of appointing successive holders of the post of Chief Rabbi in the nineteenth and twentieth centuries are sensitive historical monitors. A close examination of the work that they did, and of the manner in which they conducted themselves, is capable of clarifying a great deal about what was evolving in Anglo-Jewry and what was resisting change.

What were the criteria that they drew up for making their choice? How did Hebrew and Jewish learning compare with English comportment in the assessment of the candidates? Is it fair to say that the Jewish families who once dominated the scene were genteel aristocrats, while those who ultimately seized power from them represented immigrant parvenus? In which way did the media affect—or indeed control—the events leading up to the choice? Above all, are we now in a position to assess those who assessed others?

The first challenge facing historians desirous of answering such questions is the need to search out all the relevant sources currently available and absorb their content. They will then be required to cherry-pick those items that tell the juiciest tales and draw attention to the instances in which one set of documents appears to contradict another. Once such raw material has been carefully quarried and adequately sorted, it will be subjected to a process of analysis and evaluation. Often those who work on mining the data are not those who do the equivalent of the diamond-cutting.

Meir Persoff excels in ferreting out information and making it available in an accessible and readable fashion to both lay folk and the professional historian. He has already published important volumes that deal with the life and work of Lord Jakobovits, the overall history of the British Chief Rabbinate, and the particular tensions and controversies that have marked the tenure of the current holder of the office, Lord Sacks.

Persoff's avowed policy is generally to uncover material rather than offering his opinions as to its broader historical significance, although it has to be said that he has from time to time left the reader in little doubt about which Chief Rabbis he most admires. He is also on record as challenging the view that the British Chief Rabbinate is an essential component of today's Anglo-Jewish scene, and questioning the assumption that the office has importance far beyond its function within modern Orthodoxy.

Historians sharply focused on Anglo-Jewry will have reason to be grateful to Dr Persoff for the choice fare that he has here set before them. Whatever their views, and however they understand the personalities and interpret the events, they will find themselves in his debt for having drawn attention to such a wealth of source material and for having made available to them many items that were hitherto unknown or inadequately exploited.

Those more interested in current affairs will be aware that the choice of a successor to Lord Sacks has been occupying minds within the United Synagogue—and beyond—and may enjoy comparing today's situation with its earlier counterparts. It may even be the case that those who served, or are serving, on the selection committees will learn something fresh from this volume about the fascinating machinations of their forerunners, their own responsibilities, and the significance of their contemporary decision. Or perhaps the only thing that we can learn from history is that you can never learn anything from history.

STEFAN C. REIF
Emeritus Professor of Medieval Hebrew
and Fellow of St John's College, University of Cambridge

Israeli diplomat Yaacov Herzog (1965): the British Chief Rabbi who never was

Preface

EARLY IN FEBRUARY 2012, for the first time in the history of the British Chief Rabbinate, an advertisement appeared in the press inviting applications for the position of Chief Rabbi of the United Hebrew Congregations of the UK and Commonwealth.[1] Fourteen months earlier, United Synagogue president Simon Hochhauser had told his council that the present incumbent, Lord Sacks of Aldgate—'a hard act to follow'—would be retiring in September 2013, after twenty-two years in office, and that, despite some speculation that he would not be replaced, 'there will be another Chief Rabbi.'[2] Explaining the decision to publish a formal notice, Hochhauser's successor, Stephen Pack, later remarked: 'If you haven't advertised, you will find it difficult to say that you've done a proper trawl through the United Kingdom. That's the kind of banana-skin moment we're trying to avoid.'[3]

'When Jonathan Sacks was appointed in 1990,' commented one well-informed observer,[4] 'he was so firm a favourite, it would have been astonishing had he not got the job. Not only was he widely viewed as the heir-apparent to Lord Jakobovits, but he also had a powerful patron in Lord Kalms, who was chairman of Jews' College when Rabbi Sacks was its principal (though the good lord subsequently lost faith in his protégé). This time, the situation could hardly be more different. There may be some credible candidates, but there are no front-runners and no Kalms figure championing anyone's cause—no prince, no kingmaker.[5] In that sense, Lord Sacks leaves a vacuum rather than a vacancy. But there is still plenty of time for contenders publicly to establish their claims.

'Picking Chief Rabbis in the past has largely been up to lay leaders. It will be interesting this time to see what input there is from United Synagogue rabbis and their regional colleagues. There is a body of opinion that believes the next Chief should be a "rabbi's rabbi," more a captain of the clerical platoon than an envoy to the outside world or a globe-trotting intellectual.'[6]

In support of this view, a prominent United Synagogue rabbi—Mill Hill's Yitzchak Schochet, who chaired the US Rabbinical Council—challenged the prospect of Sacks' successor being chosen by 'a small band of merry men sitting behind closed doors,' and, advocating a United States-style presidential campaign, put his weight behind calls for a publicly elected Chief Rabbi.[7] In due course, Schochet wrote: 'I can confirm that I did not apply for the job. I have two strikes against me which don't sit well with the "establishment." The first is the fact that I'm Chabad ... [and my] other "problem" is that I am too outspoken ...

'"Unity not uniformity" has become the mantra of the US leadership. But a bone of contention among several colleagues is that this is only in words. I inevitably earned the title "maverick" because I give myself permission to communicate what matters to me and put a voice to my soul, despite rejection or disapproval. It is, I am often told, very North American. Not something we approve of in the UK. Which, I suppose, is why we're sitting ducks for verbal abuse hurled from both within and outside the community. I am not suggesting I would have ever got the job of Chief Rabbi, or that I am even qualified. But the hierarchy has its own preconceived idea of "suitable criteria," which may not reflect the reality of its membership. Hence my argument for an election even as I knew it to be untenable—anything but the current process, which is riddled with problems, if not bias and prejudices.'[8]

An elected—rather than appointed—Chief Rabbi was also the inclination of the *Jewish Chronicle*, which argued that 'at a stroke, all the problems which beset Lord Sacks would be removed. His actions would be his actions, not those of a leader forever obligated to others. He will make mistakes; but they will be his mistakes, for which he will want to take full responsibility. And he will have a mandate, having been elected to the job. A leader with a mandate is indeed a leader. An appointee is just that ...

'It is simply wrong that, in the twenty-first century, British Jews can seriously be expected to acquiesce in the next Chief Rabbi's appointment by a coterie of secret insiders. The Israelis do not. The Turks do not. The French do not. They all have different conceptions of the role, and different franchises. But they all elect their Chief Rabbi. If the upper echelons of the United Synagogue accept that times have changed and move to an election, they will strike an important blow and show that they have a serious role to play as leaders of Anglo-Jewry. If they do not, they will demonstrate the exact opposite.'[9]

As I wrote at the time in response to this argument,[10] it matters not whether the new Chief Rabbi is elected, selected, self-selected, or appointed, nor whether the process is democratic or autocratic. The thesis that an election would 'remove all the problems at a stroke' is fallacious if only because, as spiritual leader of the United Synagogue, Sacks' successor will remain as beholden to the London Beth Din as Sacks has been throughout his incumbency.

The United Synagogue's claim to represent 'mainstream Orthodox' (though largely non-observant) members of the community runs counter—and, willy-nilly, will continue to run counter—to its practice of looking over its shoulder so as not to appear any less Orthodox than those to its right. The religious direction of the US will be dictated more by that practice than by any influence the new Chief Rabbi—Finchley Synagogue's Ephraim Mirvis—might seek to wield. Whether this is as it should be is another question, but it nevertheless remains a fact of contemporary Jewish life.

Setting out its stall for the 2013 appointment,[11] the US hierarchy—describing the Chief Rabbi as 'religious head of the United Hebrew Congregations communities'—noted that, 'as such, [he] provides religious authority and guidance to the rabbinical and lay leadership in those communities,' and would 'act as the Av Beth Din of the London Beth Din and be prepared to chair sittings of the Dayanim when necessary.'

Among other duties, he would be 'the spiritual leader and religious teacher of all bodies that recognise the authority of his office; be a religious spokesman for Orthodox Judaism; be a spokesman on all matters affecting the Jewish community; lead and inspire the rabbis of his communities; and be a spiritual voice for the wider community ... In conducting these duties, the Chief Rabbi will be expected to behave with absolute personal and professional integrity, and to maintain and encourage proper and correct behaviour among all other members of the Rabbinate, other staff and general membership of all bodies under his aegis.'

* * *

In the seven Chief Rabbinical appointments preceding the latest process (as will be seen, Yaacov Herzog did not take up his 1965 post), the qualifications sought of the successful candidates varied enormously, in keeping with the requirements—and currents—of the times. Nathan Adler's election, in 1844, followed the death of eighty-year-old Solomon Hirschell, whose opposition to Britain's first Reform Jews some three years earlier had sparked a schism that took decades to subside, though was never to heal.

It was 'the unanimous desire of all classes of the Israelites'—wrote 'A Friend of Truth' to the committee of electors—'that only such men are in nomination for the office who are wholly of our own time, and not embued with the prejudices and bigotry of the darker ages ... A man who is to be considered capable to guide Israel must be possessed of the following pre-eminent qualities over all the rest of his brethren. He must be a hero in mind, and the characteristics of such are: a calm, grave, mild and consistent disposition; a penetrating understanding; a comprehensive and quick conception; a rational, reflecting and discreet judgment; and an extensive and skilful experience in government. To those who are aware that the Jewish inhabitants of England are descendants from many different countries and therefore frequently entertain different opinions on the same subjects, it will not appear too much to expect that a Rabbi should unite all these qualities, in order to reconcile this diversity of opinion.'[12]

Aligning itself with these objectives, The Voice of Jacob similarly called for a Chief Rabbi 'endowed with that energy of purpose which may give effect to his own zeal, while it guides that of others in a channel conducive to the interests which he represents. And, moreover, he must have acquired a general insight into the wants and peculiarities of the various bodies among which he has to maintain a good understanding, and a bond of sacred union.'[13]

Hermann Adler, Nathan's son and heir to the Chief Rabbinate, was not subjected to a contested election, but nevertheless faced a radically altered community in 1890 from that inherited by his father. 'How greatly has the Hebrew population of the United Kingdom expanded within the last half-century,' he remarked on taking up office.[14] 'And how heterogeneous are the elements of this population, widely differing in their culture, ranging between the two extremes of the religious thermometer, each section needing a different kind of handling!' So different were they, in fact, that by the end of his twenty-year tenure, he felt impelled to call for a successor with 'a strong personality, strong in piety and learning, one who will be equally acceptable to the East and the West, the native and the immigrant.'[15]

Nathaniel ('Natty') de Rothschild—the first Lord Rothschild, and holder of the reins within the United Synagogue hierarchy—formulated the rules guiding Adler's successor. 'If he is not acquainted with English life and English laws,' he declared,[16] 'he will not be a fit person to be the religious head of the Jews of England. That, at the present moment, is much more important than it ever was. Your Chief Rabbi, if he is not exactly an Englishman, if he has not been to an English university, should be able to speak and preach in English, and should have a knowledge of English communities. That is, in my opinion, absolutely necessary, because it is one of the duties, and one of the great duties, of the Chief Rabbi to see that all your ministers and chazanim should be able to speak English, and do all in his power to prevent the teaching and the spread of slang and jargon-like Yiddish.'

Again, a hugely different—post-Holocaust and traumatised—community confronted US president Sir Robert Waley Cohen and his acolytes, spiritual and lay, when faced with the succession to Joseph Herman Hertz in 1946. 'The tragic events in the contemporary history of European Jewry,' asserted the dayanim of the London Beth Din, headed by the Lithuanian-born sage, Yechezkel Alter Abramsky, 'have brought it about that the Anglo-Jewish community is now the last bastion of Jewish religious life in Europe.' It was their 'deep conviction that the Chief Rabbinate must have a far-reaching influence upon the grave question whether this bastion of the Anglo-Jewish community will grow stronger and form the nucleus of a new Jewish communal life in Europe, or whether it will disintegrate and end in schism and heresy.'[17]

To that end, agreed Waley Cohen, he and his electoral team had 'conjured up for themselves a very fine ideal of a man to hold this great office. He must be a man whose character rested upon a deep and sincere Jewish spiritual foundation. He must also be a profound scholar, able to take his place as head of the Beth Din, and to give authoritative guidance to all of them in religious matters. He must be able to expound the teachings of Judaism so as to attract and inspire the minds and characters of Jews and Jewesses of all ages living in the British Commonwealth and Empire and playing their part in its national life.'[18]

While referring to the Chief Rabbi's leadership of the London Beth Din, Waley Cohen had perhaps turned a blind eye to another of the requisites laid down by the dayanim. 'The Chief Rabbi,' they had stipulated, 'will, ex officio, be the president of this most important contemporary Jewish court of law. A man, therefore, who is out of tune with the strict adherence of the London Beth Din to traditional Jewish law, as handed down in Talmud and Shulchan Aruch, will of necessity cause schism in contemporary Jewish life. For the London Beth Din will accept the guidance only of a man whose orthodoxy is beyond question and recognition in the orthodox rabbinical world; and the religious future of Anglo-Jewry must be bound up with, and depend upon, the harmonious relationship of Chief Rabbi and Beth Din.'[19]

The ensuing chapters will illustrate how the dayanim's influence on the choice of Chief Rabbi thereafter grew increasingly forceful with each contest, and how their counsel was unfailingly the last port of call before an appointment was made. Despite contentions to the contrary in recent fields of Anglo-Jewish historiography,[20] the Beth Din's hold over the British Chief Rabbinate, discernible as early as—if not earlier than—the pre-war arrival of Abramsky, brought a decisive change in the direction and composition of the United Synagogue over the closing decades of the twentieth century. 'It was Dayan Abramsky above all,' acknowledges the US, 'who established the policies and customs that are followed by the London Beth Din to this day.'[21]

* * *

As indicated earlier, and as my previous studies have shown,[22] today's Anglo-Jewry is far distant, both in complexion and construction, from that over which the Adlers—or Abramsky, for that matter—held sway. Nathan Adler's incumbency, remarked the *Jewish Chronicle* following his death,[23] had extended over 'the most momentous period that has yet been recorded in the history of

English Judaism. His accession to office was almost exactly coincident with the establishment of the "Reform" synagogue in London. That event was at once the witness and the impulse to a discontent with the special interpretation of Judaism which Dr Adler was chosen to uphold.

'There can be no question that the religious opinions of English Jews have undergone slow but considerable changes during the past forty years; and it is almost equally certain that the "Reform" movement has largely helped to produce them. Still more potent has been the influence of the social and intellectual progress which has marked the annals of the community during the last few decades ...

'Dr Adler was installed in 1845 and, in the long interval that separates that era from the present time, how vast are the strides that English Jews have made in point of culture and in social power! One by one, the disabilities, both legal and prescriptive, under which they laboured half a century ago, have been removed. They are now the peers of their fellow countrymen, not only in the eyes of the law, but in the eyes of that equally potent authority—public opinion.

'It was inevitable that so mighty a revolution in their lot would be accompanied by important changes in their religious ideas. The English Jew could not possibly have taken the place in the wide world which was his by right without feeling the impact of the world's thought. He could not avoid being swept on by the great wave of inquiry which has so powerfully influenced the recent history of every religious communion.'

The spread within Anglo-Jewry of that 'great wave of inquiry' and, consequently, of religious pluralism—as well as the diverse strands of immigration, ethnicity and culture—was in time to hasten the weakening of Britain's Chief Rabbinate as 'a position of authority somewhat parallel to that of the Archbishop of Canterbury in the Anglican Church.'[24] This nineteenth-century vision, argues Norman Cohen, 'undoubtedly fostered the conception that the Chief Rabbinate was an ecclesiastical rather than a halachic eminence, which strengthened his standing in the non-Jewish world. He was without a rival as the representative of the Jewish faith.'[25] As a result, despite the intrepid march of Reform and Liberal Judaism in the early decades of the twentieth century, the inter-war years provided 'the golden age of homogeneity, unity and communal bliss,'[26] doubling the size of the United Synagogue to fifty congregations.

By the end of the Second World War, however, that scenario had changed, ascribed by Jakobovits to the altered atmosphere and direction dictated by wartime conditions. 'The fairly homogeneous, almost monolithic, character of Anglo-Jewry,' he asserted at a London conference in 1977,[27] 'was long ago transferred into a pluralistic society, especially with the heavy refugee influx before, during and after the war. The cohesion of "mainstream Judaism" as the broad heartland encompassing the vast majority of "average" Anglo-Jews has been preserved until more recent times. But, during the past fifteen years, this pattern has changed quite radically, and with increasing speed, as the centrifugal forces have gained momentum.'

'The pace of this change,' observed the Institute for Jewish Policy Research in 2000, 'has placed considerable strain on the historic central representative structures—the Board of Deputies of British Jews and the Chief Rabbinate. Questions have been raised as to why Jewish representative institutions have been unable to defuse tensions and resolve disputes that frequently surface in the public sphere.'[28]

Evident since the evolution of the modern Chief Rabbinate, these tensions have erupted unceasingly in every incumbency. Nathan Adler's peaked with Orthodox rebellion, while his son saw the 'old paths' wither away. Hertz failed to halt the Liberal advance; Brodie the emergence of Masorti; and Jakobovits the crumbling of his 'bridges of understanding.' Of Sacks' tenure, Kalms told me during the writing of this book: 'He stood on the platform of inclusivism, aiming to bring the left and right together by finding common ground. As things turned out, this was a failure and, in many ways, a disaster for the community, but the facts on that are on the record.'[29]

In light of the six Chief Rabbinates examined in this series of studies, the incumbency of Sacks' successor will do much to shape the character of British Jewry over the coming years. That the tensions will persist is, of course, beyond doubt. Whether Chief Rabbi Mirvis will be 'a spiritual voice for the wider community' depends both on the nature of his office and on the strength and confidence he will be able to manifest in being his own man.

* * *

I am again indebted to the families of the late Emeritus Chief Rabbi Lord Jakobovits, Rabbi Dr Louis Jacobs and Rabbi Dr Sidney Brichto for the unprecedented access afforded me to their personal papers during the writing of this volume and, indeed, my earlier books on the British Chief Rabbinate. I also reiterate my deepest gratitude—first expressed publicly in *Immanuel Jakobovits: a Prophet in Israel*[30]—for the help, advice, hospitality, co-operation and kindness I received over many years from the late Lady Amélie Jakobovits, whose kitchen table frequently provided a close and confidential platform over which she imparted words of wisdom that have remained a source of comfort and inspiration on both a personal and professional level. After their return to Britain in the mid-1960s, as my career on the *Jewish Chronicle* steadily progressed, she and her revered husband, of blessed memory, became cherished friends and counsellors well beyond the call of duty, and it is in large measure to them that I owe my interest, and subsequent academic activity, in the field I have chosen to study.

I also offer thanks to the many friends, colleagues, libraries and institutions that once again opened their minds, files, doors and drawers—some more secret, and secretive, than others—in the recognised search for integrity and truth, without which the story and history of modern British Jewry cannot possibly be told. In relating the facts contained herein—and relying, as ever, on the protagonists' own words—I have discerned that certain key areas are closed to public scrutiny, and can only surmise that, for reasons at present unknown, many recent documents have been withheld which perhaps, one day, will shed further light on the events reviewed.

In the preparation of this volume, especial thanks are due to Ann Harris, Rabbi Dr Reuven Bulka, Professor Leslie Wagner, Rabbi Dr Raymond Apple, Lord Kalms, Professor Geoffrey Alderman, Rabbi Dr Harvey Meirovich, Dr Miri Freud-Kandel, Professor Aubrey Newman, Dr Lionel Kopelowitz, Dr Gavriel Sivan, Dr Leonard Roselaar, Simon Rocker, Tracy Abraham, Sue Greenberg, Jenni Tinson, Evelyne Schiff, Jeff Finger, Judy Lash Balint, Jackie Persoff, Dr Igor Nemirovsky, Kira Nemirovskaya, and Sharona Vedol. London Metropolitan Archives (LMA); the *Jewish Chronicle*; the Hebrew and National Library (Hebrew University of Jerusalem); the S. Zalman and Ayala Abramov Library (Hebrew Union College–Jewish Institute of Religion, Jerusalem campus); the Special Collection Reading Room, Library of the Jewish Theological Seminary of America; and the Jewish Historical Society of England (London and Jerusalem) have extended, as always, a munificent hand. I am particularly grateful to Erla Zimmels, librarian of the London School of Jewish Studies (formerly Jews' College), whose kind help during my research into the Chief Rabbinate proved of inestimable value.

To Professor Stefan C. Reif—with whom I worked for nearly three decades on Cambridge University Library's *Genizah Fragments*—I owe a lasting debt for his characteristically stimulating foreword to this book. As an eminent scholar in the field of Hebrew and Jewish studies, and a perceptive observer of Anglo-Jewry's recent chequered history (not least that of the past three Chief Rabbinates), he is well-placed to cast a keen and critical eye over the events narrated here. His comments will be of notable concern to those charged with leading the community into a new and challenging phase, one of crucial importance to its future well-being.

MEIR PERSOFF
Jerusalem
January 2013, Shevat 5773

CHAPTER ONE

Out of the Ruins

ON SHABBAT MORNING, 22 January 1842, amid widespread controversy and deep disquiet, Anglo-Jewry's last formal *cherem*—excommunication (or 'anathema,' as it came to be known)—was proclaimed 'by the secretaries of the principal Metropolitan Synagogues from their respective reading-desks.'[1] Promulgated by Solomon Hirschell—officially the rabbi of the Great Synagogue, Duke's Place, though more popularly described as 'Chief Rabbi' or, in gentile circles, as 'The High Priest of the Jews of England'[2]—the decree followed the publication of the community's first reformist Siddur and preceded, by five days, the consecration of the West London Synagogue of British Jews and, with it, the introduction into Britain of Reform Judaism.

Descended from a family of distinguished scholars who had occupied the Great Synagogue pulpit since the mid-eighteenth century, the London-born Hirschell—then aged thirty-three and the rabbi of Prenzlow in Germany—had first applied for the post in 1794, three years after the death of Rabbi David Tevele Schiff. For financial reasons, however, the congregation's leaders delayed the appointment by several years, and it was not until 1801 that the position was advertised over much of Europe, with several prospective candidates offering their services. Of these, three were considered—though none was invited to London for an interview—and, in an election on 3 June of that year, Hirschell gained sixty-two votes as against eighteen for Rabbi Arye of Rotterdam, and just three for Rabbi Zvi Hirsch of Krotoschin, Poland.

Two years before the *cherem*, six Ashkenazim from Hirschell's congregation had joined forces with eighteen Sephardim from Britain's oldest post-Resettlement synagogue, Bevis Marks, in a revolt against what they described as 'evils' in the traditional Orthodox service. 'Regarding Public Worship as highly conducive to the interests of Religion,' they had declared, 'we consider it a matter of deep regret that it is not more frequently attended by the Members of our Religious Persuasion.

> We are perfectly sure that this circumstance is not owing to any want of a general conviction of the fundamental Truths of our Religion, but we ascribe it to *the distance of the existing synagogues from the place of our residence; to the length and imperfections of the Order of Service; to the inconvenient hours at which it is appointed; to the unimpressive manner in which it is performed; and to the absence of religious Instruction in our Synagogues.*
>
> To these evils we think that a remedy may be applied by the establishment of a *Synagogue in the Western part of the Metropolis*, where a revised Service may be performed at hours more suited to our habits, and in *a manner more calculated to inspire feelings of devotion*, where *Religious instruction may be afforded by competent persons*, and where, to effect these purposes, Jews generally may form an *United Congregation* under the denomination of *British Jews*. Anxious for the accomplishment of these objects, it is our wish that a meeting may be called for the purpose of considering the best means of carrying them into effect.³

The upshot of their appeal was the issue of a defiant letter to 'the Gentleman Elders of the Spanish and Portuguese Synagogue,' outlining the principles by which their new congregation was to be guided: 'proper decorum during the performance of divine worship'; services at 'convenient' hours and of 'moderate length'; a 'careful revision' of the daily and Sabbath prayer-book; English-language sermons; and the abolition of *aliyot* and offerings, except on the 'three great festivals.'

'Such are the views we have endeavoured to carry into effect, and we earnestly assure you they have not been suggested by any desire of schism, or separation ... but through a sincere conviction that substantial improvements in the public worship are essential to the weal of our sacred religion, and that they will be the means of handing down to our children, and to our children's children, our holy faith in all its purity and integrity. Indeed, we are firmly convinced that their tendency will be to arrest and prevent *secession from Judaism—an overwhelming evil*, which has at various times so widely spread among many of the most respectable families of our communities.'

Anticipating the reactions to their move, the rebels added: 'In thus establishing a new Synagogue, on the principles hitherto not recognised or approved by your body, we may possibly encounter a considerable difference of opinion, and a strong prejudice against our proceedings; but, having been actuated solely by a conscientious sense of duty, we venture to hope that on further consideration, our intentions and our motives will be duly appreciated, and that those kindly feelings which ought to exist between every community of Jews will be maintained in all force between the respective congregations which you represent, and the small body whose views we have herein endeavoured to explain.'[4]

It was not to be. Angered by this mutinous show of strength, which threatened to tear apart the fabric of London Jewry, a meeting of communal leaders was held on 9 September 1841, at which the edict of excommunication was drawn up by Hirschell and his ecclesiastical colleagues—held in abeyance, however, in the hope that the 'refractory reformers' would relent and return to the fold. When this hope failed to materialise, there emerged first a denunciation of the 'iniquitous' prayer-book and its errant editor, and then, several weeks later, the *cherem* itself, implemented through a series of letters circulated by Sir Moses Montefiore, president of the Board of Deputies, to the wardens of every Jewish congregation in the country:

DECLARATION

23, Bury-street, 24 Ellul 5601.
Information having reached me, from which it appears that certain persons calling themselves British Jews, publicly and in their published book of prayer, reject the Oral Law, I deem it my duty to declare that, according to the laws and statutes held sacred by the whole House of Israel, any person or persons publicly declaring that he or they reject and do not believe in the authority of the Oral Law cannot be permitted to have any communion with us Israelites in any religious rites or sacred act. I therefore earnestly entreat and exhort all God-fearing Jews, especially parents, to caution and instruct all persons belonging to our faith that they be careful to attend to this declaration, and that they be not induced to depart from our holy laws.

S. HIRSCHELL, Chief Rabbi.

We, the undersigned, fully concurring in the foregoing doctrines, as set forth by the Reverend Solomon Hirschell, certify such our concurrence under our hand this 24 Ellul 5601, A.M.

DAVID MELDOLA; A. LEVY; J. LEVY; A. S. BARNETT;
A. HALIVA.

The promulgation of the above declaration has been delayed in the hope that there would have been no necessity to give it

> publicity: circumstances, however, now require that it should be no longer withheld from the community.
> 9 Shevat 5602.

By the time of this declaration, Hirschell—old, frail and dispirited by the ongoing and taxing dispute over which he appeared to have little control—was in failing health and confined (as long before) to his study and his books. Some months later, he fell from his chair and broke his collar-bone, succumbing to his injuries on the eve of Rosh Chodesh Kislev, 5603–1842. Immediately, the Reform secession and its effects on the selection of his successor began to dominate the hearts and minds of the Orthodox fraternity—and well beyond.

Press and pamphleteers, congregational leaders and congregants, not to mention commentators as far afield as Berlin and Leipzig, spared no effort in urging strong, effective and harmonious leadership on the road to repairing the fractured community. The tone was set early by the *Voice of Jacob*, in its first issue following Hirschell's interment: 'The tomb having closed over our late spiritual head, the necessity for a well-organised, a firmly and wisely administered system of spiritual guidance, is far too urgent for any regard to what were a false delicacy, if it avoided to prepare the public mind for the requirements of this peculiar juncture.

'Peace be to the ashes of the departed! It is those who survive, who are either responsible for a most accountable short-sightedness—in failing to anticipate and provide for a crisis long impending—or else, chargeable with a shrinking from the duties, however unpleasant, which their position imposed upon them—a shrinking, which will be found to have destroyed much of that moral influence, that might else have been theirs, on questions of this character.

> Happily for them, and for all classes, but one feeling prevails, everywhere, on the necessity of appointing a successor to our departed Rabbi, and that, too, with all consistent speed. We know not, indeed, whether the very dissensions now deplored, the very errors committed in that contumacy which—producing a crisis for which the decayed powers of Dr Hirschell were no longer equal, are said to have hastened his final decay—we know not, we repeat, whether it is not those very evils, and their probable results, that have roused the public mind from that apathy which was their precursor, and which, but a few years since, would not have admitted the unanimous consent, now attainable, for the election of another spiritual chief.

> This unanimity, it is true, does, as yet, merely recognise the necessity of such uniform guidance, and shew a disposition to support and to yield obedience to it, in all consistent particulars. But that it does exist to that extent is ascertainable not only from the declarations we hear from men entertaining otherwise heterogeneous notions, but from communications to the like effect that we continue to receive ...
>
> If some qualified rabbi, of established reputation, of classical and general attainments, of experience in his vocation, of ability to understand, and discretion to use, the times, be proposed, and almost universally invited to assume the reins of government, then, while his character will guarantee his competency, his functions will enable him to set right those that are pledged to act in concert under him: his experience, and examples found elsewhere, will enable him to organise the elements at his disposal ...
>
> If no rabbi be found who can so unite, *a priori*, the suffrages of the great body of the Jews, then the adoption of a representative system must precede the selection of a spiritual chief; this plan will present more difficulties than the other, but they are by no means insurmountable. In this case, representatives from every congregation may be sent up, chosen on the principle enunciated, and pledged to have no regard to separate objects, or to individual predilections.
>
> The immediate purpose of this conclave should be to devise a constitution; there are models at hand, and if the abstract principles of justice alone be kept in view, no material differences can arise. A constitution so formed—a Chief Rabbi would be elected under it.

Of the secessionists, the leader-writer declared: 'We are much mistaken if some of the more accessible to reason among them are not already disposed to redeem their errors; personal inflexibility may yet sustain some in the wrong, but while it cannot be denied that they have put themselves out of court, and though it will scarcely, as we apprehend, be consented to invite them back, yet, if they too shall seize the emergency and seem disposed to retire from their self-chosen exclusion with dignity, there will surely not be any who would dare to refuse their peace-offering.'[5]

That this conclusion was more wishful thinking than well-informed conjecture was soon to become apparent, though the subsequent election procedure bore out the paper's view that 'a constitution so formed—a Chief

Rabbi would be elected under it.' What it had not foreseen, however, was the wrangling and finger-wagging that would prolong the process by more than two years.

In this regard, one 'well-informed provincial correspondent' was later to warn that, 'unless a Chief Rabbi be obtained very soon, schism and disgrace will await our coreligionists.' This followed his assertion, supported 'on the authority of letters from London,' that 'if the Great Synagogue do not adopt measures to provide a place of worship for those resident at the West End of London, there will be a new movement in opposition to established institutions, more formidable than any yet attempted.'[6]

Meanwhile, the process of selecting a new Chief Rabbi began in earnest, within days of Hirschell's death. 'With a promptitude which does them honour,'[7] the Great Synagogue circulated a series of 'pertinently drawn and unanimously adopted' resolutions to the congregations of the Empire, declaring that 'it is highly important and expedient that the vacant office of Chief Rabbi should be filled up at as early a period as may be possible,' and that 'it would greatly contribute to the upholding of the Jewish religion in its purity, diffusing a more correct knowledge of its precepts, and to the general harmony and well-being of the community, if a Chief Rabbi should be duly authorised as the spiritual guide and director of all the Jews of this Empire.'

Within a fortnight, views were forthcoming on 'the qualifications requisite to be possessed by the Spiritual Chief now to be elected.'[8] Foremost was the necessity 'to be a man of ascertained piety and established reputation, so that his former career shall in some wise be a guarantee for his future course.' He had to be 'thoroughly acquainted with the various branches which properly constitute Jewish Theology—a classical scholar in the accepted sense of the term.

'He must possess ability to express himself with effect, both with the pen and orally. He must have a practical knowledge of the world from personal observation. Not only must he not be a passive spectator of what may transpire around him, but he must be endowed with that energy of purpose which may give effect to his own zeal, while it guides that of others in a channel conducive to the interests which he represents. And, moreover, he must have acquired a general insight into the wants and peculiarities of the various bodies among which he has to maintain a good understanding, and a bond of sacred union.'

The *Voice of Jacob* subsequently proclaimed, 'on authority' and with 'great satisfaction,' that these principles had met with 'hearty concurrence on all sides ... and the future Chief Rabbi of our communities will, as we have reason to hope, represent that bond of union among them which will be at once their honour and their safety.'

While it was 'yet too early to canvass personal claims to what, from our peculiarity of position, either is, or will be, the most important post among European Jews, we have only to repeat, that if some one eminent name shall be found to unite the suffrages of a majority, rendering a contested election and its inconveniences avoidable, then it will be scarcely needful to do more than arrange, *a priori*, the elements of a constitution, under which the election shall take place.'[9]

Too early or not 'to canvass personal claims,' communal gossip soon ensured that no time was lost in circulating the names of possible candidates. 'Thus,' wrote the paper, 'we no longer hesitate to give the three names which occupy attention. They are Dr [Hirsch] Hirschfeld, Chief Rabbi of Wollstein; Dr [Samson Raphael] Hirsch, Chief Rabbi of Emden; and Dr [Nathan Marcus] Adler, Chief Rabbi of Hanover.' But a note of caution—justified by subsequent events—accompanied the names:

> It is not improbable that when the time arrives that an indirect canvass would not be premature, the friends of some individual candidate might, in their zeal, so injure his cause as to promise, in his behalf, an adherence to some special line of procedure, involving pledges *a priori*. It is, therefore, perhaps only useful to allude thus publicly to the settled conviction that appears to prevail—that such a pledged candidate would not be a free agent using his own observation, and conscientiously governed by his own convictions.
>
> We are assured that even the most popular candidate would be considered ineligible, even at the eleventh hour, unless he were able to give a solemn assurance that he came *unfettered*, and that his supporters had exacted no more from him than an unreserved profession of principle, and, as an only security, the guarantee afforded by the history of his past administration. Public opinion appears opposed to a popular election of such an official, except in so far as it would be secured by a special election of delegates, with whom the selection should ultimately rest—every member of the congregation having a vote in the appointment of those delegates.[10]

Despite the speed with which the names appeared—that of Benjamin Auerbach, Chief Rabbi of Darmstadt, was added later to the final list, while a further nine applicants were deemed ineligible for selection, 'not having complied in various particulars with the published requisitions'[11]—a full twenty-four months were to pass before a victor emerged.

Congregational back-biting and factional posturing were among the causes, with the recalcitrant Western Synagogue the leading culprit. One disillusioned member reported that, despite its initial support, the Western had 'stultified its concurring resolutions' by evading the appointment of representatives to the selection committee, 'and thus our congregation is left without any voice in this important business.'

Underlying this apparent indifference was 'a suspicion ... that a disposition to favour and sympathise with certain seceders from Orthodox Judaism has been permitted, undetected, to influence gentlemen whose attachment to the holy faith of Israel in its purity, and to the institutions of our fathers, is otherwise unimpeachable.

'This suspicion,' so the report went, 'is founded upon the fact that the gentleman who dictated the recent evasive reply acted (as an unelected member of the committee of our synagogue) at his own special request, for the purpose of dictating that same evasion, that gentleman being indirectly connected with the Burton Street [West London Synagogue] secession—for, though not generally recognised as one of its members, he is certainly a subscriber of a large amount.'[12] Whether or not the suspicion was well founded—and there was undoubtedly a Reform bias among the members—within a week the Western's delegates were duly appointed.[13]

The conditions and qualifications pertaining to the Chief Rabbinate, and the procedure for the election, were thereupon speedily approved by representatives of the metropolitan and provincial congregations, meeting at the Great Synagogue on 19 and 21 February 1843. Notable among the conditions was one severely limiting—and, in effect, prohibiting—any future imposition of the *cherem*:

> 1. That this Conference, having heard the Resolutions of the Committee of the Great Synagogue on 14 November last, are of opinion that it is desirable that a Chief Rabbi be appointed, duly authorised as the Spiritual Guide and Director of all the Jews of this Empire.
> 2. That the amount required for the maintenance of the dignity of the office of Chief Rabbi be raised by sums to be contributed by the various Congregations in the Empire, in such manner as shall be hereafter agreed upon.
> 3. That no person be admitted a Candidate unless he be a Chief Rabbi, and must have held such office at least six months immediately preceding the death of the late lamented Rev Solomon Hirschell.
> 4. That each Candidate shall present to the Committee testimonials of ability from Chief Rabbis and others, and shall

be expected to be well acquainted with Ancient Classical and Modern General Literature, and to have a competent knowledge of some of the Modern European Languages.

5. That he shall be able to deliver Discourses when required; and the successful Candidate will be expected to qualify himself to deliver such Discourses in the English Language, within two years from the date of his appointment.

6. That the Candidates shall not be under thirty, nor above forty-two years of age, at Rosh Hashanah 5603.

7. That a Committee, consisting of the same number and in the same proportion as compose this Conference (of whom eleven shall form a quorum), be appointed by the several uniting London Congregations to select Candidates, and that from the number of Candidates for the vacant office, not less than two, nor more than five, be returned for election.

8. That it is desirable, in the election of Chief Rabbi, the votes of each Synagogue be taken separately, agreeably to their own regulations; but that the Candidate returned by each Synagogue be taken as having each a number of votes estimated, according to the amount subscribed by such Congregation, on the following Scale:

Per Annum				Per Annum			
£5, and under	£10,	1 Vote		£50, and under	£75,	10 Votes	
£10,	"	£15,	2 Votes	£75,	"	£100,	20 "
£15,	"	£20,	3 "	£100,	"	£150,	25 "
£20,	"	£25,	4 "	£150,	"	£200,	30 "
£25,	"	£30,	5 "	£200,	"	£300,	35 "
£30,	"	£40,	6 "	£300,	"	£400,	40 "
£40,	"	£50,	8 "	£400, and upwards		50 "	

9. That this Conference is of opinion that the Salary of the intended Chief Rabbi should be not less than £1,100 per annum, which shall include the payment of an efficient Secretary, and the sum of £100 annually for a Life Assurance (such Policy of Insurance to be considered as a provision for the family of the Chief Rabbi after his decease), but shall be irrespective of what may be required

for the annual payment of an Ecclesiastical Board.

10. That the Delegation for the Great Synagogue having stated their intention to recommend their Congregation to subscribe an annual amount of £500 (irrespective of what they now contribute to the Ecclesiastical Board), the several Congregations in London and the Provinces be requested to intimate to the Secretary, by letter, or through their representative, on or before 20 March next, the amount they will be willing to contribute towards the annual fund required for the purpose.

11. That the Honorary Officers, and three of the committee of the Great Synagogue, together with the Honorary Officers (for the time being) of the other London uniting Synagogues, do constitute a permanent committee, with which the Chief Rabbi may communicate, when necessary, on any subject relative to the exercise of the duties of his office, through the medium of the President of the Great Synagogue.

12. That should it unfortunately happen that the Rav should fail in his duty, the conjoint committee, composed as above, shall in the first instance inquire into the matter; and, if they deem it requisite, convene a meeting of twenty-three Delegates (to be elected by the vestries of the London uniting congregations, in the same proportion as constitute this conference), and such body, consisting of the conjoint committee and delegates, shall, after investigation, be empowered to do what is just and necessary.

13. That the Chief Rabbi shall have the general religious direction and superintendence of each of the uniting congregations.

14. That he shall determine all questions on religious points referred to him by any member of any such congregation.

15. That he shall deliver Discourses in the several Synagogues, at such times as shall be hereafter arranged.

16. That he shall perform the Marriage Ceremony for the Members and Seatholders of all the uniting London congregations, their widows and children, under such regulations as shall be hereafter agreed upon.

17. That he shall superintend the affairs of Shechitah, both in London and the Provinces, assisted by the gentlemen of

the Beth Din, under such regulations as may be adopted by the conjoint committee of the Shechitah.
18. That he shall determine all religious matters referred to him by any of the Subscribing Provincial Congregations, and shall give *hatarat kiddushin*, without fee, on receiving a request from the President of any such Congregation, provided he see no cause to withhold such permission, and shall give *kabbalah* when a Shochet is required.
19. That he shall be recommended to visit the Public Educational Establishments, and to assist in carrying out their objects.
20. That he shall on no account denounce *cherem* (anathema) against any person; neither shall he deprive any member of his religious rights in the Synagogue, without the consent of the Committee of the Congregation to which such person shall belong.[14]
21. That he shall occasionally visit the country, to superintend the religious condition of the Provincial Congregations, at such periods as his duties in London will permit; the mode of disbursement to be arranged at a future meeting.
22. That copies of the foregoing Resolutions be forwarded to the Presidents of each of the Metropolitan and Provincial Synagogues, and to the Colonies.
23. That the cordial thanks of this meeting be given to Isaac Cohen, Esq., for his very able and impartial conduct in the Chair.[15]

Delays in implementing the election procedure were aggravated, however, by uncertainty on the part of the Spanish and Portuguese Congregation—without a Haham since the death of Raphael Meldola[16] in June 1828 ('in the twenty-third year of his priesthood,' as the *Annual Register* put it)—over whether or not to participate in the poll. Its indecision turned on 'the expediency of the congregation appointing a Chief Rabbi for itself, after its own *minhag*, as in times when the policy of that community was more exclusive.'[17] In the event, the Sephardim excluded themselves.

Commenting on their decision, the *Voice of Jacob* later remarked: "The Congregation of Sephardim, in Bevis Marks, is the only one recognised synagogue which is not a party to these important measures. Sooner or later, this anomalous position must prove untenable, as we think is now perceived by even a larger number of its members than voted for the union, for all common purposes, last year.

'The impossibility of that separate Synagogue's supporting, with adequate dignity, a Chief Rabbi such as these critical times require has been proved too lately to need a laboured comment. All now agree that a Spiritual Guide, able to command veneration for his functions, and wise to exercise power, is the great desideratum of the Anglo-Jewish communities; how admirable then will it be when the most ancient and interesting of those communities shall prove itself superior to that unworthy jealousy which the popular voice ascribes as the ground of its isolation, and shall frankly assume its true position in the van of what is certainly the most important movement of our times, as it also offers the best guarantee for the future peace of Israel.'[18]

Several months were to pass before any advance was made in selecting Hirschell's successor, leading the press to declare that 'many and anxious are the representations which reach us of the desirableness of progress in this important matter.' For its part, the Great Synagogue saw a need to widen the Rabbinate's jurisdiction, the laws of the congregation, as then prevailing, being 'adapted for a Chief Rabbi over that body exclusively.'[19] Once the 'process of repeal and enactment' was carried out, the remaining synagogues within the electoral orbit were similarly enfranchised, giving them 'full powers to prosecute this important business to a speedy termination.'[20]

This cleared the way for Samuel Helbert Ellis, as chairman of the Committee of Correspondence on Matters Relating to the Office of Chief Rabbi, to designate 31 July 1844 as the final date for the receipt of applications. Congregational wardens in Altona, Amsterdam, Berlin, Frankfurt, Hamburg, Hanover, Paris, Posen, Prague and Vienna were sent copies of the conditions and requirements, with a request that 'they afford to worthy inquirers every information contained therein.'

No person would be admitted as a candidate, the Committee ruled, unless he had held the position of Chief Rabbi on or before Rosh Chodesh Sivan, 5602 [1842]. Each applicant was required to present testimonials of ability from 'Chief Rabbies and others' and was expected 'to be well acquainted with Ancient, Classical and Modern General Literature, and to have a competent knowledge of some of the Modern European Languages.'

The Committee stipulated that prospective candidates 'shall be able to deliver Discourses when required; and the successful candidate will be expected to qualify himself to deliver such Discourses in the English Language within two years from the date of his appointment.' Finally, the candidates 'shall not have been under thirty, nor above forty-two years of age, at Rosh Hashanah 5603.' As only Chief Rabbis now filling situations were eligible as candidates, the personal attendance of applicants was not desired.

Heartened by these signs of progress, the *Voice of Jacob* seized the moment to renew its appeal for unity and harmony:

This conclusive proof that the executive committee are prosecuting earnestly the important business entrusted to them will allay much of the anxiety consequent on the slowness which had characterised the preceding steps. No one now doubts that we are to have a spiritual guide, competent to maintain piety and peace. To such reverend functionaries as these remarks may find access to, we respectfully suggest that they do not so much estimate the office by the personal advantages which it at present offers as by the glorious opportunities of usefulness that it affords ...

Religious feeling is reviving among us here, as it is among our brethren everywhere; and the very restlessness which is one of its indications will prove anything but an unhealthy symptom – provided only that a safe bias be impressed upon it by a Chief Rabbi in whom is the spirit of God, to unite our scattered energies and, as a Jew and as a statesman, to direct them into the paths of duty, harmony, and every good man's esteem ...

At no previous era of the history of the Jews in England has the tide of affairs presented such a confluence for the welfare of all our most important interests, nationally considered. May the helm be taken by a man of true piety, of uncompromising independence, and decision of purpose; and with God's blessing, a bright future dawns for the dispersed of Judah, wherever located, if only in reciprocal communication, and therefore, in fraternal confidence.

Looking back at the desires and expectations first formed, with reference to the reconstitution of our spiritual guidance, we rejoice to reflect that, so far, none have been disappointed. All the synagogues of the German [Ashkenazi] *minhag* throughout Great Britain and her colonies have given their adherence, and that too with a pledge heretofore not existing: to recognise and uphold the Chief Rabbi's 'general religious direction and superintendence' ...

When the Sephardim shall, with that frankness which of right belongs to them, unite with their brethren for the security of our common heritage, there will remain (if indeed the last at the goal) only the small body of Seceders. Our unaffected expectation that all will unite ultimately was expressed at the very first; and therefore is it that, while we have discouraged attempts, on the one hand, to drive them still further into secession, we have, on the other, not failed to restrain the more ardent from so compromising their own party as to render accommodation impossible.

Nay, we have, for our part, gladly seized upon every manifestation of conformity by the Burton Street Community, in order to evidence our satisfaction at it, as a promise of re-union; in other words, a return to that uniformity (its limits being authoritatively prescribed) necessary to our national spiritual integrity. The future Chief Rabbi of the Jews in the British Empire will have indeed a noble opportunity to advance the interests of Israel nationally. May we be blessed with one equal to the emergency![21]

As the closing date drew near for the receipt of applications, reports indicated that 'there [were] in all seven candidates up to the present moment' and that 'surprise has been expressed, considering the noble sphere for useful influence which the Chief Rabbi of Great Britain might occupy, that all the most eminent Rabbis of Europe [were] not in the field.' By way of an explanation, the *Voice of Jacob* published the substance of a letter received from 'a distinguished functionary on the Continent' by a friend in London, who had urged him to become a candidate.

The rabbi wrote that it was 'incompatible with the official dignity and self-respect of the spiritual chief of one community himself to seek after election to another, seeing that such a course is likely to loosen those ties which constitute his usefulness with his present flock, especially when the income of the office sought for is superior to that at present enjoyed.'

He alluded to the practice prevailing on the Continent in similar circumstances where 'the reputation of the rabbi being known—as well as the history of his past administration and general capabilities—the community which desires his services directly invites them; and thus the congregations over which he actually presides are reconciled to his translation to a more important sphere of operations.'[22]

* * *

On Monday, 5 August 1844, the Rev Dr Nathan Adler, Chief Rabbi of Hanover; Rev Dr Benj. [sic] Auerbach, Chief Rabbi of Darmstadt; Rev Dr Hirsch Hirschfeld, Chief Rabbi of Wollstein; and Rev Samson Raphael Hirsch, Chief Rabbi of Emden, were officially confirmed as candidates for the vacant office of Chief Rabbi. The election—by ballot, with no proxies allowed—was initially set for Sunday, 13 October ('next after the coming Festivals'), throughout Great

Britain, and the Central Committee would meet three days later to declare the result. 'The testimonials and other documents belonging to these reverend gentlemen having been epitomised,' they would be printed and transmitted to every elector and would remain for inspection, in their original form,[23] at the vestry chambers of the Great Synagogue for one month prior to the election.

The committee expressed pleasure in observing that 'so highly satisfactory are the testimonials of the selected candidates, and so high a reputation do these gentlemen respectively enjoy for religion, morality and learning, that on whomsoever the election may fall, there can be no doubt as to the competency of the successful applicant adequately to fulfil his sacred and important functions.'

The votes allocated to the participating synagogues were: London—Great (Duke's Place), fifty; New (St. Helen's), twenty-five; Hambro' (Fenchurch Street), twenty; Western (St Alban's Place), five; Maiden Lane, three. Provincial—Liverpool (Seel Street), eight; Liverpool (Hardman Street), two; Birmingham, Manchester, four each; Bristol, Dublin, Edinburgh, Plymouth, Portsmouth, two each; Brighton, Chatham, Falmouth, Glasgow (Old), Glasgow (New), Ipswich, Jersey, Newcastle, Southampton (High Street), Swansea, Penzance, one each. Some of the smaller provincial synagogues were deemed to be unrepresented 'in consequence of their pecuniary inability to subscribe annually to the extent which entitles to a vote.'[24]

With the election in sight, the qualities, attainments and potentials of the four candidates came under increasing scrutiny. 'Our position,' observed the *Voice of Jacob*, 'naturally opens to us many and various sources of information; and as the complexion of public opinion has now been for some time assuming a pretty definite character, we no longer hesitate to give it a candid expression. In doing so, we can by no means be construed as deviating from the strict line of policy which we prescribed to ourselves as an Anglo-Jewish organ from the very outset – that is to say, a scrupulous avoidance of all partisanship in such matters, our adherence to which, in this case, none could better testify, in need, than the executive officers of the committee of selection, and the immediate friends of the respective candidates.

> It appears that the very powerful recommendations which Dr Adler has secured, the dignity with which he is known to have fulfilled his sacred office in Hanover, and the strong personal influence which these and other like circumstances may be expected to exercise in a community so peculiarly constituted as that of London, have occasioned a decided bias in Dr A's favour on the part of those who, in their turn, are the influential party here.

Again, the great stress laid upon what he has achieved for education has naturally excited the hopes of those who are conscious of the serious defects in our own establishments, which have arisen from the want of such superintendence. And to these recommendations, Dr A's friends (certainly the most active party) add the official experience which so many years of uninterrupted administration must have secured.

The next upon the list is Dr Auerbach, of whom it must be declared with justice that, although he is little known to our public, yet his efforts for the promotion of education have been honourably testified by his school publications, which have been brought under our notice.

The well-known erudition of Dr Hirschfeld has already won for him a reputation with our literati; true, they are few in number and therefore, perhaps, the comparative paucity of his open advocates; but to one whose opening career is so full of promise, the Jewish world at large may look with high anticipations of future advantage, wherever his lot be cast.

The most active and the most powerful pen is indisputably that of Rabbi Hirsch; although for the reasons already stated,[25] the English public are the least familiar with its productions. To this only can be attributed the circumstance that Rabbi H appears to possess no ostensible party here ... The claims of Rabbi Hirsch, in respect to what he has achieved for education, are not overlooked, but we are neither enumerating nor weighing the qualifications of the respective candidates; our task is merely to record the impressions which they are found to have produced here.

Having, throughout, vindicated our impartiality, we may be permitted to remind the electors how desirable it is that the successful candidate should be brought in not merely by a majority, but by an overwhelming one. So very much depends upon the extent of influence likely thence to result to the Chief Rabbi of Great Britain, and her dependencies, that it might be more than expedient that the various synagogue leaders should, so far as may be practicable, previously communicate with a view to a concurrent support of the candidate whose election may prove to be secure; by which means, if not a unanimous, at least an eminently successful election may be recorded.[26]

A week after this appraisal, perceiving machinations adverse to Hirschfeld's interests, one of his supporters—Elias Davis, of Aldgate High Street—addressed an appeal to his co-electors, noting in an accompanying letter that 'the Election for Chief Rabbi is now fast assuming a colouring of party feeling and private interest which the supporters of Dr Hirschfeld have so carefully avoided.' It was therefore their duty, wrote Davis, 'not only as an act of justice to that Gentleman but also for the well-being of the whole community, to submit the following address to counteract the effects that may arise from the ridiculous and malicious reports that are daily put forth with the intention of wounding the high reputation in which he is justly held.'[27]

Three of the candidates—asserted 'the friends of the Rev Dr Hirschfeld' in their accompanying address—'are Doctors of Philosophy; but no one at all acquainted with the rank of foreign Universities will for an instant pretend to compare Giesen or Erlangen, respectable as they both are, with the high fame and illustrious pre-eminence of Berlin! At this last-named University, no Student can obtain his Doctor's degree unless he has been resident there during his course of studies, has submitted to a rigid examination, and maintained a thesis or public disputation; whereas, both at Giesen and Erlangen, diplomas can be obtained by non-residents, without either examination or thesis.'

Davis and his colleagues contended that Adler, who until March 1828 was a student at the University of Warzburg, had taken up his degree at Erlangen in the following June; and that Auerbach had continued his degree at Giesen in July 1834, having finished studying at Marburg only months earlier. Hirschfeld, however, 'who had followed his studies at Berlin till the end of the year 1835, obtained his diploma at THAT UNIVERSITY in January 1836.' Moreover, 'the same superiority which attends Dr Hirschfeld's University Diploma is also remarkable in the respective Rabbinical ordinations and letters of recommendation ...'

Other literary merits, as well as experience, demonstrated by Hirschfeld— as well as 'the unanimity, good feeling and excellent institutions for which Wollstein [the seat of his rabbinate] is now distinguished – entitle his friends to expect that similar blessings will attend his administration here. The great success that has attended their canvass inspires them with the confident hope that He who has declared himself "the Guardian of Israel" will appoint a man after his own heart, to be the Spiritual Chief of His people in this great Empire.'[28]

Following this proclamation, ten days before the scheduled poll, the secretary of the selection committee, Simeon Oppenheim, announced a six-week postponement. No reason was given, but, suspecting a rash of vote-rigging, the *Voice of Jacob*—facing competition from the newly reissued and renamed *Jewish Chronicle and Working Man's Friend* (hitherto suspended for some two years)—speculated that 'a very active canvass has been carried on in particular interests ...

'If reports are true, tactics were resorted to which are common enough, and proper enough, when there is a contest for a parish official, a municipal dignitary, or a Member of Parliament, but which are scarcely compatible with the sacred office of spiritual guide of the very parties involved in the mêlée.'[29]

Disquieted by the tactics of the unnamed supporters of their unnamed parties (widely known to be Adler's and Hirschfeld's),[30] the paper called for the emergence of a 'third party,' so as 'to procure harmony and good government for the community'—adding later that 'means must now be taken, before the final election, to ascertain which it is of the non-partisan candidates to whom the larger amount of support can be secured.'[31]

The *Jewish Chronicle* dismissed the worth of all the candidates. 'Pious, good, talented men we have, no doubt they are; but eminent assuredly they are not. We hesitate not to affirm that, previous to this election, Dr Adler was comparatively unknown; so likewise was Dr Auerbach, the compiler of a catechism. Dr Hirsch was known as the author of controversial pamphlets that evince more talent than learning, more zeal than charity; and Dr Hirschfeld was named as a rising man who gave indications of future excellence rather than of actual greatness.

'We ask not if any of these four men be competent to hold the office to which he aspires—for we are willing to believe that if they were not so, they would not offer their services, and their friends would not support them. But we do ask, are they the *most competent* that they may be *invited* to fill the office? And unhesitatingly we answer, assuredly not!'[32] 'Not the man who seeks office but him whom the office must seek,' added the paper a fortnight later, 'is the most worthy of choice.'

On the question of choice, the paper similarly found fault with the electoral process. 'How,' it asked, 'is the proposed election to be conducted? The movement minority almost entirely consists of *ba'alei batim* (free members), while the conservative majority is mostly composed of seat-holders. The power of electing a Chief Rabbi is entirely vested in the former. Is it likely that the latter will be satisfied with a choice made by their antagonists? Is it likely they, the vast majority, will submit to the authority of a man who holds his office by the votes of those whom they cry down as heterodox the moment he exercises his authority in a free and conscientious manner?

> The Chief Rabbi to be appointed should be elected by all, that he may be obeyed by all; and by no means should the choice be in the hands of a minority, to whose views the vast majority object. But, as if this serious difference of opinion—and the ills that are likely to spring from it—were not enough to require the most discreet and prudent conduct on the part

of our leaders, they set about procuring a Chief Rabbi in the same manner as if they sought for a Beadle. Candidates are invited, testimonials are required, personal influence is put into requisition, parties are formed, canvassers are busy, and all the worst features of a popular election—intrigue, calumny, corruption—disfigure the appointment to the first spiritual office among Jews.

Were the situation to be filled an ordinary one, the heart-burning and animosity which are occasioned by the election would probably die away after the choice had been made. But when the situation is the highest among us, when its influence and authority are to be active and felt by all; when, moreover, the elements of discord are so strong and so abundant, should we not bear in mind that 'the Rabbi of a party can only be the director of a portion of his people.'

And, if this be so, how is he to enforce his authority? Means of coercion has he none; degrees of excommunication are not applicable to the times, and to the country in which we live. Besides, if the Chief Rabbi is a wise man, he will not desire the power to coerce; if he is a violent man, he ought not to possess it.

What then, again we ask, is to enforce the authority of the Chief Rabbi? PUBLIC OPINION, the support of the vast majority, not that of a fraction. And to obtain that support, he must be acceptable to the majority of his brethren. His election must be pure; the means employed to bring him among us must be above suspicion and above reproach.[33]

The sparring between the papers was to prevail—indeed, to intensify—until the demise of the *Voice of Jacob* in 1848, the *Chronicle* being viewed as the advocate of reform and reason, and the *Voice* the defender of traditionalism and faith.[34] While the former vigorously opposed the poll, the latter continued its campaign for a unifying 'third party,' declaring at the height of the election 'excitement':

There has been imposed upon the sober part of the community the imperious necessity of using their influence for a compromise, one which it appears to be generally understood can only now be effected by supporting that candidate most acceptable to those who have to yield up other predilections; in other words—Rabbi Hirsch.

This rabbi is reputed a fair English scholar, and thus, sit venia verbo, ready-made; he is allowed to be an eloquent man, and an eminent divine; he is admitted to be an author of great reputation (we should almost say of European reputation); a man of experience, of independent mind, and of principles which have wrested respect even from antagonists, and which have, even at this present moment, obtained for him the call to the important office of Provincial Rabbi of Moravia.

Those who interpose at this juncture will certainly be enabled to make out a strong case on qualities such as these; and if we therefore rejoice at his being the man put forth, it is not that we would disparage the qualifications of other candidates for their hallowed duties, but because a man is put forward whose qualities are so eminent, whose claims are so well-founded, whose merits are so universally acknowledged, that not even the blindest partisan of either side could make any rational objection to his fitness.[35]

Responding to this call, a meeting of synagogue elders, and 'several other gentlemen of influence in the community,' was held in London at which friends of Adler's 'conceded to the desire of the majority then present (fairly representing dispassionate feeling out of doors)' that Hirsch should be recommended 'for a united support.' But Hirschfeld's 'most active partisans ... were not equally swayed by the moderate counsels ... and repulsed the conciliatory overtures made to them.'[36]

There followed a series of 'hole-and-corner meetings; assemblies at private houses, offices, and dissensions; adjournments to subscription-rooms; compromises proposed and rejected; manoeuvres to bring in a third candidate; and the complete failure of all machinery and scene-shifting which, it cannot be denied, has taken place in the last fortnight.'[37] Thereafter, the advocates for a compromise met once again and 'finally consented to give their co-operation in aid of Dr Adler, as the candidate who appeared to possess the most effective support and who, if elected, would command by far the greatest amount of useful influence.'[38]

And so it transpired. When the returns were opened on 4 December, Adler was found to have polled one hundred and twenty-one votes, Hirschfeld thirteen, Hirsch two, and Auerbach nil. Three synagogues—Newcastle, Birmingham, and Bristol, commanding between them seven votes—had declined the ballot. The chief point of attraction was the vestry room of the Great Synagogue, both on account of its influence on the result of the election and because the poll had been kept open one hour beyond that of other synagogues across the country. An eye-witness at Duke's Place described the scene:

> Most of the leading men of the community were assembled here, and their number continued to be augmented by arrivals from the other vestries, with reports of the results on the declaration of the respective scrutineers. Precisely as the clock struck three, Mr S. H. Ellis, who as senior warden presided, declared the ballot closed; and soon afterwards, the duties of the scrutineers having been performed, the numbers were formally declared.
>
> The chairman, by way of preface to this declaration, addressed a few words of suitable exhortation to the now crowded assembly, and also deprecated every demonstration of feeling as connected with the announcement about to be made. The propriety of this recommendation was at once felt, and it was not until the chairman, after declaring Dr Adler to be the elect of that synagogue, had implored all to merge their former predilections in favour of that Rabbi whom the majority had chosen, that the general cries of 'hear! hear!' demonstrated how cordially all right-minded men were disposed to forget past differences and unite in hailing the new Rabbi with a unanimous spirit.
>
> We heard this truly Jewish feeling expressed, in a marked manner, by the principal advocates of Dr Hirschfeld, and that, too, in the moment of their defeat. We know no praise which could be more significant than the record of that honourable fact.
>
> Mr Ellis, in acknowledging the vote of thanks passed for his conduct in the chair that day, took occasion to vindicate his impartiality from the imputations which had been publicly cast upon it. He assured the meeting that his single object had been to discharge his duty uprightly throughout; and that he anticipated the satisfaction of finding all parties concur in the propriety of merging every personal consideration, which might keep alive any but the ardent desire to maintain peace and good feeling in the community.
>
> The overwhelming majority by which Dr Adler has been brought in is one of those prominent features of the present hour which it is pleasing to contemplate. It is strikingly characteristic of the sound policy of those who, at the decisive

moment, have known how to sacrifice personal predilections to a sense of duty; who have shown how, amidst the excitement of the contest, they could still listen to the calm voice of abstract reasoning.

Their timely accession to the cause of that candidate who, at all events, would have had a majority, however small, has altogether prevented even the appearance of a party triumph; and the ready concurrence of the minority is equally indicative of that proper spirit which would invest our Chief Rabbi, not as the favourite of a party, but as the desired of the whole. Thus does he receive that confidence, and attain to that power, through which alone he can be enabled to realise our hopes.

It is, after all, scarcely within the range of possibility to secure, *a priori*, complete unanimity on questions the decision of which rests with large bodies; and though the sustained opposition of the minority may have been construed to their disadvantage, yet abstract justice cannot deny them the tribute due to conscientious conviction, nor the meed of honour earned by generosity of sentiment.[39]

Recording the outcome, the *Jewish Chronicle* declared: 'As we have not advocated the cause of either Candidate individually—as we did not play the coquette with Rabbi Hirsch at the commencement, nor flatter Dr Adler when we found him to be the general favourite, nor write for a compromise in favour of the former again, when two parties were fighting about the postponement of the election—the result can afford us no cause for exultation in triumph, nor humiliation by defeat. But we rejoice at the termination of the election, and (as we hope and pray) at the ex-termination of all discord, ill-feeling, calumny, slander and hatred which attended the proceedings.

'Now that the Chief Rabbi is appointed, the words "Adler party" or "Hirschfeld party" should be heard no more. Let all be but one party united, to welcome him with one heart and with one soul, and let them exclaim, "like one man in one voice," "Be thou our ruler, and let this ruin be under thy hand."

'Our ecclesiastical structure in this country is indeed a ruin. But if the Chief Rabbi-elect have the mind, the spirit, to build up this ruin ... if he act from sincere motives, he may reckon upon our humble support, and rely upon the assistance of all true friends of Israel, whose sages teach: "Whoever comes forward to rectify will receive heavenly support."'[40]

The *Voice of Jacob* was more charitable. 'A severe struggle has been decided,' it asserted; 'none are defeated! A field has been contested, none are injured! Each party has put forth its strength for victory, and all are gainers! ... Henceforward, the rabbinical chair adequately filled, we shall have in religious differences, if they arise, a proper arbiter for appeal;—in doubt, a legitimate guide and adviser;—in all Jewish questions, a common centre round which to rally; now receiving the impulse, now imparting it, but always resulting in simultaneous action for the good of all.'[41]

* * *

It soon became apparent that Adler may have owed much of his success to his friend and one-time patron Prince Adolphus Frederick, Duke of Cambridge, seventh son of George III and, at the time of his appointment as Chief Rabbi of Hanover, Viceroy of the kingdom, it then being an appanage of Britain.

Educated and fashioned 'in the modern mould,' Adler—born in the kingdom—had been regarded by the Hanoverian Government as the 'obvious choice' for the German post, 'an educated Jew whose breadth of learning served to enhance rather than diminish his Jewish identity and competence.' The interest shown in him by parliamentary officials and the ducal authorities was 'the fruit of his deep-rooted loyalty to the laws of his country, to the Government, and to the head of state. His accomplishments were well recognised even among royal circles in Britain itself.'[42]

Adler's first engagement on taking up his appointment in Britain, several months after the election, was a visit to Cambridge House, the home of the Duke, who had expressed a desire the see the new Chief Rabbi—'favourably known to HRH during his viceroyalty at Hanover.'[43] And five years later, at the third public examination of the Western Jewish Girls' Free School, the Duke, as a patron of the institution and chairman of the meeting, declared of Adler (also a patron): 'I must especially thank the Rev the Chief Rabbi. I have had the pleasure of knowing that gentleman, I may almost say, from his childhood, and was instrumental in promoting him to his former position; and I am very happy to see him now occupy so distinguished a position in this country.'[44]

Adler's arrival in Britain had been delayed for some considerable time through both administrative and family circumstances. He first learned of his appointment days after the election, with a high-flown letter from Ellis, translated into Hebrew:[45]

> We have agreed as one man to present to your Reverence the Rabbinical Chair in our several communities, 'the government shall be on your shoulder,' and the staff of pleasantness in your hands, for such a leader have the congregation of the Lord desired, to heal the wounds, to remove every stumbling-

block, 'to stand as a breakwater,' and to maintain the cause of
His people at all times ... You are our leader, our preceptor.
May our desire be speedily fulfilled by your superintendence
as our Chief Rabbi! May the study of the Holy Law of God be
encouraged and increased; and may the splendour of your
light shine on us and on our children! 'For the priest's lips
should keep knowledge, and they should seek the law at his
mouth, for he is the messenger of the Lord of Hosts.'

Before replying officially, some weeks later, Adler addressed two letters to Ellis of a more personal nature. The first, dated 18 December 5505 [1844], noted: 'I have been much rejoiced at the news of my having been elected Chief Rabbi of Great Britain by a very large majority ... Though I have not yet officially received my appointment, for which I shall have to wait before I can give notice to the Government of here, which must be done half a year before I can obtain my dismissal, yet I cannot help giving you my most hearty thanks for the kind advice, as well as for the holy zeal which you have taken by conducting this important matter. It is my sincere wish and my earnest prayer that the Lord may grant you a continual health to see and enjoy the fruits of your endeavours.'[46]

In a second letter, written three weeks later, Adler expressed regret that he was 'still without the official certificate of my appointment. It is true I have heard from Mr Klingerman, Secretary of the Ambassador of Hanover, that you have given it to the Ambassador, but the latter intend to forward it by the quarterly Courier, and this will come here not before many weeks. Under these circumstances, I cannot forbear longer to reply at large your kind letter.'

Expressing gratitude for the opportunity 'to be the clerical guide of so many congregations metropolitan as well as provincial, which have within themselves all the elements of a spiritual prosperity and possess so many worthy men distinguished by the happy union of religion and morality,' Adler then sought Ellis's help in matters both communal and familial. 'You know,' he wrote, 'that it is the first office of the Chief Rabby [sic] to be acquainted with the statutes and rules of the first congregation, because his duties are in many respects depending on them. But I am still unacquainted with these interior relations. I shall therefore be much obliged if you had the kindness to forward me the mentioned statutes.

'However great my anxiety is to make your personal acquaintance, yet the reason which I mentioned in my former letter, as well as the situation which I am in, in reference to the Government and the different congregations of this country, make it impossible to dissolve my engagement immediately, and I am convinced that you, my dear Sir, will agree with me that I must stay here till the month of June or July next.'

Adverting to a suggestion from Ellis 'to leaving my children here and first coming over without them,' Adler wrote: 'My wife and I are so very attached to them, as they are yet of a tender age, that we could not part with them even for a time. Perhaps some friends of mine (I venture to name Mr Aaron Joseph and Mr R. L. Moses) will take the trouble upon them to arrange my future lodging before my arrival and I come at once with my whole family.'[47]

In a more formal letter of acceptance to the selection committee, five days later, Adler wrote:

> Estimable friends, synod of councillors, who love truth and delight in equity, men of worth, the guardians of the Congregation and leaders of the community, who are appointed by the United Congregations in London assembled. May the Lord grant to you His blessing individually and collectively, and life and peace for everlasting.
>
> GENTLEMEN,
> Your worthy and estimable writings, breathing the spirit of kindness and affection, have inspired me with confidence, and demand my most grateful and heartfelt acknowledgments.
>
> Thereby have you crowned me with honour and eminence, in conveying to me the intelligence that the Lord has enlarged His grace unto me, and planted my lot in a pleasant place,—in the seat of the house of DAVID, and on the throne of SOLOMON.
>
> You have called me from the herds, to be to Israel a father and a priest; you have placed the government on my shoulder, to guard, with the staff of gentleness and the rule of honour, the holy flock of the people chosen of the Lord.
>
> Verily! my soul trembleth with hope and fear, when I reflect, How can I aspire to soar on high, to govern various precious Congregations in distant localities? or how find strength of heart to remove the ashes, and to inspire with the light of truth and faith the thousands that encompass me round about? how sustain each spirit, give delight to each soul, and pleasure to each mind,—to youth as to the aged, to the exalted as to the lowly, to the poor as to the rich,—to content all equally?
>
> But my trust is in the Lord, the God of the spirits of all

flesh, as the son confideth on the love of his father. To His word do I hearken, which speaketh in the recesses of my heart: 'Gird thy loins and strengthen thyself; droop not, for I am with thee!'

His light and His truth will lead me to cast aside the stumbling-block from the highway, to put away the thorns from the pastures of my people, to restore the fainting soul from the shadow of death to the protection of the Almighty. He will strengthen and sustain me; but deeds not words will I place before you; those will testify my righteousness on the future day, for it is not the spirit of arrogance that has caused me to aspire to this eminence, nor has vanity of pride called me to this guardianship, but solely the desire to exalt the horn of the Law, and to guard the way of the tree of life.

To you, worthy and excellent Gentlemen, with whom dwelleth the spirit of wisdom and understanding, and whose main object is peace, for it is your glory, to you I humbly supplicate, that each of you may, according to his power and means, sustain and assist me in my endeavours to lead your offspring in the path of righteousness and good conduct, to enlighten them in the way of everlasting truth, that the youth of Israel may thirst after the waters of the well of life, which princes have dug with their staves.

On you, the heads of the Assembly of Israel, I depend for aid, that I may guide our youth, like unto the eagle, which at times swiftly darts to its young, but at other periods gently indicates its presence, though invariably it so shapes its course that the arrow pierce not its offspring.

May the good Providence shield both fathers and children, and grant you every blessing, and that good fruit may be your reward, which at maturity will be to you a sustenance and protection, until the throne of His glory, that was from the beginning, be established!

The words of your friend, who is now of your number, whose heart is with you, and whose soul longeth to dwell in your courts.

> With profound esteem and desire to serve you,
> NATHAN MARCUS ADLER.[48]

Adler arrived in Britain on 7 July 1845, nearly three years after Hirschell's death. He was welcomed at Dover by a delegation of representative Jews headed by Sir Moses Montefiore as sheriff of the county and president of the Board of Deputies.[49] Montefiore 'had resolved on paying this graceful compliment to one called on to fill so sacred and responsible an office among the Jews of this Empire.'[50]

On the day preceding his installation, another delegation—this time of deputies alone and again headed by Montefiore—called upon him to present a testimonial, inscribed on vellum, 'congratulating him on his entry upon the sacred duties of his vocation.' Delivered on behalf of 'nearly the whole of the Jewish community in this country'—a veiled reference to the schism that had so recently rocked London Jewry—the document declared: 'Your talents, piety, experience and high position warrant us in anticipating the highest results from your ministry, and we feel that it is our duty, the performance of which affords us the sincerest gratification, to avail ourselves of the earliest opportunity to offer you our fervent wishes for your welfare, and that of your lady and family.'

Clearly moved by this display of solidarity, Adler replied: 'I feel highly honoured by the very gratifying manner in which you have been pleased to express your very kind sentiments and wishes on my arrival in this country, and on my entrance upon the duties of my sacred office. The more extensive, influential and important is the body which you represent, and the greater your own merits—not only towards our brethren in this country but throughout the world—the more highly must I esteem and value these marks of your kindness towards me.

'I already feel the full weight of the high and important office which has been confided to me, but I hope that, through the assistance of God, my earnest efforts will be attended with those beneficial consequences which we all have so devoutly at heart. That your great endeavours on behalf of all our congregations may be continued by the divine blessing will be my constant prayer.'[51]

Nathan Marcus Adler (1845): 'A stranger in the midst of a strange assemblage'

FROM THE PULPIT — I

Guardian of the Law

Sermon delivered at the Great Synagogue, London, by the Rev Dr Nathan Marcus Adler on the occasion of his installation into office as Chief Rabbi of Great Britain, 8 July 1845–4 Tammuz 5605[1]

My Beloved Brethren:

It is with a mind deeply moved by mingled feelings of bashfulness and timidity that I commence my first address to you; and if you will reflect on the great change which the last few days have wrought in my position, you will acknowledge that such feelings are fully justified. But ten days since I stood in my native city; my words were addressed to the ears and hearts of those who had known me from my youth, and who were cognisant of every particular of my life and my labours. I, too, could rely on their attachment, and could lay claim to their love. But this day I stand up, for the first time in this great capital of the world, a stranger in the midst of a strange assemblage, whose love I have yet to gain—in the midst of a congregation which comprises men and women, on whom the eyes of all Israel, nay, of all the world, are now resting, who constitute the pride and the hope of my people. Must not such a scene make me feel abashed? There, too, I addressed my hearers in their mother tongue. My words could not be misunderstood. They passed direct from heart to heart, from mind to mind; but here I am as yet constrained (until practice shall conquer difficulties) to speak to you in the German language. How easily may my words be unfavourably received, how readily miss the road to your hearts; and shall such thoughts not make me tremble? Or if I cast my looks backward, and reflect that I am now in a place where so many pious, learned and noble men have already spoken, taught, striven and laboured, amongst

---

1   [Delivered in German and translated by Barnard van Oven, with this introductory 'advertisement': 'The Translator respectfully offers this English version of Dr Adler's admirable Discourse to those Members of his Congregations who are unacquainted with the German Language. It is hoped that they may be thus enabled to appreciate the piety, good sense, logical precision and kindly feelings of their reverend Pastor; but no attempt has been made to compete with the style of the original, which is at once elegant, powerful and persuasive.' The sermon opened with a Hebrew prayer.]

whom I will only name my uncle and my predecessor, who for forty years guided his flock with faithfulness and love—whose name and wisdom are still cherished in Israel—must not such reflections make me anxious? Or if I look onward, and reflect that I enter upon a sphere of action, on the due performance of which the spiritual welfare of so many thousands, both near and far, depends—of parents and of children, of great and of small; and if I measure against these many and high duties the feebleness of my powers, the narrow limits of my capabilities, must not my heart be most deeply and solemnly moved—must I not feel myself fearfully embarrassed to select the best mode of address? But I put my trust in Him who, from my youth onwards, hath ever been to me a staff, a support, and a help. I put my trust in Him who most delighteth to give aid to the feeble, because so shall they, by his power, become strong. I put my trust in Him who said to the priest, 'And they shall put my name upon the children of Israel, and I will bless them.'[2] I put my trust in Him who said unto Jeremiah, 'Fear thou not, for I am with thee';[3] who, through the mouth of the wise, recommends 'to cast thy mental bread upon the waters'; to 'give a portion to seven, and also to eight; for thou knowest not what evil shall be upon earth.'[4]

I trust in those friendly expressions with which you have but just now gladdened my heart. I trust that you will meet my timidity with love; and so add to my weak words a force and power which I am unable to give to them. Therefore, I beseech you, allow me shortly to explain, 'With what purposes, and with what hopes, a minister enters on the duties of his sacred office.'

These purposes and hopes are expressed in a passage of the prophet Zechariah, which impressed itself strongly on my mind when you honoured me by your choice: 'Thus saith the Lord of Hosts, If thou wilt walk in my ways, and if thou wilt keep my charge, then thou shalt also judge my house, and shalt also keep my courts; and I will give thee admission to walk among these that stand by.' After the prophet had been promised that the Lord would renew the splendour of the first temple in a second—after the prophet had already in spirit beheld that temple, the splendid golden ornaments, the candelabra, and the numerous lamps, then did the Lord shew to him by what means the glories of the new temple should be brought about—by the High Priest Joshua. The prophet saw how he would be inducted into office—how his filthy garments would be removed, and his clean vestments put on—saw how his opponents would point to his wants, defects, and imperfections—how the Lord would reprove them, and put forward the High Priest as a brand rescued from the

---

2   Numbers 6:27. [All citations are as in the original German and English text.]
3   Jeremiah 1:1.
4   Ecclesiastes 11:1.

fire. He saw how the angel placed on his head a fair mitre, the symbol of priestly virtue, and said unto him, 'If thou wilt walk in my ways, and if thou wilt keep my charge, then thou shalt also judge my house, and shalt also keep my courts; and I will give thee admission to walk among these that stand by.' Although, my beloved brethren, I am far from daring to compare myself to the High Priest Joshua, yet I resemble him in his imperfections, for which you must make all due allowance, if I am to fulfil my sacred and important office. I resemble him in the sacred commission given. The words of the text contain all the sacred duties of the High Priest of former days, and which are, with suitable circumstances, to be fulfilled by the minister of our time, as well as the hopes which he hath to cherish. And even I, my brethren, enter my new office with the following purposes:

I. To walk in the ways of God.
II. Truly to maintain his law.
III. To superintend the institutions for education.
IV. To watch over the places of worship.
V. And, lastly, with a deep hope that I shall make my way into your hearts.

O let my words be deeply implanted in your hearts, that they may there blossom and produce fruit, even sevenfold.

I. The minister of this day, like the High Priest of old, enters on his office with an intent to walk in the ways of his God. In which of the ways of the Lord is man able to walk? How is a feeble mortal, son of earth, able to imitate the Deity? Is it in power? Human power is but weakness. Is it in wisdom? Human wisdom is but folly. Is it in strength? The human arm reaches not far. Is it in justice? Man drinks often of injustice as though it were water.[5] It is only through the goodness of God, and his love towards all his creatures, that man can learn to understand, and, as far as his weak powers allow, to imitate Him. When the man of God desired to know the ways of the Lord, and said 'I beseech thee, show me thy glory,' God answered him and said, 'I will make all my goodness to pass before thee.'[6]

This, the love of God, which is made manifest in the great laws of nature, as in the small ones which affect us personally—which preserves order alike in the great circles of the universe, and in the narrow limits of the circumstances around us—which displays itself in the holy law, in all that it commands or

---

5   Job 15:16.
6   Exodus 33:15.

forbids, permits or demands (for all tend alike to promote the welfare of mankind)—this love it was the duty of the High Priest, and is now the duty of the pastor, to know and to proclaim, to seek for, and to inquire into. Three books, which are laid open to his researches—the book of nature, the book of history, and, above all, the book of the law—must be his constant study. He must read in them day and night,[7] must learn them by heart, and take them to his heart. And if man is permitted to acquire but the first elements of this knowledge, the first syllables, or a few letters only, even that will afford him the means of comprehending the depth and grandeur of Almighty love, and will lead him onwards to that which is the beginning and end of all wisdom, The Fear of God. And if man is permitted to perceive but one branch of the tree, but one spark of that flame, but one arm of that stream, by that portion he may judge of the whole, by that single one he may judge of all combined. But he must, as far as he is able, go in the ways of the Lord—he must move about in the commands of God; and must, like the priest, love peace and seek for peace.

But how shall the pastor succeed in his efforts if his own life be not an example—if he points out a path which he does not follow? Can it be more than a mere false appearance if his sermons, his knowledge, his labours, are opposed to his actions, or if his deeds and his words stand in opposition to each other? Can he recommend and procure mutual love and peace if his own conduct be not that of love and charity—if he do not, like a true follower of Aaron, strive to promote peace? How shall he gain followers to the duties of religion if it is needful that he himself be reminded of them? Ere thou seek to take the splinter from another's eye, remove the mote from thine own.[8]

No; he must himself tread the desired pathway of the Lord. He must adorn himself before he can adorn others. He must so conduct himself as to make knowledge honourable—he must be filled with sacred love before he can recommend it to others. It is only where warmth of feeling exists that such warmth can be communicated—only where the spirit of life pervades that it can be excited, or burst forth in others.

He must cast off his unclean garments before he puts on the clean vestments of others. In one word, investigation and activity, word and deed, conviction and conduct, must go hand in hand; and then surely and silently they will do their work.

And I, my beloved brethren, have a settled purpose to go before you—to lead your footsteps in the ways of the Lord, and to walk therein as I have done

---

7   Deuteronomy 18:16.
8   Eruchin 19a.

from my earliest youth. This expression may sound perhaps too boastful to you; nay, it must sound so, if I did not add to it that it is for you not only to resemble me, but rather to surpass me. When the prophet with the tongue of fire was asked, 'Whom shall I send, and who will go before us?',[9] he replied, 'Here I am, send me,' but did not venture to add, 'I will go before thee'; so I do not venture to assert that in all the pathways of the Lord I will go before you. Many of you may, will, can, and must surpass me; but I have taken upon myself the holy resolve to walk in the ways of the Lord, and to guide your steps in the ways of love and peace.

II.   The minister of this time, like the High Priest of old, enters on the duties of his office with a purpose to watch over all sacred things. It was his duty, as you know, to keep watch over the law, spiritually and actually from without and from within. The sacred things, the ark and the table of the covenant, the shewbread, etc., were entrusted to his care. Under his direction, the Levites officiated (guardians also of the holy things); but he had also to watch them spiritually, and to determine between things permitted and forbidden, common and holy, clean and unclean.[10] His duty was to protect them from injury, that no one should, as it were, devour the sacred things.[11]

Man turns to his pastor in all positions of life—in joy and in sorrow—in times of happiness and of misfortune—at the beginning of life[12] and at the closing hour.[13] In his contests against the general enemy, as well as against the inroads of disease;[14] and this is, in many respects in these days, the true priestly calling—He should be, He must be, the watchman, the guardian, the preserver of the holy law.

It is indeed arduous, very arduous, to take good care of it in a time when some rest their hopes on rapid innovation, and others on steadfast adherence to whatever time has sanctified, even though it may be contrary to the law. It is indeed difficult, very difficult, to take good care of it, whilst urged on by some to constant advance, and implored by others to remain immovable. It is indeed difficult, in such circumstances, to find the golden mean. But if he be seriously resolved to do his duty to God and to his holy law, then will he place himself in the watchtower, preserve the sacred inheritance undimmed and uninjured, secure it from all injury, and defend it from every attack.

Yes, on every change in life—on entering the congregation—the celebra-

---

9   Isaiah 6:8.
10 Compare Ezekiel 44:23.
11 Numbers 4:35.
12 Exodus 13:13.
13 Leviticus 10:6.
14 Compare Leviticus 12.

tion of marriage—at the coming in and the going forth—his voice shall be raised to declare, to watch over, to protect and to promote the commands of God.

In all important circumstances, he will judge according to his fullest knowledge and direct conscientiously. He will distinguish the false from the true, the bad from the good, the wrong from the right, the dark from the light—he will stand between the living and the dead, and bid the religious pestilence to cease.[15] But he will take every thing seriously to his heart,[16] all names inscribed on the tablet of his breast—he will, in all cases, consult the law as the Urim and Thummim of old; and as that oracle speaks and decides will he judge and determine.

Yes, my beloved brethren, I also do purpose to become a guardian of the law, to protect, promote and advocate it. This may seem to you grandiloquent boasting; yea, it must seem so, if I did not add that even should much escape me, should I lack power to bring my purpose to its complete fulfilment, one thing I cannot want—one thing which man has, above all other gifts, at all times within his reach—and this is a holy will. The will to become a pious guardian in the true spirit fills me, rushes and throbs through all my veins; and therefore my God will vouchsafe to me the fulfilment of the prescribed task.

III. The minister enters also on his office with the purpose to govern God's holy House. All know that the term 'my house' did mean the Temple, within whose walls in the inner and innermost courts the priesthood was employed. These brought the various offerings of sin or praise. It was their duty to guard against any faulty offering, any strange fire, which the Lord had not commanded being introduced,[17] that the fire on the altar of the Lord be duly fed and never extinguished,[18] to take care that the light should be burning from evening until morning outside the curtain which hung before the Ark of the Covenant;[19] in a word, it was their duty to take the charge and care of all within the house of God.

If in these days the pastor would fulfil those duties of the priests of old, his labours must be directed to another house of God: he must erect the temple in other places; and these are the establishments for education. He must strive to make every house become a house of God—to make every father and mother a priest to light up the divine fire in the infant breast; remove those clouds

15 Numbers 17:13.
16 Exodus 28:12.
17 Leviticus 10:1.
18 Leviticus 6:6.
19 Numbers 8:2.

which conceal the most holy God from that youthful mind wherein He so much delighteth to dwell. He must guard against any strange fire being introduced, and watch that the true flame burn clear and bright from morning until evening, and from evening until morning.

Home is the first and most important school; there, example works more effect than precept, and bad example more powerfully than good. He must take charge of God's houses. These are the establishments for education, whether preparatory or high schools—whether he establish them or improve them—whether he found or support them—whether he call them into being or uphold their existence; so that a pious spirit pervading all classes may pass from the school to the domestic home, from the home into business life—that, by means of the lispings of infancy, the kingdom of God may be upheld, and by means of the voice of the scholar, the moral world. The true houses of the Lord are the institutions for instruction, in which priests and teachers, directors and guides, instructors of youth and of the people, should be educated, so that they may attain to the highest degree of religion, and remain endued with the greatest knowledge and piety until their God call them to his service; the institutions for those who are to undertake the priestly office, who, although seemingly poor, are yet rich in their endowments.

It is his duty to have a care in such institutions that the holy *Law* be and remain the one Sun whence all rays of light emanate, and to which they return; that the Law be the light of all other knowledge and science. Your children may learn to know every tree and flower that grows, from the cedar of Lebanon to the hyssop on the wall,[20] but they must know and recognise Him who has created all. They may speak and use many foreign languages, as is fitting for so distinguished and powerful a nation, whose ships are found throughout the world,[21] and in whose dominions the sun never sets; but they must use and love that one language in which God made himself known, which, whether in tears or in laughter, in joy or in sorrow, in pleasure or in pain, belongs to our innermost selves, and expresses our sentiments and feelings. Your children may study the records of all people, especially of their native country; but their own history must not be a sealed letter, a closed book to them:[22] in a word, it is the duty of the pastor to superintend and to take care of establishments for education—to direct what should be taught and how—so that a spirit of true piety and wisdom may be diffused throughout all schools and pervade all homes.

And I, my beloved brethren, do purpose to superintend your establish-

---

20   I Kings 15:13.
21   Compare Ezekiel 27:3.
22   Isaiah 29:12.

ments for education; this sounds bold—it would be bold if I did not add 'that God supporteth the weak.' It is not power, it is not number, but the spirit of the Lord which commands success.[23] Can you, I may ask, stop the revolving sails of a windmill? You answer, no; surely no. But I say, take hold of the springs, the innermost springs; and not only any one of you, but a mere child, can arrest its course or set it in motion. Truly, the task I here prescribe to myself is difficult; but my God demands this good service from me, and that raises in me a confident hope that I shall succeed.

IV. The minister enters on his office with the purpose of watching the forecourts of his God.

You are aware, my beloved brethren, that whilst in the Temple, the Holy of Holies was open only to the high priest, whilst the holy precincts were trodden by the priesthood, who passed much of their lives within them; the forecourts were open to all—to men and to women—to adults and to children—to the Levites and to the Israelites: there they assembled and waited to hear the words of the priest, listened also to the tones of avowal and declaration with which the Levites accompanied the presentation of the offerings, and the Hallelujahs raised to the dispenser of all things. There the burthened brought his burthen, the sorrowful his sorrow, the afflicted his tears, the oppressed his suffering, and the joyous his gratitude; for from the lips of the priest abundance of knowledge went forth, and instruction was sought from his mouth.

The forecourts of our God, in these our days, are the synagogues—the houses of the Lord; this is our little Temple. This is the school for the adults, who come here alike and equally—men and women, strong and weak; they who are looked up to and they who are looked down upon; here there is not, there shall not be, any rank or station; here all are united as brothers and sisters, learning to put faith in that One whose eye never sleeps nor slumbers—who is aware of the slightest movement, the most trifling emotion of the heart—whose paternal hand leads and guides mankind in all difficulties—whose arm is a staff, an aid, and a support—whose heart warms with love to all his children, and upholds and maintains their love.

Here let him come who is bowed down, that he may be sustained—him who is loaded with sorrow, that he may be lightened of his burthen—the doubting, that he may obtain peace—the sinner, that he may meet with pity and forgiveness—the solitary mourner for lost and loved ones, that he may find hope and comfort. Here too the joyous shall come to pour forth his gratitude, the happy to express his delight.

Therefore it is the duty of the pastor to watch well the forecourts, to have

---

23   Zechariah 4:6.

a care that they accomplish their holy purposes, that every thing be banished from God's holy house which might prevent holy respect and decorum, which might diminish holiness and devotion; and also, that nothing be permitted to enter there which is contrary to the holy Law.

Therefore it is the office of the pastor to take upon himself[24] the anxious duties of these holy places, to make known the commands of the Lord in their purity—to direct attention to the holy writings—so that the light of the Law may shine forth not only within this place but without also, giving light and warmth in the business of life, so that the pious purposes resolved on by him may be thus brought into happy fruition.

And I, too, my beloved brethren, have the purpose to watch over your forecourts, to take charge of your synagogues, to have a care above all that all honour and respect due to holy places be not diminished. It is also my purpose, fearlessly and without hesitation, to lay before you the word of the Law, unclouded and pure even as the wise have transmitted it to us, as our ancestors have taught it to us, as the noblest minds have presented it to us. It is therefore my purpose to explain it in the different houses of the Lord, now here, now there, so that none shall be void of instruction; and to strive that it may be studied more, be better known, and more easily brought into actual use in the affairs of life; to strive that our love for our fellow men may flourish, prosper and increase, and prejudices disappear. This again sounds boastful; it would be so if I did not rely on that God, who has proved himself to thousands, who assuredly knows that I seriously seek to serve Him. He will support me and help me to accomplish the duty which I have prescribed to myself.

V.   But the minister of these times, like the high priest of old, enters into his office with the earnest hope of winning his way to the hearts of his flock. 'I, said the Lord, will give you admission to those that stand there.' This expression has many meanings.

The Lord would give Joshua admission to the assembly of priests, who previously had only observed his unfitness and imperfections, his faults and crimes, but not his capabilities—admission to the hearts of his contemporaries, the distinguished men, upon and by means of whom he should act and bring about the great designs of God—admission finally to the angels above; there, where man mounts from step to step, from power to higher power, from height to greater height, to receive the reward of all his labours. The pastor equally requires this hope, this reliance on the love and confidence of his flock. Then say, my beloved, if this love be absent, this confidence be wanting, this assurance be denied, how can he labour in his vocation, or even produce

---

24   I Samuel 2:32.

small fruits? Would not his powers and his willingness be exhausted by vain efforts to attain the wished-for object? If their hearts are closed against him, and the way to the strings of life and thought, to the mind and to the heart, be barred against him by the fiery sword of distrust, how shall he begin, prosecute or accomplish the arduous duties of his calling? How uneasily must he walk in the ways of the Lord if he fears that every step he may take will be mistaken, misunderstood, and falsely judged?

Will he be able to judge correctly, to determine rightly, and to make smooth the difficulties which occur in the various and manifold circumstances of his office, if he has to fear that by acquiring the love of one he may lose that of another? How can he improve the existing institutions, how establish holy places, if mistrust impede his course—mistrust in his words, labours, and occupations; or if haste and impatience desire and demand of his works that they should be like the rod of Aaron, which was no sooner planted than it bloomed, budded, and bore fruit?[25] How can he make the houses of God the scenes of his labours if he have to fear that he shall be thought to say too much here, too little there? No, the hope that he will gain admission to the hearts of his congregation, that he will be met and supported by them with feelings of affection, is indispensable to the pastor if his labours are to be rich with blessings and are to endure. His conduct, his life, his labours must be such as shall make him worthy to become of the number of the noble and angelic above; but they must reciprocate his love. Heart to heart must be the watch-word. And this, my beloved brethren, this is my hope, that I may win admission to your hearts; and the more honestly, the more zealously I have determined to devote my exertions to your service, wholly and unreservedly, the more does my soul desire to gain your love and confidence; for without these your expectations will be disappointed, and unconquerable difficulties will frustrate my endeavours. I hope all from your love; that you will aid me by counsel and support, by help and action, and will bear me onwards in love and confidence.

But how can I doubt your love or confidence? Have they not summoned me from the small house of my fathers? Have they not placed me here this day? Have they not, on my arrival here, before inauguration in my office, given me proofs of kindness? All these great antecedent preparations are to me but friendly pledges and promises of future good will. Well, then, let us make a covenant—a durable covenant to all you now here present, and to those absent ones to whom I equally hold out the hand of brotherhood. I pledge myself that I will walk in the ways of the Lord, that I will keep guard over the holy Law, that I will direct your schools—will watch over the forecourts of the

---

25   Compare Numbers 17:23.

Lord. I feel assured that you will meet my efforts with trust and confidence; and I will strive to justify your confidence, and, yet more, to gain the approval of the Almighty, so that, when dust shall again return to dust, and my ashes shall rest amongst you, my soul shall gain admission to my ancestors and predecessors,[26] who amongst the angels rejoice in the heavenly reward of their earthly labours.[27]

---

26 Daniel 12:3.
27 [The sermon concluded: 'With this hope, join with me in the prayer which, in your language, I will address to the Lord.' There then followed a lengthy prayer in English for the welfare of the Queen and the Royal Family, the Government, the people of Britain, and 'all the congregations which Thou hast intrusted to me.']

CHAPTER TWO

Between Old and New

IN OCTOBER 1879, some thirty-five years into his Chief Rabbinate, Nathan Marcus Adler—having recovered from, but still incapacitated by, 'a severe illness that compelled me to be away from London for several months'—addressed an urgent plea to the chairman and executive of the United Synagogue.

'During the period of my absence,' he wrote, 'I endeavoured as far as lay in my power to prevent any of the religious interests of the community from suffering neglect ... I am thankful to say that, by the blessings of Providence, I returned to town before the Festivals, much invigorated. But I am earnestly warned by my medical advisers that the state of my health makes it imperative upon me to relinquish a portion of my public and outdoor functions, and renders it necessary that I should be absent from London during the inclement months of the year.

'I shall endeavour, God willing, to direct and to supervise, as heretofore, the spiritual affairs of the congregations under my charge, and specially to decide all questions connected with our religious observances ... But I shall no longer be able to attend at my office regularly throughout the year to take charge of matters of detail requiring immediate consideration. In these circumstances, you will, I am sure, agree with me that it is desirable that means should be devised for avoiding any inconveniences that may arise ...

'With this in view, I would ask you to recommend to the Council to take measures for enabling me to secure the proper discharge of those duties which I am unable to perform, so that the affairs of the community hitherto committed to my charge shall not suffer any neglect.'[1]

The executive committee, 'having given the subject introduced to them by Dr Adler the most careful consideration,' laid before the United Synagogue council the following recommendation:

> For thirty-five years, Dr Adler has served the Jewish community ably, zealously and unremittingly as their revered

Spiritual Chief. During this long period, the congregations of London, under his pastoral charge, have grown in number and in importance. While the circumstances of the different synagogues have undergone a change probably greater than in any previous similar period, their attachment to their sacred faith has remained unimpaired and has been cemented under his wise and enlightened supervision, and feelings of unity and mutual affection have been developed and matured.

The Council cannot but regret that the state of Dr Adler's health prevents his affording the same continuous attention as heretofore to the incessant duties of his high office; but they feel that his long and indefatigable labours well entitle him to command that assistance which he states he is reluctantly compelled to seek, and they congratulate themselves that his wise counsels and advice will still be available to the whole community in any matters of weighty importance.

In considering the best means of reconciling the exigencies of the public service with the comfort and convenience of Dr Adler, the Council have fortunately not had a difficult task. If Dr Hermann Adler were entirely unconnected with the Chief Rabbi by the near ties of relationship, his great learning and high abilities, his conciliatory disposition and the manner in which he has succeeded in gaining the affection of a large and important congregation would designate him as eminently fitted for the discharge of the responsible duties from which Dr Adler is compelled to seek relief.

But in addition to these advantages, Dr Hermann Adler, as the son of the Chief Rabbi, must have already acquired a large amount of experience of the Chief Rabbi's important sphere of duty and will possess facilities for assisting his father which no other gentleman could enjoy.

The Council, therefore, assuring the Chief Rabbi of their entire confidence in the learning, judgment and abilities of his son, Dr Hermann Adler, recommend that he appoint him as his delegate, 'to attend at his office on his behalf, to issue authorisations of marriage, and to represent him at the Court of the Beth Hamidrash and at the meetings of the Board of Shechita, and generally to take charge of matters of detail requiring attention in his absence.'[2]

The Council have abstained from directly making the

definitive appointment themselves, inasmuch as the appointment of Chief Rabbi was originally made by some of the Synagogues now in the Union in conjunction with other Metropolitan and Provincial Congregations ...[3]

The recommendation, though soon adopted, was not without opposition—in one case, from an unlikely source. Seconding a motion to refer back the proposal, Baron Henry de Worms, a cousin of the Adlers and a warden at the Central Synagogue,[4] asserted that, in adopting it, they 'would practically appoint a locum tenens for the Chief Rabbi; this was well beyond the powers of the Council. The other congregations interested in the election of Chief Rabbi should be first consulted.'

The course proposed, he added, was 'injudicious and unwarranted. The Council should not name any gentleman to be delegate of the Chief Rabbi, both on grounds of general inexpediency and because it would lead to division in the community.'

While 'fully agreeing' with those of his colleagues who had praised Hermann Adler's abilities, Benn Davis—who had called for the reference back—'objected to the course by which the executive committee purposed to anticipate posterity. It was, perhaps, a consummation devoutly to be wished that Dr Hermann Adler should be the future Chief Rabbi, but he [Davis] protested against the manner in which it was proposed to bring about that consummation. The future election of a Chief Rabbi should not be anticipated, and the free choice of the electors should be left entirely unfettered.'

Dismissing the objections, council chairman Lionel L. Cohen described them as 'insidious, and showing a lamentable want of information on the question before the meeting. It would be excessively disrespectful, after the letter of the Chief Rabbi, to leave Dr Adler to appoint a representative for the discharge of certain duties, and to leave him to bear the odium which might be produced by his appointing his son.'[5]

Following this exchange, the proposal was speedily approved and was related to the Chief Rabbi by the United Synagogue's recently elected president, Nathaniel Mayer de Rothschild [later Lord],[6] with expressions of regret and in the 'sincere and earnest hope that, with the blessing of Providence, you will soon be restored to health and vigour.'[7] In letters to non-US congregations in London under his charge, and to others in the provinces and overseas, Adler thereupon wrote: 'I have made the appointment thus considerately counselled, feeling assured that this measure will prove beneficial to the community. As for myself, I hope, with Divine help, to continue the general supervision of the religious affairs of the Community, and to devote to it such time and strength as may yet be spared to me.'[8]

That period of time and strength was to extend over eleven years, during which—though confined to West Brighton, and 'notwithstanding the appointment of his son as Delegate—the venerable Chief Rabbi continued to take the liveliest interest in all the affairs of the Jewish community, and every important question was still submitted to him almost to the last day.'[9]

Regular reports from his secretary on the correspondence received at his London office were read to him as late as the Saturday night preceding his death, which occurred at his home on Tuesday morning, 21 January 1890, when, Adler having blessed his sons and daughters[10] and recited the Shema, 'his Father in Heaven called him to his eternal rest as a beloved infant is hushed to sleep.'[11]

* * *

Born in Hanover in 1839, Hermann Adler was six years old when he witnessed from 'yonder gallery, nestling close to my dear mother, gazing with childish wonder on the strange ceremonial that was being enacted below—the installation of a new Chief Rabbi.'[12]

Forty-six years were to pass before he found himself similarly installed. At the outset, he began studies at University College School in London and then (at least, for the first part of his bachelor's examinations)[13] at University College itself. There, one of his contemporaries was Julian Goldsmid,[14] later to become his—and his predecessor's—adversary as president of the West London Synagogue.

Hermann's 'first and last teacher was his revered father, who began to teach him the Decalogue when he was four years old, and studied Talmud with him practically to the very last day of his life.'[15] His other mentors included Barnett Abrahams,[16] a dayan of the Spanish and Portuguese Congregation; Marcus Kalisch, the Chief Rabbi's secretary;[17] and David Asher,[18] of Leipzig—as well as Rabbi Solomon Loeb Rapoport and Rabbi Samuel Freund, from whom he received *semichah* after two years at the Prague yeshivah (1860–1862).[19] During this latter period, he also gained his doctorate from the University of Leipzig.

For much of the next three decades, Adler combined his ministry at Bayswater—where he was appointed as 'Lecturer' in 1864, at the age of twenty-five—with duties as tutor (and later as president) at Jews' College, and with honorary positions in the wider community.[20] Defeating Birmingham-based Abraham Pereira Mendes, scion of a distinguished Sephardi family, for the Bayswater post, he (or at least his supporters) regarded the contest as a 'referendum' on his father's Chief Rabbinate.

'This was by no means a key to leisure,' wrote the congregation's chroniclers,²¹ 'as his honorary officers had agreed from the start that his services were to be at the disposal of the whole metropolitan area. He was already a Chief Rabbi in the making.' The synagogue, noted another commentator,²² 'was both large and influential. Hermann's gift for preaching and homiletics suited his congregation. The new generation was prepared to step into the place of the old.'

Between the old and the new, radical changes in the Anglo-Jewish landscape confronted the Delegate Chief Rabbi as he took up the reins. 'How greatly has the Hebrew population of the United Kingdom expanded within the last half-century,' he was later to remark. 'And how heterogeneous are the elements of this population, widely differing in their culture, ranging between the two extremes of the religious thermometer, each section needing a different kind of handling!'²³

It was this juggling of extremes that came to dominate intra-communal relations—and to temper their effect on the election and its principals (not to say principles)—as the need gradually arose to replace the Delegate Chief Rabbi with a Chief Rabbinical successor. Indeed, the 'two extremes of the religious thermometer' were to play a significant role in shaping what became, in effect, a one-horse race.

* * *

By the time Nathan Adler's Chief Rabbinate drew to its close, the initial effects of the Reform secession had long since dissipated. In the years immediately following the *cherem*, 'brothers and near relations ceased to visit one another, the closest families were broken, and much hardship and bitterness ensued.'²⁴ But in 1845, within weeks of Adler's installation (though coincidentally), the Sephardi Beth Din—overseeing the religious affairs of the congregation from which most of the reformers had come—'manifested a disposition to relax that stringency of the exclusion enforced against the Seceders, individually, which is still maintained towards them in a corporate capacity, and towards their synagogue as a non-conformist one.' As an act of compassion, the dayanim 'formally sanctioned the attendance at a funeral of several Seceders as chief mourners, and tacitly recognised their claim to participate in all the melancholy offices usual on such occasions, except the recital of the kaddish.'²⁵

Four years on, after a lengthy battle waged by two of the congregation's leaders, Hananel de Castro and Haim Guedalla, 'the few antiquated gentlemen, the main supporters and upholders of the "anathema,"'²⁶ were prevailed upon to repeal the penalty, as a result of which 'the ecclesiastical authorities performed the ceremony requisite to purge the reformers of *cherem* ... This act enabled families that had long ceased holding mutual communication to resume friendly intercourse; and one of the leaders of the Reformers paid at once a visit to one of the chiefs of the Orthodox party, between whom family ties had not prevented the birth of a bitter religious feud.'[27]

Thereafter, despite the Ashkenazi Beth Din's disinclination to follow suit, relations between Adler's constituents—now controlled at the organisational level by the United Synagogue, established by Act of Parliament in 1870—and the Reformers softened considerably over the course of his incumbency. 'The strong feelings which were evoked fifty years ago against the Reform movement,' its leaders declared in 1892, 'have long since died a natural death. For many years past, the closest domestic ties by marriage, and the growth of general enlightenment and forbearance, have combined to reunite the two sections of the community into one; one for all practical purposes of communal action and religious sympathy despite the deviations in external forms of public worship.'[28]

While this assertion was wide of the mark, as will become evident, cooperation had reached a close enough point to prompt six 'influential members'[29] of the synagogal bodies—from across the spectrum, and largely through spirited self-interest—to suggest taking steps 'with the object of uniting the entire Anglo-Jewish Community under one Spiritual Chief.'

The spectrum, by this time, had widened considerably, with, on the left, the first murmurings of Liberal Judaism in the recently formed Jewish Religious Union, and on the right, a rapidly growing ultra-Orthodox confraternity represented by the Federation of Synagogues and the Machzike Hadath ('Upholders of the Religion')—the latter, mainly immigrants from Poland and Russia, labelling the English Jews as 'reformers,' and Adler himself as 'the Chief reformer.'[30]

The Machzike Hadath had resulted from a revolt by these immigrants against what they regarded as the tolerance and easy-going traditionalism of the United Synagogue's 'inclusive Orthodoxy.'[31] Even Nathan Adler, from his sanctuary in Brighton, had urged his East European colleagues 'kindly to preach in the synagogue and house of study, to publicise the evil that is befalling our brethren who have come here, and to warn them not to come to the land of Britain, for such an ascent is a descent.'[32]

The new arrivals objected strongly to (among other perceived failings) the younger Adler's identification with the leaders of his anglicised community, and indeed of the Anglican faith, by dressing himself in church-like clericals, using the title 'The Very Reverend,' and addressing others in the ministry—not least those eminent rabbis outside his flock, and well above him in learning and piety—as 'The Reverend Mr.'

The catalyst for the revolt was Adler's refusal, during the interregnum, to respond to requests for more stringent supervision of butchers licensed by the London Board for Shechitah. As a result, a group of East Londoners, supported by German-born followers of Samson Raphael Hirsch—one of his father's rivals for the Chief Rabbinate—founded the secessionist body, acquiring their own rabbi, Abraham Aba Werner, as well as a synagogue, Talmud Torah, and kashrut infrastructure.[33]

The Federation of (Minor) Synagogues[34] had had an earlier provenance, emerging in October 1887 from a meeting at the Spital Square Synagogue, within the Whitechapel constituency of Shechitah Board president Samuel Montagu, MP (later ennobled as Baron Swaythling of Swaythling).

Drawn to its call were worshippers from the *chevras* (small prayer-houses) and minor congregations that had sprung up across London's East End, but had, as one contemporary put it,[35] 'no effective share in communal affairs and no organisation for voicing their views or making their influence felt. Dissatisfaction was general; rumblings, low but deep, forecasting threatening storms and eruptions, manifested themselves from time to time, and there were open threats of opposition movements and institutions.'

Perturbed equally by the native-born Jews' undeniable laxity in religious observance, these immigrants soon forgathered as the *Chevros Bnai Yisroel* (Societies for the Children of Israel), aimed at promoting their spiritual and physical welfare, funeral and burial rights, kashrut and ministerial services, and representation on the Board of Deputies and Board of Guardians.

Relations between the United Synagogue and the Federation of Synagogues were frosty from the outset. Questioning the latter's *raison d'être*, the US council declared: 'At a time when the desire of the community is to unite as much as possible its various organisations, and to make further provision for the religious requirements of the poor in the East of London, it surely seems inopportune to create and extend a body whose policy must inevitably tend to disunion and disintegration.'[36]

These remarks were prompted by the Federation's short-lived appointment of its first Minister, the German-educated Mayer Lerner[37]—who, as a diplomatic sop to the US in their joint war against Reform, was placed under Adler's jurisdiction[38]—and its broadening espousal of the East Enders' cause in the increasingly bitter hegemonic battle between the two synagogal bodies.[39]

Recognising the threat to its hitherto unquenchable dominance, the United Synagogue leadership, with Lord Rothschild at its helm, retaliated by formulating what came to be known (though never implemented) as the 'East End Scheme,' the proposed construction of a 'Colossal [1,000-seat] Synagogue' in Whitechapel under US control, with ancillary social, cultural and welfare facilities.[40] As the debates over the scheme and the Chief Rabbinical election both boiled over, and eventually coalesced, so too did the tempers—and temperatures—of the protagonists and issues involved.

* * *

In a letter to Rothschild, dated 22 April 1890, and signed by, among others, Montagu as acting president of the Federation, and Sir Philip Magnus,[41] a council member of the West London Synagogue, the six 'influential members' of the community wrote that there was 'now abundant evidence of the existence of a widespread desire for (a) a comprehension of the English Jews under the guidance of one presiding Chief Rabbi, who shall be the Chief Spiritual adviser of all the Jews residing in the British Empire; and (b) a certain latitude to individual congregations within well-defined limits to vary the present order of Divine Service in some details.

'It may be useful to point out that though there are some differences of outward practice and of ritual observance between sections of Jews, differences which may perhaps be the outcome of their surroundings, the main principles of the Creed of all are not merely similar but identical, and that the brotherhood of Israel is far stronger than any divergence of liturgy or rite.'

Acting, they acknowledged, 'entirely without any representative authority,' they suggested to Rothschild that the time had arrived 'when you can usefully invite the Spanish and Portuguese Synagogue; the Federation of Synagogues (whose acting president is one of the signatories of this letter); the West London Synagogue of British Jews, of the Council of which some of us are members; the other metropolitan and the provincial synagogues to join with the United Synagogue, of which you are the President, in the election of a consultative Committee, who shall endeavour to formulate a plan of comprehension of the Jews of the British Empire.'

The 'comprehension,' dealing largely with modes of ritual and liturgy, included a proposal that 'the Chief Rabbi shall be the Spiritual head of the whole of the Jews of the British Empire, but in respect to the Portuguese and West London Congregations in a consultative capacity only, such congregations respectively retaining their autonomy.'[42]

In support of the plan, a petition signed by 472 members of the United Synagogue was delivered to Rothschild the following day, urging that the US constitution 'be so amended as to render possible the admission of the West London Synagogue of British Jews as a constituent synagogue.' It also sought the establishment of 'a representative Board for the control and regulation of public worship which shall, in consultation with the Chief Rabbi, exercise in matters of Synagogue discipline and ritual the powers hitherto solely vested in the Chief Rabbi.'

The US executive responded by 'considering the steps which should be taken to convene a meeting of delegates of the Congregations represented at the Chief Rabbi's Board for the purpose of conferring upon the preliminary steps to be taken to elect a Chief Rabbi.'[43] A fortnight later, on 6 May 1890, the council authorised Rothschild 'to invite representatives from the Metropolitan and Provincial Synagogues to consider, in conjunction with the Honorary Officers of the United Synagogue, the proposals contained in the letters addressed to the President in reference to the appointment of Chief Rabbi.' The move came at the end of a lengthy debate over the merits of those letters, one of which had urged Rothschild 'to proceed at once to the election of a Chief Rabbi.'

During the debate, Montagu delivered a back-tracking justification for co-signing the letter to Rothschild alongside the Reformers. 'Three things I desire,' he told the council. 'The first is that we should elect a Chief Rabbi as early as possible. I also think that we should select one who would be most able to keep together the majority of the Jews in the British Empire, and that we should not seek for pledges inconsistent with the past life of the individual himself. We should be prompt, because the anxiety that prevails in the community should be allayed as soon as possible; and, at the same time, we should remember that the position of the gentleman who is now discharging the duties of the Rabbinate is not a dignified one.

'I need not dwell on the second point, for it is patent to everyone that we must have a man who will promote peace and concord. I lay stress on the third point, because if we asked for pledges and they were refused, we should be bound by such refusal, whilst if the Chief Rabbi yielded to the pressure of circumstances, he would lose all influence.

> If these be my opinions, it may be asked why did I sign a letter to the President, of which you have heard, with the object of uniting the entire Anglo-Jewish community under one Spiritual Chief. I may tell you that the inception of this programme occurred in the lifetime of the late Chief Rabbi, and had no reference whatever to the Rabbinate. One of the signatories, it is true, suggested that we should delay our action until the appointment of a successor to the late Dr Adler, but this suggestion did not meet with acceptance.
>
> There is nothing in our letter to which the Chief Rabbi *pro tem* could offer the slightest objection, and it therefore need not alarm the most orthodox of my friends. The intention of our letter is an honest endeavour to unite all the Jews of the Empire under one Spiritual Chief and one lay chief, the Spiritual Chief to be an adviser in a consultative capacity

to all outside his jurisdiction. The Portuguese congregation may, perhaps, not have recourse at present to such an arrangement, but they did so in the past, and might do so again in the absence of Dr Gaster,[44] and under other circumstances.

I see no objection to representatives of the Berkeley Street Synagogue being invited, providing they will follow the lines laid down in our letter, which was signed by three influential members of that Synagogue. What I would like of those who will meet under the resolution of my noble friend is that, if they are outside the jurisdiction of the Chief Rabbi, they shall be bound by his authority on imperial Jewish questions while retaining their autonomy. We have adopted something similar at the Board of Deputies, where representatives of the Berkeley Street Synagogue have been admitted without any evil results.

I confess that years ago I was opposed to the recognition of the Berkeley Street Synagogue as a corporate body, but in latter years I have come to consider that if a body of Jews exists who adopt the Mosaic laws, their synagogue should be recognised even if it be closed on second days, and even if the congregation reject the rabbinical laws.

I still regret the schism of fifty years ago. I believe that if those who founded the West London Synagogue had remained with us, we should have had the improvements in our service much earlier than we did. I look on the present movement as holding out the olive-branch to the Berkeley Street Synagogue. I believe that if it sends delegates to the conclave, it will be for purposes of union, not of division—that the synagogue will not be led further away, and that the cleavage will not be increased.[45]

The West London Synagogue and the Federation of Synagogues were among those subsequently invited by Rothschild 'to elect gentlemen to represent them at the Conference which I propose summoning to give effect to this resolution.'[46] The West London's response was preceded by a 'long and animated' debate within its council, at which, it was later reported,[47] a motion was tabled by the chairman, Sir Julian Goldsmid, 'to return a courteous negative to the invitation of the President of the United Synagogue.

'To this proposal, an amendment was moved by Mr L. Schloss accepting the invitation, but limiting very greatly the powers of any delegates who might be appointed ... A very strong feeling was shown by both parties to preserve the autonomy of the congregation.' Attending the debate in a non-voting capacity, the West London's ministers, David Woolf Marks and Isidore Harris, spoke forcefully against the invitation, Marks (the senior minister) declaring that 'if the suggestions contained in the letter signed by three of his congregants were carried into effect, he would have no alternative but to retire from his ministrations.'

After this meeting, Rothschild wrote (18 June 1890) to the West London Synagogue's Herbert G. Lousada, stating that 'the terms of the letter addressed to me by yourself and five other gentlemen have my approval, and I shall be glad to see delegates from your Synagogue at our Conference. They will be able to defend Mr Marks's position, but they will certainly have a sinecure, for no one, in or out of his congregation, would desire to interfere with a position earned by several years of service, not only to your congregation but to the whole community. With regard to the preservation of the autonomy of your Synagogue, I may remind you that this was one of the points specially stipulated in your letter.'

Lousada confronted widespread opposition to the content of the letter when, the following week, nearly one hundred West London seat-holders voted, by a large majority, to reject the invitation. 'Ultra-Orthodoxy prevails in the East End, whereas it does not on the other side of London,' declared Goldsmid. 'For this reason, it would be serving the best interests of Judaism not to accept the invitation of the president of the United Synagogue because, by doing so, we might promote a split in another direction.'

Referring to Adler, Goldsmid added: 'I do not want a spiritual leader. Mr Lousada has said that the Chief Rabbi will have a consultative voice only, but to consult him and not to follow his advice would be an impertinence to the Chief Rabbi, whilst to consult him and to follow his advice would be an insult to the congregation.'[48]

Following the vote, Goldsmid wrote to Rothschild: 'We wish to acknowledge with much satisfaction both the courtesy shown in this invitation and the desire for closer relations between our body and the constituents of the United Synagogue. At the same time, it appears to the great majority of the members of this Congregation that the principle upon which it has been founded must, of necessity, prevent its being represented at a meeting intended to prepare the way for the election of a new Chief Rabbi, as the congregation has uniformly declined to accept the spiritual authority of such an officer, however personally distinguished.'

Appended to this letter was the text of a resolution 'that the Congregation, whilst desiring to maintain and, if possible, to strengthen the cordial relations now happily subsisting between it and the United Synagogue, cannot be represented by delegates at a Conference which is called to consider the conditions of the appointment of a Chief Rabbi.'[49]

Rothschild's invitation was also turned down by the Reform congregation in Manchester and by the four Sephardi synagogues—at Bevis Marks and Bryanstone Street in London, and at Manchester and Ramsgate.[50]

Soon after his volte-face, Montagu felt obliged to explain to 'the most orthodox of my friends'—in starkly different terms—the inclusion of his name on 'a certain letter addressed to the President of the United Synagogue,' as well as his attendance at the US council meeting at which the letter was discussed. Moving a resolution that the Federation accept Rothschild's invitation (subsequently passed by thirty-four votes to nil), he told his Board that he had attended the meeting because he had been asked to do so by Adler, 'who begged me not to absent myself from any meeting at which important communal matters were discussed.' A similar request had come from 'the noble President of the Council,' who had discussed with him the plan he proposed to adopt with reference to the letter.

> He [Montagu] desired to assure the Board that he had signed the letter and made his remarks at the Council meeting in his individual capacity and in no way as the representative or as President of the Federation. He had acted purely on his personal responsibility in the matter, and the freedom or liberty of the Federation remained perfectly untrammelled.
>
> As he was anxious to retain the confidence of even the most orthodox member of the Board, he would recall the views which prompted him in the action he had taken. His main object was to unite under one Chief the community for communal, but not for religious, purposes—for the promotion of whatever would be for the general advantage of the Jews of the Empire ...
>
> He held that the recognition of so influential a body of Jews as the West London Synagogue was absolutely necessary. That they had severed themselves from the general body of the community was to be regretted, but to ignore them would be to act like the proverbial ostrich which, burying its head in the sand, thought that it could not be seen.
>
> At the same time, he condemned the Reform movement as he had always done, and would do. He had taken the action he did at the Council because he did not for a moment wish to risk the threatened resignation of Lord Rothschild. Such a step would not have helped the cause either of orthodoxy or of the United Synagogue.
>
> He was prompted by feelings which, he hoped, all would

give him credit for—considerations of the good of the community as a whole. If there was to be a split, he did not desire that the responsibility of it should be thrown upon the Federation, which should tranquilly follow its course of always supporting orthodox Judaism.

Montagu argued that Rothschild's invitation was 'an important recognition of the Federation,' which had been asked to send proportionately as many representatives as any other congregation. His main object in the whole matter was 'to protect the Jewish religion, and the presence of eight orthodox representatives at the conference would support that object.'[51]

Despite the Federation's ongoing battle with the US over the East End Scheme, and its deference to Chief Rabbinical jurisdiction in the appointment of its Minister, Montagu craved influence for his organisation in the process by which the higher office was to be represented, managed and occupied. This desire accorded with that of Rothschild himself, anxious to widen the Chief Rabbinate's authority to cover—and, more importantly, be recognised by—all sections of Anglo-Jewry, though it defied the wishes of others on the US council who saw in it 'a union of shadows, without substantial benefit to anyone except Montagu and the Federation.'[52]

To ensure representation in the Chief Rabbinical election—tied to terms laid down in the United Synagogue's Deed of Foundation and Trust[53]—the Federation was required, as were all participating bodies, to demonstrate that it was 'contributing to the maintenance of such respective office.' As an influential member of the US, having participated in the negotiations that had led to its establishment,[54] Montagu himself had long voiced support for the Chief Rabbi's authority, and now—despite (or, more certainly, because of) his additional role in the Federation—he sanctioned further steps to secure its place at the electoral table.

At a meeting of his Board before the process began, he won approval for a £10 payment to the Chief Rabbi's Fund,[55] telling his colleagues that 'the question agitating the community, the election of the Chief Rabbi, was of the deepest concern to the Federation, and that he hoped they would be consulted in the matter. He could but hope that Dr Hermann Adler would be their spiritual chief, a gentleman of the first order and an orthodox scholar.'

Touching on a subject that had begun to raise hackles in the community, Montagu added—'from what Dr Adler had said to him in the course of conversation, and from what he knew of Dr Adler—that if he were elected Chief Rabbi, he would preach alternately in the East and in the West, and that he would, as far as practicable, divide his home between the East and West End.'[56]

Four months later, addressing the Chief Rabbinate Conference, Rothschild told the invited delegates that 'the idea [for the more representative gathering] was chiefly my own, and I was emboldened to summon you because I became aware that there was a widespread and deep-rooted feeling in the community that the time had come when even the humblest portion, and certainly the most orthodox, should invite the other branches of the community to join with us in attempting to unite us all—I will not say under one head, but under one spiritual Chief ...

'You may ask me what is the use of convening us here today after the Portuguese and Reform synagogues have refused to join. Perhaps there may be but very little for you to decide, but I thought that even after the refusals which I had received, it would be to the advantage of the community at large to proceed to the election of a Chief Rabbi after gentlemen from different parts of the country had met together and enabled us to gather their ideas as to what they looked forward to in the future.'

Having gathered their ideas during the course of the day, Rothschild then moved two resolutions—the first carried 'amid cheers,' the second 'by a large majority'—that, 'in the opinion of this Conference, it is desirable that the President of the United Synagogue be requested to take the necessary steps preliminary to the election or appointment of a Chief Rabbi, and with other bodies in the United Kingdom contributing to the maintenance of such office as to the mode of election or appointment and all details concerned therewith'; and that, 'in the opinion of this Conference, it is desirable that the Chief Rabbi should reside in the neighbourhood of the East End of London, where the bulk of the Jews reside.'[57]

For several months thereafter, the various committees within the United Synagogue, as well as congregational members, ministers, dayanim, and not least Adler himself, were engaged in the minutiae of the recommendations that were to form the backbone of the election. Finally, after a protracted meeting on 3 February 1891, the US executive committee adopted the 'Report to the Council on the Election of a Chief Rabbi,' which included the following recommendations:

> That the mode of election be analogous to that adopted for the last election of a Chief Rabbi, each synagogue contributing to the Chief Rabbi's Fund electing a delegate with voting power proportionate to the contributions of the bodies represented. (The twelve delegates to be appointed by the constituent congregations of the United Synagogue would thereby have two hundred and eighteen votes, and the other congregations a total of about fifty votes.)
> That the salary of the Chief Rabbi is to be £2,000 per an-

num, to cover all expenses incidental to the office. He 'shall be required to have a house as a residence, with an office in the City, as near as practicable to the East End of London.' The whole of the salary is to be paid for him direct by the United Synagogue, the subscriptions from contributing congregations heretofore paid to the Chief Rabbi's Fund being paid by them to the United Synagogue.

That the Chief Rabbi shall on no account denounce *cherem* (anathema) against any person, neither shall he deprive any member of his religious rights in the synagogue.[58]

With regard to proposals for future modifications in the ritual, the council recommended that 'whenever a question shall be raised by the Board of Management or Committee of a synagogue contributing to the support of the office of Chief Rabbi as to any proposed alteration in the form of worship or ritual, the Chief Rabbi shall consult upon such question with a Committee to be convened by him and to consist of the Preachers of the Metropolitan and Provincial (contributing) Congregations, unless he shall deem it proper to authorise such alteration without consultation with the proposed Committee.'[59]

None of the recommendations, bar the first, was seriously challenged when the US council met to adopt the report some days later. Montagu, however, was incensed by a change relating to representation, giving 'power to congregations in the United Kingdom contributing to the maintenance of the office of Chief Rabbi to be represented for the purpose of election by delegates with voting power in proportion to the several annual contributions of the bodies represented, a mode of election analogous to that adopted on the occasion of the last election of a Chief Rabbi.'

Rising to amend this resolution, Montagu called for delegates to be invited 'on the same principle as adopted at last year's conference' (where the Federation was accorded eight places). While 'frankly admitting,' he said, 'that the report on the whole was fair and reasonable,' he argued that 'the introduction of a money qualification as a voting power is a great blot on the entire series of resolutions. Things have greatly altered since the last election of a Chief Rabbi, the suffrage has been extended by the abolition of privileged membership, and by the granting of equal voting powers to seatholders irrespective of the payments contributed by them.'

Montagu held that it was 'quite impossible in a large congregation to find one representative who is a fair reflex of the multifarious opinions entertained in that congregation. The selection of delegates should, as before, be on the basis of the number of members in each synagogue.'

Opposing the amendment, US vice-president Henry Lucas described as 'preposterous' the argument that the United Synagogue, which paid four-fifths of the Chief Rabbi's salary, 'should practically place the power of election in the hands of the remaining fifth.' Council member Noah Davis asserted that, if the amendment were adopted, 'the same power would be given to the Federation of Synagogues—which, as an afterthought, sent a donation of £10 subsequently to the death of the Chief Rabbi—as to the United Synagogue, which contributed £1,600 towards his salary.'

After Montagu's bid was voted down by thirty-seven votes to six, he told the council that the £10 sent to the Chief Rabbi's Fund 'was intended as an annual subscription, and has since been repeated.' This assertion was dismissed by Lucas, who contended that 'the letter accompanying the first payment described it as a donation, and as such it was mentioned in the recommendation of the Executive Committee empowering the Federation to take part in the election of the Chief Rabbi.'[60]

In a subsequent letter to the press, Montagu wrote that he had recommended at the US council that all contributing bodies should be represented by delegates in proportion to the number of their members, with a maximum of eight representatives. This, he claimed, was the plan adopted at the 1890 conference, where it had been 'deservedly popular.'

> The recent reactionary policy was condemned with faint praise by Lord Rothschild, but was supported by thirty-seven in a meeting of fifty-seven members of the council. My object was to make the election popular, not the advancement of the Federation of Synagogues. Its representation of eight for which I pleaded was fixed by the United Synagogue for the Conference to decide as to the powers of the Chief Rabbi.
>
> We are now in the position that, by some kind of gerrymandering, the Great, New, and Hambro' Synagogues, under the immediate supervision of the Chief Rabbi, are to have forty-eight votes, and the Federation (of twenty synagogues) two votes, total fifty—not a quarter of the voting power of those synagogues which have perhaps less need of a Chief Rabbi.
>
> This is not all. Each constituent synagogue is to be represented by one delegate with varying voting power from forty to four. Was ever such a system dreamt of by an enlightened community until the Executive Committee recommended it?
>
> One would think that to state the fact would be enough to demonstrate its absurdity. I admit that the United Synagogue should have a preponderating voice. So it had at

the Conference, but that it should invite outsiders to attend at an election, to be overwhelmed by the privileged three or four who will decide the election, is an absurdity against which I protest.

Conceding that 'it matters little now, when there is only one suitable candidate,' Montagu added: 'Prior to the next election, I trust that our successors will upset so preposterous a system. Supposing at some future time there should be a reform and an orthodox candidate for the Rabbinate, are the great majority of Jews in East London to be controlled by the few in one district?'

As representative of the New West End Synagogue, and deputising for the Federation vice-president, Hermann Landau (whose two votes he was about to cast), Montagu was among the forty delegates who met on 4 June 1891 'for the purpose of electing a gentleman to fill the position of Chief Rabbi.'[61] Rothschild himself was absent, as his deputy, Henry Lucas, explained, 'owing to the calls of other duties.'

Alluding to what some had described as 'the unnecessary delay' in holding the election, Lucas referred to differences that had arisen over the powers and duties of the Chief Rabbi. 'Various suggestions were made, and owing to these and other circumstances to which I need not refer [the East End Scheme], the peace of the community was threatened, and the atmosphere surrounding it charged with heavy storm clouds. In the time that has elapsed, better counsels have prevailed. The difficulties that have arisen have been smoothed down, and the clouds, I am happy to think, have dispersed.[62] The consequence is that you can now proceed to the election with a concord that could otherwise not have existed some months ago.'

Charged with proposing that 'the Rev Dr Hermann Adler be elected Chief Rabbi of the United Hebrew Congregations of the British Empire,' Bayswater's Benjamin Cohen referred to their presence not merely as delegates, but 'to give effect to the voice of the whole Jewish community pronounced in language loud, clear, unmistakable, and at times impetuous ... It is because we know that Dr Adler has never been a partisan, because we know that he will always be a just and impartial ruler, and that he will blend the necessities of the present with the traditions of the past that I submit his name with confidence on this occasion.'

Seconding the motion, Montagu ascribed his own selection 'for this agreeable task not only to the fact that I represent an important synagogue in the West End, but also because I am the representative of numerous synagogues in the East End. This is an emphatic testimony to our unanimity in the choice we are making.'

After expressions of admiration for Adler from several provincial delegates,

Lucas called for a vote on the resolution, 'which was carried by acclamation, every delegate upstanding.' Rubber-stamping the result, he then added: 'It has been my good fortune to be a member of the Bayswater Synagogue for a period of twenty-seven years, and during the whole of this time Dr Adler officiated in the capacity of minister. I have heard more sermons from his lips than other gentlemen in this room, and they enabled me to judge of his fitness for the office to which he has just been elected.'[63]

Hermann Adler (1891): 'Let me feel that every hand I grasp is that of a true friend'

FROM THE PULPIT — II
The Ideal Jewish Pastor

Sermon delivered at the Great Synagogue, London, by the Rev Dr Hermann Adler on the occasion of his installation into office as Chief Rabbi of Great Britain, 23 June 1891–17 Sivan 5651

My dear brethren, it is just forty-six years ago since I sat in yonder gallery, nestling close to my dear mother, gazing with childish wonder on the strange ceremonial that was being enacted below—the installation of a new Chief Rabbi. I then comprehended but little of the discourse that was preached on that occasion; but since that time I have often read and re-read the words that were spoken by my beloved father and revered predecessor. He dilated on the feelings of diffidence and trepidation with which he entered upon his office, being a stranger in a strange land, the language of which he, as yet, but imperfectly understood, and amid surroundings that were altogether novel to him. There are, I believe, several here today who can recall the fervour with which he implored Divine help and blessing—a help and a blessing which were indeed so signally manifested to him from the moment that he set foot on these shores to the time when his soul returned to its heavenly home, sacred and pure.

My position is of an essentially different character. I have grown up in your midst. I have endeavoured to draw my mental nurture from the rich stores of our dear England's thought and learning. In my paternal home, as a disciple and student, and subsequently, during a period of gradually increasing responsibilities, every detail has become familiar to me of the exalted office which I have been called upon, by the Providence of God and the voice of the community, to occupy. I am standing in the presence of friends. Many of you are knitted to my soul. We take sweet counsel together. Your loyal friendship has proved a stay, a solace and a delight. And yet I must aver that I am inspired by sentiments of anxiety and misgiving no less keen and poignant than those which thrilled the heart of our late Chief Rabbi. And you can all appreciate, even as I hope you will fully sympathise with, the motives and causes which prompt those anxieties and suggest those misgivings.

May I not well stand appalled at the responsibility cast upon me, to direct the religious government of the many English communities scattered over every part of the globe, extending even beyond the British Empire? How greatly has the Hebrew population of the United Kingdom expanded within the last half-century! It has been trebled, if not quadrupled. Take only the metropolis. It is no longer a city, but a province, with its synagogues from Hampstead, in the north, to Lewisham, in the south; from Hammersmith, in the west, to Stepney—and soon, I trust, to Poplar—in the east. And how great an increase has there been in the number of our institutions, both educational and benevolent, each of them needing some supervision, and making some rightful claim on the Chief Rabbi's time and thought! And how heterogeneous are the elements of this population, widely differing in their culture, ranging between the two extremes of the religious thermometer, each section needing a different kind of handling! Verily, as I think of the multitudinous duties and responsibilities that await me; as I reflect on the grave problems by which I am confronted; aye, and as I hear of all that I am expected to achieve, I ask, with Job, 'Is my strength the strength of stones, or is my flesh of brass?'[1]

Dear friends, if I were to depend on my own unassisted powers, I should indeed be tempted to despair. But I rely with trustful confidence upon the help and guidance of my God and the God of my fathers—God, my exceeding joy, who has brought me thus far, and whose blessing you have this day invoked on my behalf; and my soul is no longer cast down nor disquieted within me. And I crave the affectionate forbearance of the members of my flock, that they may not expect more of me than can be planned by one poor human brain; that they may not demand of me more than can be wrought by two weak human hands. But I also feel upheld—I say it with deep humility—by the all-absorbing desire which God has implanted in me since my earliest years, and which my parents fostered within me since ever I drew conscious breath, the aspiration to become a worthy teacher in Israel, the yearning to spend myself for the glory of Judaism, the welfare of its professors, and the good of my fellow-creatures.

It has been truly said that the worth of a man in relation to his fellows depends upon the ideals which he cherishes. Let me then point out to you what I have conceived to be the ideal of a Jewish pastor, which I shall strive to follow, though I can never hope to attain it. This ideal, it seems to me, is set forth in a few words written in Exodus 28:30: 'And Aaron shall bear the cause of the children of Israel upon his heart before the Lord continually.'

These words, in their literal sense, refer to the Urim and Thummim which the High Priest was to bear on his breast, and which, according to traditional

---

1   Job 6:12. [All citations are as in the original text.]

interpretation,[2] would seem to have been none other than the precious gems on which the names of the twelve tribes of Israel were engraven. These he should bear on his heart, which, in Scripture parlance, denotes the centre and source of all intellectual and emotional life. 'He shall bear the names of the children of Israel upon his heart for a memorial before the Lord continually,' ever mindful that the interests, not of any one powerful and influential section, but of the whole House of Israel, have been entrusted to his keeping. And if his brain and heart would thus be entirely engrossed by solicitude for the well-being of his people, if all disturbing elements—selfishness, prejudice, and the fear of man—had been banished from his soul, then God would vouchsafe to him his clear and perfect guidance,[3] and he would be worthy to lead and to counsel Israel in every season of difficulty and perplexity.

Dear brethren, there are many essential differences between the functions of the High Priest of old and the duties incumbent upon the Jewish pastor of our time. But it appears to me that the obligation is as imperative on the present-day religious guide as it ever was on the High Priest, that *'he shall bear the cause of the children of Israel upon his heart before the Lord continually.'* He must ever meditate on the needs of his community, sensitive to all that will redound to Israel's honour or besmirch his fair name. He must not judge of events and decide upon his course of action with the assumption of sacerdotal infallibility. He must humbly bring the cause before God. Before Him who is the fountain of wisdom; so that, striving for the divine light, he will not be wise in his own conceit. Before Him who is the Sun of righteousness; so that, despising the soft flatteries of an easy popularity, he will consider not what will be the easiest and pleasantest policy, but what line of action will stand the scrutiny of Heaven. Before Him who is the God of mercy and lovingkindness, so that the poor and the oppressed will confidently look to him for help and for defence. Before Him who worketh great things, so that he will not fold his hands in idleness, but will be forever striving and toiling, acknowledging no master above him, save the Lord his God.[4] 'Before the Lord continually.' He must be ready to sacrifice his ease without murmuring, and to surrender his leisure without questioning, impressed with the force of the words spoken by an ancient sage:[5] 'When once a man has been placed at the head of affairs, and has been vested with the robe of office, he dare never more say, "Let me now have a care for my comfort; why need I concern myself for the affairs of others?" Ah, no. All the needs of the community henceforth devolve upon him.'

2   Yoma 73b.
3   Ibid.
4   Horayoth 11a, b.
5   Shemoth Rabbah c.27.

Momentous and paramount as are the spiritual interests of his flock, he will not confine his activity to these, but devote much anxious thought to their temporal condition. His sympathies and his energies will not be pent up within the narrow limits of his own pastorate, but will extend far beyond to the lot of his brethren in countries afar off—sympathies and energies never more urgently needed than in these troublous times, when the hydra of intolerance and persecution, alas, again lifts up its hateful head. Imbued as he is with a fervent love for his country, he will work with gladsome energy in every cause that can tend to add to his country's welfare, and alleviate the miseries of his fellow-men. And thus he will prove himself the rightful successor, not merely of those pious men who guided our community from the days of Menasseh ben Israel, but likewise of those who lived before the expulsion; of men like Rabbenu Yom Tob, the martyr hero of York Castle; of Jacob, Presbyter of the Jews of all England, whom King John termed *dilectus et familiaris noster*, 'our well-beloved and intimate friend'; of Rabbi Elias, named Elyas le Evesk by the chroniclers, who lifted up his voice in solemn protest against the spoliation of the third Henry.

But it is to the spiritual claims of his flock that the ideal pastor will devote his chief solicitude. He will watch over God's house, imbued with the anxious desire that the Divine Service held within its walls shall enable the worshipper to realise the lofty ends to which his communion with his Father in heaven shall serve—to purify, to consecrate and to elevate to a higher plane his life outside the synagogue. He will therefore strive that every service be characterised by dignity and reverence, by fervour and devotion. His voice will be heard when he has entered the sanctuary, awakening the careless and stirring up the slothful, seeking to kindle in his hearers' hearts the enthusiasm that stirs and quickens his own soul. He will unfold to them the high significance and spiritual purpose of the statutes and ordinances of his faith, the observance of which he has been appointed vigilantly to safeguard and jealously to defend, as heirlooms to be faithfully transmitted from generation to generation. And he will teach that a mere blind and mechanical fulfilment of these ordinances will not be acceptable in the eyes of the Supreme, unless they serve as a stimulus to the higher life—a life of self-control and abstinence, a life of uprightness and of integrity.

It is the cause of the *children* of Israel which he will most earnestly bear in his heart, eagerly solicitous that *they* may be won for God and his Law. To attain this end, he will watch over the schools, that they may ever remain nurseries of genuine piety and sterling virtue. Nor in his care for the children of the poor will he be unmindful of the sons and daughters of the leisured classes, who stand in need not less but more urgently, of the wise and wholesome restraints of religion. His care will not be confined to the young during the brief period of schooling. He will watch over the pupils at that critical period when they are launched upon the world with all its lures and enticements, endeavouring still to instruct, to guide and to mould. Not by vague exhortations, but by seeking to influence each individual that comes under his ken. For the counsel of the wise king will powerfully come home to him:[6] 'Be thou diligent to know the faces of thy lambs: set thy heart to the flocks.'

He will rally around him the poor and uncultured, sympathising with them in their struggles, mitigating their troubles, and advising them in their perplexities. Nor will he hold aloof from those who are accounted the spoilt children of fortune, but seek to shame them out of their wasteful luxury and hard selfishness. He will essay to win back to the fold those on whom their Judaism sits but lightly, by holding up our faith in its real garb, and showing how its teachings are in harmony with all that is good and noble and true in modern thought.

And thus, in accordance with the Scripture texts we heard just now, he will be at one and the same time a shepherd and a watchman. A shepherd who goes out before his flock; a leader, not one who allows himself to be swayed by every passing wind of doctrine, but a man of tender heart, who guides his sheep to green pastures and cooling streams, carrying the young, the weary and the footsore in his arms. And a watchman, a sentinel standing on the lofty tower, patrolling the battlements, ever alert with eye and ear, a vigilant guardian of the citadel of religion and morality against the surprise of every foe; a doughty champion of the mission Israel has still to accomplish on earth—to spread the knowledge of the unity of God, the supremacy of virtue, and the brotherhood of man.

This, in the fewest possible words, is the ideal of the true Jewish pastor which I have set before me. In how far shall I be able to realise it? I answer in the prophet's words:[7] 'O Lord God, Thou knowest.' It is not in the power of poor humanity to realise its high ideals.

> On the earth the broken arcs;
> In the heaven a perfect round.

But of this I am assured, that if I but aspire to the highest, God in his mercy will account the pure intent as though it had been fully achieved.[8]

Who would deny the fact that the task which awaits me is, in sooth, gigantic? I speak not as one who is ignorant of the work that confronts me.

---

6   Proverbs 27:23.
7   Ezekiel 37:3
8   Kiddushin 40a.

During the last twelve years I have learnt what the English Rabbinate means, what it entails, and what it requires. How fully applicable to it are the words of Rabbi Gamaliel:[9] 'Think you that I commit governance unto you? Ah, no! I give servitude unto you.' Not that I dread work. From my earliest years, I have bowed my shoulder to bear. To the community, I have given the vigour of my youth and the strength of my manhood. For the community I will live; for the community I will die. But do not exact too much from me. Do not entirely deprive me of a few interspaces consecrated to those studies which are the rejoicing of my heart. Do not expect me to be continually in evidence. The Chief Rabbi's office is not the stage of a theatre; the sphere of a pastor's work is not the arena of a circus.

I can but re-echo the words spoken by him who will ever remain the highest ideal of a nation's guide: 'I am not able to bear all this people alone, because it is too heavy for me.'[10] And, therefore, I am fully confident that I shall not succeed in accomplishing aught of sterling value unless you will all extend to me your right loyal aid. Dear ministers and fellow-workers! Second me in all these various labours, which I have imperfectly sketched, with your deliberate counsel and your willing help. Let me feel that I have in every one of you a zealous coadjutor, who will devote heart and soul to the work demanded of him. I ask every individual member of the community to extend his loyal help to me. Let me feel that every hand I grasp is that of a true friend! Give me your loyal help, members of my flock in the provinces, whose representatives I rejoice to welcome here today, and whom I hope soon to visit in your homes! Give me your loyal help, brethren across the seas! Though my voice cannot reach you, yet will my written word, my counsel, and my guidance, ever be freely given to you. And oh! that a dear wish of my heart may be fulfilled to me ere I pass away, to behold with my eyes the various colonial communities that are so often in my thoughts, so constantly in my prayers.

Give me your confidence, I ask of the various sections of the community, with their many divergent opinions. That such diversities exist it would be but foolish and ostrich-like to deny. But I would entreat them to deal with a forbearing spirit toward each other, devoid of suspicion, devoid of distrust. To my brethren in the West, I say: Do not stigmatise the denizens of the East as bigoted fanatics, lost in the slough of mediaeval superstition. Granted that some of them may be inferior in refinement and culture to their wealthier brethren, they certainly teach many a precious lesson of staunch, manly religious allegiance and of glad willingness to make heavy sacrifices for the sake of their faith. To my brethren in the East, I say (though, happily, the East cannot

---

9   Horayoth 10a, b.
10 Numbers 11:14.

claim a monopoly in the possession of strictly observant Israelites): Do not look upon those who are not in entire agreement with you as though they were outside the pale of Judaism. Give them credit for being as solicitous as you are yourselves for the welfare of our common faith. And to both East and West I appeal: Let not your divergence of opinion lead to schisms and divisions, to discord and disruption. May the union of hearts continue and strengthen! At no crisis in the annals of our race was it more necessary than it is now to present a united front to the world. And confide in me that my most earnest strivings will be directed to secure this end. 'Truth and peace' are the aims for which I will toil. For gratitude I ask not. From the noble it comes spontaneously; from the ignoble it never comes at all. But for this I do ask and entreat you all: Give me your loyal trust! Give me your prayers! Let me feel that your supplications are joined to mine in this most solemn hour![11]

11 [The sermon concluded with a prayer for the welfare of the Queen, the Government, the Jewish people across the globe, and the Jewish communities throughout the United Kingdom, followed by the Priestly Blessing.]

CHAPTER THREE

Who Pays the Piper

THE CONFLICT BETWEEN, and over, East and West was to dominate the twenty-year tenure of Hermann Adler. Faced with challenges from within and without—from the strengthening elements of Reform and Liberal Judaism no less than those of ultra-Orthodoxy, and from ministers in his own camp dispirited by the rigidity of what came to be known (and scorned) as 'Adlerism'—he trod a difficult and delicate tightrope which, while threatening at times to snap, survived many attempts to cut it loose.

Disputes over liturgical reform, ministerial appointments, rabbinical credentials, shechitah supervision, intra-communal relations, the Beth Din's authority, Sabbath-afternoon services—these and other difficulties during his incumbency left East and West as divided at its close as they were at the start. Acknowledging the inadequacy of his mission, it was little wonder, then, that Adler's last message to both sides was a cry from the heart. In February 1911, sitting alone in his study, he penned a letter which, he instructed his family, was to be opened immediately after his death. Five months later, some of its contents were shared with the community at large.

'I am strongly convinced,' he wrote, 'that, to ensure the welfare of Judaism in this country, it is essential that a successor in the Rabbinate should be appointed with the least possible delay after my demise. He must be a strong personality, strong in piety and learning, one who will be equally acceptable to the East and the West, the native and the immigrant. And realising the grave difficulty of meeting with such a personality, I pray with all my heart: "May the Lord God of the spirits of all flesh set a man over the congregation, who may go out before them, and who may go in before them, and who may lead them out and bring them in, that the Congregation of the Lord be not as sheep which have no shepherd."'[1]

Some months earlier, a proposal had been made to the United Synagogue by the Federation of Synagogues which might—if accepted—have gone some way towards advancing Adler's wishes. At a meeting with the US executive, held at the offices of its president, Lord Rothschild, the honorary officers of the Federation and its secretary, Joseph Blank—who later recorded an account of the discussion²—sought, among other questions, 'to come to some arrangement upon the [Chief] Rabbinate' or, as Lord Swaythling put it at the meeting, 'to prevent friction in the election of an eventual Chief Rabbi, when our respected Chief, who is over seventy, is not able to work any longer at his post.'³ The result, wrote Blank, was summed up in a letter from the US secretary, Philip Ornstein, to Swaythling, which included the following passage:

> The question of the Rabbinate appears to be that which presses mainly upon the representatives of the Federation. It is, in the opinion of the Hon. Officers, inexpedient to discuss that question at the present time. But, apart from that objection, they feel that it would not be possible to pledge the United Synagogue, or the community at large, to the proposal suggested, which is 'the mutual agreement for the election of a first Minister of the Federation to be Delegate Chief Rabbi and eventually Chief Rabbi.' The Anglo-Jewish community, as a whole, have to be considered in regard to this question.

Having rejected the proposal, and now losing no time in filling the vacuum, the US honorary officers 'deemed it necessary that steps should be taken without delay to have the duties of the important office of Chief Rabbi duly carried out without intermission. They have therefore decided to appoint the Revs M. Hyamson and A. Feldman, the dayanim, to act until further notice, jointly and severally, in carrying out the duties and functions appertaining to the office of Chief Rabbi, so far as those duties and functions in any way relate to the United Synagogue and the institutions with which it is connected. The Honorary Officers will in due course give their careful attention to the question of the appointment of a successor to the late Chief Rabbi, but any consideration of this question would at the present be entirely out of place.'⁴

The interim naming of Moses Hyamson, in particular, was not without relevance to subsequent events, and was to have a significant impact on the lobbying and outcome of the Chief Rabbinical succession once any consideration of the question was deemed not 'out of place.'

On their appointment as dayanim in 1902, the two 'reverends' had been described by the chairman of an Aldgate protest rally as 'men in whom the East End has, and can have, no confidence.' While the United Synagogue council was anxious to improve the condition of Jews in the East End, said the Rev L. Frumkin, 'if the election of unqualified dayanim is the means to that end, then it is better to leave the East End as it was. The United Synagogue has no right to experiment on the East End by the novel introduction of English under-trained rabbis without receiving the East End's sanction.'[5]

Responding to this rebuff, Hyamson declaimed in his installation sermon as dayan: 'The men of light and leading in the East End, they who stand out prominently by reason of their knowledge, energy and initiative, are earnestly implored not to retire to their tents, or build every one a high place for himself, but to accord the valued assistance of their loyalty and good will. Combination is better than competition. The latter, though certainly stimulating energy, involves enormous waste of force; the former secures the same results with a maximum of efficiency and economy. I ask you to aid in the worthy task of welding the community into one harmonious whole.'[6]

Days after Adler's death, United Synagogue vice-president Albert Jessel referred, somewhat over-zealously, to the Chief Rabbi's peace-making role in the conflicts that had plagued his period in office. 'Questions of difficulty,' Jessel told his council, 'must continually spring up in every organisation, in this among others, yet it was to him as the ultimate tribunal that we always could appeal, not only for our internal difficulties, but also for those difficulties which, from time to time, arose in connection with other bodies.

'He did not always have an easy task, because there are in our community many men of profound convictions and determined opinions, and many men who possibly in a heated moment give expression to views which make subsequent negotiation and settlement difficult. But by that persuasiveness to which I have alluded, and that extraordinary influence which sprang from a sense of devotion to duty, he was always able to assuage hostility and reconcile opposing elements.'

This led Jessel to 'the question in the minds of every one of us—the succession to this high office. It is not an easy question. There is no person who stands conspicuously forth in the community as when the late Chief Rabbi was appointed. It is, as I say, not an easy question. There are many persons whose views are entitled to be consulted. It is not a question we can hurry. I expect none of you can have read that passage from Dr Adler's will, which has appeared in the press, without echoing the hope that a man would be found able to reconcile conflicting interests. The late Chief Rabbi was such a man.

'What I think we will all agree on is that we must bear ourselves patiently. It is not a thing to be hurried, and, above all, not a thing to be discussed in any spirit of acrimony, either because we stand for a particular set of principles, or because this community or that individual thinks that one candidate or one possible candidate would best fill the office.

'We shall be paying a poor compliment to the memory of him whom we mourn if we allow any feeling of strife on this occasion. And I do hope—in this council such an expression may be unnecessary, but my words may reach beyond this room—I do hope that we shall see in the community a reflection of that desire for peace which was one of the great characteristics of Dr Adler.'[7]

Meanwhile, at a specially convened meeting to mark Adler's death, the leaders of the Federation of Synagogues expressed—in decidedly circumspect terms—their own 'profound grief' and 'deep sense of loss.' Since the establishment of the Federation, they declared, 'its members have received the advantage of [the Chief Rabbi's] ready co-operation in their efforts to raise the standard of synagogue buildings in East London. The late Dr Adler consecrated the majority of the new synagogues erected under the auspices of the Federation and, on the occasion of these and other visits to the Federation synagogues, heartened and sustained the members by his deep-seated and earnest sympathy with their difficulties and by his practical suggestions for the amelioration of their lot.

'The members of the Board pray that Mrs Adler and the members of her family will be sustained in their bereavement by the knowledge that their loss is intimately and universally shared. Not alone in the United Kingdom, but throughout the civilised world, the death of Dr Adler is mourned as a loss to his community, to Judaism generally, and to the cause of public philanthropy at large.'[8]

* * *

As in the past, several months were to elapse before the United Synagogue felt equipped to launch the electoral process. During the interim, delegates representing varied interests within the East End, the ministry and the wider community submitted memoranda to the US on the Chief Rabbinate itself, and on issues of rabbinical authority, administration, and government. And as the names of prospective candidates became known and canvassed, the Jewish press once again launched a vociferous debate on the merits and failings of the parties involved, as well as on the methods of selection, election and, indeed, rejection.

In November 1911, prior to the inaugural Chief Rabbinical Conference, the US council requested its executive committee—in line with precedent—'to confer at an early date with representatives of other bodies in the United Kingdom contributing to the maintenance of the office of the Chief Rabbi, as to the duties and emoluments of such office, and as to the mode of election.' The colonial congregations were not invited, 'as it was thought that the delay which would have been occasioned by corresponding with them might be very great, and there appeared to be a general feeling that steps should be taken at once with the view to filling up the vacancy in the Chief Rabbinate.'

Referring to Hermann Adler's election, the council noted: 'It is obvious that the weight of the duties appertaining to the office has become far more burdensome than was the case in 1890. The Jewish population has increased, the field for the activities of the Chief Rabbinate has become wider, and its responsibilities greater. There are continually new claims upon the attention of the Ecclesiastical Representative of the great majority of the Jews of the Empire.

'The reorganisation of the London Beth Din which has taken place under the direction of the United Synagogue doubtless materially helped the late Chief Rabbi in the performance of some of his duties, but it is felt in some quarters that the Rev Dr Hermann Adler had, nevertheless, more work put upon him than even he, with all his energy, could properly discharge. The Conference will be aware that suggestions have been made with a view to obtaining greater devolution in the labours of the Rabbinate, and will probably think it well to consider some of these proposals.'[9]

Central to the proposals was the submission by the standing committee of the Conference of Jewish Ministers of a 'scheme for the religious administration of the community.' The scheme, described by the press as 'remarkable' and by others as 'perverse,' envisaged the establishment of an Ecclesiastical Board and a central consistory which would deprive the Chief Rabbbinate of many of its exclusive and unfettered rights.

All questions submitted to the Board—composed of rabbis and preachers, with the Chief Rabbi at its head—would 'be decided by the majority of members present at a conference of the said board.' The consistory's task would be 'to assist the Chief Rabbi and Beth Din in a range of religious, communal and judicial duties,' while the Chief Rabbi's supervision and control would be 'in council with the central consistory.' The Chief Rabbi, moreover, 'shall be selected from those present members of the British ministry who possess the rabbinical diploma and a British university degree.'[10]

Hyamson and Feldman roundly condemned the proposals and promptly resigned from the standing committee, the former asserting that the scheme 'sets up as the ecclesiastical governors of the orthodox community a new and heterogeneous body—the so-called consistory—comprising men the bulk of whom will be without the rabbinical qualifications, and some of whom may possibly be ministers of the Reform congregations whose principles of religious law and practice are not the same as those of orthodox Jews.'

Alluding to the addition of the words 'in council with the central consistory,' Hyamson declared: 'This perversion of the plain, literal meaning of an important sentence in a serious document [the Deed of Foundation and Trust] is, as I pointed out at the meeting of the standing committee, offensive to the legal mind and seems, to my moral sense, ethically unsound and unjustifiable ... The proposed scheme will take men away from duties in their own synagogues and congregations and impose upon them functions for which they are not as well fitted. This would weaken the community instead of strengthening it, lead to confusion and possibly to the disruption of Anglo-Jewry.'[11]

In a letter to the Revs J. F. Stern and S. Levy, the Conference of Jewish Ministers' honorary secretaries, Feldman wrote: 'It is my firm resolve to take no part whatever in the presentation of the scheme by the standing committee to the honorary officers of the United Synagogue.'[12]

Concurrently with the ministers' submission, representatives of the Association for Furthering Traditional Judaism in Great Britain met with the Chief Rabbinate sub-committee to voice the concerns of the strictly Orthodox.[13] Rabbi S. Bloch, of Birmingham, 'expressed in clear and unmistakable language the opinion of the rabbis and Orthodox laymen that, in accordance with Jewish law, there is no room for a Chief Rabbi who could be a Rabbi over all other rabbis in the country, according to whose sole authority and rule all the affairs concerning Judaism should be managed.

> According to our Law [said Bloch], all questions affecting the religious life of Jews are governed and decided by the local rabbis in each town, who enjoy full and absolute autonomy in the discharge of their duties. Moreover, the experience of all countries where an official Chief Rabbi existed showed that Judaism suffered there through the Chief Rabbinate, and Orthodox Judaism entirely disappeared.
>
> For these reasons, we have arrived at a conclusion that the best means for safeguarding the highest interests of Judaism would be to abolish the Chief Rabbinate and, if our opinion would be accepted, then we would, of course, advise not to appoint any Chief Rabbi at all ... [But] animated as we are by the desire of maintaining peace in the community, we would forgo our objection to the principle of the appointment of a Chief Rabbi only on the following conditions:
>
> 1. That the Chief Rabbi to be elected should be a man of great piety, strict orthodoxy, and live in accordance with the injunctions of our religious code (Shulchan Aruch), from which he must not deviate either to the right or to the left. He must be a great Talmudic scholar, and then we will honour him in accordance with his deeds and merits.
>
> 2. That the Chief Rabbi should not interfere in any ques-

tions affecting the religious life, or in all matters appertaining to the Shulchan Aruch, in the provincial towns where there are God-fearing rabbis who are great in learning and who shall alone decide all these questions.[14]

* * *

The inaugural Chief Rabbinate Conference, held on 14 January 1912, at the Great Central Hotel's Wharncliffe Rooms, was lauded by the *Jewish Chronicle* as 'an historic gathering, its proceedings throughout marked by a dignity and an earnestness that are not always notable characteristics of Jewish meetings. Every individual delegate appeared to realise to the full the importance of the business in which he was taking part, and to appreciate the great consequences that are dependent upon the appointment of a successor to Dr Adler.'

Painting his vision of the future Chief Rabbi, Rothschild told the gathering that the incumbent 'must be acquainted with English life and English laws, and be able to speak English; and if he is not acquainted with English life and English laws, he will not be a fit person to be the religious head of the Jews of England. That, at the present moment, is much more important than it ever was.

'Your Chief Rabbi, if he is not exactly an Englishman, if he has not been to an English university, should be able to speak and preach in English, and should have a knowledge of English communities. That is, in my opinion, absolutely necessary, because it is one of the duties, and one of the great duties, of the Chief Rabbi to see that all your ministers and chazanim should be able to speak English, and do all in his power to prevent the teaching and the spread of slang and jargon-like Yiddish ...

'I can only ask of you to consider today, and when you go home after the discussion you may have here, and when you meet again, the great duty which is thrown upon you to select a gentleman worthy of the post, who will train those who come after you in the true traditions of Judaism and who will make them, at the same time, good, honest and loyal citizens of this great country.'

In a session devoted to the mode of election, the joint vice-president, Felix Davis, proposed that—as with the disputed procedure in 1890—the voting power of the respective delegates 'be in proportion to the several annual contributions of the bodies represented.' The ballot at the election, at all meetings of the delegates, and for all purposes, 'should be in accordance with a scale of one vote for bodies contributing under £10 per annum; two votes for £10 to under £15; three votes for £15 to under £20; four votes for £20 to under £25; and the payment of every additional £5 entitling that body to a further vote.'

And once again, as in 1890, Lord Swaything—this time Louis Samuel Montagu, the son and heir of the Federation's founding chief[15]—stood up to oppose the resolution, following an exchange of letters some weeks earlier, between the heads of the United Synagogue and the Federation, on the issue of representation.

On receipt of its invitation to the Conference, the Federation told the US that 'if it is to be properly represented on the body dealing with the election of the Chief Rabbi, this must not be in proportion to its contribution to the Chief Rabbi's Fund—which was fixed with special reference to the circumstances under which the contribution is made—but to the immense interests it represents in the religious life of the community. It necessarily follows, then, that the elective influence must be in proper ratio to the membership, which numbers 6,500 in the fifty-one synagogues represented.'[16] The Federation indicated that, since the Conference would deal only with details concerning the election itself, it would be content with a minimum of five representatives. The United Synagogue countered with a suggestion of three, and to this the Federation agreed.

With the question of a money franchise now raised at the Conference, Swaythling perceived a political retraction. 'As far as the Federation of Synagogues is concerned,' he declared, 'we take one very strong line on this subject. You are not electing a Chief Rabbi of the contributors to the Chief Rabbinate, but a Chief Rabbi of the Jews of England.

> I therefore desire to move as an amendment 'that the voting power of synagogues contributing to the salary of the Chief Rabbi shall be calculated in proportion to the numbers of seat-holders of such congregations.' When it comes to the individual to be elected Chief Rabbi, it is the number of seat-holders of synagogues owing allegiance to that Chief Rabbi that must be considered, not the length of their purses ...
>
> Your Chief Rabbi is to be the spiritual head of the Jews of this country whether they are English or foreign, or the children of foreign parents. They are all alike. They are all—in spite of what Lord Rothschild has said—equally interested in the election of the Chief Rabbi.
>
> It is far from my desire in any way to seem to be speaking in an unfriendly spirit, but I have tried to make it perfectly clear what our instructions were from the Federation. Mr Davis has explained the point of view of the United Synagogue. It is for that reason that I have tried to find this middle path—that those who contribute should be consid-

ered according to their numbers and not according to their purses.

Seconding the amendment, Federation vice-president Hermann Landau said that if it were adopted, he 'would be prepared personally to guarantee that the United Synagogue would obtain £1,000 in contributions to the Chief Rabbi's Fund.' Amid laughter, Davis responded that he 'hoped Lord Swaythling would endorse that guarantee. Their experience in the past was that promises were made which were not fulfilled.' Put to the plenum, the amendment was lost by fifty-eight votes to eight.[17]

This brief debate, and another that followed, brought the proceedings to a close, Jessel having remarked that the Conference might in due course 'desire to express its view on the question of election or selection. He personally thought it extremely desirable that the elective body should be able to select one candidate and thus avoid the disagreeable situation that would be caused by a contested election.'

The 'disagreeable situation' was, however, destined to be the readier course.

* * *

'Having regard to the proceedings at the Conference on Sunday last,' the Federation's leaders promptly wrote to the United Synagogue, 'we desire to confirm the letter of 23 November last, referring to the adequate representation of the Federation of Synagogues on the body dealing with the election of the Chief Rabbi. We desire to protest against any mode of election dependent on the amounts contributed by any body or bodies to the Chief Rabbi's Fund.

> Were the United Synagogue electing an official of its own body, or a Chief Rabbi over the various synagogues within its Union, it would be a perfectly logical course to proportion the elective power to the amount of the several contributions towards the cost of the remuneration of such officer or Chief Rabbi. The present election is not thus limited. A spiritual head for the Jews of Great Britain is to be elected.
>
> The precedent of the last election for Chief Rabbi does not apply in this instance, for on that occasion the occupant of the office of Delegate Chief Rabbi was by a general consensus of opinion clearly marked out for the office, and the election was more or less a matter of routine.
>
> It is not, we submit, a question of any particular body wielding a predominant influence over the election—or of

one set of members 'swamping' another. Under any well-conceived and logical method of representation, all members of the Jewish congregations in the United Kingdom would have such a share in the election as their numbers justified; the members of the Federation synagogues, under proportional representation, would form but a small minority of the whole; under a scheme of proportional representation, a minority could fairly be expected to accept the decision of the majority, but not otherwise.

We are quite certain that the United Synagogue is desirous of electing a Chief Rabbi acceptable to every section of the community; but without having regard to the comparative smallness of the section of the community it represents, it has determined to keep the election in its own hands. The Federation of Synagogues, therefore, cannot share in the responsibility of an election in which it has practically no voice.

We sincerely trust that after the United Synagogue has made its choice of a Chief Rabbi, the Federation will be able to accept him in the same spirit as in the past. Under the present circumstances however, the Federation must withdraw from participating in the election.[18]

Thus it was, by the time the Chief Rabbinate Conference resumed four months later, that the Federation of Synagogues had, in Jessel's words, 'retired in a temper'[19] from any further deliberations. Swaythling told a meeting of his board that the Federation's position continued to be that, as the United Synagogue would not give them 'the voting power to which they were justly entitled,' they would abstain from participating in the election.

They were willing, however, 'to accept any man elected if he were an orthodox Jew and if he possessed great rabbinical knowledge, and would assist if required, either directly or indirectly. The honorary officers, and other members of the Federation, were ready to place any knowledge they possessed at their disposal, but they could not accept responsibility for this election unless the United Synagogue could see their way to meeting the just demands of the Federation, which he had not seen any disposal on their part to do so far.'[20]

That the US hierarchy were not so disposed was reinforced at the opening session of the Conference, with Rothschild's remark ('not of a harmonious nature,' he admitted) that the Federation's leaders 'have had the audacity to suggest that if the gentlemen assembled here, who represent the entire body of Jews in England outside the Federation, and who come from the great centres of Jewish population, were to send a few people to a round-table conference, they could arrange everything. Mr Hermann Landau and his colleagues were invited here, and if they choose to absent themselves from our deliberations, we need not go out of our way to sit at a round table with them.'

Dealing mainly with administrative matters, the Conference spent considerable time discussing the path to finding a successor to Adler. The question had been raised, said Jessel, 'whether they could not to some extent get on with the election before the next meeting of the delegates. And here arose a matter of considerable delicacy and difficulty.

> What steps were they to take in order to get before them the names of gentlemen who would be willing to accept the post on the conditions they offered? It was not likely that the community at large would assent to an invitation being given to one person. They were anxious that the person to be appointed should be known to the community in these islands, known by having had an opportunity of visiting, as far as possible, the congregations in London and the provinces. They wanted to be able to have seen him and heard him.
>
> He did not think [said Jessel] that the community would tolerate the election of someone who was merely nominated on the report of a small body, however representative they might think that body to be. So they thought that anyone who had a fair chance of being elected ought to be heard.
>
> They knew those who were available. One gentleman had been here, and another was now here. There might be others. They did not know who might desire to come forward. Various names had been mentioned. Some of these gentlemen did not wish to become candidates. Some would only consider the post if an invitation were sent to them and to no one else.
>
> They could not elect to the Rabbinate on those conditions. It would be by popular election. The view of the Committee was that the best means of getting over the difficulty and of avoiding hurting anyone was by publishing a notification of the vacancy in the press inviting gentlemen who wished to apply to send in their names. That would clear the ground and enable them to get on with the list of names prior to the appointment of the next Conference.

If the applicants were not satisfactory, it might be for the next Conference to say that others should be invited here and preach in the various synagogues. It was a very difficult question. They did not want to do anything unworthy of the community, but they thought this was the best way out of the difficulty.

Commenting on 'the character of the gentleman to be elected,' Jessel stated that, while no recommendations had been passed on the subject of qualifications, they had 'merely expressed the opinion that one of the things the gentleman ought to be able to do was that he should be competent to speak and preach fluently in English. Most of them would agree with this, but in some quarters the view was entertained that in the suggestion that the gentleman should be able to preach fluently in English, it proscribed the foreigner who could speak but not preach fluently in English. He would be quite prepared in any notice that might be issued to omit the word "fluently."'

Jessel then moved a resolution that 'the Jewish press be invited to make an official announcement of the vacancy of the office of Chief Rabbi, with an intimation that gentlemen desirous of applying for the position should send in their names, with full particulars of their qualifications, to Mr P. Ornstein, the Secretary to the Delegates.'

The motion was passed, but not before a Manchester delegate had described advertising for a Chief Rabbi as 'an undignified procedure ... a humiliation to the Jews of this country. Would the Church advertise for an Archbishop?' Felix Davis denied they would be advertising the post, and Lord Rothschild maintained that 'this procedure was adopted on a previous occasion and should be good enough now.'[21]

* * *

Unbeknown to many of the Conference delegates, although alluded to by Jessel, one of the overseas figures to loom large in the Chief Rabbinical election—Joseph Herman Hertz—was in London both before and during their deliberations. A native of Hungary, Hertz had settled with his family in New York. In due course he became the first rabbinical ordinand of the Jewish Theological Seminary and briefly served Syracuse's Adath Yeshurun synagogue before being drawn to the Old Hebrew Congregation at Witwatersrand, Johannesburg.

Some eleven years later, he was offered the pulpit of New York's prestigious, and strictly Orthodox, Congregation Orach Chayim, passing through Britain on his way home from meetings with its members. In an interview with the *Jewish Chronicle*, devoted mainly to a stinging attack on Reform Judaism and its rabbis, he had voiced his indecision over accepting the offer, asserting that 'what will finally determine me will be where I can do best work. All else I shall put aside—that and that only will decide me in acceding to the call, or in yielding to the call back.'[22]

In the event, he accepted the post, reasoning that he could 'better serve the Jewish cause, can better serve Judaism, in New York than in Johannesburg.' Little knowing—though perhaps desiring—what 'all else' might lie in store, he prepared to set sail towards an uncertain future, with unforeseen results.

A second visit to Britain, as he later told the press,[23] had proven to be a pivotal opportunity. During ten days spent there in December 1911, he was approached by 'some of my old friends in London who urged me to apply for the vacant Chief Rabbinate.' He was 'brought into touch' with Lords Rothschild and Swaythling and, 'as a result of the conversations I had at the time,' had received an official invitation to visit England.

'Personally, I have so far been to them no more than a name. They have known nothing about my personality, and it is only right that they should have gathered as much information about me as possible from various sources.'

Hertz said that, as far as he understood, the leaders wanted 'an active man, a man of energy, capable of instilling new life in the community. The English Jews are beginning to perceive that the "years of plenty" are over, that the happy times when the Jews in England sat safely "under their vines and fig trees" have gone. There already exists a permanent immigration question, and internal new lines that affect the Jews who are already settled there. The future Chief Rabbi must concentrate in great part the energy and activity of the whole community. He must constantly be on his guard.'

Of himself, Hertz conceded—after some modest hesitation—that his career as a rabbi offered proof that he was 'the possessor of enthusiasm and energy.' His years in South Africa testified to his being 'of an active disposition. Under such congenial circumstances as can be found in England, I could achieve a great deal.' Without elaborating, Hertz ended the interview by hinting 'of a certain scheme I am contemplating for the advancement of Judaism in England in the event of my being elected Chief Rabbi.'

The 'quasi-official' invitation to visit Britain, as the JC downgraded it, had reached Hertz in February 1912—coinciding with his New York installation—and by April he was back in England for a three-month stay, 'with a view to becoming a candidate for the office of Chief Rabbi in this country.' For that purpose, the Orach Chayim board had accorded him the necessary leave of absence and had intimated that, 'if he should not undertake the high office of Chief Rabbi, means will be found on his return to New York for much enlarging the field of his work, to which will be attached even better conditions than those at present prevailing.'

It was further announced in London that 'Dr Hertz—whose religious attitude may, perhaps, be best described in the words applied to his own master, Dr Sabato Morais, as cultured Orthodoxy'[24]—would give a series of sermons at the Great, Bayswater, Philpot Street, Hampstead and Dalston synagogues, as well as at other metropolitan and out-of-town congregations. A 'forceful and eloquent preacher,' he had met a number of provincial delegates to the Chief Rabbinate Conference who had gathered in London as he reached Britain's shores.[25]

In his opening sermon at the Great Synagogue, entitled 'Kiddush Hashem and Chillul Hashem,'[26] Hertz remarked that 'while we have succeeded in making non-Jews respect Judaism, our problem today is nothing less than to make Jews respect Judaism. We are witnessing an alarming loss of faith of Israel in Israel. We stand appalled at the mass of unbaptised apostasy in English-speaking countries.'

With his second address, at Bayswater a week later—in the presence of its resident preacher, Hermann Gollancz—views were beginning to coalesce over the quality and substance of Hertz's oratorical style, 'a good means for any man to prove if there is anything "in him" for the purpose of an office in which the pulpit must of necessity play a large part.'[27] Based on the biblical text, 'You shall hallow the fiftieth year and proclaim liberty throughout the land,'[28] the discourse was hailed as 'a powerful homily on the value of Jewish self-respect, calling on the "emancipated" Jew not to despise his heritage but to honour it and obey the responsibilities it involves.'

Referring to Hermann Adler's former occupancy of the Bayswater pulpit and comparing the 'pulpitry' of Adler and Hertz, the JC's special correspondent found that 'they bore scarcely the slightest likeness. The late Chief Rabbi always carefully wrote out his sermons and read them with great deliberation. Dr Hertz preaches extempore with sharp, staccato diction, with nothing of the clergyman's manners.

> Dr Adler's delivery was not clear, but his voice was deep and sonorous. Dr Hertz can be readily heard. Never does he seem lost for a word, a quotation, or an illustration, and somehow when he ended his sermon, which occupied just about half an hour in delivery, one felt that he had by no means exhausted either his subject or himself, and that he could without much effort straightaway have delivered another sermon of equal length from the same text without repeating himself.
>
> When Dr Adler ended his discourse, he gave one the impression that he had said all he had to say on the topic under

his consideration, that he had told, as it were, the whole story. Dr Adler kept rigidly to his text. When he gave it out, he gave the key to his whole discourse so far as the subjects upon which he intended to speak were concerned.

Dr Hertz took as his text the institution of the Jubilee. Who could have guessed that he would have taken his hearers into questions of the relative value to Judaism of the Ghetto Jew and the emancipated Israelite, of the relative progress in civilisation of the Congo Negro astride his bicycle, and the Americanised son of Jacob ensconced in his sixty-horsepower motor? No two preachers that can be thought of present for comparison so many actual pulpit opposites as Dr Hertz and the late Chief Rabbi.

Even as Hertz's visit was being widely discussed, discordant voices began to be heard over the possibility of a contest between him and Hyamson—though neither had as yet been officially named—with calls for a compromise candidate who might prevent the eruption of a divisive campaign. The intervention of 'Moderator,' a pseudonymous letter-writer to the *Jewish Chronicle*, appeared to set the ball rolling.

'As it is impossible,' he wrote, 'that there should be any man capable of filling even part of the expectations raised, it behoves the community to consider very carefully which part ought to receive the first consideration. Why not look out at least for a man who, by his Jewish scholarship, by his strict religious life, by his piety, by the unquestionable validity of his titles, and by a record of public work of many years' standing, might claim at least as much consideration for the vacant post as any of those hitherto mentioned? If he should combine with those qualities also fine physique and youthful age and enthusiasm, it were well, though he may be lacking in administrative ability and in the supposed merit of suppleness.

'A man such as Dr Drachman of New York might be found to respond to this description, and a call extended to him would be no more than a simple act of fairness to the community, while lessening the responsibility of those with whom the final selection rests. In putting this name forward, I have, it is only right to say, the peace of the community largely at heart. It is only right to say, too, that I am moved by deep anxiety lest a rash choice should jeopardise the future welfare and prosperity of Anglo-Jewry, thus endangering the highest interests of Judaism in this country.'[29]

Whether or not a call was thus made—and differing versions of events, as later offered, leave a cloud of uncertainty—the name of Drachman, then rabbi of the Oheb Zedek and Zichron Ephraim congregations in New York, was soon to emerge in United Synagogue circles. Within weeks, Ornstein circulated to the Conference delegates the names of 'the reverend gentlemen who desire to have their claims considered for the office of Chief Rabbi,' listing in alphabetical order those of Joseph Abrahams, Samuel Daiches, Bernard Drachman, Hermann Gollancz, Joseph Herman Hertz, and Moses Hyamson.[30]

Days later, the selection committee quickly eliminated Abrahams, who had paid a brief visit to London, but who (as Jessel was later to remark[31]), while having 'many qualities which would have fully enabled him to discharge the duties of the office, did not meet with that support which would have justified us in putting him prominently forward.' Daiches was also rejected[32] and, debating whether to allow Gollancz to proceed, the committee then agreed, by ten votes to three, to remove his name as well. The committee felt that, 'notwithstanding the personal respect in which he might be regarded, it was undesirable he should be appointed to the position. His age, his health—in more than one respect we felt he was not strong enough.'[33] At the time, the three were, respectively, chief minister of the Melbourne Hebrew Congregation and president of the city's Beth Din; lecturer in Bible, Talmud, Shulchan Aruch and homiletics at Jews' College; and minister-preacher at Bayswater Synagogue, in succession to Hermann Adler. Abrahams was born in London (1855); Daiches in Vilna (1878); and Gollancz in Bremen (1852)— all with eminent rabbinical pedigrees.

After further discussion, the committee agreed to submit to the elective body the claims of Hyamson (1863) and Hertz (1872), with a recommendation that 'no meeting of that body be convened until an opportunity has been given to Rabbi Dr B. Drachman [1861] to come to England and to preach in various synagogues; that if he fails to respond to that invitation, these names be submitted without any further meeting of the committee, and if he accepts it, that the committee hold a further meeting at the conclusion of his visit.'[34]

That Drachman's name appeared on the list of 'claims to be considered' suggests that the initial approach may have come, if not directly from him, at his personal instigation. In later accounts of the episode, however, he writes of his 'mixed feelings' when, in the early summer of 1912, 'I received an official letter from the United Synagogue formally inviting me to come to England and preach in various synagogues with a view to becoming a candidate for the Chief Rabbinate.

> On the one hand was the realisation that a very great honour was being conferred on me in being so considered. On the other hand, and more important yet, this high post offered an unequalled opportunity of rendering great and enduring service to Judaism and the Jewish people. But crowding out

these happy thoughts was another, less happy: if I should be the chosen one, I should be obliged to tear up my roots, to forsake my native land and my kindred, and to pass the rest of my days on foreign soil, among those whom I had never before known.

The material benefits which the position would bring had no attractive power. My financial position was such that I was under no necessity of seeking a place for the purpose of earning a living. I felt myself an American in every fibre of my being. At the possibility of leaving home and country forever, America loomed up before me. America, loved and cherished above all lands! The glorious and irreplaceable home of liberty, beauty and happiness, the loss of which could not be compensated for by all the treasures of earth.

My beloved wife looked upon the matter in the same light. Although she made no audible objection, deeming it improper to seek to influence my decisions in matters connected with my vocation, I could see that the prospect of leaving America and her family was very distasteful to her. My children, it is true, felt differently. The glamour of the exalted post of Chief Rabbi of the British Empire fascinated them, and they would have been delighted to see their father occupying it. For me, the matter was the choice between duty and inclination.

I decided to follow the call of duty. That does not mean that I took it for granted that I would be chosen for the post. I knew very well that I was only one of several candidates who would be considered, and that it was not at all certain that I would be the successful one. I decided, however, that should the choice fall upon me, I would disregard considerations of personal convenience or preference and would dedicate whatever abilities I might possess to the service of this great community of Israel. Accordingly, I answered the letter of the United Synagogue expressing thanks for the invitation and stating that I would come to England after the fall holy days.[35]

Accompanied by his daughter, Beatrice, Drachman arrived in Britain in October 1912 and undertook a number of preaching engagements in London—at the Great, Bayswater, New West End, St John's Wood, Poets' Road, and Stepney synagogues—as well as in Birmingham, Leeds, Manchester, and Liverpool. 'My emotional reaction toward the task which I had set myself,' he later recalled, 'was clearly indicative of my inner attitude and sentiment over against the whole undertaking.

'I was at first, and in a lesser degree during my entire stay in England, in a state of extreme nervous tension and agitation. It was not that I did not respect and think highly of much of what I observed in England and in its Jewish community. In particular, I admired and profoundly esteemed the august institution of the Chief Rabbinate and thought regretfully of its absence in America. But I felt, and could not rid myself of the feeling, that I did not belong in that country and environment, that only a rigid sense of loyalty to duty could induce me to remain there and accept the post of Chief Rabbi, should it be tendered me.'[36]

Despite what he described as 'a severe nervous attack' that preceded his Duke's Place sermon, and 'what a strain and trial this meant to me,' he delivered his address 'with perfect self-possession, without the slightest indication of the pain that was racking my frame. My sermon was a phenomenal success.'[37]

Discussing the occasion in the light of 'the vital necessity for avoiding the contested election with which we are threatened,' the *Jewish Chronicle* was quick to concur. 'The sermon he delivered at the Great Synagogue last Sabbath,' the paper declared,[38] 'created of Dr Drachman a most favourable impression. On all hands we hear that those who since his arrival here last week have been privileged to meet the Rabbi have not been slow to recognise in him a gentleman of dignified bearing, of restrained, cultured demeanour and, above all, an earnest, zealous Jew, broad-minded, albeit pious, singularly primed with a knowledge of Anglo-Jewish conditions and with, for one who practically all his life has lived in America, quite a remarkable knowledge of the affairs of the community.

'That he is a scholar of no mean attainments is on record; that he has stood fast by his religious principles, despite the allurements of Reform in the United States to yield them, we know; that his rabbinical acquirements are unexceptionable, the diplomas he possesses go to prove. If the first impression thus formed of Dr Drachman's qualifications for the Rabbinate become confirmed, and if they are shared by the community generally, it ought not to be impossible for a "call" to be extended to him, and a contested election thus avoided.'

Similar plaudits followed Drachman's appearance at St John's Wood, where (the special correspondent reported) 'a record congregation—if the term may be employed with adequate regard to the reverence of the occasion—greeted the third candidate for the Chief Rabbinate. On being called up to the Reading of the Law, a notable demonstration of respect for him was manifested by the congregation instinctively rising as he passed from his seat to the reading desk. As this is a sign of honour generally reserved for those occupying the position of Chief Rabbi, Dr Drachman must, in the circumstances, feel very proud of the distinction paid him.'

Referring to his sermon, the correspondent added: 'To say that Dr Drachman made any great impression, as the term is usually understood, upon the congregation would not be to say the truth. Indeed, his great success—which, to be sure, was marked—lay in a contrary direction. He infused into the large congregation a sense of friendship. He left them with the feeling that they were no strangers to him, neither was he a stranger to them—that, indeed, they were old familiar friends, he as Preacher and Rabbi, they as congregants and worshippers.

'This evoked in its turn a sense of mutual confidence and good understanding which may yet go very far. The qualities of the heart and the soul manifesting themselves in their own unerring manner count for much; sometimes far more than exhibitions of mind and intellect in [the] face of which the average man must perforce shade his eyes or turn elsewhere.'[39]

Further signs of welcome and anticipation greeted Drachman wherever he went. Tête-à-tête with the United Synagogue president—'this distinguished representative of Anglo-Israel'—he outlined his concept of the Chief Rabbinate and went away 'with the impression that, as far as Lord Rothschild was concerned, my election as Chief Rabbi was certain.' Similarly, 'my visit to Lord Swaythling and his charming family was most pleasant, and his good will to me was manifest.' And at an East End meeting attended by (as Drachman put it) 'an immense crowd'—which he addressed in German since he 'did not consider Yiddish a language in the true sense of the term'—'they were even more wholeheartedly in my favour than their English-speaking coreligionists, and the Yiddish press came out with articles warmly endorsing my candidacy.'[40]

The *Jewish Express*, indeed, had remarked that 'Dr Drachman's appearance and gentlemanly bearing have created a good impression in all circles, and the East End is satisfied with his vast knowledge. It preferred Dr Drachman to the two other candidates, believing that the Rabbi is the ideal man for the position.' The *Jewish Journal* noted that 'Dr Drachman brought with him all qualities which the English Jews sought in a Chief Rabbi, and wished the candidate success. It attributed to him a tendency of uniting the English Jews, orthodoxy, the desire to foster Jewish education, and a spirit of independence.'[41]

Away from the metropolis, Drachman was again convinced of his enormous success. 'I can truthfully say that the reception given to my addresses and the expression of my concept of the place and function of the Chief Rabbinate in English-Jewish life was very favourable. It would be no exaggeration to say that it was enthusiastic. According to all indications, the provinces were solidly united in their demand that I should be the next Chief Rabbi.'[42]

In Manchester, 'there seemed to be unanimity of sentiment that I was to be the next Chief Rabbi. Indeed, this sentiment seemed to have preceded my arrival, presumably based on reports from London, and to have even reached some circles of the gentile population. When we visited the Exchange, the official who acted as the guide said, in a tone of deep respect, to the committee who accompanied me: "This, I presume, is the gentleman who is to be your Chief Rabbi."'[43]

After some six weeks in Britain, Drachman and Beatrice set sail for New York, where, he perceived, 'interest was general, among Jews and, to a considerable extent, among non-Jews, in the outcome of the election.'[44] In London, meanwhile, where communal interest was at fever pitch, Jessel told his colleagues that Drachman 'had promised to forward a communication regarding his application for the post of Chief Rabbi';[45] while the *Jewish Chronicle* understood that 'Rabbi Dr Drachman has intimated his willingness to submit himself for election as Chief Rabbi, and that a meeting of the Selection Committee is to be called immediately.'[46]

The committee did not meet until three weeks later, when Jessel reported that Drachman's rabbinical diplomas had been examined and found to be 'quite in order.'[47] He then read from correspondence with the rabbi, 'the purport of which showed that the resolution of the committee passed on 23 June [1912] was at once communicated to Dr Drachman and that the Chairman had also made it clear to him that he would have, if recommended by the Committee, to engage in a contest with other candidates; but at the conclusion of his visit, Dr Drachman refused to enter a contest, though he suggested that a caucus might be arranged to test the feeling of the elective body.'

After further discussion, the committee agreed, by sixteen votes to one, that 'Dr Drachman's name be not submitted to the Election Conference'; and, on a unanimous vote, that 'Rabbi Dr Hertz be specially recommended to the Conference for election.' A further motion—that 'an opportunity should be given to Rabbi Dr Hyamson to withdraw his candidature, and that, in the event of his so doing, Dr Hertz's name be alone sent up with an intimation that Dr Hyamson had withdrawn'—attracted a lengthy debate before eventually being carried, with two dissentients.[48]

In advance of this meeting, sections of the Jewish press had carried a report, later picked up by *The Times*, that 'an impasse had been reached within the Selection Committee; that no agreement could be come to by the members of the Committee; and that it had been decided to withdraw the names of candidates previously submitted tentatively for the Rabbinate and endeavour to form a new list of contestants.'

Commenting on the report, the *Jewish Chronicle* observed that 'a certain section of the less well-informed Jewish press accepted this information, which, upon the face of it, must have been false. How was it possible for the Committee to find themselves in hopeless disagreement before they had met? Equally, how was it possible for them to come to a decision before they had gathered to discuss the situation?'[49]

Almost certainly responsible for the blunder, if unwittingly, was the standing committee of the Conference of Jewish Ministers, which had unsuccessfully sought a postponement of the election so that a deputation might convey its views to the Chief Rabbinate Conference on Hertz's candidature. When this was refused, the ministers had sent a protest letter to the Jewish press, with a copy to the Conference.

'The eve of the election of a Chief Rabbi,' they had declared, 'ought to mean the eve of the peaceful settlement of a great communal problem; and the appointment of a successor to the late Dr Hermann Adler should have provided the comforting compensation to the community for a great personal loss. But, as matters stand at the moment of writing, we are far distant from either, to the deep regret and the intense pain of the members of the Jewish ministry, to the detriment of the prestige of the Anglo-Jewish community, and to the serious—perhaps irreparable—prejudice of the gravest of Jewish interests.

'We are bound to express our strong feeling that in no other religious denomination would there have been possible the contemplation of an appointment of this character without regard to the opinions and the special knowledge of those most immediately concerned ... Our contention is that the recommendation of the election of the Rev Dr Hertz as the final conclusion of the Selection Committee is one that, to our great regret, we cannot bring ourselves to regard as a suitable solution. It is our opinion it should be a *sine qua non* that the Chief Rabbi should possess qualifications of outstanding eminence, and we cannot persuade ourselves that these are possessed by the recommended candidate.

'It is only fair to the Selection Committee to say that we have been made aware, though only at the last moment, of the terms of Dr Hertz's testimonials. But these notwithstanding, we are unable to alter our conviction that he does not reach the standard of the requirements of the Chief Rabbinate and the needs of the community. We therefore urge the postponement of the election, from the present candidates, and ask that renewed efforts be made to secure a nomination which will meet with general approval.' The letter was signed by A. A. Green, president; M. Abrahams, vice-president; Michael Adler, treasurer; J. F. Stern and S. Levy, honorary secretaries; and G. J. Emanuel, past president.[50]

After garbled reports of this protest had surfaced elsewhere, the JC published the ministers' letter, clarifying why it had done so after announcing that it would exclude any criticism of either candidate once the Selection Committee had reached its decision. 'We were informed,' wrote the editor, 'that if we did not publish the letter, a communication would be forwarded to the general press intimating that the Jewish press had been closed to its Ministers. It was with a desire to avoid, as far as possible, a further accession of scandal of this nature in the general press that we reluctantly decided to adopt the course requested by the Ministers.'[51]

Following the reports, Jessel was questioned at the United Synagogue council and compelled to relate 'precisely what has happened with regard to the proceedings yesterday of the Selection Committee. I do so with the more anxiety and readiness because of the unfortunate mistakes which have come into the papers—not our papers only, but those that appeal to general readers, such as *The Times* of today, which has a wholly erroneous account of what happened.'

Explaining why the Selection Committee had decided to recommend more than one name, as it had originally envisaged, Jessel said that it had felt that 'irritation would be experienced in some quarters if only one name was sent up, and it would be said that the thing was "cut and dried."' However, 'it had wished the Conference to know the views of the committee as to which is the more desirable of the two names, and we recommended that of Dr Hertz.'[52]

Jessel added that the committee had expressed 'a very strong desire that representatives of the electing synagogues would not come to the conference with tied hands.' This desire was incorporated into a resolution accompanying the election invitation that 'in the event of a contest, the Selection Committee hope that the Delegates would be at liberty to come to the meeting unfettered by any pledge to their congregations as to how they should vote.'[53]

As the election drew near, voices for and against Hertz grew ever stronger. From New York came a striking approbation by Solomon Schechter, head of the Jewish Theological Seminary,[54] 'whose position as one of the leading living Rabbis,' asserted the *Jewish Chronicle*, 'is unassailable, and whose orthodoxy is unquestioned.' His testimony of Hertz, which Jessel had asked the paper to publish, 'will be read before the Electoral College on Sunday next and may therefore be regarded from all points of view as indisputable.'

Hertz, wrote Schechter, 'is a fine Hebrew scholar, even in Rabbinics, a great preacher, and an accomplished student in many respects. He must also have had a large experience in pastoral work, to which his long activity in a British colony, composed of most heterogeneous elements, has given him ample opportunity ... The best school for him will be the London Chief Rabbinate, with its wide possibilities and manifold problems and variety of opinions, in which he would be compelled to bring some harmony and unity.

'I may further add that, as far as I understand, there are now Radical tendencies prevailing in English Jewry, such as were unknown in a former generation. And I believe that, unless you have a man of his oratory, able to present the ideas and ideals of ancient Judaism in an intelligent and lucid manner, and even to enlist modernity itself in the defence of Conservatism, Traditional Judaism will soon be a matter of the past.

'It is not a question of denouncing Radicalism, which is out of date, but of giving Conservative Judaism a fair chance by explaining and interpreting it in such a manner as to awaken the sympathies and arouse the loyalty and devotion of the congregation to our great heritage. And I thoroughly believe that Dr Hertz is the man able to accomplish this great task.'[55]

What Jessel did not reveal was that, in an earlier letter, Schechter had praised Hertz while demeaning Drachman. 'Dr. Hertz,' he had told Jessel the previous summer,[56] 'is decidedly the greater scholar, even in rabbinics, the greater gentleman and the greater preacher ... The difference between the two candidates is so greatly to the advantage of Dr Hertz as to exclude all comparison. I know of no greater calamity which could happen to British Jewry than the election of Dr Drachman to the Chief Rabbinate. Even the extending of an invitation to him is humiliating to English Jewry in the eyes of those who know the man and his position here.'

Despite Jessel's proposed appeal to the electoral college, critics of Hertz did dispute the 'indisputable' and made known their views to the US president. A group of twelve notables, including three who had served on the Selection Committee, drew up a letter of protest and, at a meeting at his New Court office, urged Rothschild to postpone the election on the following grounds:

> (a) That the proposed appointment involves the filling of an Office of the highest authority in the Religious affairs of the entire Anglo-Jewish community, and cannot fail to influence the future of Jewry in all parts of the British Empire, and indeed in all English-speaking countries.
> (b) That the sphere of activity and the influence for good of any Chief Rabbi must depend upon the general recognition of his scholarship, ability in organisation, and powers as a spiritual guide.
> (c) That neither of the two candidates submitted by the Committee of Selection possesses the qualifications necessary to secure for him the allegiance of either the Clergy or the general body of the Community, or to fill adequately an office of such great dignity and importance.
> (d) That Rabbis of the necessary eminence, who, on account

of their high position, cannot apply for the post, are available, if a call were given, instead of an invitation to a contest. (e) That the result of an Election made in existing circumstances must inevitably be the creation of division in the Community, the diminution of the authority of the titular Chief Rabbi, the dissolution of the single tie which has hitherto united all Communities of English Jews, and the limitation of the office to one of merely local influence.

The petition was signed by Alfred Eichholz, Charles Henry, Seemy Japhet, B. Kisch, Ernest Lesser, Frank I. Lyons, Redcliffe N. Salaman, Sir Stuart M. Samuel, MP, Otto Schiff, Oscar Selinger, Sir Adolph Tuck, and Lucien Wolf.[57]

In advance of their interview, the group had circulated the letter to a wide cross-section of the community, seeking support for their course of action.[58] At the meeting, Tuck, who led the delegation, told Rothschild: 'How far-reaching is the opinion voiced by this deputation is adequately demonstrated by the following data. Although the Memorial, with covering letter inviting signatures, was sent out in part on Friday last [7 February], while by far the larger portion of copies were posted only the night before last, the response has been remarkably prompt and emphatic. Nearly 1,200 signatures to the Memorial—that is, upwards of twenty-five per cent of the number sent out—have been already received, and are now placed before your Lordship, while I understand that every post is bringing in further additions.

'The significance of these figures is further made clear by the fact that upwards of 1,000 members of the United Synagogue have signed. Of these, thirty are wardens of the US, or members of the Council; the delegates to the election itself number twelve; and the presidents and wardens of other synagogues outside the US number fifty-eight. Other Jewish public men outside the US number thirty-four, and the signatures of leading communal workers in the provinces number over one hundred.'[59]

In an account of the meeting,[60] Japhet wrote: 'Sir Adolph Tuck acted as spokesman, but he was never an eloquent speaker, so he read his statement, which was very lengthy. Lord Rothschild, being rather deaf, did not understand a word. He was nervous and impatient. After a few minutes, he lost his temper and shouted, "Stop! I know all you have to say, but I have made up my mind. The election will take place and unless Dr Hertz is elected, I shall resign the chairmanship of the United Synagogue and shall, as the head of my house, prevent any of my family from holding office there ..." With increasing excitement, he ordered us to leave the room. "Go away, leave me alone, I am sick and tired of you all! Out you go!" And we went, some of us disgusted, some furious, and some inwardly amused.'

The *Jewish Chronicle*, in its own brief account of the proceedings, wrote that 'it is understood that Lord Rothschild intimated that he was opposed to any postponement and that, in any case, the matter must rest with the Electoral College, which is to meet on Sunday.' The paper also sought the views of the three signatories—Samuel, Tuck and Lyons—who, though having served on the Selection Committee, had voted for a postponement.

Samuel (the Western Synagogue's delegate) said that 'my efforts have been directed towards preventing a split in the community. None of the candidates appeared to me to be an Archangel Michael, but I was prepared to adopt the one that had the best chance of conciliating the community ... However, in view of what Lord Rothschild said to the deputation, I am prepared to bow to the will of the majority and do the best I can to make the situation a tolerable one. I think I have done sufficient to show that I am a man of moderation.'

Tuck declared: 'I opposed the recommendation of the Selection Committee from the first and was instrumental in staying the hands last July by voting for the invitation to Dr Drachman, whom I did not know from Adam at the time, and who might have suited for the position of Chief Rabbi.' (Drachman was later to write of Tuck and Herbert Bentwich, who had travelled to America 'to view the candidate in his home environment': 'There was something about them which set them apart and marked them as especially noble, both as English gentlemen and as Jews.'[61])

Lyons had also opposed both candidates, but 'having gone to a certain point, I do not propose to pursue any action likely to lead to any embarrassment, and shall therefore advise all my friends loyally to accept any decision that may be arrived at on Sunday.'[62]

* * *

One hundred and fifteen delegates from across Britain and the dominions—commanding between them four hundred and eighteen votes—were due to attend the meeting of the Electoral College on 16 February 1913; in the event, several were absent, and many others abstained. The gathering was briefly addressed by Rothschild and by the United Synagogue's legal adviser, Algernon Sydney, before Jessel took the stage to present a detailed account of the search.

Following Adler's death in July 1911, he said, 'we all wanted to have someone in England in whom we had confidence, but we all felt then that there was no one in England who would have that confidence. We, the honorary officers of the United Synagogue, felt that if we could have done what we should have liked, we should then and there have recommended one of our own men for the post, though I know people would have said we were trying to impose a Chief Rabbi upon them.

'Two names were before our minds, but we felt we could not conscientiously recommend either of these gentlemen for the post. That was concurred in by every member of the United Synagogue. There was the further difficult question in regard to one of the candidates before you today—Dr Hyamson. I desire not to hurt anybody's feelings, but it is idle to deny that Dr Hyamson would not receive the support of what is termed the East End. We all felt it at the time.

'Lord Swaythling has referred to some previous correspondence and negotiations. He did not carry them back far enough. At the time of Dr Adler's death, we were in complete unanimity. The desire of the United Synagogue was to consult the Federation, and he told us then that the Federation would not support Dr Hyamson. With great respect to Lord Swaythling, I am not always sure that he correctly interprets the views of the Federation, but in this case his view was supported by every East End worker with whom we came into association. That was the difficulty which we felt with regard to the appointment of Dr Hyamson. All the workers of the Federation and everybody of importance took that view, and it has been held right along to this moment. We were bound to look elsewhere.'

After briefly considering Abrahams, who (said Jessel) had met with little support, they turned their attention to Hertz, then en route to taking up his New York appointment. He was introduced to them by a member of the United Synagogue[63] and was interviewed by Felix Davis and himself. 'We brought him to New Court and introduced him to Lord Rothschild. And where do you think we took him after that? We took him to 60 Old Broad Street. And why do you suppose we did that?'

Brushing aside laughter from his audience, Jessel continued: 'It was not to view that historic building, nor was it to watch how Lord Swaythling conducted his financial operations. It was in order that if Dr Abrahams did not prove suitable, his Lordship should consider whether Dr Hertz was a proper person to invite over on a subsequent occasion. I mention that circumstance in order to show the intimate connection between us and Lord Swaythling at that time.'[64]

After conducting an international search for suitable candidates—which, said Jessel, had covered America and Europe, including France, Germany, Holland, Italy, Rumania, Turkey, Russia, Denmark, and Austria—they had settled on six names and, in sending up two of those names, had 'thought it wise to invite Dr Drachman to come over.

> The resolution was made clear to him. He knew there was to be an election and could have withdrawn his candidature if he thought fit. I took upon myself the responsibility, in a

long letter addressed to him, of telling him that he must not assume he would be adopted, and calling his attention to the position he would occupy. He quite knew what was up. He quite understood he was up for an election. He acquiesced. He assented.

He came over here and preached in various synagogues and, without any communication direct with us, we heard a rumour that he was undesirous of going up for a contested election. I saw him on that, because it came as a thunderbolt to me. He said it was quite true he did not like to come up for an election. He had never said that right through till shortly before the close of his visit.

I told him to put his views into writing. His view was that we ought not to have an election, but that we should have a caucus as a preliminary, and if it were decided that we preferred a particular candidate, that candidate should be elected. I told him that we knew of that sort of thing in America, but that it was an impossible proceeding, and I did not think we could very well entertain it.

I am very sorry he did not discover what his views were earlier, because he received a large amount of support. But he will have had the advantage—which he appreciated—of having met a number of English people he was very anxious to see.[65]

Drachman's version of events, based (as he later claimed) on information that had reached him, differed radically from Jessel's. 'There was,' he contended, 'a strong sentiment in my favour among the electors; indeed, a clear majority was warmly desirous of electing me. But certain legal difficulties, or ostensible difficulties of a legal nature, made it impossible for them to carry out their will. The electors opposed to my election, though only a small minority, made skilful use of these difficulties to prevent my election.

'As I have stated, I was not a direct candidate for the position. My attitude was that I was not seeking the appointment but that, if I were called by the Jewish community of Great Britain to stand at its head, I would, as a matter of duty, of religious obligation, accede to the call. This attitude corresponded to my true feelings.

'My opponents secured a ruling from the legal counsel of the United Synagogue, a Mr Algernon Sydney if I recall correctly, that such a call could not be issued. The constitution of the United Synagogue, Mr Sydney ruled, did not provide for such a call but only for selection of a Chief Rabbi from candidates who had applied for appointment. As I had not made any such application, he decided, my name was not before the College of Electors, and therefore choice must be made between the two other gentlemen considered, Rabbi Dr Moses Hyamson and Rabbi Dr Joseph H. Hertz. The College of Electors saw itself obliged to bow to this decision.

'The reaction to this result in America was a diversified one. Among the general public, it was one of surprise. The reports coming from England had all been to the effect that my election as Chief Rabbi was practically certain. The contrary result, therefore, naturally aroused great wonderment. Many of my friends were grievously disappointed. They had thought that selection of me for this exalted post was a well-merited distinction and they were grieved and, to some extent, resentful at this unexpected outcome of their hopes.'[66]

Having disposed of Drachman in his address to the delegates, Jessel reverted to Hyamson's bid and to the rabbinical certificates of the contesting candidates. 'All these diplomas were found to be absolutely in order, except that in the case of one of the candidates there was a certain qualification.' To cries of 'Dr Hertz' from the floor, Jessel remarked: 'You're wrong, it was Dr Hyamson. It was only a small matter. He was to carry on his rabbinical functions only under the direction of the Chief Rabbi. Dr Adler, perhaps wisely, put that in.'

Jessel then referred to 'another resolution passed by the Selection Committee in order to remove certain misapprehensions' (having decided that Hertz should be 'specially recommended' to the elective body). Of course, we did not want to hurt Dr Hyamson's feelings; I should be the last man to do so. We recognised his learning and his industry, and we did not desire to injure his feelings. The question had been mooted to us in private conversation that, in certain circumstances, Dr Hyamson would be willing to retire.'

At this point, M. J. Landa, the delegate for Abertillery and a relative of Hyamson's, challenged Jessel to mention names. 'I desire to say this,' declared Landa, 'to avoid any misconception. I am desired by Dr Hyamson to say that it is quite untrue. It was unauthorised.' Jessel replied: 'We were told that in certain events Dr Hyamson would be willing to retire. I accept your statement that it was unauthorised.

'We passed this resolution, which it was not intended should be public, "that in the event of the motion being passed, an opportunity would be given to Dr Hyamson to withdraw his candidature and, in the event of his doing so, only the name of Dr Hertz should be put forward." With a view to assisting Dr Hyamson's position, an interview took place between Mr Evelyn de Rothschild, Mr Albert Woolf and myself [members of the Selection Committee] and Dr Hyamson. At that interview, Dr Hyamson absolutely refused to consider the question of retirement, so that this resolution failed. But it has been put forward that we were willing to give him a bribe to retire. This is absolutely false.'

Asked by Landa whether they had made Hyamson any conditions, Jessel said: 'Dr Hyamson was fully aware what his position would be in the event of his being beaten. I told him to think it over and let me know his decision. On the following day, he let me know his decision, in which he said he affirmed his determination of the previous evening. And he did not retire. I should not have alluded to this, only it has been promulgated far and wide that we wished to give a bribe to Dr Hyamson to retire. It was absolutely without foundation. I have endeavoured to go through this long story because I wanted to vindicate our action in the matter.'[67]

Davis added his voice to the debate on Hyamson, in the hope, he said, that he 'might be regarded as speaking on behalf of those who had composed the selection committee. They would have been proud and pleased if, after due consideration and after thinking of the high position to be filled, and the tremendous importance of the advice they had to give, they had been able to advise them to vote in favour of Dr Hyamson.

'Unfortunately, they had not been able to do so. They granted that Dr Hyamson was a learned man and a great rabbi, who had had a greater chance than any other man of succeeding to the Chief Rabbinate. He had worked in the East End for many years and it might not be his fault that he had not gained, during those years of work, the love and respect of the East End of London, without which it was impossible for a Chief Rabbi to work. For other reasons, they did not think they could give preference to Dr Hyamson.'[68]

'Amid evident signs of intense interest,'[69] the delegates were soon after called upon to signify their preferences. The roll-call having concluded, Rothschild declared that two hundred and ninety-eight votes had been cast for Hertz, and thirty-nine for Hyamson, with sixty abstentions and twenty-one absentees.

The Chief Rabbi-elect, it was later announced, would be leaving New York by the *Mauretania* on 5 March 1913, accompanied by Mrs Hertz and their family.

*   *   *

Three days after the vote, Rothschild wrote officially to Hertz with an account of the election and with the Conference's report outlining the powers, duties, conditions and emoluments of the new incumbent. 'You will have heard with gratification that, after the election was over, the delegates of our widespread congregations with practical unanimity pledged themselves to support you, and I trust that the rest of the community, clerical and lay alike, will give you similar support and will assist you in your onerous task.'[70]

Signing himself Chief Rabbi-Elect, Hertz responded: 'I have the honour to acknowledge the receipt of your valued communication, which accompanied me on the *Mauretania*. Permit me to thank you for your good wishes and kindly expressions, contained in your letter of notification of my election as Chief Rabbi of the United Hebrew Congregations of the British Empire. It shall be my life-work to strive to reach, with the help of the Almighty, the high ideal set me by my sainted predecessors in the exalted office of the Chief Rabbinate. And in these endeavours I trust and pray that for many years I may have the benefit of your wise counsels.'[71]

To the Anglo-Jewish press, Hertz wrote: 'Prayerfully, I answer "Hineni!" ["Here I am!"] to the summons extended to me under the guidance of Providence by the Electoral College of British Congregations. I am deeply conscious of the vast and sacred responsibility which the office of Chief Rabbi imposes upon its incumbent, and equally so the immense difficulty of any attempt worthily to succeed Hermann Adler.

'From my heart of hearts, I pray that the God of our fathers may sustain and guide me! With His help and the help of my spiritual and lay co-workers, whose willing aid I now invoke in the communities throughout the Empire, my life and my strength shall be consecrated to the upholding and maintaining of the sway of Torah over our lives and the sanctification of the Divine Name, both within and without the ranks of Anglo-Jewry.'[72]

The result of the election, declared the *Jewish Chronicle*, was, 'above all, a triumph of, and for, the community—a triumph of the community over itself, over the bickering, the feud, and the unworthy spirit that had manifested themselves especially during the last few weeks of the Rabbinate controversy. It was a triumph for the community in the assurance that the ugly incidents to which we have referred are past, that there will be a general rally to support and encourage, in the best sense of the word, the choice that has been made.'

Notwithstanding the sustained role the paper had played in attacking Hyamson and his candidature, as well as, if less stridently, belittling Hertz, its leader-writer declared: 'Nor must the vote of the Electoral College be held in any way as casting anything like a slur upon Dr Hyamson, or as indicating any lack of recognition of the services to the community he has performed during a lifetime that has been spent on its behalf ...

'Rumours have been sedulously set afloat that Dayan Hyamson, as a consequence of Sunday's decision, intends no longer to retain his present position in this community. We hope they are untrue, or if they are not, that he will repent of any such determination, for which, in reality, there is not the remotest reason. So far as he is personally concerned, he has retained through all the respect and esteem of Anglo-Jewry ... We hope that for many years there may be given to us the advantage of his long experience and knowledge. We can ill spare them, especially in present circumstances.'[73]

'Repent of any such determination,' Hyamson did not, and even as Hertz—weeks later—was delivering his installation sermon at the Great Synagogue in London,[74] the defeated candidate was being feted by friends and colleagues in New York, where, it was reported, 'a rumour is gaining circulation that Dayan Hyamson may assume here the position which was left vacant by the new Chief Rabbi of England, namely that of spiritual head of the Congregation Orach Chayim.'[75]

The rumour was quickly confirmed, and the following month Orach Chayim unanimously elected Hyamson as its rabbi for life, 'recognised at once as a great leader in Israel who has won the hearts of all he came in contact with. God bless all England for having given him to us.'[76] Two years later, by a further quirk of history, and despite acknowledging the institution's Conservative bias, he additionally took up an appointment at Hertz's alma mater, the Jewish Theological Seminary, becoming professor of codes and 'perhaps the most Orthodox member of the seminary faculty.'[77]

As for Drachman—who, by another quirk of fate, had been one of Hertz's teachers as dean of the JTS[78]—his failure to become Chief Rabbi may possibly be ascribed, quite simply, to second thoughts. From the outset, he was clearly undecided about leaving America—'loved and cherished above all lands'—but, in a moment of vanity, may have been lured by the glories that lay ahead. And perhaps, as he later suggested, there were deeper emotions that underpinned his decision.

'My dear wife's reaction,' he wrote,[79] 'was one of unconditional relief. She would have accompanied me, had I been chosen for the post and accepted, without a word of objection or complaint—such was her loyalty to her concept of wifely duty—but now that the sacrifice was not to be required of her, she was frankly happy. She bade me "forget it," dismiss the matter from my mind, and resolve to be happy with her in our own dearly beloved America, our precious native land.

'As for my own reaction, it was also mainly one of relief. There was, naturally, a certain degree of humiliation in the thought that I was apparently a defeated candidate. But when I reflected upon the manner in which my rejection had been brought about, that it had not been the result of a straight, direct vote but of a mere legal technicality, and when I reflected further on the reasons which actuated my opponents, that they found no fault either with my character or ability, but did not want a Chief Rabbi of firm and uncompromising devotion to the principles of Orthodox Judaism, I came to the conclusion that my lack of success, instead of being a dishonour, was really a tribute of honour and high esteem.

'One result my failure to reach the Chief Rabbinate did not have. It did not embitter me in the slightest. I felt that the English-Jewish community had honoured me signally in inviting me, without any solicitation on my part, to become a candidate for the highest position in its power to confer, and I was sincerely happy that I had had the opportunity to get in touch with this great community of Israel, to observe its workings from within, and to make the acquaintance and, in many instances, gain the friendship of so many noble men and women of its members. I felt that my life was greatly enriched by this experience. Neither did my experience in England lessen or weaken my desire to do what I could in behalf of my brethren and faith on the west side of the Atlantic.'

Joseph Herman Hertz (1913): 'Ours is an age of doubt and disillusionment'

FROM THE PULPIT — III
Moderation in Judgment

Installation sermon delivered at the Great Synagogue, London, by the Very Rev Dr Joseph Herman Hertz, Chief Rabbi of the United Hebrew Congregations of the British Empire, 14 April 1913–7 Nisan 5673

'Remember ye the Law of Moses my servant, which I commanded unto him in Horeb for all Israel, with the statutes and judgments. Behold, I will send you Elijah the prophet before the coming of the great and dreadful day of the Lord; and he shall turn the heart of the fathers to the children and the heart of the children to their fathers, lest I come and smite the land with a curse.'[1]

These concluding verses of the Book of Malachi will, within a few days, be read as part of the prophetical lesson on Shabbat Hagadol, the Sabbath preceding Passover, our Festival of Freedom. They take us back twenty-three centuries to the times of the last of Israel's seers of old. The lamp of religious enthusiasm burned but dimly in that age, and both priests and people were treating sacred things with a weary indifference. The high hopes of the returning exiles from Babylon had not been fulfilled, and doubt, despondency, and spiritual lassitude paralysed the souls of men. Though from the rising of the sun until the going down of the same, God's name was great among the Gentiles,[2] it was Israel that began to doubt whether there was a righteous Governor of the world, and was losing Israel's belief in Israel. 'I have loved you, saith the Lord. Yet ye say, "Wherein hast Thou loved us?" Your words have been stout against Me. Ye have said, "It is vain to serve God, and what profit is it that we have kept His charge?"'[3]

It is in such a generation that Malachi reaffirms and boldly proclaims the divine election and the deathlessness of Israel. 'I am the Lord, I change not; therefore ye sons of Jacob are not consumed.'[4] Confronted by sordid irreligion and cruel selfishness, he preaches the reality of the unseen and the brother-

---

1 Malachi 3:22-24. [All citations are as in the original text.]
2 Ibid., 1:11.
3 Ibid., 1:2; 3:13
4 Ibid., 3:6.

hood of man. 'Have we not all one Father, hath not one God created us all? Why, then, do we deal faithlessly every man against his brother?', he asks.[5] The culmination of his prophecy is: 'Remember ye the Law of Moses which I commanded unto him in Horeb for all Israel, with the statutes and judgments.' That to him is the indispensable condition of the glad tidings of the reconciliation of fathers and sons with which his book closes. For it is the home divided against itself, the estrangement of the youth from the elders, that especially fills him with pain and horror as something unnatural—a curse which, if unremoved, must blight the land.

Was he a voice crying in the wilderness?, we wonder. We have no contemporary written record concerning his work. Our oral literature, however, repeatedly records the tradition—unassailable by sober historical criticism—that the forces that made for spiritual regeneration eventually gathered round Malachi and his fellow-leaders of the Restoration, and formed the institution known to posterity as the Great Synagogue. It was the men of the Great Synagogue and the scribes, sages and teachers that succeeded them, we are told, who composed the liturgy, arranged the weekly readings of the Torah, edited various books of the Scriptures, and all but fixed the Biblical Canon. It was they—the rabbis declare—who finally eradicated idolatry from the Jewish breast, planted reverence therein and prayerfulness, and 'restored the crown of the Torah to its pristine splendour.'[6] Even the secret of these reorganisers of Judaism, the cultural programme which regulated their world-historical activities, has come to us. It is this: 'Be ye moderate in judgment; raise up many disciples; and make ye a fence to the Torah.'[7]

Do we not feel that in more than one respect that long-vanished age was a very real anticipation of our own times? Ours is an age of doubt and disillusionment. Times are out of joint. Theological foundations are rocking. Dreams of humanity, that but yesterday seemed within grasp of realisation, are dissolving into thin air in face of the malacious race-hatred that is being fanatically preached, and the purposeless human slaughter cynically practised in the opening decades of the twentieth century. Within the House of Israel also, old sanctions are weakening, home influence waning, and there is an alarming subsidence of the sense of worship. The generations are separated as by an abyss; hosts of our men and women of tomorrow are losing belief in Israel's future, and drifting into unbaptised apostacy. We are, moreover, living in the midst of a new Exodus, a new Exile even. The last fifty years have witnessed the forcible migration of over a million of our people from a Slavonic

---

5   Ibid., 2:10.
6   Berachoth 33a.
7   Aboth 1:1.

into an Anglo-Saxon environment. The ways of Providence are large—still that remains a unique transition; and in the life of the spirit all transitions are critical. The centre of gravity of Judaism is changing. The Jew is becoming *urbanised*, more than ever a dweller of cities. There are today nearly a dozen communities with 100,000 souls or more, one with over a million. In these vast cities, the entire religious and ethical, as well as the industrial, life of our masses is undergoing a fundamental transformation. Our loyal 'Remnant' are thus on every side confronted by problems—of adaptation, education, and organisation—on a scale well-nigh unprecedented in the Diaspora. Whence shall our help come?

With eternal timeliness, there resounds across the ages the message of Malachi: 'Remember ye the Law of Moses which I commanded unto him in Horeb for all Israel, with the statutes and judgments.' And the genius of Israel demands of us today nothing less than the same threefold response that the men of the Great Synagogue rendered in their generations!

'Be ye moderate in judgment.' Obedience to this would alone bring with it the fulfilment of the promise, 'Behold, I send you Elijah the prophet.' For remember, Elijah the prophet of zeal and fire of the ordinary Bible-reader is not the Elijah of the rabbis or of Jewish folklore. There, he is the helper and healer, the reconciler and peace-bringer.[8] This Elijah-spirit is our greatest need. The Jew very often can see only one thing at a time. He is intensive in his loyalties and antipathies, in his differences—and indifferences. Pre-eminently does he need constant reminders that infinitely more important than all the issues that divide us are the things that should bind us, unite us; that it is as noble a striving for brother to rediscover brother as to preserve an unbroken connection with Israel's past. And to all parties alike comes this warning for moderation in judgment. The revolutionaries need it. Theirs is the cry of 'New lamps for old.' But there is no inherent, sacramental virtue in change as change. The new is not always the true. 'The seal of the Almighty is Truth,' say the rabbis.[9] But He has no Keeper of the Seal; and even the latest theory of the youngest revolutionary thinker may be mistaken. And, ye men of older years and views, be moderate in judgment. 'New occasions teach new duties,' and new conditions require new methods. In classical phrase, 'the *methods* of the quiet past are inadequate for the stormy present. The occasion is piled high with difficulties, and we must rise with the occasion. As our case is new, so we must think anew, act anew.' Let us, therefore, whether we be traditionalists or revolutionaries, first of all disenthral ourselves, on the one hand, from masterly inactivity or from methods obsolete, even in Russia; and, on the other, from the spell of

8   Eduyoth, end.
9   Yoma 69b.

new remedies which have proved pathetically futile, and worse than futile, in Germany and America—and we shall save our young for the future. For our children's sake, therefore, be ye deliberate, moderate, charitable in judgment.

The second great master-word of the men of the Great Synagogue was, 'Raise up many disciples.' Very zealous were they in the spread of religious knowledge.[10] And rightly so. For in Judaism ignorance is never the mother of devotion. Ignorance of Hebrew, of the Bible, and of Jewish thought, then as now, invariably tends towards ultimate desertion. One of the gravest symptoms of the present is the gradually diminishing knowledge of the sacred language in our Western communities. Hebrew is the key to all the eternal values we have contributed to human life. And if we are to throw that key into the ocean of forgetfulness, the end of this century can have but one thing in store for us—the grave.[11] A Hebrew-less Jewry, moreover, would be a sin against humanity. We dare not allow the most sacred, the most potent and most radioactive things in this world to die; and they would die if the knowledge of Hebrew were utterly to disappear among us, the predestined and everlasting custodians of the Hebrew word. Our religious education must be broadened and deepened! We suffer from partial, fragmentary views of Judaism and of the Jewish world-conception. Hence a new phenomenon has arisen at the present day—the 'Jewish' funeral orator of Judaism. It is only when once more we see Judaism in its totality that, instead, we will bless and render thanks to our Maker for the happiness of our portion, for the beauty and glory of our heritage. 'The world's memory must be kept alive,' says a great scholar-statesman of our day;[12] 'we are in danger of losing our identity and becoming infantile in every generation. This is the menace under which we cower everywhere in this age of change.' *Israel's memory must be kept alive*, otherwise we are menaced with loss of our identity, with becoming infantile in our semi-religious or irreligious aberrations. But not only intensively, in content; extensively as well, in regard to the human area of operation for such education, there is a crying need for improvement. As things are today, the vast majority of our boys and girls in their adolescent period—in fact, nearly all our youth in the secondary schools—are left without any religious guidance. We neglect to fortify them for the warfare of life by grounding them in the elementals and fundamentals of Israel's faith, past and outlook. Religiously, they are 'abandoned' by us; and, in turn and time, they are abandoning us, drifting over to our enemies; worse still, too many of them, alas, suffer moral shipwreck in the social abyss of our large cities. We look to our institutions for

---

10 Sanhedrin 104b.
11 Henrietta Szold, *A Century of Jewish Thought*, 1896.
12 Woodrow Wilson, 'Princeton in the Nation's Service,' *The Forum*, December 1896.

advanced Hebrew learning—those store-houses of the knowledge, memory and the wisdom of our race—more and more to rear unto us religious leaders of faith and fervour; men of knowledge and reverence and power; men endowed with the gift of vision, interpretation and religious contagion, who will all along the line, from the base to the apex of our educational pyramid, hear the vital summons, 'Raise up many disciples.' Then a reawakened Jewish consciousness will be ours, bringing with it a reawakened Jewish conscience!

Now, deliberation and memory, moderation and knowledge are but means in the service of our ideal—Jewish living under the Law. Like the men of the Great Synagogue, therefore, we will remember the Law of Moses, with the statutes, judgments, 'fences.' Ours will be no Platonic admiration of the Torah; ours no 'fulfilling' of the Torah by abolishing it. For well we know that, when the framework of the ancient Law falls away, when the immemorial rites, customs and ceremonies go, we are left without God in our lives. We may—for a time—remain an ethical, but we are no longer a religious, people.[13] And then our days are numbered; for in our religion alone lies the secret of our deathlessness. When Malachi's contemporaries asked for proof of the love of God, he bade them contrast the history of Israel with that of the neighbouring Bedouin tribes. And verily, with all their outward similarity and kinship of blood, how different were the ultimate fates of Israel and of Moab, for example. 'The history of Moab loses itself obscurely and fruitlessly in the sand; that of Israel issues in eternity.'[14] Why? Israel had the Torah, statutes, judgments, 'fences'; ceremonies which in a world of maddening brutality sweetened the life of the Jew; customs which linked generation to generation in filial piety; observances which in the face of countless cataclysms and dispersions unified, as nothing else could, the scattered atoms of the House of Israel—dykes built by inspired engineers to save us from all the waters of heathenism and animalism.

Only a religious Israel is invincible. Only a religious Israel is a great dynamic power for personal holiness, social righteousness and humanitarian endeavour. Only a religious Israel is a national asset of infinite value to the State whose citizens we are. Israel's Book of Books, though forever preserving its sacred contents unchanged and unaltered, has been translated into every tongue and has become an integral part of the language, literature and life of every white nation. The true Jew, it has been well said, resembles in this respect his ancient Revelation. Preserving in his breast an unchanging love towards his glorious past and sacred heritage—Israel's Law and Israel's lore—he is at the same time an integral part of the life and spiritual endeavour of every people among whom Providence has allotted his home. And as for the Jews in this

---

13 *The Spirit of Judaism*, by Josephine Lazarus, the ultra-Liberal sister of Emma Lazarus.
14 Julius Wellhausen, *Encyclopædia Biblica*, 'Moab.'

Empire—which is earth's nearest realisation hitherto of might coupled with justice and humanity[15]—finely has a noble Anglo-Jewish soldier expressed it:[16] 'Loyalty to the flag for which the sun once stood still can only deepen our devotion to the flag on which the sun never sets.'

My exposition of the prophetic word—'Remember ye the Law of Moses'—is at an end. Though I have not spoken directly of the sacredness of this hour to me, and its significance to the religious life of the congregations far and near that at this moment pass under my charge, I have yet indicated to you some of the aims that shall beckon me on in my exalted office, shown you the spirit in which I shall serve them, and traced a few of the larger lines on which I shall attempt their realisation. I need not further specify the work before me in all its multitudinousness, whether as *teacher* of the Book to the people of the Book; as *interpreter* of Israel, the great misunderstood of history, to the larger, often hostile, world around him; as *champion* of my people, guarding the honour, upholding the prestige of Anglo-Jewry; as *defender* of the Faith, who cannot permit any 'cutting of the dykes' for the display of the hypothetical steersmanship of anti-Nomian theorists; or, lastly, as *peacemaker*, with the Elijah-ideal before me of the harmoniser who reconciles and restrains the various centrifugal and disruptive tendencies in our modern life.

Too well do I know that I do not bring to these tasks the mature statesmanship and wonderful diversity of gifts of my predecessor in the high and holy office I have been called upon to fill. Neither can I, an untried man, hope for the involuntary reverence that was paid to the august presence and erudite profundity of his sainted father. Standing in the place of such men, on the threshold of the vastest of ministries, I can only plead for charity and patience towards myself. Ideals such as those of the men of the Great Synagogue require years, not days, for accomplishment. In the words of Hillel, I would implore you, 'Judge not thy fellow-man till thou art in his place,'[17] and forget not moderation. We simply cannot succeed without sympathetic understanding and co-operation. Tower-builders, even when such are labouring for the greater glory of God, must understand one another. Confusion of tongues can wreck any scheme.

And I beg for loyalty. In my fight against ignorance and irreligion, crime or race-hatred, those Amaleks whose onslaught is ever directed against the innocent, the weak, the helpless, my hands may become heavy and weary. It is essential that a united Jewry be ever ready loyally to support my hands and steady them. Once more I beg for sympathetic understanding and coopera-

---

15   Berachoth 58a.
16   Colonel A.E. Goldsmid.
17   Aboth 2, 5.

tion. Vast are the potentialities of British Jewry, with its hegemony in contemporary Israel, with this community the axis round which so many of Israel's endeavours revolve. The eyes of our brethren throughout the world are upon us—their hopes and prayers are all with us. Who shall live up to the great trust? Who dares fail to try? In the words of Hermann Adler, I ask you all—young and old, men and women, laymen and scholars, ministers and rabbis—'what can be grander or more glorious than to become fellow-workers with God in securing the immortality of Judaism?'[18]

When the masters of the Jewish academies entered on their duties, they prayed, 'May it be Thy will, O Sovereign of the Universe, that no evil arise at our hands, that we neither fall into error nor cause others to stumble, that we declare not the pure impure, nor the impure pure, and that all our work and doings tend toward the increase of amity and fellowship.'[19] A similar supplication is mine at this, my solemn reconsecration and rededication to God, the Torah and Israel. May the Sacred Cause entrusted to me never suffer at my hands. May He keep me from error, so that I advance all things that are pure, and restrain all forces that tend towards unrighteousness and ungodliness. May truth, peace, brotherhood increase through my service, that His Law be magnified and His great Name be sanctified for ever more.[20]

---

18 *Jews' College Jubilee Volume*, p.cxxxii.
19 Berachoth 28b.
20 [The sermon concluded with an additional prayer.]

CHAPTER FOUR

No Imaginary Man

DESPITE HIS INSTALLATION appeal to the 'revolutionaries' and 'the men of older years' for moderation in judgment, a plea that was to dominate his Chief Rabbinate, the early years of Hertz's tenure—spanned by the First World War—engaged him in fields other than the purely religious. Anti-Semitism, alien agitation, Zionism, and the trenches sucked up the energies, and the lives, of many in the vanguard of ritual reform, and, as a result, theological debate subsided within Anglo-Jewry. A ceasefire on the military front, however, saw hostilities resumed in communal ranks, with the synagogues ringing out to the notes of religious disarray.

In the summer of 1919, the demand arose for a definition of 'Traditional Judaism,' associated with a project—the Jewish War Memorial Scheme—aimed at creating a British School of Jewish Learning to redress the acute post-war shortage of ministers and teachers. 'There is not the slightest doubt in our mind,' declared Hertz, 'in regard to the connotation of "Traditional Judaism." The words mean what they say—the teachings and practices which have come down to the House of Israel through the ages: the positive, Jewish beliefs concerning God, the Torah and Israel; the sacred festivals; the traditional service; the holy resolve to maintain Israel's identity; and the life consecrated by historic Jewish observance—all of these in indissoluble union with the best thought and culture of the age, and with utmost loyalty to King and Country.

'This is a working description of Traditional Judaism, the Judaism of a Saadiah, a Maimonides, a Menasseh ben Israel, a Moses Montefiore, or a Nathan Marcus Adler. What is more, it may fairly be called the Anglo-Jewish position in theology, as even those who three generations ago separated from the Orthodox body have in the main zealously stood for these principles and practices.'

Adding fuel to the furnace he was determined to stoke, Hertz challenged his Liberal opponents: 'If a man is a follower of the reformers of Germany and America, if *religiously* he is a German-American Jew—this would be a far more correct designation than the self-righteous and question-begging name "Liberal Jew"—he need not, of course, support this Jewish War Memorial.

'Far otherwise must be our attitude *if our ideals are Anglo-Jewish ideals—the ideals of the fathers of Anglo-Jewry*, the ideals of a Menasseh ben Israel, a Moses Montefiore, or the founders of this synagogue.[1] We shall then help "according as we are able, according to the blessing wherewith God has blessed us." And we shall do so because we realise that on its success largely depends the entire future of Judaism in England and the Empire at large.'

Writing to an associate during the last quarter of the decade, Hertz confessed to an all-consuming battle 'in defence of Traditional Judaism against the Liberal onslaught' that had precluded much else from his communal agenda. 'This duty,' he stated, 'took up all my energy, and took precedence over all other tasks.'[2] He had launched it, he wrote elsewhere, 'in view of the religious unrest of the age, aggravated in the Jewish community by misunderstanding from without and within,' leading to the need for a presentation of Judaism that endeavoured 'to bring out the truth and eternal timeliness of Israel's historic beliefs and institutions.'[3]

Thereafter, for a full ninety months, Hertz conducted his campaign against the Liberal 'onslaught.' Yet his vigorous efforts were to little avail. With each passing year, the movement announced increasingly concrete progress in its appeal to the masses, with growing attendances, communal recognition and international support.

In 1921, a Liberal congregation was launched in Stamford Hill, with its own permanent synagogue six years later. Following an approach from the Board of Deputies and a change in its constitution giving women the franchise, the congregation voted for representation on the Board in 1922. By 1925, 'Progressive' services initiated jointly by the Liberals and Reformers at St George's Settlement[4] in Whitechapel, the heartland of East-End Orthodoxy, were attracting up to 1,000 worshippers on Sabbaths and festivals; and in the same year, an impressive sanctuary seating 1,400—the largest in London—was consecrated by the Liberal Jewish Synagogue in St John's Wood. Crowning these achievements was the founding, a year later, of the World Union for Progressive Judaism, the brainchild of its first honorary secretary, Samuel Montagu's daughter, Lily.

While the Liberals continued to make spectacular gains across the board, the Reform advance—though far more modest—proceeded apace, resulting in growing harmony between the movements which was soon cemented by joint membership of the World Union. Over the ensuing decade, avenues were opened with the long-term aim (never fully realised) of linking the two bodies through an association of Liberal and Reform synagogues.

In the face of this seemingly unstoppable reformist bandwagon, Hertz's protagonists looked on in dismay. None of his approaches, bemoaned the *Jewish Chronicle*, 'deals in any sense with the particular problems and duties thrown up by the present hour ... Merely to recite the beauty and grandeur of Orthodoxy built up for the purposes of another hour, or even admiringly to parade the ingenuity of its exponents, to employ a colloquialism, cuts no ice.

> And it is from the ice-bound lethargy, the cold and frigid *laissez faire*, the frozen stagnated life-blood of modern Jewry, that it is supremely the duty of those who stand for Orthodox Judaism to endeavour to release their brothers and sisters. For the vast majority of these are anxious, above all things, to be loyal; but they are faced with problems arising from the duties of the hour which, let us put it quite plainly, are in so many instances irreconcilable with not perhaps the principles, but certainly the practices, of Orthodoxy.
>
> The task is not one for a man, however learned, however gifted in point of eloquence, whose spirit is otherwise than big and lofty. Its accomplishment, or even an essay towards its accomplishment, would bring honour and glory even to a great man; and it is a task urgent beyond measure.
>
> The more we realise the truth of all that Dr Hertz has told us about 'Liberal' Judaism on the one hand and the affirmations of Judaism on the other, the more clearly we must come to understand how important and vital it is that our rabbis and leaders should, in the words of Dr Hertz, 'deal with the problems and duties that the present hour brings to the loyal sons and daughters of Israel,' so as to 'help them to make their Judaism a matter of living experience.'[5]

Alarmed by defections from their own congregations and by the growing strength of the Liberals and Reform, United Synagogue leaders—spearheaded by their president, Sir Robert Waley Cohen, who had conducted a long-time and often vitriolic battle against Hertz's methods—sought in 1940 to close ranks as wartime exigencies exacted their toll. Differences existed, however, over the means and ends of the crisis strategy.

'The United Synagogue, and with it many of the institutions on which Jewish religious life in this country depends,' asserted Waley Cohen to the US council, 'stand at a very critical crossroad: the whole of our future depends on the community showing itself as ready as our forebears to rally to the cause of Judaism.' One positive move was that 'every minister has pledged his time and energy to the work of recalling the community to the synagogue.'[6] 'Recall to the Synagogue' thus became the slogan of a spirited movement towards that goal. But if Waley Cohen and Hertz were ever at odds over means to an end, these were seldom more highlighted than in the new endeavour.

From the outset, the Chief Rabbi, seeking to assert his own authority within the Orthodox community, launched an oblique broadside against his US nemesis. 'The architects of the United Synagogue, Sir Anthony de Rothschild and Lionel Louis Cohen,' he told the council, 'provided it with a constitution that permits no ecclesiastical interference in matters of finance; and, at the same time, these great-hearted Jewish gentlemen had a horror of lay interference in religious law. They therefore placed the entire religious administration and educational supervision under the control of the Chief Rabbi; and, of course, his remained the religious leadership and public representation of the community ...

> The whole *raison d'être* of a Jewish community is the advancement of Judaism. And by Judaism we mean, first of all, the web of fast and festival, precept, symbol and ceremony that is the foundation of the Jewish way of life. That way of life has come down to us from our fathers of old.
>
> It is rooted in the Hebrew Scriptures, and the inheritance of Israel as the depository and guardian of the truths held by it for mankind. It has been nurtured by the instruction of God-enlightened prophets and seers, sages and saints; and upheld by the teachings of self-denying generations. In a word, it is the fruit and outward expression of a religious civilisation aglow with the passion for righteousness, a religious civilisation in which are enshrined world-old, original, spiritual forces which to this day have lost none of their effectiveness.
>
> Given such a conception of Judaism, we at once see that the financial side of synagogue administration is not all-important; and that we can have nothing but contempt for those zealots of business efficiency in religion who would tear down the two Tables of the Law from the front of our houses of worship and replace them by the balance-sheet. Besides, deification of business management, coupled as it so often is with colour-blindness to Jewish spiritual and cultural values, is unwise even from the purely business point of view.
>
> As long as a born Jew is still possessed of some reverence for things Jewish, as long as there is still a spark of Jewish feeling in him, so long may there be in him loyalty to his people and generosity in the support of its institutions. But

when his heart is void of every religious memory, there is refusal to support even Jewish philanthropic institutions, which are then dismissed by him as 'sectarian' charities.[7]

Further disputes between Hertz and his lay leaders led eventually to a *cri de coeur* from the Chief Rabbi, urging them 'to give up your quixotic fight against the windmill of "priestly dictatorship."' It was, he added, 'pure hallucination.'[8]

* * *

'His strength sorely taxed by the many anxieties that beset his office,'[9] Hertz died at home in his sleep on the morning of 14 January 1946, aged seventy-four. His wife and confidante, the former Rose Freed of New York, had predeceased him in 1930, 'cut off in the midst of her years,'[10] leaving a fraught and increasingly fractious Chief Rabbi to face the effects on his divided community of the catastrophe unfolding in Nazi-occupied Europe. It was under these circumstances that the perception had gained ground of Hertz's domination by the extreme right-wing, feelings accentuated by the ravages of war.[11]

Despite this view, the *Jewish Chronicle* remarked in the week of his passing: 'It can be recorded without dispute that while—as with the general population in these islands—there was no great religious revival during his years in office, and while there was even a continuation of the weakening of religious ties which he could not arrest, he did succeed, as perhaps few others might have succeeded, not only in maintaining but in enhancing the supremacy and leadership of the British Chief Rabbinate. Many people in these islands, and still more abroad, realise what an invaluable asset to Jewish prestige and to the strength of British Jewry the Chief Rabbinate provides, and the years of office of Dr Hertz have very forcefully brought this fact to light.'[12]

With the hindsight of subsequent events, centring on several individuals at the core of the electoral process, the eulogies to the late Chief Rabbi took on added significance. In a collection of essays and addresses belatedly published in Hertz's memory, one Chief Rabbinical hopeful, the Federation of Synagogues' Principal Rabbi, Kopul Rosen, declared: 'During the past two years, those who have been seriously concerned with the direction and the future development of our community have thought of him [Hertz] frequently and wished that the strong, courageous and deeply Jewish leadership which came from him was still with us.'[13]

Seeking to probe 'the secret of the late Chief Rabbi's personality, and of the striking success he achieved in his ministry,' another candidate—Alexander Altmann, Communal Rabbi of Manchester—argued: 'I think the answer lies in a biographical fact. As a young man, he joined the Jewish Theological

Seminary of New York, which had just been founded by a band of enthusiastic protagonists of conservative Judaism in America, and he came under the spell of great teachers, above all of the saintly and learned Dr Sabato Morais, who seems to have impressed his own personality upon his disciple ... At that time, American Jewry held out but few prospects of success to a protagonist of conservative Judaism. It required self-denial, courage and conviction to choose the career which Dr Hertz did choose.'[14]

The London Beth Din's Isidor Grunfeld asserted of Hertz: 'He spoke out fearlessly and quite regardless of what circles he might offend. He simply could not contain himself at the sight of injustice and disingenuousness, and nothing was more hateful to his noble nature than moral cowardice.'[15]

Waley Cohen, a prominent leader of one such circle, touched on this point at a meeting of his council within hours of Hertz's death: 'Let us admit that so forceful a personality could not fail at times to come into some anxious conflicts, but the controversies in recent times were hushed by the news of his critical illness and are silenced by his death, whilst the impression of his outstanding efforts stands out in ever greater relief.

> If I, who worked in close personal consultation with him for more than twenty-five years, may for a moment strike a personal note, I would say that, though it would be idle and insincere to pretend that we did not sometimes hold strongly conflicting views, I always felt that both of us were grieved to find ourselves viewing events and actions along divergent lines; I am sure others had the same experience. Through all these years, no one who saw much of him could fail to be conscious of the sincerity by which he was always moved, and in later years—when bitter controversies arose—we always felt conscious that it was in that sincerity itself that the difficulties of adjustment had their origin. In the last days of his life, he felt a great desire to bring reconciliation to Anglo-Jewish life; and I have been told that a letter which he had approved and which aimed at peace and reconciliation in our midst lay ready for his signature when the hand of death fell and carried him to his eternal peace.[16]

Although never dispatched, a draft of that letter fell into the hands of the Federation of Synagogues' president, Aaron Wright, who was to play an ambivalent role in the subsequent election as, concurrently, a United Synagogue representative on the Chief Rabbinate Conference committee.[17] Over a lengthy period, Wright had witnessed the growing mutual antipathy between Hertz and Waley Cohen and, describing himself as 'privileged to be his [the Chief Rabbi's] intimate adviser in the last few years of his life,' he wrote later of Hertz: 'He had grown steadily in strength and stature and ... increasingly asserted his authority, a course which brought him into conflict with the lay leadership of the United Synagogue personified by Sir Robert.

'The two protagonists were well matched—Dr Hertz, compact, direct in speech, courageous, fiery in his zeal to protect the faith, a scholar justly proud of his writings, and intent on leaving his "footprints on the sands of time." Opposed to him was Sir Robert, a man of extraordinary ability, immense driving power and capacity for work ... There was no doubt of his loyalty to his own conception of Traditional Judaism. To say that Sir Robert was very determined is to understate the position; it was both his strength and his weakness that he could not readily perceive the distinction between his own convictions and revealed truth.'

Following a dispute at the end of 1945 over the Chief Rabbi's request for ministers to include in their sermons reference to the then current crisis in Zionist affairs—a proposal countermanded by Waley Cohen and his joint vice-president, Frank Samuel—a fierce debate erupted within the US council, following which the second vice-president, Ewen Montagu, wrote to Hertz on 14 November 1945: 'At the meeting of the council at which I took the chair last Monday night, I read to the council the following statement which was wholeheartedly agreed to by all the honorary officers:

'"1. We accept and support the authority of the Chief Rabbi on all religious matters as laid down in the Constitution of the United Synagogue and, in particular, in paragraph 3 of the Deed of Foundation and Trust ... 2. We accept the fundamental principle of the freedom of the pulpit and fully recognise the right of Ministers to preach the ideals of Zionism in the pulpit. 3. As our telegram of 5 October 1945 to the Wardens of the synagogues of the United Synagogue and our circular letter of 25 October 1945 to the members of the Council have been misinterpreted as involving an attack on the Chief Rabbi, or as being contrary to our above views, we of course readily state that those documents were not so intended, and that our views are, and always have been, as stated in the above two paragraphs."'

Responding—in his unsent letter—to a request by the US honorary officers to confer with him, 'with a view to re-establishing between us that close co-operation which is essential for peace in the Community,' Hertz wrote:

> I thank you for your letter of Nov. 14th, 1945, and I am more than sorry that the present state of my health does not permit me to see the Honorary Officers as they suggest. I feel it is not desirable in the best interests of the Anglo-Jewish community

that this matter should be left in abeyance any longer, and I am accordingly writing to you on the matter.

As you know, I have no personal ambitions at all at this stage of my life. My only object is to transmit to my successor the constitutional rights of my high office undimmed and undiminished. It would appear to me that the rights and responsibilities of the office of Chief Rabbi are acknowledged by the resolutions of the Council and in such form that my successor whenever he may have to take office is duly protected.

I trust that there will be entered on the Minutes of the Council of the United Synagogue a copy of their letter to me of November 14th and this my reply, so that it will stand in the future as an acknowledgement and declaration for the preservation of the rights of my high office.

I think, in the interests of Anglo-Jewry, that this unhappy and unfortunate occurrence may now be considered closed.[18]

* * *

From the moment of Hertz's death, 'the rights and responsibilities of the office of Chief Rabbi' recaptured the attention of the opinion-makers of Anglo-Jewry. 'Dr Hertz's career,' declared the *Jewish Chronicle*, 'did more than preserve a tradition: it exemplified, as never before, the vital functions of the Chief Rabbinate and its absolute indispensability to the welfare of Jewry in Great Britain and the Empire. It would be the crassest folly, therefore, to contemplate abolishing this precious office, or reducing its power, however difficult the task may prove once more to fill it. For the community, as a whole, it represents the chief, if not the only, unifying power in British Jewry. To non-Jews, it is the symbol of that unity and the direction to which they more and more turn for the expression of Jewish views and wishes.

> To eliminate or in any way reduce it, therefore, would be to invite disunity and confusion, to weaken the ties between the community and the State, to court the attentions of those who wish us ill, and to throw away an invaluable instrument of progress. Least of all in these critical and cloudy days can we afford to play fast and loose with an institution that has served us well and that holds within itself, as Dr Hertz has shown, infinite promise for future service. The task of selecting a successor, we know, will be hard indeed, and in weak-

ness or despair, or perhaps from other motives, voices may be raised for the appointment of an interim or acting Chief Rabbi. Any such facile arrangement must be sternly resisted. It would only open the way to controversy and intrigue which should be taboo in such a connection. The stop-gap Chief Rabbi would, even if suitable, suffer all the undesirable and indelible afflictions of prolonged candidature. The community must also be on its guard against any weakening of the powers of the Chief Rabbinate, a policy which would be sheer fatuity, robbing it of all its value and heading the community straight for chaos and disintegration.

As for the process of election, the precedent exists, and it is in keeping alike with the spirit of Judaism and the spirit of the country that it should provide the basis for the procedure. But conditions have drastically changed since Dr Hertz was appointed, and it will therefore require the most careful consideration and adaptation if it is to fulfil its function in 1946 as wisely and fortunately as it did in 1913. In recent months, steps were taken for the initiation of informal conversations on the subject between some of the principal Synagogue authorities in the country, and as soon as may be fitting these should now be vigorously pursued, with free and open interchange of views, so that the community may understand how the existing precedent can evolve to meet the present conditions.[19]

In the event, disregarding the paper's cry against the 'facile arrangement' of a 'stop-gap' Chief Rabbi, the United Synagogue speedily informed its honorary officers[20]—and, through them, its associated congregations[21]—that it had requested Dayan Harris Lazarus[22] 'to act until further notice in carrying on the duties and functions appertaining to the office of Chief Rabbi, so far as those duties and functions in any way relate to the United Synagogue or the institutions with which it is connected.'

In accordance with the Deed of Foundation and Trust, wrote US secretary Philip Goldberg, 'steps will in due course be taken with a view to the appointment of a successor to the late Dr Hertz,' in the hope that, meanwhile, 'congregations who acknowledge the authority of the Chief Rabbi ... will repose in Dayan Lazarus in this emergency the same authority, and regard him as their spiritual Chief.' To that end, Waley Cohen summoned a meeting—'a good plan,' he called it—'to confer with some of the heads of other important religious institutions in Anglo-Jewry, both in London and the Provinces, on some of the problems connected with the Office of Chief Rabbi.'²³

Pre-empting the input of the institutional heads, the dayanim of the London Beth Din—who were later to have a decisive impact on the appointment—lost no time in addressing a memorandum to Waley Cohen, spelling out their views on 'the qualities required in a Rabbi, and especially in a Chief Rabbi,' and on 'the collaboration of the new Chief Rabbi with the Ecclesiastical Court of which he is to be the President.' The signatories were Yechezkel Abramsky (the senior dayan), Julius Jakobovits (who died eleven months later), Isidor Grunfeld and Morris Swift.

The tragic events in the contemporary history of European Jewry, commented the dayanim, had 'brought it about that the Anglo-Jewish community is now the last bastion of Jewish religious life in Europe,' and it was the Beth Din's 'deep conviction that the Chief Rabbinate must have a far-reaching influence upon the grave question whether this bastion of the Anglo-Jewish community will grow stronger and form the nucleus of a new Jewish communal life in Europe, or whether it will disintegrate and end in schism and heresy.

> The strong trend towards undiluted traditional Judaism makes it imperative to find a man as the spiritual head of Anglo-Jewry whose orthodoxy and religious outlook cannot be questioned by any section of Jewry. A Chief Rabbi must not be assumed to be orthodox merely because he happens to be working with an orthodox Beth Din. His orthodoxy must be based on his own convictions and on his own mode of life. What is valid in any orthodox Rabbi is especially important in the case of a Chief Rabbi, namely, that the title of 'Rabbi' is not an academic degree which testifies to knowledge only, irrespective of the holder's beliefs and mode of life, but that 'Rabbi' is a title sui generis which connotes belief in, and practice of, Jewish doctrines and observances.
>
> However great a Jewish scholar may be in Bible exegesis and rabbinics, if he does not believe in the Divine Origin and binding force of written and oral law alike, he ipso facto destroys his eligibility to the title of 'Rabbi' and much more so to that of 'Chief Rabbi.' It is first and foremost his personal sincerity and adherence to orthodox Jewish beliefs and practices which will ensure for the new Chief Rabbi the following of Anglo-Jewry and Empire-Jewries in their present-day structure. Moreover, owing to the unspeakable tragedy of Israel's fate in our own days, the new Chief Rabbi must, like

his unforgettable predecessor, be a fearless champion of the rights of the remnant of Israel, and a fighter for their better future both in the Diaspora and the Land of Israel.

In the selection of the new Chief Rabbi, the dayanim declared, it was necessary to find a man who not only had an understanding of the Anglo-Jewish community, 'but who, by his personality and religious outlook, also gives the assurance of smooth collaboration with the members of the London Beth Din, known as the Court of the Chief Rabbi ...

'The Chief Rabbi will, ex officio, be the President of this most important contemporary Jewish Court of Law. A man, therefore, who is out of tune with the strict adherence of the London Beth Din to traditional Jewish law, as handed down in Talmud and Shulchan Aruch, will of necessity cause schism in contemporary Jewish life. For the London Beth Din will accept the guidance only of a man whose orthodoxy is beyond question and recognition in the orthodox rabbinical world; and the religious future of Anglo-Jewry must be bound up with, and depend upon, the harmonious relationship of Chief Rabbi and Beth Din.'[24]

From the initial meeting of United Synagogue and organisational leaders, held at Woburn House, London, on 12 February 1946, emerged a six-man sub-committee and a list of possible candidates for the Chief Rabbinical post,[25] named (and, in some cases, ticked and/or incorrectly spelled) as 'Rabbi de Sola Pool; Rabbi Altman (√); Rabbi Herzog (√); Rabbi Israel Abrahams (√); Rabbi Rabbinowitz, Johannesburg (√); Rabbi Dr Soloveitchik, Boston (√); Rabbi Kopul Rosen (√); Rabbi Grunfeld (√); Rabbi Irvin Miller, Far Rockaway (√); Dr Jung (√).' Crossed out in the document were the names of 'Rabbi Brodie; Rabbi Porush, Sydney; Rabbi Unterman, Liverpool.'

Of those named, Isaac Herzog, the Chief Rabbi of Palestine, was evidently the front-runner. Born in Poland in 1888, he had emigrated to Britain with his family as a ten-year-old, settling in Leeds. After studying Talmud primarily with his father, Rabbi Joel Leib Herzog, he had attended the Sorbonne in Paris and then London University, from which he earned his doctorate for a pioneering study on the rediscovery of *techelet*, the blue dye once used in the making of *tzitzit*. For two decades, beginning in 1916, he had served as a rabbi in Ireland, soon becoming Chief Rabbi of the Irish Free State and, in 1922, Chief Rabbi of Ireland. Fourteen years later, he left for Palestine to succeed Abraham Isaac Kook as Ashkenazi Chief Rabbi.

In a letter regarding the British Chief Rabbinate, dated 1 April 1946, Waley Cohen told Herzog that 'at the last meeting of the Informal Committee, a very general desire was expressed that I should write to you and ask you to allow me to put forward your name for consideration by the formal electing body for this great Religious Office, with a view to a call being given to you by them. I very much hope you will be willing to authorise me to do that and to say that you would be prepared to accept such a call ...

> In the anxious years that lie ahead, the future of Jewry—not only in the British Empire but throughout the world, and especially in Palestine—is clearly going to depend very largely upon relations with leading public men in this country, and upon the understanding which we can give to the people of Britain of the spiritual service which we can render to the world.
>
> These, and many other considerations, were present to the minds of our Committee when I undertook to write to you, and it is with a very great sense of widespread unanimity that I now invite you to allow your name to go forward to the Electoral Body. If, as I hope, you are willing to allow that, it would be most desirable for a Conference to take place between us, and I hope you may find it possible to visit this country soon after Passover when I, as President of the United Synagogue, and my colleagues, Mr Frank Samuel and the Hon. Ewen Montagu, the Vice-Presidents, as well as the leaders of the other Jewish religious communities in this country, would hold ourselves at your disposal for examining with you all the relevant considerations that arise.
>
> It is right that you should have some idea of the financial arrangements for the Chief Rabbinate of the United Hebrew Congregations of the British Empire. These are, of course, not by any means crystallised for the future, and we should wish to consider them with you. The British Community will certainly make ample provision for the expenses of administration necessary for the discharge of such widespread responsibilities, and £3,500 per annum has been suggested as the emolument that should attach to the office itself.
>
> We realise, of course, that you may hesitate to abandon the work on which you are engaged in Palestine even for the opportunities of so great an Office as that of which I am now writing to you. But I am sure you will recognise how important, in the years to come, must be the influence of Great Britain in all matters appertaining to Jewry in Palestine and elsewhere, and I feel sure you will share my view that the Chief Rabbi of the British Empire with his headquarters

in London may have still greater opportunities of serving the cause of Jewry and of Judaism than even those which are open to the Chief Rabbi of Palestine.

Waley Cohen concluded: 'Greatly looking forward to your favourable reply to this letter, and with warm regards.'[26] Four weeks later, apologising for the delay in replying, 'due to the strike of the postal services here which only came to an end the other day,' Herzog—while 'deeply gratified' at the offer—was less than positive about its outcome. Prefacing his remarks by assuring Waley Cohen that 'I shall always treasure in the family archives your beautiful and eloquent epistle,' he continued:

> I was glad to see that you appreciate the difficulty in my even contemplating departure from Eretz-Israel. Had I been living now outside of the Holy Land, no matter what position I might have been occupying, my answer would have been immediately and definitely in the positive, for this is beyond doubt the most important and distinguished rabbinical chair in the whole of the diaspora and, as you have so forcefully pointed out, offers a field for the most vital activity. But, Sir Robert, I have already for nine years been the incumbent of the office of Chief Rabbi of Eretz-Israel, the land so dear, so sacred, to my heart, and indeed to every Jewish heart. Could I bid farewell to the land to enter which the first and the greatest rabbi of all times prayed with such historic fervour?
>
> Moreover, at this most critical and bitter juncture in our tragedy-laden history, our prophetic cradle-land—over the religious affairs of whose young and virile Jewish community I have the honour to preside—offers the only means for alleviating the endless agony of our suffering brethren; it alone, as I told the Anglo-American Commission, possesses the magic quality of reviving the dry bones of the remnants of the cruelest slaughter in the annals of Mankind, that as in the vision of Ezechiel [sic] they might rise and throb with spirit and vitality and become a blessing to Israel and the whole of humanity.
>
> With me, of course, the prime consideration is the interests of our sacred religion and our people to which I have devoted my life till now and shall, with the help of God, continue so until the end of my days. I fully appreciate your

thesis as to the place which Anglo-Jewry occupies today in world-Jewry and the possibilities of service for our people which residence in the metropolis of the Empire, in the capacity of Jewish religious head, holds out.

I am fully aware how vitally our destiny is bound up with decisions taken in London. I am also informed of that stirring towards religious revival in the hearts of so many young English Jews, a tendency which I have no doubt could, under proper spiritual guidance and inspiration, be fully crystallised. Yet, after weighing up the whole matter most earnestly, I feel that Jerusalem has even greater possibilities in these respects. I cannot set down in writing all my thoughts. I shall elaborate them fully to you when I come to London in a few weeks' time, and I have the feeling that you will come round to my view.

Herzog added that he would also take the opportunity of his visit to London 'to discuss with you many more matters of the highest possible importance affecting Judaism and the Jewish people. On these I should very much like to have your valuable counsel. I may mention, in passing, that during my recent visit at the Vatican, the question of anti-Semitism occupied a prominent place in the discussions.'[27]

Days later, Waley Cohen received a handwritten note from the Anglo-Jewish Association—whose secretary, Sefton D. Temkin, had been closely acquainted with Hertz during his later years as Chief Rabbi[28]—to the effect that Herzog had landed briefly in England before flying to Paris, where he would remain 'for about a month' before returning to Britain.[29] At noon on Friday, 21 June 1946, the two leaders—Chief Rabbi and Chief Rabbinical kingmaker—finally met, and Waley Cohen used the occasion to bolster his case. In a subsequent memorandum to his fellow honorary officers,[30] the US president summarised their discussion.

The Rabbi, he reported, had impressed him 'very much indeed. His English had very little trace of a foreign accent and he seemed full of vigour.' Waley Cohen believed he had moved Herzog slightly from his written decision, which, he opined, 'was influenced by what he thought the people of the Yishuv would think of his leaving the Yishuv to take up a post in the British Empire.'

Since the Chief Rabbi had just come from an interview with the Colonial Secretary [George Henry Hall, ennobled later that year as the first Viscount Hall of Cynon Valley]—whom Herzog described as 'somewhat light'—Waley Cohen 'had impressed upon the Rabbi how valuable it would be if he could serve the Anglo-Jewish Community, with London as its centre, and bring his undoubted forcefulness to bear on the Foreign and Colonial Offices.' In that way, he suggested, the problems which they now considered were getting too troublesome 'could be taken out of the hands of the men who were dealing in a superficial fashion with them, and could be passed to more responsible people who would deal with them more fundamentally.'

Herzog replied that he was leaving London six days later and would 'give to the whole matter put to him by Sir Robert reconsideration before he left England, and would advise Sir Robert before he left whether he was prepared to re-examine the matter.' Waley Cohen asked that if the decision was 'definitely not to go forward, he [Herzog] could doubtlessly say so at the end of the week, and this he agreed to do. On the other hand, his decision might take the form that he was interested, in which case the idea was that he would then be prepared to discuss the matter again with Sir Robert when he returned to London in a few weeks' time.' Herzog indicated that he 'quite saw that, if he did not intend to go forward, the Anglo-Jewish community would wish to take other steps very soon.'

Asked by Herzog what names were being considered for the British Chief Rabbinate, Waley Cohen declined to give a definite answer. Herzog responded that he was 'very much against the Seminaries being asked to give names and recommended to Sir Robert's consideration a Rabbi Raphael Gold, of Dallas, Texas, who, he said, was "a Talmudist of standing but not great; a product of great Yeshivoth; a Professor of Psychology in the University of Dallas and one of the State Universities of New York; a great speaker in English, Yiddish and Hebrew; and was writing a gigantic work on Psychology in the Talmud."' Waley Cohen told his colleagues that if Herzog decided not to proceed, 'it might be a good idea for this American Rabbi to be asked to come to this country so that people can see for themselves what he is like.' In the event, the 'good idea' was never pursued.

Some three weeks after their meeting, the US president reported that, on Sunday, 14 July, he had again met Herzog, who 'had come to the definite and final decision contained in his long letter of 28 April.' As a result, they 'should now go for Rabbi Brodie wholeheartedly'; Waley Cohen would himself be seeing Brodie on the following day and, 'if he is willing, we should tell him that this is the proposal of the honorary officers.'[31]

The second of five children of Aaron and Sheina Brodie, of Newcastle upon Tyne—'a couple noted for their piety and Jewish Orthodoxy'[32]—Israel Brodie had attended the Bath Lane elementary school and Rutherford College before joining Jews' College and its secular partner, University College, London, in 1912. At both institutions, he had shone as a scholar, gaining a number of awards before moving on to Balliol College, Oxford. Before completing his higher degree, he was persuaded to join the Army as a chaplain, thus laying the foundations for similar work in the future and a growing reputation for his ability to lead and influence young people.

In 1923, after receiving *semichah* at Jews' College, he had left for Australia to become senior minister of the Melbourne Hebrew Congregation and head of the local Beth Din, where he remained until 1937, when he returned to Oxford to complete his doctorate. These studies were again delayed, this time by his appointment, successively, to the Army Chaplains' Corps, the Royal Air Force chaplaincy and, with the rank of lieutenant-colonel, as senior Jewish chaplain to the forces.

Following his declaration of support for Brodie's nomination, Waley Cohen reported that 'Rabbi Brodie had announced his willingness to allow his name to be considered.' A number of points, he told his colleagues, were 'very strong arguments in favour of Rabbi Brodie: he was a very fine scholar, perhaps one of the best rabbinical men ever to come from Jews' College; he had acquired the deep respect of all men serving in H. M. Forces; and he was very forceful and very able in dealing with Government departments.'

Waley Cohen added that, 'on the strong advice of Rabbi Dr Herzog,' he had not approached Rabbi Louis Finkelstein, of the New York [Jewish Theological] Seminary, and that, while they were in London, he had interviewed Rabbis Harry Freedman and Israel Porush, of Australia, and Israel Abrahams, of South Africa—none of whom, in his opinion, was of 'the required calibre.'[33]

* * *

The summer and early autumn of 1946 brought little progress in the electoral process or in the formal compilation of a list of candidates. But towards the end of October, with support for Brodie evidently in abeyance, Waley Cohen's focus alighted upon another of the nominees listed some months earlier—Joseph Soloveitchik, of Boston.

Widely known and revered as 'The Rav,' the Polish-born talmudist, then aged forty-three and the scion of a Lithuanian dynasty of rabbinical scholars, had been educated at universities in Warsaw and Berlin before emigrating to Boston in 1932, where he became the rabbi of the Orthodox community. In 1941, he had succeeded his father, Moshe, as professor of Talmud at Yeshiva University's Isaac Elchanan theological seminary and, by the time of Hertz's death, had combined that post with the chair in philosophy at its Bernard Revel Graduate School.

Misspelling Soloveitchik's name in a letter to Judge Charles E. Wyzanski of Cambridge, Massachusetts, Waley Cohen wrote: 'As you may no doubt be aware, the lamented death of Dr Hertz, the late Chief Rabbi of the United

Hebrew Congregations of the British Empire, has left our Community with the difficult task of electing a successor.

> One of the names which has been mentioned to us as a man who might possibly be suitable for the post is Rabbi Dr Soloweizick, who I understand is a leading Rabbi in Massachusetts; but before approaching him, Mr Otto Schiff[34] has suggested that I might write to you and ask you ... for your frank opinion as to his suitability for this very important appointment.
>
> We know, of course, of Rabbi Soloweizick's reputation as an outstanding Talmudic scholar, and that is one of the qualifications necessary, but there are other equally important needs. Our Chief Rabbi is required to be an organiser and leader in our Community, but he also occupies an outstanding position as the Representative of the Jewish Community in English public life, and it is of vital importance that the man holding the position should possess not only eloquence and scholarship, but tact and a pleasing personality and the ability to work amicably and effectively with men of affairs, and especially the experience necessary to work in friendly relations with leading men in all walks of public life in this country and elsewhere.
>
> Our late Chief Rabbi had many high qualities, but he became a difficult character and in consequence created many serious difficulties for the Jewish Community, and whilst we of course need a man of strong character, we are most anxious that we should avoid those dangers in appointing a successor at the present critical time.

Wyzanski replied that he had had no contact with Rabbi Joseph Soloveitchik ('to use the spelling that appears in the telephone book'), but had made 'a consensus of views of certain leaders of the Greater Boston Jewish community in whose judgment I have confidence.' All had praised Soloveitchik's scholarship, talmudic knowledge and acquaintance with Jewish and non-Jewish philosophy, while his familiarity with Jewish ritual was 'also of a very high order. But,' wrote Wyzanski, 'that familiarity, coupled with what some people call his intellectual intolerance, has made him most critical of many conservative as well as reformed rabbis in this community. The result has been that personal feelings have at times run rather strongly against Rabbi Soloveitchik ...

'So far I have said nothing about the Rabbi's "tact ... pleasing personality and ... ability to work amicably and effectively with men of affairs"—the qualifications to which you specifically referred in your letter. All my informants thought the Rabbi quite deficient in these qualities.[35] The best that any of my sources would say was that while a positive-minded person, he would listen to reason if the reason was compelling. Another person said that he was charming when subjects were discussed conversationally, but obdurate when they were discussed from the viewpoint of community action.'[36]

The year quickly turned before any progress became apparent, Waley Cohen having spurned the judge's offer that 'if you from other sources get information which leads you to believe that you still want to consider Rabbi Soloveitchik and would like me to do so, I should be glad to see him personally.' But, at a meeting of the US honorary officers in the closing days of 1946, it became clear that Brodie and Kopul Rosen were well in the running.

Just a year before, Rosen—aged thirty-one and barely eighteen months in the post of Communal Rabbi of Glasgow—had become Principal Rabbi of the Federation of Synagogues, following the rejection of that role by Soloveitchik.[37] Despite having attended the yeshivah of Etz Chaim in London and, for three years, of Mir in Poland, Rosen had faced formidable opposition from the Federation's own rabbis who, in Aaron Wright's words,[38] 'were grasping at some phantom figure who would combine the profound scholarship of the yeshivot of Eastern Europe with the modern outlook of the West,' and who believed that 'if such a man could not be found, better to make no appointment at all.'

Even as the Federation's leaders had been on the point of confirming Rosen in the post, their rabbinate fired telegrams to several council members protesting against the title of 'Principal Rabbi.' Wright wrote later of the situation: 'I do not think that Rabbi Rosen—Kopul as we called him—had any illusions about the difficulties confronting him. There was a good deal of disunity in the Federation, and it was unlikely that he would receive consistent lay support. It was clear that the rabbis of the Federation would not readily flock to his banner; for the most part, they were of the old school, very much his senior in years and with claims of their own.'

Within the United Synagogue hierarchy, views fluctuated over Rosen's and Brodie's perceived qualities. Addressing his fellow officers, Waley Cohen said that he was 'definitely of the opinion that Rabbi Kopul Rosen was ultra-orthodox and that we ought to face the fact that, if he were appointed as Chief Rabbi, he might drag the US into ultra-orthodoxy, which might mean the ultimate splitting-up of the US and cause a large number of its members to join the Liberals.' He added, as an aside, that Brodie was 'orthodox, but not ultra.'

Ewen Montagu felt that 'it would be very much better, if there were any danger of a cleavage in the United Synagogue, to face it now rather than let the US die out later on.' Brodie, he believed, 'certainly did not seem to possess the initiative, drive, etc., that was so essential.' Waley Cohen replied that Brodie had 'got the military synagogues working; but the sub-committee did not feel that they could back him and it was definitely essential that all sides of the question be considered. Rabbi Kopul Rosen is certainly spectacular, but we do not want to be misled.'

Broadening the issues, Waley Cohen observed that, while many people would support Rabbi Brodie, 'Mrs Brodie was not really suitable.[39] Mrs Rosen, however, was in an entirely different category from Mrs Brodie,[40] and this in itself might be a decisive factor.' They were due to see Rosen at his home, and Waley Cohen thought it likewise necessary to see Rabbi and Mrs Brodie. 'If everybody felt that the position should go to Rabbi Rosen, however, he would like to obtain some outline of the procedure to be adopted, and the possible dates of meetings.'[41]

Following their consultation with Rosen, Montagu reported that they had been 'enormously impressed with his personality' but had had 'doubts regarding his depth, learning and judgment.' A further meeting with Brodie had left them 'very impressed. He had a good personality when one was in conversation with him and we felt that those who did not know Brodie as well as Rosen should meet him in like manner.' Montagu doubted, however, whether Rosen 'would last as Chief Rabbi' or 'would carry the older people with him.'

Waley Cohen commented that, although at their last meeting he had recognised Brodie's 'inadequacy,' he was 'favourably impressed by the great character behind him'; and, with regard to Rosen, he had 'had more admiration for him after their long talk than when he had heard him speak in public.'

The discussion then turned briefly to a consideration of Manchester's Communal Rabbi, Alexander Altmann, whose candidature his fellow Mancunian, Abraham Moss, strongly supported. Born in Austria-Hungary, the son of the Chief Rabbi of Trier, Altmann had in 1931 received his doctorate from the University of Berlin and *semichah* from the Hildesheimer Rabbinical Seminary. He had then served as a rabbi and professor of Jewish philosophy in Berlin, before fleeing Germany shortly before the war.

Asked by Moss whether Altmann had been 'entirely eliminated,' Montagu said that his personality 'was not as strong as the other candidates' and that he 'lacked leadership.' Wright remarked that on the last occasion they had met, 'apart from discussing Rosen and Brodie, the matter generally dealt with was Rabbi Soloveitchik, and no one present then felt sufficiently strongly about Altmann's qualities to press his claim.' Moss replied that, while Altmann 'had not got great determination and forcefulness of character, he was very determined in defence of views about which he felt deeply. He had great academic qualifications and great personal charm. It would be unjust to eliminate him without learning more about him in the same way as the other two.'[42]

The following day, Lazarus sent Waley Cohen ordination details regarding Brodie and Rosen. The former had been a student of Jews' College and had received his rabbinical diploma shortly before his call to Melbourne in 1922. 'His subsequent career is well-known to us.' Of Rosen, Lazarus wrote: 'He was born in 1913, entered the Yeshivah Etz Chaim in 1929, and on the strong recommendation of Dayan Abramsky went to the yeshivah of Mir in 1935. He received rabbinical diplomas from three well-known rabbis: 4 July 1938, granted by Rabbi Meir Abawicz; 15 August 1938, granted by the famous Rabbi Simcha Zelig, Dayan of Brisk; 20 December 1938, granted by the principal of the Mir Yeshivah, Rabbi L. G. Finkel, who states that Rabbi Rosen had been a student for three years, had done very well indeed, and had received rabbinical ordination from the two rabbis mentioned above.'[43]

* * *

More than a year after Hertz's death, the confidential nature of the committees' discussions, and the lack of progress in finding a successor, prompted the launch of a public debate—in both clerical and lay circles—over the need for speedier action.[44] Meeting in London in February 1947, the Union of Anglo-Jewish Preachers 'unanimously resolved that the continued vacancy in the office of the Chief Rabbi of the United Hebrew Congregations of the British Empire constitutes a grave menace to the spiritual welfare of British Jewry' and called on the vestry of the United Synagogue 'to convene without further delay the appropriate meetings in order to fill the vacancy in the said high office.'[45]

That the resolution achieved its desired effect was evident from a motion—proposed by Waley Cohen, seconded by Montagu, and passed unanimously three weeks later—that 'the Executive Committee be requested to confer at an early date with representatives of other bodies in the British Empire contributing to the maintenance of the office of the Chief Rabbi, as to the duties and emoluments of such office, and as to the mode of election and all details connected therewith, and that the report of the deliberations of such Conference be laid before the Council in due course.'[46] Waley Cohen said that the procedure, as far as he could see, 'will be on exactly the same lines as on the last occasion.'[47]

Of the decision to move forward with the conference, the *Jewish Chronicle* observed: 'In 1911, a similar resolution was passed four months after the death of Dr Hermann Adler, but on the present occasion it has taken fourteen months for a like move to be made. The delay is all the more regrettable since conditions are incomparably more pressing now than they were then, and the leisurely procedure that has so far prevailed is altogether incompatible with the urgent demands of the time.

> While the present move—belated though it is—will be widely welcomed, much must depend on the vigour with which this resolution is implemented. For the resolution refers to the conference being summoned 'at an early date'; to its then discussing 'the duties and emoluments of the office of Chief Rabbi, the mode of election, and all details connected therewith'; and finally to its reporting back to the United Synagogue Council 'in due course.' Thereafter, if the procedure of the last occasion is followed, it will be necessary for an Electoral College to be summoned and to transact its business.
>
> After the passing of the corresponding resolution in 1911, it was another fifteen months before Dr Hertz was elected. Such a further delay on the present occasion surely cannot be tolerated. The need for the most energetic action on the part of the Executive Committee of the United Synagogue in carrying out the terms of last week's resolution must be apparent to all who appreciate the urgencies of the present situation.
>
> In view of the attitude that has been adopted during the past fourteen months, no apology need be made for labouring this point. Indeed, misgivings cannot but be increased by the fact that the Council of the United Synagogue was not informed at last week's meeting of a resolution that had been forwarded to it by the Union of Anglo-Jewish Preachers, which called attention to the danger to the spiritual welfare of Anglo-Jewry by the continued vacancy in the office of Chief Rabbi.
>
> Although the passing by the United Synagogue Council of the resolution was the first official, constitutional and public action taken in this matter, yet it is an open secret that numerous private talks and arguments have long been proceeding behind the scenes. These have not conduced towards an orderly and dignified settlement of any of the questions connected with the appointment, especially as they have introduced a most undesirable atmosphere of irresponsible partisanship.
>
> Rumour has naturally been rife, and a list of alleged candidates supposedly favoured by different interests has

been discussed by all and sundry. The number of names on the list has fluctuated almost from week to week, and the licence given to gossip has concentrated public attention on personages and prevented a really serious consideration of the solemn requirements of so exalted an office.

Some of the outstanding requisites that must be forthcoming from any worthy candidate for the Chief Rabbinate may be enumerated. First and foremost, his status in the field of Jewish learning must be unchallengeable. He must be a Talmid Chacham in the highest sense of that term. Not only must he possess the fullest Jewish religious knowledge, but he must also be able to impart it.

Merely abstract or academic knowledge which was incapable of inspiring others to noble living would be valueless. Nor would Jewish wisdom alone suffice, unless it were accompanied by high qualifications in wider fields of general learning and culture, for it is essential that our religious leader should be able to meet the world of scholarship on equal terms. Administrative ability and experience and high qualities of statesmanship and diplomacy will be required from the holder of this office.

It will be one of his greatest tasks to be the representative and interpreter of British, including Commonwealth, Jewry—and emphasis must be placed on each of the last few words. The position of British Jewry is distinct from both that of American Jewry and that of European Jewry; British Jewry cannot afford to remain without its own independent spokesman for an indefinite period.

And Britain's association with Palestine will invest our Chief Rabbi with a special importance in relation to Christendom and the Moslem world. He must be a man of fearless and independent character, who will be the true mouthpiece of Jewish religious tradition. One who merely gave rhetorical expression to the opinions of strong-minded lay leaders would not save the cause of Judaism.

The incumbent of the Chief Rabbinate must without question be capable of presiding over the Beth Din, which is the recognised tribunal for decisions on questions of Jewish faith and practice. But he must likewise be fully acquainted with British life and thought. While his active love of the Holy Land will necessarily be in accord with immemorial

Jewish tradition, his practical support of the Yishuv will find expression through sober counsel and wise statesmanship. Doubtless such a temperament will be most easily found in one who has been born and bred in British traditions, and whose experience has been widened by past or present service of his people in the Empire overseas.

Let it not be supposed that here has been given a portrait of an imaginary man such as our times could not produce. The hour will not fail to produce the man, and when the Electoral College meets—and may it be very soon!—it should have little difficulty in making its decision.[48]

CHAPTER FIVE

Fateful Days

BY THE SPRING OF 1947, through of series of unexpected developments, the tide of sentiment had begun to turn against Kopul Rosen. After the submission of its appeal to the United Synagogue in furtherance of the election process, the Union of Anglo-Jewish Preachers (UAJP) sought—and obtained—a meeting with Waley Cohen so as to strengthen its influence in the choice of Hertz's successor. Its delegates were Isaac Livingstone, Myer Lew, Arthur Barnett, and Isaac Fabricant, the ministers of, respectively, the Golders Green, Hampstead Garden Suburb, Western, and Brighton and Hove congregations.

As a body, they explained, they wished to be consulted 'on the attributes and otherwise which should be looked for in a future Chief Rabbi, to whom they were going to be asked to give their allegiance.' They did not seek to be told the names of anyone on the shortlist, but would be prepared—if asked—to submit their own list, which had been drawn up at a meeting of some forty of their colleagues from London and the provinces.

Waley Cohen told them that such a procedure was 'fraught with danger, because either side might regret having taken the step if the talk they were having ever became known outside the office.' While agreeing that there were indeed dangers inherent in the course they had proposed, the ministers nevertheless sought approval to submit the results of the second of their two ballots, which had reduced the number of recommended names from six to three.

On receiving Waley Cohen's sanction, they gave the names, in order of preference, as Rabbi Israel Brodie, Rabbi Dr Leo Jung,[1] and Rabbi Dr Israel Abrahams.[2] Brodie, they believed, was 'the most suitable person available for the post, a scholar with a very fine background of service to the Anglo-Jewish community and the Empire, broadened by much travel, with a good knowledge of rabbinics and a good secular education.' On the question of public-speaking, they conceded that 'he was not necessarily a first-class draw.'

Side-stepping these preferences, Waley Cohen said that the informal sub-committee had considered the name of Rosen, who had 'apparently made a great impression on certain people, as he was undoubtedly quite a personality. He had the ability to hold large audiences, and this was considered to be a very great asset in his favour.'

The ministers replied that their conference was 'unanimous in rejecting the possible candidature of this young man for the high and important post of Chief Rabbi.' His secular educational background, they asserted, 'could be disregarded. His knowledge of rabbinics was not very profound or wide-ranging, and although he certainly had a fine manner of address, this would pall after a short while, and people would begin to realise the mistake that had been made. His character was most immature and inclined, in their opinion, to be shallow. Nor did they think that the Beth Din would accept such an appointment lightly—and if it were nevertheless made, the lack of mature knowledge would be even more clearly shown up.'

These various defects, Waley Cohen admitted, had 'of course been brought to the knowledge of the informal sub-committee, but as against these, Rabbi Rosen's personality and power to hold people, particularly youth, were of very great importance. Moreover, the Federation of Synagogues group were showing strong support for his candidature and, in the circumstances he had explained—which required the honorary officers to consider the need for getting unanimity in the community—it might prove advantageous, despite the defects mentioned, to make the appointment.'

Dismissing the prospects of Jung and Abrahams, and of any ministerial input in the election process,[3] Waley Cohen briefly mentioned Soloveitchik, of whom, he said, inquiries had been made 'of very reliable sources in America.' These had shown that, 'while the man was of the highest possible calibre as a scholar, etc., his statesmanship and personal attacks were very poor indeed, and the sub-committee had reluctantly come to the conclusion that they could not possibly envisage asking him to come to this country for consultation.'[4]

Waley Cohen's passing mention of strong support for Rosen heralded the onset of a long and contentious battle that included among its combatants the rabbinates and lay leaders of both the Federation and the United Synagogue. The catalyst was a letter from Jack Levine, president of the Garnethill Synagogue, Glasgow, to his US counterpart in London, drawing attention to 'a most serious matter in connection with the appointment of a Chief Rabbi.

'I am informed,' wrote Levine, 'that some of the Rabbis of the Federation of Synagogues are going round the country obtaining signatures of the local Rabbis in favour of the appointment of Rabbi Kopul Rosen. This, of itself, is open to deprecation, but when the signatures are being obtained by misrepresentation, then the matter is serious. The local Rabbis are being induced to give their signatures on the plea that another of the candidates, Rabbi Israel Brodie, is not orthodox. This is most reprehensible, apart from being deliberate untruth. I do not know, and naturally I would not say, that Rabbi Kopul Rosen is aware of this statement which is being made, but he must be aware of the activities of the Rabbis of the Federation of which he is the Head Rabbi, and this ought to be stopped, and steps taken to prevent a continuance of these activities ... I write to you, as President of the Council of the United Synagogue, to inform you of what is being done, and I trust that you will take such action, as lies in your power, to put an end to improper actions of this kind.'[5]

The signatories to whom Levine referred, twenty-three in all, included many influential figures in the rabbinate, among them J. H. Cymerman, M. Fisher, B. Rogosnitzky, S. Rubin, J. H. Twersky and A. Rapoport. Several of their number had, only months before, strongly opposed Rosen's appointment as Principal Rabbi of the Federation.

Their memorandum to Waley Cohen, they told him now, 'had been drawn up and signed by a number of orthodox Rabbis of various congregations and communities who have been actively engaged in Jewish religious life for many years and who are deeply concerned for the welfare of Anglo-Jewry. In view of the fact that steps will soon be taken to appoint a Chief Rabbi, we regard it as a sacred duty to express our opinion upon this important subject.

> ... Unity and co-operation are primarily dependent upon the appointment of a Chief Rabbi who can understand all sections of the community and can claim their confidence. He must be a man who combines traditional Jewish learning with a modern cultured approach to life; he must also possess those qualities of character which will enable him to deal with people of all opinions and backgrounds with tactful sympathy and wise counsel. Such a person would be a unifying force and a blessing to Anglo-Jewry.
>
> Knowing as we do the Rabbinic personalities all over the world, we are of the unanimous opinion that there are but two persons who can command such widespread confidence. They are Rabbi Dr J. Soloveitchik, Communal Rabbi of Boston, and Rabbi Kopul Rosen, Principal Rabbi of the Federation of Synagogues.
>
> Rabbi Dr Soloveitchik is a remarkable Rabbinic scholar and a man of brilliant intellectual attainments. Rabbi Kopul

Rosen, in addition to his wide Rabbinic scholarship, has already an established reputation and has endeared himself to all sections of Anglo-Jewry and beyond. He has gained the confidence of old and young within our community. He has shown that he possesses the sober judgment and tactful approach which are so indispensable in one who deals with different groups and varying opinions.

We repeat that in our unanimous opinion only the above two Rabbis are suitable to fill the exalted office of Chief Rabbi and bring about that harmonious co-operation which is so vital for Jewry both here and the world over.[6]

Word of the rabbis' round-robin soon reached the London Beth Din, and Abramsky, Grunfeld, and Swift procured a meeting with Waley Cohen, lamenting the fact that 'Rabbonim are travelling around the country trying to obtain names for a petition asking that Rabbi Kopul Rosen be appointed Chief Rabbi,' and 'stating emphatically that they [the dayanim] thought the whole matter was being engineered by the person most concerned.'

The dayanim told Waley Cohen that 'the rabbis canvassing on Rosen's behalf were the very people who had originally come to the Beth Din prior to Kopul Rosen's appointment at the Federation and had demanded that the Beth Din should publicly proclaim that this man was unsuitable for the appointment as Principal Rabbi to the Federation of Synagogues. This the Beth Din had refused to do. Shortly afterwards, when Kopul Rosen was appointed by the Federation, these same Rabbonim became his best friends because he was able to divert certain monies in their direction, and they had thus been bought over to supporting him.'

Waley Cohen showed the dayanim a letter he had received from one of the signatories—J. H. Cymerman, rabbi of the Philpot Street Sephardish and Rumanian Synagogue in London's East End—seeking a meeting at which he and his colleagues could discuss the Chief Rabbinate. Feeling 'bound to grant the interview requested,' Waley Cohen invited the dayanim to be present, a suggestion which Abramsky rejected out of hand, but for which Grunfeld asked time to consider.

The dayanim said that they had been discussing Rosen among themselves and 'had come to the conclusion that the position was so serious, and that Kopul Rosen was so likely to be appointed Chief Rabbi, that it might be necessary for someone in authority to make a public statement on the question.' Waley Cohen admitted that 'he, too, had come to the conclusion that the situation was serious and he thought that the dayanim should now arm him with a letter giving certain views in regard to Kopul Rosen.'

After further discussion, Waley Cohen urged the dayanim 'not to close the door entirely to the Beth Din working in some way with the young man.' They responded by 'reiterating their feeling that they should make some statement on the matter, and it was agreed that they should write to Sir Robert (after first submitting a draft letter to him) stating that Rabbi Rosen had neither the Rabbinical nor the academic ability to be appointed to the post which was in mind.'

They also asked Waley Cohen to consider postponing the election for at least six months, since 'they felt that in any shorter period, Kopul Rosen's chances were very considerable, but that for every day after such a period, his powers would wain [sic] and eventually he would no longer be in favour.' Waley Cohen intimated, however, that 'a postponement would not be possible and that it was hoped to get the election completed before the end of the summer.'[7]

Days later, Cymerman and five of his fellow-signatories—Rabbis C. I. Etner, I. L. Margulies, A. Singer, J. Lainer and S. Rabinow—met with Waley Cohen. Singer explained that the purpose of both their memorandum and their interview was 'to urge upon Sir Robert, as the leader of the men engaged in the task of finding a new Chief Rabbi, the importance of choosing a man who would be able to weld the community together again into one whole.'

Waley Cohen replied that, on reading the memorandum, he had agreed with the views initially expressed, but that, 'on looking at the list of signatories, he was wondering whether some of them had not appended their signatures too lightly, and whether they were in a position to say that there were only two men capable of filling the position, since they possibly did not know half of all the candidates who were in the minds of the leaders of the community.'

Lainer disputed this, and pointed out that 'careful consideration had, of course, been given to the question by everyone concerned. No suggestion was intended by the document as to the standing of any other person not named as a possible candidate for the Chief Rabbinate, and no aspersion whatever was cast on other candidates.'

Noting that 'the task of choosing a Chief Rabbi was a very heavy one,' Waley Cohen closed the discussion by seeking an assurance from the signatories—'and, indeed, from everyone in the community'—that they would rally round the man eventually elected as Chief Rabbi and give him their utmost support. The rabbis said that they would 'of course rally round.'[8]

* * *

A day earlier, Waley Cohen had written to Rosen, enclosing a copy of Levine's letter and noting that 'similar reports have reached me from other directions but not in quite so definite form.' He added: 'I am sure you would be the first to disapprove of these activities and would be grateful if you would let me know what steps you can take to put an end to them.'[9]

Rosen replied that 'your letter, with the enclosed copy of the communication from Glasgow, came as a surprise and shock to me. I was aware that certain meetings of orthodox Rabbis had taken place and that the issue of the Chief Rabbinate had been discussed. I heard in a vague manner that my name had been mentioned during those discussions, but this letter from Glasgow is something quite new. I have called a meeting of Rabbis of the Federation of Synagogues for next week, when I shall make a thorough investigation into this matter. I shall communicate with you further.'[10]

Following that meeting, Rosen apprised Waley Cohen of the rabbis' assertion 'that what they have done in connection with the Chief Rabbinate could not be regarded as a purely Federation activity and that they therefore did not feel answerable to me. Furthermore, they stated that two of the Rabbis who initiated this activity are not members of the Rabbinical Council of the Federation. When I reprimanded them for the statements they have made in the course of their activities, they said that they were prepared to stand by everything they had done and to bear responsibility for any statement made by them.

'They insisted, however, that they could not understand my censure or the objection which had been made. They insisted that, as orthodox Rabbis, they have a complete right to discuss the position of the Chief Rabbinate with their colleagues, and they pointed out that all their statements had been made in a circle of Rabbis and were expressions of honest opinion. In view of their attitude, I thought that all further discussion would be purposeless.'[11]

Dismissing this rejoinder, Waley Cohen wrote back to Rosen: 'I think, and I am sure you will agree with me, that these propaganda meetings are most derogatory to the Chief Rabbinate, and I think it is exceedingly unfortunate that the Rabbis should be conducting a campaign of that kind on your behalf.

> If you have no means to prevent it, all I can do is to offer you my sympathy, but if you have any influence over them, I hope you will deprecate these proceedings. They are creating a most unfavourable impression and the conception, however unjustified, that the Rabbis who are acting in this way may have your approval. It was to prevent these undignified activities that it was decided not to advertise the vacancy, but these practices seem to be at least as disparaging to the

dignity of the office. What I think is far more disconcerting than the fact of this propaganda is the untrue statements that have been made, such as, for instance, the reference mentioned by the President of the Glasgow Congregation to attempts to deny Rabbi Brodie's orthodoxy.

Those who descend into the arena of controversial propaganda naturally lose control of the situation, and a most unsatisfactory campaign is liable to result.[12] I do appreciate, and deeply sympathise with, the most embarrassing position in which these gentlemen have placed you, and unless they are prepared to accept your friendly suggestion that they should desist from these activities, I realise how difficult it must be for you to influence the situation in any way. Nevertheless, I think you should know what is going on, as I feel it to be discreditable to all concerned, and I am sure you will do all you can to discourage it.[13]

Stung by these remarks—which, the Federation's Principal Rabbi told him, 'disturbed me very much,' and which had left him with a feeling that 'perhaps some facts had been kept from me'[14]—Rosen summoned a further meeting with 'a few of the Rabbis, men in whom I have complete confidence,' to whom he read out Sir Robert's response. The upshot was a four-page rebuttal from Cymerman to Waley Cohen, detailing the content of the meeting and the participants' conclusions—written 'because we feel that your letter is based on completely false information, and I have been asked by my colleagues to put the true facts before you.'

Referring to Waley Cohen's repeated use of the term 'propaganda,' Cymerman wrote: 'We emphatically deny that the Rabbis have conducted any meeting that can by any stretch of imagination be regarded as a propaganda meeting. Neither have we done anything that lowers the dignity of the office of the Chief Rabbinate ...

> No statement has been made by any one of the Rabbis to any layman. No meeting was convened other than small confidential gatherings of Rabbis themselves. *We have issued no statement to the press, and since presenting the memorandum to you, nothing further has been done by any of us either as individuals or as a body.*
>
> How can this dignified procedure be described as a campaign or propaganda meeting, and how can it react detrimentally on the office of the Chief Rabbi? ... What objection can there be to Rabbis discussing amongst themselves

the future of the Chief Rabbinate? Surely, had the Rabbis displayed no interest in the appointment, you might have had cause for greater anxiety ...

The suggestion that the Rabbis have conducted a campaign on behalf of any person is liable to cause much resentment. Our deliberations in private were conducted in an atmosphere which can only be described as sincere and solemn. We were guided throughout by what we considered to be the best interests of Jewry and Judaism.

We would be happy to know that all discussions on this problem are conducted on such a high plane of sincere and impersonal approach. We maintain that we have done nothing that can be interpreted by men of good will as liable to detract from the dignity of the Chief Rabbinate in any way ...

We trust that, in view of all that has been said, you will appreciate that your letter to Rabbi Rosen was unfair, because it was based on false information.[15] We trust that you will reply and express your satisfaction with the true facts as we have presented them to you.

Finally, my colleagues have asked me to assure you that they are deeply sensible of the importance of maintaining the dignity of the Chief Rabbinate, and that the reason for our submitting a memorandum to you was in order to make our co-operation possible and to ensure that the exalted office of the Chief Rabbinate shall be the dignified and influential one which Anglo-Jewry needs today.[16]

Determined to have the last word, Waley Cohen responded: 'As you asked me my view, I do not think it at all wise for Rabbis to travel about for the purpose of discussing in groups the personalities of people who may possibly be considered for the office of Chief Rabbi.

'I am very glad to hear from you of the move you have taken to avoid anything in the nature of violent propaganda, and it is certainly most regrettable that an unfavourable impression has been created. The unfortunate feature of these matters is that it is difficult for those who originate the discussions to make sure that their actions are not misunderstood.

'My conception of a Rabbi's duties relates to the spiritual life of the Community, rather than to the appointment of individuals, which I think is the task of the laymen, and that was evidently the view of our fore-fathers, who laid down our Constitution—I think a very wise document.

'The memorandum addressed to me is quite a different matter, and if nothing had been done beyond a meeting between yourself and your colleagues in order to prepare a memorandum for consideration by those who are charged with the duty of appointing a Chief Rabbi, I think the unfavourable impression would not have arisen. I gather that that is the course the Ministers have followed, and that their intention is to address a memorandum to us, which I will of course see receives the same careful consideration as yours.'[17]

Meeting with his fellow honorary officers days earlier, Waley Cohen had raised the question of the Beth Din's opposition to Rosen and the feasibility of offering him a dayanship if he agreed 'to retire from candidature of the Chief Rabbinate.' They decided that 'it would be possible to give him the same salary as Dayan Swift is receiving.' The matter of mentioning publicly 'anything detrimental to Rabbi Rosen's character was also discussed, in view of the fact that, if he were not suitable for the Chief Rabbinate, he would surely not be suitable for a dayanship.'

Waley Cohen said that he 'believed this could be overcome by reason of the fact that Rabbi Rosen would be in close and daily contact with most learned men, who would be able to shape his character. If, however, Dayan Abramsky's statement regarding Rabbi Rosen's character were serious, the whole question would have to be reconsidered.'

With regard to the Union of Anglo-Jewish Preachers, Waley Cohen stressed the need 'to obtain a round-robin signed by the Ministers to the effect that Rabbi Rosen's appointment would be a bad appointment and that they sincerely hope he will not be appointed.'

As to Altmann, following receipt of a letter from Moss urging an interview with Manchester's Communal Rabbi, the honorary officers decided that, 'although it is felt it would be straining the Community to the utmost, it was agreed that Rabbi Altmann's claims should be considered,' preferably before the last week in May.[18]

*   *   *

On 15 April 1947, Aaron Wright, as president of the Federation of Synagogues, delivered a lengthy statement that foreshadowed radical changes in his movement's approach to the election. Since the passing, three weeks earlier, of a resolution authorising an annual Federation grant of £1,000 towards the maintenance of the Chief Rabbinate, there had been, Wright told his council, 'disquieting developments.'

After detailing the financial and electoral procedures historically underpinning Chief Rabbinical elections—and pointing out, in relation to the current process, that 'Sir Robert Waley Cohen has insisted throughout on strict secrecy being maintained'—Wright asserted: 'Private discussions have their value, but they must not be allowed to prevent informed public discussion of the fundamental public issues which arise. And the time has now come for the facts to be placed before the community as a whole ...

'Without any consultation whatever, the United Synagogue honorary officers have issued invitations to the preliminary [Chief Rabbinate] conference, with ninety-three going to people connected with the US in one way or another, and three to the Federation, which comprises some seventy synagogues, with a membership of about 15,000. I regard this as nothing but a deliberate insult to the Federation, a calculated piece of provocation.

'I can only conclude that the intention is to make it impossible for the Federation to take part in the preliminary conference and the electoral college. The United Synagogue honorary officers seem determined to "pack" the electoral college so that they can control a majority of the votes over and above all the rest of the community put together ...

'It is necessary for me to use plain words. In the last thirty-five years, the community has developed and matured. Synagogue membership in London has quadrupled. In our great provincial communities, we have vigorous centres of Jewish life. The time has long since passed when a handful of men can ride roughshod over the rest of the community. No diktat will be accepted. The policy of fait accompli will not be tolerated today.'

Calling for the creation, by the Federation and 'other orthodox bodies,' of a Synagogue Council of Great Britain—'whose prime duty should be to guard orthodox Judaism against attacks from without and, much more dangerous, against insidious attacks from within'—Wright warned of the consequences if the United Synagogue 'remain adamant in their determination to dominate the electoral college and refuse to give representation on a democratic basis to the orthodox synagogue bodies concerned.

> Then it will be the duty of such a Synagogue Council of Great Britain to take steps to elect a Chief Rabbi on the basis of fair representation to the orthodox synagogue bodies concerned. We shall take such steps only if we are compelled to. With a full sense of responsibility, and conscious of the gravity of the issues involved, I give this solemn and public warning to the honorary officers of the United Synagogue that they must respect the wishes of the community as a whole, and that they are gravely mistaken if they imagine that lethargy will enable them to impose their will on the community.
>
> It is not too late to prevent a split in the community. I

have proposed to Sir Robert Waley Cohen that no further steps should be taken in regard to the preliminary conference until a further meeting takes place of the London and provincial representatives who were called together in February 1946. At such a meeting, the fair basis of representation at the preliminary conference should be considered and agreed; the invitations already sent out for the preliminary conference should be cancelled and new invitations should be issued.

The Federation of Synagogues has shown not by words but by deeds that it regards the unity of the community as very precious. We have played our full part in setting up the London Board of Jewish Religious Education. We are prepared to recognise and support the Chief Rabbi and to make a substantial contribution to the maintenance of his office, whether we agree or disagree with the final choice of Chief Rabbi, provided fair representation is given to the orthodox bodies concerned.

We earnestly hope that wiser counsels will choose the path, not of sectional domination, but of true statesmanship, and that the community as a whole will be given the opportunity of determining the choice of Chief Rabbi.[19]

In a statement to the US council five days later, its honorary officers again stressed their organisation's unique links to, and responsibilities towards, the Chief Rabbinate, noting that, apart from paying marriage-authorisation fees, it was 'perhaps rather instructive that, in the thirty-four years since the last occasion of a vacancy in the office of Chief Rabbi, the Federation of Synagogues has made no financial contribution whatsoever to its maintenance ... Indeed, not even a serious suggestion of any contribution was made in all that period, nor has any formal recognition of the religious authority of the Chief Rabbi, whether permanently binding or not on the Federation or its synagogues, ever been made.'

Dismissing Wright's complaints about secrecy in the electoral process, and his 'indignation' at the constitutional provisions surrounding the issue of invitations, the honorary officers urged the council, and the community, 'not to be led into anxiety by the utterances of those who enjoy greater freedom and less responsibility than is yours.

'A great religious office cannot be filled by the methods of the hustings. The times are anxious and difficult; but as soon as the preliminary ground has been explored, the council will be asked to exercise its wisdom and responsibility, and we do not doubt that once again, as so often before, it will, in doing so, render a great and lasting service to the religious life of Anglo-Jewry.'[20]

* * *

The Beth Din's opinion on Rosen's fitness to hold the 'great religious office' was not long in coming. In a letter to Waley Cohen, J. H. Taylor, clerk to the court, wrote: 'In reply to your enquiry, I am desired by the Dayanim to inform you that it is their considered opinion that Rabbi Kopul Rosen is not a suitable candidate for the exalted office of Chief Rabbi of the United Hebrew Congregations of the British Empire.'[21]

Hard on the heels of this rebuff came another from the Union of Anglo-Jewish Preachers, 'consequent upon our interviews with you and your colleagues, indicating which of the candidates mentioned by you—Rabbis Brodie, Altmann and Rosen—possess in the requisite degree the qualifications essential to the office of Chief Rabbi.

'In this regard, we would refer you expressly to the following qualifications referred to in our memorandum: (a) a sufficiently profound Rabbinic knowledge to exercise the necessary legal authority in the capacity of Ab Beth Din; (b) modern Jewish scientific learning; (c) academic and general scholarship and culture; (d) ability as spokesman for Jewry and Judaism to the wider world.

'It is our considered opinion that whereas Rabbis Brodie and Altmann, in the order named, do possess all the above qualifications, Rabbi Kopul Rosen does not possess them all.'[22]

These views weighed on the minds of the US honorary officers when, during their discussions five weeks later, they placed Altmann well above Rosen and, hesitatingly, even above Brodie. While the informal sub-committee had been split over Altmann's qualities—Wright was 'definitely not impressed,' while Alter Hurwitz, of Leeds, was 'enormously impressed'—Waley Cohen was struck by Altmann's 'independence of thought' and 'immense tolerance,' though he admitted that 'the rabbi's outlook was heavy and scholastic and he appeared to lack a sense of humour.'

Brodie, he thought, was 'still the most suitable candidate,' but it was unclear 'whether we could get him through the general body. In all probability, it would be possible to get Altmann through, although there would be definite opposition from the Federation.' As for Rosen, 'we could stand firm against him in view of the opinions from the Ministers and the Beth Din.'

Waley Cohen and his vice-president, Frank Samuel, 'agreed that they would not be unhappy to see Rabbi Altmann as Chief Rabbi,' though Samuel still favoured Brodie 'because it is definitely better to have a British person to fill the position, and especially one with Colonial experience.' Waley Cohen said that 'if it were a case of backing Altmann without a split in the community, or backing Brodie with a split, then he would take Altmann.' Either way, the honorary officers agreed, 'the line to be taken at the next sub-committee meeting is to try to get Kopul Rosen out of the running by means of such information as we possess.'[23]

Six weeks later, pursuing this path, Samuel told the informal sub-committee that, 'having now seen the three persons concerned, the US representatives felt that Rabbi Brodie was the most suitable. Rabbi Rosen was a fine speaker, but it was felt that he was shallow and needed "maturing." Neither Rabbi Brodie nor Rabbi Altmann would make a great Chief Rabbi, but either would make a safe one.'[24]

At a subsequent meeting, Waley Cohen reported that he had seen Rosen and had explained that, in view of the Beth Din's and ministers' letters, 'no one apart from Mr Wright felt able to support his candidature; that the United Synagogue were much influenced by his age; that all were impressed by him and would like to think of him as a man who might be appointed to the Chief Rabbinate on the next occasion.' He had urged Rosen 'to think the matter over and to meet him again in ten days' time.'

Rosen had replied that he was 'not much influenced by what the ministers or the Beth Din said, but he recognised the difficulty for an electing committee. The ministers did not know him, and he thought that the Beth Din were influenced by unjustified motives—they wanted a Chief Rabbi who would not assert himself and would not override them.' Rosen contended that he had 'never been a candidate for the position, but there were a lot of Rabbis in the Federation who aspire to do things in the future, and they might wish to assert the position of their Chief Minister.'

Of the remaining two, Waley Cohen told the sub-committee, Brodie was the better—'the other one is too academic and too Germanic in his background. It would be a great thing if there were only one man and it were possible to put him forward with the full support of the community.' He added: 'We should try very much to create conditions of co-operation between the Federation and the Beth Din. It might then be possible to endeavour to get Rabbi Rosen on the Beth Din.'[25]

* * *

Despite Waley Cohen's expressed desire to avoid 'unnecessary delay in the election of a Chief Rabbi,' it was not until October 1947, nearly two years after Hertz's death, that the US secretary, Alfred Silverman, dispatched formal invitations to the first meeting of the Chief Rabbinate Conference, including seventy-eight provincial, fourteen overseas, and two independent London congregations, fourteen district, fifteen affiliated, and seven associate synagogues of the US.

He also invited the Federation of Synagogues—'which body had not previously contributed to the maintenance of the office but had expressed their desire to do so in the future—to send ten representatives, in order that representation at the Conference would be on the widest possible basis and that the future Chief Rabbi should command the maximum measure of support from the Community.'[26]

Addressing the Conference some four weeks later, Waley Cohen reiterated that 'the qualities and qualifications required of a Chief Rabbi are of a very high order. He must be, above all, a man deeply imbued with a truly spiritual outlook: he must be a master in the field of rabbinic learning and of Jewish scholarship, and a man respected in the world of general culture and learning.

'In addition to all this, he must be a man of ripe experience and high qualities of statesmanship, and he must be well endowed with the qualities of leadership. He must be a man of fearless independent character, with unflinching strength of purpose. He must be acquainted with British life and thought and be able to expound his point of view as the representative of Jewish religious life in the British Empire to public men in this and other countries in such a way as to command their attention and their respect.'[27]

As its first task, the Conference set up a committee of twenty-five[28] 'to consider and report on the duties, privileges and conditions attaching to the Office of Chief Rabbi; the emoluments of the Chief Rabbi and his Office; the sources from which, and the terms on which, such emoluments shall be derived; and the relationship with the Chief Rabbinate of the congregations supporting his Office.'[29] The most straightforward of these tasks appeared to be that of determining the Chief Rabbi's emoluments, provisionally set at £3,000 per annum.

Early in January 1948, however, a letter reached Silverman that was to alter the landscape of the election. Referring to specific aspects of the work to be examined by the committee, his Federation counterpart, Julius Jung, wrote: 'I am desired by the Honorary Officers to send you herewith enclosed statement on the "privileges" of the Chief Rabbi.

'You will notice that no comment has been made on the "conditions" attached to this office, as these were regarded as being of secondary importance. The Honorary Officers wish to comment on the "conditions" on a subsequent occasion, but feel that the matter of "privileges" is vital as it affects the very nature of the office. I am asked therefore that this matter be placed as the first item on the agenda of the next meeting.'³⁰ The statement read as follows:

> 1. The Chief Rabbi shall act as the spiritual head of the Hebrew Congregations in the United Kingdom and the British Commonwealth. His duties shall include representing the community at civic functions, presiding at the sittings of the Beth Din, attendance at his office, visitation of Synagogues and preaching therein, pastoral visitation of the provinces and communities of the British Commonwealth, correspondence within the United Kingdom, the Dominions, Colonies, and other countries.
>
> 2. In all matters of religious ruling and halachic decision as hereinafter more particularly defined, the Chief Rabbi shall act only in conjunction with a Beth Din appointed as hereinafter mentioned. The Chief Rabbi shall have no right of veto over the decision of a majority of the Beth Din; such right of veto being contrary to Jewish law. The majority decision of the Beth Din in such matters must be binding on the Chief Rabbi. In matters of disagreement by the Beth Din, the voting being equal, the Chief Rabbi shall have the right of a casting vote as presiding chairman.³¹
>
> (a) Matters which come under the category of 'religious ruling and halachic decision' are religious questions affecting the community, the certification of Shochetim, the supervision of divine worship in the Synagogues, and the superintendence of Kashruth and Shechitah.
>
> (b) Appointments to the Beth Din shall be made by a committee representing the synagogal bodies which were responsible for the appointment of the Chief Rabbi.
>
> The Federation of Synagogues considers it necessary that the relationship of the Chief Rabbi with all Synagogal bodies shall be a uniform one. It is understood that the above suggestions do not accord with the privileges conferred upon the Chief Rabbi in the United Synagogue's Deed of Foundation and Trust, and it is suggested that steps should be taken to amend the Deed of Foundation and Trust so as to accord with the above proposals which are in accordance with Jewish law and in our opinion with modern circumstances.³²

Following receipt of the statement, the Chief Rabbinate Conference committee held a series of meetings, during which the Federation delegates 'stressed that it was impossible for a Chief Rabbi to give a binding decision, but that the Chief Rabbi himself must always accept the majority view of the Beth Din, and their memorandum should therefore be accepted by all synagogues claiming to form part of the United Hebrew Congregations of the British Commonwealth and Empire.'

The United Synagogue representatives, and some others, retorted that 'not only did the US constitution prohibit them from accepting such a denial of the authority of the Chief Rabbi—whose authority they were constitutionally bound to recognise—but that such a change in the recognition they give to the Chief Rabbi would not be acceptable to them.' Several members of the committee pointed out that 'if the Federation of Synagogues insisted on imposing on other synagogues the alteration which they desired in the status of the Chief Rabbi, a fundamental cleavage must result.'

Seeking to break the deadlock, the committee agreed on the adoption of a principle 'which would enable those who had always given, and still wished to give, full recognition to the authority of the Chief Rabbi, to continue to do so, but would at the same time allow the Federation, if they so desired, to safeguard their right to obey a decision of the majority of the Beth Din if it conflicted with that of the Chief Rabbi.'

This was embodied in a resolution, passed unanimously, 'that the Federation of Synagogues, and any other Synagogue or group of Synagogues whose constitution so permits, may reserve the right to be free from the obligation to accept a decision of the Chief Rabbi if it differs from a decision of the Beth Din.' The Federation delegates consulted their executive committee to ascertain whether the resolution was acceptable to them and would convey their response to the US honorary officers.[33]

Within a week, the executive indicated their unwillingness to accept the recommendation and sought a meeting with the United Synagogue. Three days later, this decision was formally conveyed to the US honorary officers, who urged the Federation to reconsider.

Agreement, they stressed, had been reached on all other issues and it was 'all-important that the Chief Rabbi should be able to speak to the world on behalf of Jewry in the British Commonwealth and Empire. The other congregations, who unreservedly accepted the authority of the Chief Rabbi, were prepared to agree to co-operate with the Federation of Synagogues even if it wished to reserve the right not to be bound by a decision of the Chief Rabbi if differing from that of the Beth Din.'

The Federation responded that, while it would like to have co-operated with the rest of the community, it insisted nevertheless that the other synagogues had to accept in relation to the Chief Rabbi all the stipulations laid down in their memorandum. If they were to co-operate, it was essential that the authority hitherto always vested in the Chief Rabbi should now be withdrawn and be vested in the Beth Din.

Meeting a week later, following a telegram from Waley Cohen 'in view of the extremely serious turn which events have now taken,'[34] the committee rejected the Federation's demand for a fundamental change in the authority of the Chief Rabbi, and decided that it 'could not do otherwise than to proceed without the participation of the Federation of Synagogues.' It would, however, retain the proposed recommendation 'in the hope that, at some future date, the Federation of Synagogues may be willing to co-operate with the remainder of the community, all bodies respecting the conscientious beliefs and constitutional position of the others.' As a result, the composition of proposed committees to be established in connection with the Chief Rabbinate—a Chief Rabbinate Council and an ancillary Consultative and Advisory Committee—would be reduced, without Federation participation, from twenty-nine representatives to twenty-two.

Despite these moves, and having consulted their executive, Federation delegates attended a meeting of the Chief Rabbinate Conference the following month, at which they tabled a number of amendments to the duties, privileges, and conditions attaching to the Office of Chief Rabbi: 'that a properly constituted and representative Beth Din shall be established; that consultation between the Chief Rabbi and this fully representative Beth Din shall take place on all matters of Jewish law and religious principles; and that any pronouncements on such matters shall be issued by the Chief Rabbi in accordance with the majority ruling of such a Beth Din.'[35]

Waley Cohen ruled that the Conference could not discuss the first amendment 'as the question of the constitution of the Beth Din was not one for the Conference, nor was it within the terms of reference of the Committee set up by the Conference.' After lengthy discussion, it rejected the third amendment by a large majority, and similarly the second amendment, but with the proviso that the words 'with whom the Chief Rabbi shall consult on all matters of Jewish law and religious principle' be added to the clause[36] 'The Chief Rabbi shall be the President of the Beth Din.'

The Federation delegates sought leave to ask their executive 'whether or not they will accept the authority of the Chief Rabbi as now set out in the report, and agree to contribute to the maintenance of the office in accordance with the financial provisions thereof, thereby qualifying for further participation in the Conference.'

The Conference then ruled that the words 'ultimate and unfettered' be restored into a clause relating to the Consultative and Advisory Committee, whose function was 'to enable the Chief Rabbi to exchange views with the elected leaders of the Anglo-Jewish Community with their lay knowledge and general experience and, at the same time, to enable these officers concerned with and responsible for the general administration of their synagogues to gain a greater understanding of the religious considerations on which the Chief Rabbi bases his [ultimate and unfettered] decision.'

The bracketed words had been deleted 'in order to meet the wishes of the Federation representatives, who objected to any suggestion that the Chief Rabbi's decision should be unfettered in religious matters, although it was explained to them that the words were intended to refer to the relationship between the Chief Rabbi and the Consultative and Advisory Committee. As the deletion had been adopted in an effort to keep the Federation of Synagogues in the Conference, and as this effort had failed, the Committee decided that the words should be reinserted in order to make it clear beyond a peradventure that the Consultative and Advisory Committee is in fact what its name implies.'[37]

* * *

Addressing the Chief Rabbinate Conference committee in March 1948, Waley Cohen began by announcing 'the official withdrawal of the Federation of Synagogues from the support and recognition of the Chief Rabbinate.' He then turned to an appraisal of each of the leading candidates, noting that 'the informal committee of some twenty lay leaders of the Anglo-Jewish community ... had endeavoured to obtain unanimity as to the person to be appointed, but, having managed to reduce the very large number of names suggested, had been unable to progress beyond the final three.'[38]

Of Altmann, Waley Cohen suggested that 'his qualities are more suited, and even much more notable, in the study and lectern than on the platform or in the pulpit and in public counsel,'[39] and that 'his German background coloured his outlook very much indeed, making him unacceptable to a large number of young people in this country—and we are very anxious that we should have, if possible, a Chief Rabbi with a British background.'

In relation to Rosen, Waley Cohen drew attention to the Beth Din's and ministers' opposition; to the widely held criticisms of Rosen's academic and Jewish scholarly qualifications; and to his youth—'for a Chief Rabbi, this is a disadvantage.' He added, however: 'We were all very much impressed by his innate qualities and we hope that, in his present position, he will grow in stature and that, if we can succeed from disparaging him in any way, he will prove a most valuable religious officer of the community and render great service to it and acquire knowledge and respect which might enable him to aspire to this office.'

Turning, finally, to Brodie, Waley Cohen lauded his 'high academic distinctions,' his 'remarkable impression on audiences and communities,' and his 'power' as a chaplain and in influencing young people, 'in whose hands we must recognise lies the immediate future ... The United Synagogue, who have a great responsibility in this matter—indeed, a very heavy responsibility—feel that, all round, he is much the best candidate available and would be a very hopeful appointment. It would rally large sections of the community not presently active in our religious life; it would be acceptable to the orthodox and ultra-orthodox; and it would be particularly acceptable to the overseas Empire—making it a very fine appointment in every possible way.'

Adjourning the meeting, Waley Cohen declared: 'It is a matter of great urgency that a Chief Rabbi be appointed, and I wonder whether we should not be rendering great service to the community if we could rally to a single call of this kind ... On the last such occasion, there was a contested election, which created great bitterness and drove away from Anglo-Jewry one of the most effective ministers we had in our midst.'[40]

Days later, Waley Cohen made a similar appeal to 'an absolutely private and confidential meeting of all those [three hundred representatives from the London area] who are entitled to a voice in the far-reaching and important appointment of the Chief Rabbi.' After summarising his assessment of the final nominees, he added: 'All three, I am bound to say, were attractive to all of us. We felt conscious of their fine qualities and we had, at first, some difficulty in coming down to making a final choice ... I do not think I could hope to say much more about Rabbi Brodie in order to carry you through the process of elimination which led many of us—I think most of us—to feel that he would be the best possible man for the post.'[41]

Describing this meeting to Moss, whose support for Altmann had thus far remained solid, Waley Cohen wrote: 'I told them that the right course now was to recommend to the Conference giving a call to Rabbi Brodie. They were asked to vote as to whether they would wish that to be done and, after a number of interesting speeches—of which a remarkable one was contributed by Aaron Wright, giving his full and unqualified support[42]—there was a unanimous vote in favour of the proposal.

'I do not remember ever before experiencing such an overwhelming unanimity from a meeting of this large dimension. I think that everybody was immensely moved both by the speeches and by the final vote ... I appeal to you now to support the clearly overwhelming desire by the great bulk of the community that we should give a call to Rabbi Brodie. If you can do that, I am sure you would influence your constituents to give you as unanimous a confidence in that course as the London bodies have given to theirs.'[43]

Waley Cohen's appeal, however, initially had less than the desired effect.

At the final meeting of the committee set up to consider voting rights and the selection of a candidate, Moss noted that a Manchester gathering of around ninety people 'had decided unanimously to support Rabbi Dr Altmann.'

Other provincial delegates reported that similar support had come from parts of Scotland (though not from Glasgow or Edinburgh, which had sided with Brodie), Southsea and Sunderland; that Leeds had gone unanimously for Brodie, as had Bournemouth, Brighton, Liverpool, North Wales, Newcastle, Northern Ireland, and the Dominions; and that Birmingham and the Midlands were 'strongly in support of Kopul Rosen, though, since the view had been expressed that a call should be extended to one man—and as Rabbi Brodie appeared to be that person—they would not press their support for Rabbi Rosen.'

In the end, there emerged 'the unanimous view of the committee that a call should be extended to Rabbi Israel Brodie,' and a recommendation that 'the Conference hereby empowers and instructs its Chairman to take all the steps necessary to effect [his] appointment.'[44]

Such steps were taken in early May, with the issue of invitations to a meeting at the end of the month, at which Waley Cohen expressed his happiness 'at being able to tell the Conference that the recommendation of the Community was a unanimous one. There has never been a time when I could feel happier than at this fine conclusion to arduous labours which have continued for the past two years.

> As was to be expected, all participating had conjured up for themselves a very fine ideal of a man to hold this great office. He must be a man whose character rested upon a deep and sincere Jewish spiritual foundation. He must also be a profound scholar, able to take his place as head of the Beth Din, and to give authoritative guidance to all of them in religious matters. He must be able to expound the teachings of Judaism so as to attract and inspire the minds and characters of Jews and Jewesses of all ages living in the British Commonwealth and Empire and playing their part in its national life.
>
> In addition, he must be a personality who would command the admiration and inspire the confidence of leading public men in this country, among whom he would be taking his place, and he must give to them, and to the people of this country, an understanding of the spiritual service which could be rendered to the nation and to the world by Judaism, and by Jews who were faithful to its teachings.

He must be able to represent their Jewish community with strength, firmness and tact and to give them an increasing sense of pride in, and understanding of, their Judaism. He must be ready to take the leading part in their councils to which his great office entitled him, and, finally, he must be a man who made the world feel that the Jewish community was an asset in every country of the British Commonwealth of Nations.

In Rabbi Brodie, the community felt that they had found a man who possessed all these qualities.[45]

Waley Cohen's recommendation to the Conference—'to effect the appointment of Rabbi Israel Brodie as Chief Rabbi of the United Hebrew Congregations of the British Commonwealth and Empire'—was thereupon adopted 'amid loud applause.'[46] Buoyed by this response, he wrote immediately to the Chief Rabbi-elect inviting him to accept the appointment.

'You will have heard with gratification that the Delegates of our widespread Congregations have pledged themselves with unanimity to support you, and I trust that the whole Community, clerical and lay alike, will give you its support and will assist you in your onerous task of maintaining the strength of Judaism throughout our lands and discharging the many and varied duties of the High Office to which you have been called and which, under the blessing of the Almighty, I hope you will occupy in health and strength for many years.'[47]

Accepting the invitation, 'with a profound sense of responsibility and humility,' Brodie responded in the knowledge that 'these are fateful days indeed in the history of Israel and mankind, in which persuasive and courageous leadership is essential. The late Dr Hertz exemplified such leadership ... and I trust that I shall not be found inadequate as his successor.'[48]

Earlier in the year, Brodie's preparedness to accept the offer had been less readily forthcoming. While referring to 'the religious considerations on which the Chief Rabbi bases his ultimate and unfettered decision,' the Conference committee had added a clause to their recommendations—subsequently ratified by the council—that 'consultation between the Chief Rabbi and the Consultative and Advisory Committee shall take place in relation to the following matter, among others: any public pronouncement proposed to be made on behalf of, or in relation to, the Jewish community by the Chief Rabbi either in his own name or in association with other Jewish bodies.'

This provision had troubled the Union of Anglo-Jewish Preachers, which unanimously passed a resolution expressing 'grave concern' at its inclusion, and asserting that 'such enforced consultation weakens the authority of the

Chief Rabbi, derogates from the prestige associated with his high office ... and must act as a serious reflection upon his status, dignity and effective influence.'[49]

Voicing similar concerns, the *Jewish Chronicle* had declared: 'The principle effect of forcing the Chief Rabbi to consult with such a committee as is proposed would be to damage his status, and even if he did take the opinion of the committee, his own inherent good sense and his desire for the welfare of Anglo-Jewry would prompt him, despite the committee, to seek out those men in the community who, in his opinion, are the greatest experts on the particular matter, irrespective of whether they are the official advisers or not. Once the choice [of Chief Rabbi] is made, restrictions which suggest any belittling of the man or the office will only serve to undermine the Chief Rabbinate and with it the authority and dignity of the whole Anglo-Jewish ministry.'[50]

Brodie, too, had expressed dismay over any restriction on the Chief Rabbinate's powers and the 'shackling and restraint' of its occupant's 'ultimate and unfettered decision.' He objected 'not to consulting with others, but with having to do so. Waley Cohen's response was friendly, conciliatory, but quite firm, insisting that there could be no alteration in the conditions of the appointment and that it was essential to have Dr Brodie's reply. Given verbal assurances and written confirmation that his authority was unfettered, Dr Brodie agreed to accept an invitation to become Chief Rabbi.'[51] One of his first pronouncements after the election was to the effect that, while he would willingly consult the committee, he would make his own decisions.[52]

* * *

Following the election, Waley Cohen corresponded with Lazarus, the long-serving Deputy for the Chief Rabbi, who had written 'to confirm my official retirement by the end of this month [June 1948]. Mrs Lazarus and I are deeply thankful that Providence has spared us to render service to the community during the period of the interregnum and are grateful to the community who have shown us both their affection and approbation of our efforts. We retire officially; but even in our retirement, loving service is still the life-long urge in our hearts.'[53]

Responding, Waley Cohen expressed his council's appreciation 'for the great work you have done for the community, and especially the readiness with which you accepted the onerous task of deputising for the Chief Rabbi during the interregnum. I know that this must have involved many sacrifices both for you and Mrs Lazarus, and the community, as well as in an especial degree the United Synagogue and its Honorary Officers, are deeply grateful to you both for all that you have been and all that you have done for the community.'⁵⁴

In another aspect of the mopping-up operation, Waley Cohen wrote also to the War Office, officially requesting Brodie's release from military duties. 'The necessary instructions,' he was informed, 'will be issued forthwith.'⁵⁵\

Israel Brodie (1948): 'Our tasks are very heavy indeed; but the end is glorious'

FROM THE PULPIT — IV

Out of the Darkness

Sermon by the Very Reverend Rabbi Israel Brodie on the occasion of his installation as Chief Rabbi of the United Hebrew Congregations of the British Commonwealth of Nations, New Synagogue, London, 28 June 1948–21 Sivan 5708

On Sabbath last, I worshipped in the Great Synagogue, to which I have always been attached for deeply cherished reasons connected with the formative years of my early ministry. My visit there was intended to emphasise the historical and factual association of the Chief Rabbinate with our Cathedral Synagogue. Alas that through indiscriminate enemy action in the recent war, the former House is no more, and I am precluded from following in the paths of my sainted predecessors who dedicated themselves to their exalted ministry within its hallowed precincts. However, I am thankful that the spirit and atmosphere of the 'Great' abides in the present temporary structure, surrounded though it be by melancholy-piled rubble. May the day not be distant when a permanent building will arise, greater even than the glory of the former House in which will be heard, continuously and throughout the generations, the voice of prayer and traditional melody, the living word of Torah and wisdom.

I am profoundly happy that this synagogue, so closely and prominently associated with Anglo-Jewish history for two centuries, has been chosen for this solemn ceremony. In spite of its mildly dissident beginnings, the congregation early recognised and supported the authority and office of the Chief Rabbinate. Throughout the decades, the New Synagogue has been an important pillar of the United Synagogue and has made a notable contribution to the progress and expansion of traditional Judaism in the Metropolis. Its present vigorous maturity is not shamed by the early enthusiasm of its founders.

And here I would like to say how grateful I am to my colleagues, tried and beloved members of the Anglo-Jewish ministry, who have been associated thus far in the ceremony of today. More particularly would I like to pay sincere tribute to Dayan Lazarus for his great services to the community and the office of the Chief Rabbinate during the interregnum following the passing away of that great man, my sainted predecessor, Joseph Herman Hertz. Dayan Lazarus brought to the office of Deputy for the Chief Rabbi that singleness of devotion to the cause of Judaism which has characterised his long and successful ministry. We pray that the Almighty will give him and his gracious lady many years of happiness. I am confident that they will still continue to render service to an already grateful community.

When I recall gatherings of our people which I have addressed in recent years in this country or in the DP camps in Central Europe, where the remnants saved like a brand from the fire wait for their redemption, or when speaking, as I was privileged to do, to a congregation in the Great Synagogue in Tel Aviv, I marvel at the miracles which the Lord hath wrought for us. I bless the Knower of secret things; for we of the House of Israel have had many 'Dunkirks' and been extraordinarily saved. Our foes—and they were many—sought most cunningly and diabolically to blot us out from being a nation. They had almost succeeded, had not the God of Israel been with us, and in His mercy spared us, the remnant, to live and see His judgment executed against His and our enemies. The enemy had been almost at the very shores of this island, and it seemed that nought could save us from the fate which befell so many of our brethren in Europe and elsewhere; but the Lord looked down from His heavenly habitation and confounded the intentions of the enemy; the hated foe was scattered, and the 'thousands of Israel' in this country were saved. By the grace of God, we were all spared the horrible visitations which descended upon large and important communities in Europe, communities that were famed centres of Jewish learning and faith. By reason, then, of our rare fortune, we have now become the most important surviving Jewish community in Europe. I say in the words of the Psalmist, 'Bless ye God in full assemblies, even the Lord, ye that are from the fountain of Israel.'[1] We, and the generations that are yet to be, should be filled with gratitude and humble thanksgiving to the Almighty for the gift of life and the will to hope. Songs of thanksgiving to the Lord for His goodness to us should never cease; we should be humble before God's inscrutability, in that we have been chosen for survival. Should we not be stirred by a tremendous realisation of our privilege, and feel that we ought, in so far as in us lies, be worthy of His favour by more intensive service to God and man? Does not a call come to us who have drawn joy from the well of salvation, to seek the Lord, who hath not hidden His face from us, but illuminated our path and enabled us to tread into safety? Here one might pause, briefly, to reflect on the potentialities for good in the Anglo-Jewish community. Its past has not been unworthy. Led by notable spiritual and lay leaders, it has had great hours when it was recognised by all as possessing a homogeneous character, and could take the lead in responding to the cry of brethren in other

---

1   Psalms 68:27. [All citations are as in the original text.]

lands who turned to it—and not in vain—for material and moral aid in their struggles for elementary right and justice. Our community owes some of its lustre to men and women who, a few generations back, came from lands of Europe and brought with them traditions of piety, love of learning, self-sacrificing adherence to Jewish practice. They created basic institutions devoted to Torah, Service and Charity. In the comparatively congenial atmosphere of tolerance and opportunity which they enjoyed in this country, they and subsequent arrivals—our fathers and grandfathers and great-grandfathers—soon adapted themselves to its ways and institutions and were not a little influenced by the British outlook. There was no conflict of loyalties, however; they prayed for and sought the welfare of the country of their adoption, and many took a keen interest and active part in all the variety of national life. In their devoted service to suffering Jewries elsewhere, the constituted leaders of our community could turn confidently to the government of the day, as well as to leaders of opinion both spiritual and temporal, for sympathy and intervention. Thus, they that went before set the pattern of an Anglo-Jewish tradition which has persisted; they helped to create in us a sense of continuity and provided us with a background. Conscious of our legacy and grateful in our portion, you and I must believe that the community throughout the Commonwealth and Empire is yet destined for still greater things in the service of Israel and mankind. This belief is reflected in the congratulatory messages I have received from responsible members of other communities, from our brethren in Bergen-Belsen, from some of the struggling communities on the Continent, from the Dominions, and also from the Land of Israel. They look to the English-speaking communities for a lead: they challenge our faith, our sincerity, our morale, our sense of brotherhood. We of this generation have the opportunity of giving a convincing and memorable response to their challenge, despite these perplexing, momentous times. Compared with our age, our predecessors lived and worked in days stable, steadfast, and spacious. We, like our fellow-citizens of other creeds, are passing through a bewildering chapter of crises, economic, moral and spiritual. Hatred and hostility abound to delay, if not to frustrate, our natural longing for a continuation—in this post-war world—of the comradeship and mutual helpfulness we knew in the dread days of national danger. Pity is dried up in the hearts of many to whom one formerly looked for its comforting exercise. To their disappointment and disillusionment, our Jewish ex-Servicemen are called upon to spend much of their energies in the fight against anti-Semitism and prejudice which still threaten both the peace of our community and the stability of the realm. Our Jewish consciousness is excited in a negative, fretful way, and our self-awareness is stimulated by a resented outside pressure. But we should not have to depend on our enemies for our attachment to the Jewish community. We might well heed the encouraging words of the great prophet Isaiah: 'And it shall come to pass in that day that the remnant of Israel, and they that are saved of the house of Jacob, shall no more again rely upon him that smote them; but shall rely upon the Lord, the Holy One of Israel, in truth.'[2] For our pride, for our peace and to be worthy of our appointed role, we have to be responsive to spiritual imperatives positively and joyously. We must not be dejected; we must not indulge in self-pity or bitterness, because there are elements in this country whose behaviour is repugnant to the British tradition of freedom and fair play: not they are the real England that we know. Thank God, there are millions of citizens of this great country whose life and character have been moulded by the religious and ethical teachings of the Bible, who refuse to bend the knee to the idols of hate and calumny. Men of good will of all creeds can and will co-operate for the common good and display the fine virtues of enlightened patriotism. Amid the present restlessness and uncertainty, there are also promising signs among us, and not least among our youth, of a searching for a firm credo, for a philosophy of life, for the word of the Lord. It is here that the spiritual leader should be aware of an urgent and pulsating opportunity. He must encourage the men and women of this generation to see God's handiwork in the events that are taking place before our very eyes. The latest and most momentous evidence of His Providence is being enacted in a tiny strip of territory, in the land of Israel. 'Who will despise the day of small things?'[3] Nearly 2,500 years ago, some few eager exiles returned from Babylon to a Palestine, which, from a material point of view, bore little resemblance to the dreams and visions of the future with which the prophets of comfort soothed the wounds and humiliations of the captivity. But the small community was destined to develop a way of life and a faith which made Israel a light unto the nations. In the words of a biblical scholar, 'It became the centre of a widely dispersed religious commonwealth which was a unique form of social structure, and has had an incalculable influence in history. It is not too much to say that if this handful of devoted and practical men had not faced and carried through their almost hopeless task, the world would never have seen three of the most potent factors in all subsequent history—Judaism, the Christian Church, and Islam. In the Jews' Return from Exile, then, we have an event which, though its scale was so minute as to be almost invisible on a chart of world history, was, on any showing, a decisive turning-point, of which the historian must take serious account.'[4] What a soul-stirring precedent to fire our enthusiasm and kindle our vision!

---

2   Isaiah 10:20.
3   Zechariah 4:10.
4   Dodd, *The Bible Today*, p.50.

The true leader in Israel has to renew and strengthen our religious and moral preparedness to meet the challenge of the hour. Our lives have to be cleansed and sanctified. We need a spiritual purification to remove mean and sordid thinking, the battening sloth of smug selfishness, and the besetting sin of disunity. We have to strengthen those traditional defences which our sages tell us require constant support and firmer attachment—Torah, Prayer, Good Deeds, and Worthy Conduct. They must not be neglected or cheapened or become atrophied. Our tasks are very heavy indeed; but the end is glorious, and the enterprise worthy of all our endeavour.

It is not my intention today to refer to any detailed programme whereby I seek, with the collaboration of my colleagues and the community, to translate our high hopes into activities through communal and extra-communal channels. I wish rather to use this solemn occasion to direct our minds to a fundamental need which will or should be the inspiration of all our service to God and our fellow-men. It is contained in the text which I have chosen: 'Acknowledge Him in all thy ways, and He will direct thy steps aright.' The recognition of God as ruling our lives must be basic in all our proposals and all our plannings—and on all levels. The prophets and teachers of Israel are never wearied in their requirement of man to know God in order to know himself, and of nations to know God to avoid catastrophe. In this context, to know God does not mean an intellectual or even theological searching of the nature and being of the Godhead; it means rather a conviction of His presence and pervasiveness as a real factor in our individual and social experience in human history and its interpretation. It is revealed in a selfless readiness on the part of man to subdue the passion of overriding acquisitiveness, to serve those who are in need, to promote moral practice generally. 'He judged the cause of the poor and needy; then it was well. Is not this to know Me?, saith the Lord.'[5]

Our text is described by a sage of the third century of the current era as the foundation on which depend the essential parts of the Torah, the Revelation of His Divine Will. If we acknowledge Him in all our ways, all acts and thoughts, habits and words, however ordinary, assume significance.[6] This teaching, absorbed in our every member, must make us pause when, for example, we are tempted to commit a wrong against God's law, to belittle the individuality or dignity of our neighbour, to take advantage of a situation of scarcity to enrich ourselves dishonestly. It implies being our best in prayer and in work, for we know before whom we stand, who knoweth the imaginings of the heart. It is the key to open the gates to the salvation of Israel and of mankind.

Needless to say, the spiritual leader also must be eminently guided by, and

---

5 Jeremiah 22:16.
6 Berachoth 63a.

intoxicated with, the knowledge of God in all that he says or does. His is the duty to tend the Lamp of Truth and evoke the feeling of God's Presence in the hearts and minds of his people. He must help them to rise in spiritual stature and generously give of his own spirit in order that they might share in the knowledge of God. 'Would that all the Lord's people were prophets, that the Lord would put His spirit upon them.'[7]

The great seer, Isaiah, looking to the glory that is to be, predicts a world happy and at peace with an Israel restored and a humanity tamed and united. 'They shall not hurt nor destroy in all My holy mountain; for the earth shall be full of the knowledge of the Lord as the waters cover the sea.'[8] The prophet foresaw this dazzling ideal. May it be given to us to believe in it and work for it, with passionate sincerity.

And now, my dear friends, I stand in this historic pulpit and see before me a vast assembly who have gathered to hear my message on this day of my installation. I will confess to you that for long I shrank from the thought that I might be invited to the exalted office of Chief Rabbi, filled with such distinction by predecessors, among whom were scholars and saints, the light of their generation, known and praised in the gates for their piety and learning; spiritual and moral leaders who had the courage to admonish, and the gracious gift to persuade and instruct; men who illumined counsel with words of wisdom and experience; defenders of the Faith, ready spokesmen of the people.

I had preferred to return to civilian life to resume my career by the still waters of academic tranquillity, confined within the four cubits of halachah, and from thence to be privileged to communicate the abiding truths of our faith and civilisation as embodied in Torah and tradition, in literature and history, to aspiring students—alas, too few—for the Jewish ministry. For mine has been a strenuous life, particularly during the last eight years. My dream and hope were to come back at last to the 'distinctive gates'[9] of the beth hamedrash, and to spend my years as a humble student and teacher in Israel. But God has willed it otherwise; and I say to you, before this representative assembly and congregation, and in the presence of the Most High: 'Behold me, here I am, to serve you.' I bring to you all of myself, with whatever gifts I may possess, and with all my weakness and shortcomings. 'I planned my ways, but my feet are returned to Thy testimonies.'[10] I step readily into the full blaze of public life, and, in a strenuous, noisy and anxious time, I enter freely upon my life's task to learn and to teach, to fulfil and to do.

---

7   Numbers 11:29.
8   Isaiah 11:9.
9   Berachoth 8a.
10   Psalms 119:59.

At this solemn moment, I turn with trustfulness to our Father in Heaven, the Source of all goodness, our Strength, our Shield, our Fortress, and pray with fear and hope for His help and protection in the sacred work to which I give myself, to the honour and glory of His Name. With some confidence and no small justification, I look to you, colleagues and laymen, and to the whole community in these 'islands of the seas' and the Empire beyond, for loyalty and co-operation, for sympathetic judgment and patience.

I ascend this day to my great and high office, I stand by the Menorah of our Faith, prepared for service. Like my predecessors, I will be at my post day in, day out; and as long as it shall please the Almighty, I will keep alight the lamps whose rays of righteousness dissipate the darkness of ignorance and the shame of unworthy fears, diffusing in their stead wisdom, knowledge, the fear of the Lord, the strength of salvation, as the firm faith of our times. Listen with me to the voice of wisdom as I conclude my message. 'Have I not written for thee excellent things of counsels and knowledge, that I might make thee know the certainty of the words of truth, that thou mightest bring back words of truth to them that send thee.'[11] These words echo my earnest prayers for the success of my dedicated efforts as leader, and for the encouragement of your response as hopeful followers.[12]

---

11 Proverbs 20, 21.
12 [The sermon concluded with a prayer.]

CHAPTER SIX

A Blank Cheque

THIRTEEN YEARS INTO his Chief Rabbinate, most notable for its comparative calm, Israel Brodie suddenly found himself at the heart of a storm. The Gateshead-educated[1] Louis Jacobs, whom he had inducted into office at the New West End Synagogue, and later appointed to the Jews' College faculty, had published allegedly heretical views in a little-known book entitled *We Have Reason to Believe*. The resultant conflicts,[2] perhaps the most serious in the Chief Rabbinate's history, brought the Brodie incumbency to a bitter close.

Jacobs had vacated his New West End post in 1959 in the hope—and expectation—of leading Jews' College when its principal, Isidore Epstein, retired some two years later. While the appointment required the Chief Rabbi's sanction, this was regarded as a formality by the college council, and when Brodie refused without advancing his reasons, Jacobs promptly resigned.[3] Apprised by the London dayanim of his 'unacceptable' position on *Torah min hashamayim* (Divine Revelation)—which, they declared, was 'in conflict with authentic Jewish belief'[4]—Brodie cited, apart from Jacobs' published views, inadequate standards of outstanding scholarship, 'and other qualifications required of a candidate for the office of principal,' in justification of his veto.[5]

Early in 1962, while the controversy was at its height, Brodie, by then in indifferent health, took refuge on a cruise to Australia. Rumours began to circulate, and soon reached Rabbi Immanuel Jakobovits at New York's Fifth Avenue Synagogue, that the Chief Rabbi 'no longer felt able to resist the pro-Jacobs clamour, would announce from abroad that he had withdrawn his opposition, and would follow this up with notification of his own resignation from office. Dr Jacobs' progression to the Chief Rabbinate would thus be assured, since no other candidate of similar stature existed—as the community was being led to believe—or, in any event, would wish to become involved in such a poisoned atmosphere.'[6]

Jakobovits' informant was Norman Cohen, a prominent Anglo-Jewish activist and close friend and adviser, who told him that 'at the moment, things here are extremely confused. It may be that they will be settled when Dr Brodie returns, but, on the other hand, they may get even worse ... If this position [the Jews' College principalship] is allowed to go by default to Dr Jacobs, it will be very difficult to avoid the Chief Rabbinate going the same way.'[7]

To counter this possibility, London supporters of Jakobovits had days earlier proposed that the Jewish Agency's Torah department—which annually sponsored guest speakers from abroad—invite him to Britain 'with very definite intent' and with 'more at stake than a mere lecture tour.'[8] Jakobovits had responded to Cohen: 'I feel greatly complimented by your and your friends' thought of me, and I need not tell you that the suggestion of serving in the greatest rabbinate in the world (with the possible exception of Israel) is certainly an exciting and attractive one.

'My decision would have to depend on the prospects and opportunities the appointment would give me. I am too young [forty-one] and have too large a family [five children at the time] to submit for the rest of my life to Brodie's agonies and anxieties. I would therefore need some reassurance on that score—probably from the right as well as from the left—before I could really feel happy about any firm candidacy.

'That is not to say that I would not meanwhile wish to pursue the matter with the greatest interest and at the same time await developments. I realise only too well that the number of possible candidates is, if anything, shrinking; and the narrower the choice, the greater, presumably, my bargaining power would be to obtain acceptable terms (I am thinking solely of working conditions, not financial terms).'[9]

Jakobovits was less than happy, however, about the complexion of the United Synagogue hierarchy, whose president, Ewen Montagu,[10] was a strong supporter of Jacobs. On being told by Cohen that business tycoon Isaac Wolfson might succeed Montagu, and had expressed himself as 'a good friend to you,' Jakobovits replied: 'I know he is well disposed towards me. I have had a number of contacts with him over the years.

'What is of rather greater moment to me is the possibility of his succeeding Montagu, not so much because that might improve my prospects, but because that would greatly affect my interest in the position. Under the present United Synagogue regime, I have, frankly, still grave reservations about linking my fortunes to Anglo-Jewry's "Orthodoxy," while if a man like I.W. assumed the leadership, my prospects of success and contentment would be immeasurably greater.'[11]

In due course, Jakobovits delivered his lectures in London and later described the visit as 'successful.' But, he added, 'I could not really be certain that I wished to exchange the settled satisfaction of my life in New York for the hazards of the British Chief Rabbinate.'[12]

* * *

Eighteen months on, with Wolfson firmly in the seat as US president,[13] Anglo-Jewry and the Chief Rabbinate were reeling from a second 'Jacobs Affair,' following the New West End's attempt to re-engage him as its minister. The question of a successor to Brodie—who, after fighting off the congregation's rebellious bid,[14] had indicated his wish to retire—rose high on the communal agenda, and the United Synagogue council took its first steps in 'the complex process'[15] by convening a Chief Rabbinate Conference to map out the route.

Following the accustomed path of forming a committee to consider the duties, privileges, conditions and emoluments of the Chief Rabbi and his office and, more significantly, 'the steps to be taken to select and appoint a Chief Rabbi,'[16] the Conference made no apparent progress for several months, little helped by yet another dispute with the Federation of Synagogues, whose demand that the Chief Rabbi should be subject to a majority decision of his own Beth Din on halachic matters—which had led to the Federation's 1948 electoral boycott—was again said to infringe the United Synagogue's Deed of Foundation and Trust.[17]

At best, there emerged a trickle of names, with Jakobovits high in expectations, despite several denials. The *Irish Times* ruminated that, while the former Chief Rabbi of Ireland regarded 'the whole matter as academic' and was 'at present interested in fulfilling his mission in New York,' he might make up his mind 'in the light of several factors, including the controversy over the position of Chief Rabbi Brodie and his relationship to certain schools of thought.'[18]

The Observer, also recording Jakobovits' name, commented that he was 'less strictly Orthodox than another American rabbi being mentioned—Rabbi Joseph Soloveitchik—who, however, had recently turned down an offer to become Chief Rabbi of Israel and who, it is understood, would not even consider taking Dr Brodie's place until he had studied the recent controversy over Dr Louis Jacobs.' The report added: 'Rabbi Jacobs is, of course, now out of the running for the Chief Rabbinate, since Dr Brodie refused to license him last month as minister of the New West End Synagogue.'[19]

The impasse appeared to be broken when, in March 1965, the selection committee announced that it had drawn up a list of eleven names of possible candidates, reduced to ten with the hitherto undisclosed withdrawal of Soloveitchik. The other 'suitably qualified rabbis' were later given (in alphabetical order) as Bernard Moses Casper (South Africa), Isaac Cohen (Ireland), Shear Yashuv Cohen (Israel), Shalom Coleman (Australia), Yaacov

Herzog (Israel), Immanuel Jakobovits (United States), Norman Lamm (United States), Israel Porush (Australia), Louis Isaac Rabinowitz (Israel), and Emanuel Rackman (United States).[20]

The list was not published until May, but the doubtful nature of its veracity is illustrated by a disavowal from Rackman, who, along with Soloveitchik, was surprised to see his name mentioned at all. 'That future historians may have the correct facts,' he told the *Jewish Chronicle*, 'I never was a candidate and never authorised anyone to submit my name. While Sir Isaac was in the United States, I met him to discuss the possibility of my accepting an invitation to lecture in London after the election of a Chief Rabbi. I write this with due regard for the importance of the position of Chief Rabbi. Yet my own situation and commitment in the United States make impossible any consideration of a change.'[21]

The belated release of the names, moreover, rendered most of them passé. In March, Jakobovits was already being tipped by the *Daily Express* as 'the man most likely to be Britain's next Chief Rabbi,'[22] a view confirmed by its New York correspondent, whom he told in an interview: 'I am not a campaigning candidate for this position, but one thing I can tell you is this: whoever gets the job will be a traditionalist.'[23] *The Observer*, meanwhile, had reported that 'Sir Isaac—who, in effect, has a blank cheque to survey the field—would most like for the post a senior official of the Israeli Foreign Office, Rabbi Jacob Herzog, son of a former Chief Rabbi of Palestine.'[24]

That Wolfson had been given 'a blank cheque' was a moot point in United Synagogue circles, following reports that, in February, he had told the Chief Rabbinate committee—concerned about delays in finding a successor—'Don't you worry. I will find you a good Chief Rabbi in good time.'[25] At a subsequent meeting of the Conference, delegates expressed concern over the committee's recommendation that Wolfson 'be entrusted with the task of preparing a short-list of suitably qualified candidates,' and demanded from him an assurance that the next Chief Rabbi 'will not be the choice of one individual imposed on a take-it-or-leave-it basis.'

Wolfson's response—'I am sure that if the Conference reposes its confidence in me, I will be able to satisfy everyone'—prompted one disgruntled delegate to remark that 'if Sir Isaac's February declaration was incorrectly reported, he should deny it. If it was correct, what is the use of having a committee? While not doubting his ability to choose a director or manager of a commercial undertaking, the sacred task of selecting a Chief Rabbi must not be left to one man.'

US vice-president Alfred Woolf, who was moving the recommendation—eventually carried by an overwhelming majority—replied that he was 'not concerned with any report that had appeared and would therefore not ask Sir

Isaac to deny it. The recommendation itself was a denial of what had been read in the press.'[26]

Even as this debate was taking place, it became evident that Wolfson's talks in the United States had involved more than just Rackman. In an address to his New York congregation, Jakobovits revealed that, 'while to this day no official approach has been made to me—or, as far as I know, to anyone else—many people in England, and even here, have urged me to declare my willingness to accept the position if it were offered to me.

> At times, I was bombarded with inquiries on my intentions from press reporters on both sides of the Atlantic, Jewish and general. However, I did not deem it necessary to cross my bridges before I got there. Hence, I answered invariably that I was very happy in my present post and that I would prefer to stay here. But if I were ever officially called to London, I would feel morally bound to give the offer my most serious consideration.
>
> This answer I also gave to Sir Isaac Wolfson—whose friendship with me goes back much longer than his presidency of the United Synagogue in London and his ex-officio chairmanship of the Chief Rabbinate Committee—when, in the course of his last two visits here, he asked me quite informally, and without any commitments on either side, where I might stand if a call came to me. I made it very clear that I would be happy if he found some other adequate candidate and left me out of consideration.
>
> Throughout this time, I kept our [synagogue] president constantly informed on all developments. His counsel and understanding have been of immense help to me at all times. We both felt that, without any formal approach, it was entirely premature and unrealistic to discuss the matter officially with our board and congregation. But lately we felt it might be wiser to reach a definite decision now than to wait for more pressures to build up. It would be easier for me to say a firm 'No' now than to refuse the position if and when offered to me.[27]

Confronted with this dilemma, Jakobovits had long since struggled to come to terms with the situation. A year earlier, he had written to Cohen: 'The truth is—as I have always been at pains to point out—that now, as before, my heart is not set on returning to London, especially under present conditions.

The only consideration which might eventually force me to change my mind is, in my father-in-law's [Rabbi Elie Munk's][28] terms, a moral duty not to let the office go by default—that is, if Orthodoxy simply has no other candidate to offer. So far, Sir Isaac has not been in communication with me on the matter, and I certainly would not feel called upon to take the initiative in contacting him.'[29]

Several months later, Jakobovits wrote again to Cohen in reference to murmurings from British supporters over 'my "harmful" handling of my "candidature." They complain, in so many words, that I do not observe the rules of the game properly, but they forget that I have not agreed to play the game at all! I wonder when my friends and foes alike will begin to be convinced of my sincerity when I declare, time and again, that I am really not considering myself a "candidate," or a "contender," or a "contestant," or what have you.

'Nothing has happened in the past few months to induce me to change my earlier position. I continue to hope that a better candidate will be found (I wish I were certain of his identity). If the powers-that-be will decide to turn to me, I shall feel morally bound to consider their challenge most earnestly, but I do not propose to do anything to manipulate things in my "favour."'[30]

Matters came to a head in April 1965, when Jakobovits was called upon to make, as his put it, 'a moral decision.' In talks with his congregation, he had drawn up a proposal which would rule out any consideration of the British Chief Rabbinate, and this, he told them, 'is to be the moment of truth.'

The plan envisaged the establishment of an institute 'through which, I believe, you and I can best combine our resources to make a significant contribution to enriching Jewish religious life and thought in America. It would harness the intellectual resources of the religious community in a continuous effort to co-ordinate Jewish and secular thinking; re-examine Judaism through intensive research in the light of contemporary conditions; open up lines of communication between religious intellectuals and the wider public; resolve conflicts between Jewish teachings and modern thought—in sum, create a movement which will blaze new trails of the compatibility and relevance of Judaism to the problems of our morally and religiously bewildered age.'

This dream, Jakobovits said, 'will exact great efforts from all of us. I am prepared to dedicate my energies to the academic and organising part of its fulfilment, but I am not willing or able to assume the responsibility for providing and administering the material requirements. This is an obligation to which I would like you to commit yourselves. My concern this evening is that you collectively undertake such a commitment, so that you can give me the signal and say: "Rabbi, you can go ahead; we are fully behind you." Our congregation is now nearly seven years old. We have spent this first sabbatical cycle on consolidating our own existence. It is now time for us to expand our horizons and to make our creative mark on the community to which we belong.'

Jakobovits said that, if he confirmed his decision with his congregation that day, 'it is my definite resolve to communicate it to London tomorrow or the day after tomorrow. So far, the facts. Now let me confide in you my considerations, the pros and cons as I see them, the arguments for and against weighing on me.

> I would not be honest or human if I did not admit that this was a most difficult decision to make, probably the most fateful in my life. The British Chief Rabbinate may well be the highest rabbinical post today; it is certainly the best-organised and most powerful rabbinical office in the world. Its incumbent not only sits at the controls of British Jewry's religious destiny, but he may decisively affect the direction of Jewish life in Europe and, indirectly, even in Israel and America. The office confers far more powers, and offers a greater challenge for leadership, than any rabbi here has at present.
>
> On the other hand, I am planted here in the very heart of the world's largest Jewish community, leading what is today already perhaps the best-known Orthodox congregation to be found anywhere. I am surrounded by friends who give me as much affection and respect as I can bear or as any rabbi can wish for. Here I am a free agent. Unlike the Chief Rabbi in England, I can choose the scope of my work. I can exploit my strengths, such as lecturing or writing, and I can avoid my dislikes, such as communal politics or fund-raising.
>
> I must tell you frankly that, among my many friends and relatives on both sides of the Atlantic, opinions on what I should do or seek are sharply divided. Some suggest that I should have my head examined if I passed up this historic opportunity to assume an office of such distinction and influence, if I chose to remain the spiritual head of some two hundred and twenty families instead of the leadership over half-a-million Jews. They also tell me it would be morally wrong to refuse a call to lead Anglo-Jewry at this time of crisis, and by my refusal possibly to let this key position in the religious world go to the wrong person by default.
>
> Others are equally insistent in recommending me for psychiatric treatment if I exchanged the comforts, distinction and opportunities of my present position with you for the headaches and quarrels of a community of minor importance

compared to American Jewry. I realise, of course, the decision must be mine, and mine alone. No one can make it for me. But you can help me make the right decision. You can give me the certainty in five, ten or twenty years from now that I was right in deciding as I did.

For me, as a rabbi, this is primarily a moral decision. If I am to justify my decision to stay here before my conscience now and in future years, I must be certain that I can achieve at least as much here in terms of religious reconstruction and spiritual leadership as I could in London. This is the crux of the problem confronting me.[31]

Having gained his congregation's support for the project—which, in the event, never materialised[32]—Jakobovits conveyed his decision to Wolfson the following day, with a postscript that, 'in view of my anxiety to end all speculation involving my name, I propose to release this letter to the press as soon as I have your confirmation of its receipt.

After much soul-searching, I have decided to request you kindly not to consider my name for election as the successor to Chief Rabbi Dr Israel Brodie.

You will recall that I have repeatedly and consistently stated, privately and in public, as well as in my informal conversations with you, that my personal preference would be to remain in my present office in New York. I added, however, that I would feel morally bound to give the most serious consideration to any official call your Committee might extend to me. From this attitude I have not wavered ever since my name was first mentioned in connection with the forthcoming election.

While it had been my intention to wait and determine my final decision only if and when the position were formally offered to me, certain more recent developments have prompted me to reach a decision at this time. You will surely realise that the uncertainties of the situation have continued long beyond the time anticipated by you. In these circumstances, rumours and speculation—not to mention the persistent harassment by reporters and editors—have assumed forms which are increasingly embarrassing to me, to my congregation and, in my opinion, to the dignity of the Chief Rabbinate itself. Moreover, I felt that the elimination of my name from your consideration at this stage (albeit I was never officially asked to declare my candidacy) would cause also you and your Committee less embarrassment than a negative response in the event of my selection.

These factors merely explain why I have made my decision at this time; they have no bearing on the decision itself. This is based strictly on personal and communal considerations. Above all, I have come to the conclusion that my disposition is better fitted to meeting the challenge of spiritual leadership and academic activities posed to me in my present position at the very heart of the world's largest Jewish community. The opportunities here offered to me are practically unlimited to pursue my communal and literary interests. For example, my congregation only quite recently agreed to sponsor an institute of contemporary Jewish thought which I plan to establish with the aim of harnessing the intellectual resources of the religious community for studying and disseminating the relevance of Jewish teachings to present-day thought and living.

Finally, my decision is not meant, of course, in any way to reflect on the high distinction of the British Chief Rabbinate. It ranks, I believe now as before, as by far the best-organised and exalted rabbinical office in the Diaspora today. I will forever be deeply sensible to the great honour done to me by those who thought me worthy to be even considered for so high an office.

I trust that you will understand my position, and I conclude this letter with fervently wishing you every success in your historic deliberations that will determine the religious destiny of Jewry in the British Commonwealth and beyond.[33]

* * *

Faced with this turn of events, the selection committee set their sights in other directions, having followed certain signposts as the saga unfolded. As early as the previous November, Yaacov Herzog had been mooted as 'a possible successor' to Brodie, although, when asked to comment, had replied that he was 'unaware my name has been mentioned as a candidate.'[34]

The committee was said to have received his name from an unexpected source—Sarah Herzog, the widow of Israel's Chief Rabbi, who had telephoned Wolfson, an old family friend, to suggest that her younger son would make 'an excellent Chief Rabbi of Britain.' Wolfson, according to close sources, had 'immediately pounced on the idea.'[35] Herzog's wife, Pnina, held a similar view, believing that 'Yaacov was a prodigy, a man of exceptional gifts, and that his distinctive personality was unfulfilled in most of the posts he had held so far. Here, at last, was a proposition that she felt was more appropriate to his personality and abilities.'[36]

Jakobovits was later to write: 'Yaacov Herzog was an admirable rabbinical scholar but, although holding *semichah*, had never had any practical experience in the rabbinate. Rumour credited his mother with a burning desire to see him carry on the rabbinical tradition, inherited from both his father and his maternal grandfather, Dayan Samuel Hillman. His nomination was of special interest to me, for several reasons. We had been friends ever since we studied together at the Etz Chaim Yeshivah in London, just before the Second World War. I had always rated him as one of our leading intellects, and the only statesman in or near Israel's seats of power to see contemporary Jewish events through specifically Jewish eyes.'[37]

Herzog, director-general of the Israeli Ministry of Foreign Affairs, was reported to have 'stayed on at his Mayfair hotel for a few days' after accompanying Prime Minister Levi Eshkol on a visit to London. The *Daily Express* declared that 'a new row among Britain's Jews is brewing over the likelihood that their new Chief Rabbi could be an Israeli diplomat who has never been a minister of a synagogue ... Until a few days ago, the most likely candidate seemed to be Dr Immanuel Jakobovits, but since Dr Herzog flew into London, the position has changed in his favour, although many Jews feel it would be "ridiculous" for him to be appointed.'[38]

The *Daily Mail* wrote that 'the battle behind the scenes to appoint a new leader for Britain's 450,000 Jews in succession to seventy-year-old Dr Israel Brodie became more confused with the arrival in London of Dr Herzog. It is known that he has been approached by several leading British Jews who oppose the appointment of Dr Jakobovits.'[39]

To add to the speculation, Louis Rabinowitz told journalists in Jerusalem, where he was living after sixteen years as South Africa's Chief Rabbi: 'If my name is put forward, I shall not object.'[40]

At a meeting a month after Jakobovits' withdrawal, and two days before a crucial gathering of the Conference committee, Wolfson intimated to his United Synagogue colleagues that 'the rabbi's letter does not necessarily signal the end of his involvement' and that 'he would probably take the position were it offered to him.'

Meanwhile, said Wolfson, a visit to Israel had brought him into contact with the Ponevezher Rav [Rabbi Yosef Shlomo Kahaneman],[41] who had recommended Herzog for the post. He had also received a 'glowing' tribute to

Herzog from Edmund de Rothschild,[42] describing him as 'a man of the highest calibre and one who will be able to lead our community and achieve greater unity than it has enjoyed for many years. Not only would he bring a tremendous sense of purpose to us, but the whole image of British Jewry would be enhanced if it had such a man at its head. I very much hope that Dr Herzog's candidature can go forward with the unanimous support of all concerned.'[43] Further discussion ended with an appeal to the committee from the US president to support this recommendation.

On the day he sent his letter to Wolfson, de Rothschild dispatched another to Herzog, in terms not unlike those conveyed by Waley Cohen to Herzog's father a generation earlier. 'When you were in London during the visit of Prime Minister Eshkol,' he wrote, 'we had a short discussion on the possibility of your becoming Chief Rabbi of the British Commonwealth. The full understanding which you then showed not only of the problems of Judaism in the modern world, but more particularly also of all the considerations which such an appointment involves, convinced me that you would be the person best fitted for this office.'

Repeating his comment on unity, de Rothschild added: 'The whole image of British Jewry would be enhanced by the standards which you have set yourself and by all that you stand for. Through the work which you have done in Israel, you have access to so many world leaders; you understand how, in a constantly changing world situation, co-operation between people of good will everywhere is vitally necessary; and you have an appeal to and an influence upon the younger generation. For all these reasons I sincerely hope that you can see your way to becoming our Chief Rabbi if you are formally invited so to do. For my part, I should like to assure you that in that event you could count on all the assistance and co-operation that it lay in my power to give in the task before you.'[44]

Perhaps the most alluring of the messages Herzog received at this time was one from Israel Brodie. Addressed to 'My dear Jacob,' the Chief Rabbi's handwritten letter opened with an expression of regret 'that we could not meet during my recent stay in Israel.

> Among other things, I wanted to hear from you further on the question which you and I discussed when you were good enough to call on me at the Accadia [Hotel] some months ago. Although I have not attempted in any way to interfere or advise in the matter of my successor, I have naturally been concerned to know that someone was to be chosen who would be eminently suitable.
>
> When your name was first mentioned, I felt that you

would be the man to lead the communities in the United Kingdom and in the Commonwealth. I was very impressed when at the Accadia you took me into your confidence and informed me that you were earnestly considering the proposal and that you were hoping to give a final answer at the end of February. I do not know whether you have as yet come to a decision.

I thought I ought to let you know what I was asked to convey in person should I have seen you in Israel. It was a message from the learned members of the Beth Din and also the Haham, Dr S[olomon] Gaon, to the effect that they would welcome your appointment.

As you know, I will be retiring at the end of this month. It is important that the interregnum between my retirement and the appointment of my successor be as short as possible.[45] It is for that reason that I—and I know also that Sir Isaac—are especially anxious to have your definite answer.

I pray that the Almighty will direct you and help you in reaching a decision on which so much depends. I need hardly add that should you accept, I will make myself available in any matter in which you think I can be of assistance.[46]

Meeting in London on 16 May 1965, the selection committee considered at length the names of the rabbis mentioned to Wolfson as being 'suitably qualified to be elected to the Office of Chief Rabbi.' It unanimously decided to recommend that Herzog be invited to accept the appointment,[47] declaring it 'unnecessary on the present occasion that the mode of election should be by an elective body,' and charging a seven-man delegation with the task of leaving 'almost immediately' for Israel to offer him the post.

As with earlier Chief Rabbinical appointments, the committee's unilateral action provoked the displeasure of the Union of Anglo-Jewish Preachers. A delegation of its members, together with representatives of the United Synagogue Council of Ministers, had met with Wolfson the previous month and—said their chairman, Leslie Hardman—'were given an unequivocal assurance that as soon as the ten possible candidates had been short-listed, we would be consulted.

'Knowing Sir Isaac to be a man of his word, we cannot think what happened to have made him change his mind. The first time I heard of the [proposed] appointment of Rabbi Herzog was when it was announced on the television. To have let the ministry down, as it would appear to be the case, is, to say the least, most bewildering. I have no objection to the appointment of Rabbi

Herzog, but would not the occupant of this high position be pleased to know that his ministers were consulted and agreed to his appointment?'[48]

The delegation's visit to Israel was delayed for several days while Herzog recovered from an appendectomy performed some two weeks earlier. It was meanwhile reported that he was 'still undecided whether to accept the invitation,' his response dependent upon whether or not he would be appointed as ambassador to Washington. Confirming that he had read such reports, he indicated that 'my decision on the Chief Rabbinate, which will shortly be taken, will be determined within that context and in that context only.'[49]

During this hiatus, from his sick-bed, Herzog sought the advice of intimate friends and colleagues. 'I advised him to accept,' stated World Jewish Congress president Nahum Goldmann, 'because for several years he would be one of the foremost leaders of world Jewry.'[50] Foreign Minister Golda Meir, under whom Herzog served, opposed the idea. 'My mind was set against it; I thought he ought to stay in Israel. When we talked at his house, I did not see any inclination on his part to go for it. He and his wife also faced the question of taking the children out of the country. Then I saw that he was torn between his own will and a sense of duty ... I must confess that I left with a heavy heart.'[51] She later described him as 'among the most intellectually sophisticated men I have met.'[52]

* * *

On the morrow of the committee's decision, Wolfson wrote to Herzog confirming the dispatch of two cables, one stating 'Happy and honoured to inform you that the Chief Rabbinate Conference committee of thirty-five unanimously recommended you as sole name to present to the Conference for election as Chief Rabbi,' and the second expressing regret that Herzog's indisposition had delayed the delegation's visit.[53] A week later, Alfred Woolf, George M. Gee, Mark Kleiner, Morris Lederman, Samuel Davies and Harry Landy, accompanied by US secretary Alfred Silverman, arrived in Israel, to be met by Maurice Jaffe, the head of Hechal Shlomo—the seat of Israel's Chief Rabbinate, named after Wolfson's father and established with Wolfson funds.

The next day, Woolf reported in due course,[54] 'we were greeted most graciously by Mrs Herzog at the apartment in Usisskin Street and, on the Rabbi joining us, the secretary formally introduced the members of the delegation.

> I then acquainted the Rabbi officially with the purpose of the delegation's visit and, in the course of my remarks, particularly emphasised two factors. The first was the spontaneous nature of the unanimity under which the call to him was

being made; and the second, the fact that all agreed that his acceptance was the one certain way in which to ensure a united Anglo-Jewish community.

The Rabbi, in reply, said that he was very touched by the call made to him, and conscious of the great responsibility that was entailed in his acceptance of it. He had especially, since Sunday night 16 May, when he had heard from the press and radio that he was to be given a unanimous call, given long and deep consideration to the matter, particularly in so far as it affected his wife and family.

His own devotion to the State of Israel—in whose service he was engaged, and in the solution of whose problems he had always wanted to be able to share—and the wrench that would be entailed by his acceptance, were immense. Nevertheless, after consultation with his wife and with certain eminent people, to whom he owed allegiance and who were likely to be affected by his decision, he had decided to accept the call, and hoped that the Almighty would guide and sustain him in his efforts.

He told us that his final decision had been reached only just before our arrival in Jerusalem, and had been the subject of all his thoughts since the Sunday before when, in hospital, he had learned of our committee's decision.

The delegation consisted of men who can fairly be claimed to be experienced in communal affairs, but one would not have recognised any of us as such from the emotion we felt and, I am afraid, showed on hearing the words of Rabbi Herzog. His humility; his grasp of the problems and anxieties besetting Anglo-Jewry and world Jewry; his obvious heartfelt devotion to the State of Israel; his heart-searching on the question of where he could be of greater service, without regard to his personal position; his decision to make what we of the delegation recognise as great a personal sacrifice as a man of his calibre has ever been called upon to make; his stated desire to attract youth—all these factors, combined with a straightforward practical and even analytical approach, made the occasion in Jerusalem on Monday afternoon, 24 May 1965, one which will live forever in our memories.

Let it be understood that we entered the presence of the Rabbi with some trepidation, for we all saw clearly the responsibility which lay on us to come home with an affirmative decision, and the bleak consequences of what might accrue if we did not do so.

The trepidation, as was evident from Herzog's response, was clearly misplaced. 'I am deeply moved,' he told the delegation, 'by this unanimous call. After deep contemplation and heart-searching, I have decided to respond.[55] Providence has directed me from the course in life which I have pursued for many years and has guided me back to the world of religious thought, a world with which my innermost essence has always been linked.

'I will consider it a privilege to serve the Jewish communities of Britain and the Commonwealth, which have a long and distinguished tradition. It will be a privilege to perform this service in a great land of freedom which has made, and continues to make, so vital a contribution to world civilisation.

'I hope I shall enjoy the full co-operation of all segments of the community. I need hardly say that I shall not be dominated by groups, institutions or individuals. I shall be guided by my religious conscience, by the precepts of Judaism, and by the concept of *Klal Yisrael*, ever aware of the inner meaning of the epoch of Jewish history now unfolding.

'The wrench of departure from Israel made my decision difficult indeed. However, I am motivated by an inner urge to serve the cause of Judaism and of the world of the spirit, against the canvas of faith and Jewish eternity. I pray that it will be given to me to advance the cause of Judaism, to deepen Jewish learning, and to contribute to the strengthening of the spiritual ties between Jewish communities the world over, and between the Jews of the British Commonwealth and Israel reborn. May the Almighty sustain me in my task.'[56]

Responding in similar terms to a message from a representative group of United Synagogue rabbis who, on the delegation's return, had offered their congratulations and co-operation, Herzog wrote: 'It has been a difficult decision indeed to make, but my religious conscience did not leave me free not to respond to a call of this nature. I look forward to a partnership of the historic mission of deepening the knowledge of Torah and Jewish learning and of advancing the cause of our immortal spiritual heritage.'[57] He had earlier told the *Daily Express*: 'A unanimous call from the entire British Jewish community—this was something I could not have turned down. It was not a matter of choice, but of conscience. I was ordained a rabbi, and felt it my duty to accept. After all, I was brought up in the British Isles. I know the Jewish community in Britain, and it will be a pleasure to serve them.'[58]

Days later, Wolfson told the Chief Rabbinate Conference that 'so much has been said, and so much written on the subject of the Chief Rabbinate since last we met, that I must confess to having some little difficulty in sorting out my own ideas from all those which have been pressed—I almost said forced—upon me, especially in the past two weeks.

'However, we have maintained what I am sure it will be agreed has been an even course and, speaking for the committee, I am happy to report the unanimous nature of its recommendation. We, all men of experience, record with gratification that, in presenting our report concerning the name of one man alone, we have done so without a dissentient voice—no, even that does not describe the atmosphere at our meeting. It is perhaps more accurate to say that only affirmative speeches were made, each hoping that the man of our unanimous choice would accept the call.

'I propose now to put to you the resolution, and sincerely hope that the spirit which moved the committee you appointed will inspire this great gathering to emulate its example and so give the new incumbent an encouraging welcome.'

Having received by acclamation the Conference's unanimous approval, Wolfson continued:

> The rabbi we have today chosen as our spiritual leader, and who is going to bring to our service his undoubted talents, is doing so, we recognise, with some humility, at no mean sacrifice. It is my contention, knowing him as I do, that there is only one thing that he will require of us in return: he will ask for our complete co-operation, our complete trust, our complete confidence, our complete loyalty, and our complete readiness to follow his leadership.
>
> He is entitled to ask this of us, and I want to be sure that we do not fail him. With him at the helm, we can hope to face up to the perplexing problems of this age without anxiety, and we can hope to attract and keep our youth within the fold.
>
> With him, we can hope to combat the evils of creeping assimilation and apathy and, in particular, we can by the force of his personality, deep learning, sagacity and real spirit of dedication make sure that we are no longer susceptible to the attacks of those who would desire to make inroads into our ancient heritage and who may, though perhaps disappointed at our decision, be prepared to give the new regime a fair chance.
>
> And out of this perhaps we may have the privilege in our days of seeing a truly United Hebrew Congregations of the British Commonwealth of Nations.[59]

Chapter Six

* * *

Those who were 'perhaps disappointed at our decision' were, indeed, prepared to give the new regime 'a fair chance.' After its sustained battering of the Chief Rabbinate during the Jacobs Affairs, the *Jewish Chronicle* commented guardedly: 'The problems are many. The community is leaderless, torn and confused, and everything that makes up Jewish life—knowledge, observance, family cohesiveness, sense of continuity—is receding. He [Herzog] has become heir to a situation where his potentialities for leadership and diplomatic skill will be employed to their limit.

'Some may be apprehensive that his very lack of experience may induce him to put too much trust in those who have had a great deal, and that he may in the course of time become the prisoner of one group or another. We believe this fear is unfounded ... [His] ready appreciation of the ideal of *Klal Yisrael*, of the unity of the Jewish people, raises the hope that we may be on the threshold of a new age in which Anglo-Jewish Orthodoxy will once again lay greater stress on what unites than on what divides.'[60]

From the communal left-wing emerged similar sentiments. The Union of Liberal and Progressive Synagogues offered Herzog 'our full co-operation in all of your endeavours, which are motivated by your devotion to the concept of *Klal Yisrael*. We trust that the differences which exist between the various religious communities will not obscure the strong bonds which unite all Jews. May you succeed in your expressed determination to strengthen the spiritual ties between Jewish communities the world over.'[61] The Chief Rabbi-elect replied: 'I am deeply grateful for your kind message and for your offer of co-operation in the cause of *Klal Yisrael*.'[62]

Welcoming Herzog's success, particularly after these expressions of support from across the divide, Jakobovits later remarked: 'I was greatly cheered when Herzog—a friend of mine, and adviser to four prime ministers of Israel, for whose extraordinary intellect and reputation I had the highest esteem—agreed to accept this key post, especially at a time when Anglo-Jewry was still in turmoil over the "Jacobs Affair" and many had written off the future of the British Chief Rabbinate altogether. After several years of communal commotion, nothing did more to break the back of the religious crisis in Anglo-Jewry, then still seething, than the mere announcement that a man of Jacob Herzog's eminence was to be the new incumbent of the beleaguered office.'[63]

From his vantage-point in New York, Jakobovits' joy was clearly tinged with an element of relief. Told by Cohen that, following his withdrawal from the race, the United Synagogue honorary officers had 'lately become tepid' towards him, he riposted: 'I must admit to reciprocity. As the whole drama (or comedy, as my brother Joseph called it) tediously unfolded, I certainly became more and more disenchanted with the position. This, combined with my disinclination from the outset to mortgage the rest of my life to *machloket* [controversy] and the flagellations of the JC and other malcontents, eventually prevailed on me to pull out while there was still time.

'The alleged "tepidness" (or is it sour grapes?) did not prevent Sir I. W. from trying to get me to withdraw my withdrawal in a twenty-minute call from London on the Thursday before the die was cast for Herzog! At any rate, I hope that in future neither my friends nor my detractors will ever again charge me with saying one thing and meaning another; I think I have now vindicated the sincerity of my statements that I did not seek the position. Incidentally, for my part,' he added, enigmatically, 'I still believe that had I not publicly withdrawn when I did, I might have landed myself in the same inextricable position in which Herzog eventually found himself ...'[64]

Following the appointment, Jakobovits received a printed card from Herzog expressing 'deep appreciation for your kind message of congratulations.' Appended was a handwritten note: 'Deeply moved by your very kind message. It was a difficult decision indeed, but I found no alternative but to accept. I have appreciated our friendship over the years and look forward to its deepening into the future. We will surely be in close contact.'[65]

The formal notification of Herzog's appointment came in a letter to him from Wolfson sent on the day of the election, accompanied by 'a pledge to support you in all your undertakings ... and all assistance in the vital task which lies before you of maintaining and enhancing the strength of Judaism throughout our lands.'[66]

Wolfson wrote also to the dayanim of the London Beth Din, inviting them 'once again to act as the Chief Rabbinate-in-Commission until such time as our new Chief Rabbi is officially inducted into office. I know that the community can repose complete trust in your being able to carry out these duties in exactly the same manner as has been the case when you acted during the absence of Chief Rabbi Brodie.'[67]

That very day, Brodie stepped down. His last sermon as Chief Rabbi had been preached the previous Shabbat at the Western Synagogue, where he spoke of the 'happy relationship' that existed between himself and the congregation, and his final engagement was a B'nai B'rith dinner in London. Expressing 'mixed feelings' about laying down the responsibility for the Chief Rabbinate which he had carried for seventeen years, he declared that, though he had experienced 'much anguish' while discharging his duties, it was not easy to give up his work. 'Through all the years, I learned to take it on the chin. While I shall not be sorry no longer to be responsible for this important office, that does not mean I shall lose interest in the community or be unconcerned about its welfare in spiritual and moral terms.'[68]

Reviewing Brodie's travails as Chief Rabbi—for which it was hardly free of blame—the *Jewish Chronicle* was in a conciliatory mood: 'A man whose every instinct disposed him to tranquillity was at once thrown into a raging conflict which tore the community asunder and whose effects have not yet entirely abated. Yet he pursued his course with tenacity and resolution, at great cost in peace of mind, personal happiness and health. In all he undertook, Rabbi Brodie has been a dedicated servant of the community, of the Jewish people, and the interests of Judaism as he saw them.'[69]

In August came an announcement that Herzog was expected to arrive in London in the first week of November, and would be formally installed a few days later.[70] A draft letter from the United Synagogue, dated 6 September 1965,[71] noted that 'the Installation Service has provisionally been arranged to take place at the St John's Wood Synagogue, Grove End Road, NW8, on Tuesday, 16 November.'

* * *

All this came to a sudden end when, on 31 August, Professor Hermann Zondek, an eminent Israeli endocrinologist, wrote to Wolfson, then holidaying in the south of France: 'Over the past six weeks, Dr Herzog's health has seriously deteriorated and during this time he has been under my constant medical supervision. It is my clear judgment that his state of health does not permit him to undertake the position of the Chief Rabbinate, as planned, now or in the near future. He is obliged to take a prolonged rest under medical supervision and under no account can undertake a public office of an exacting nature.'[72]

Three days later, a second letter was penned by Herzog himself. 'It is with deep pain,' he told Wolfson, 'that I have to inform you of my inability to undertake the position of the Chief Rabbinate of the United Hebrew Congregations of the British Commonwealth of Nations.

'Since this position was offered and accepted last May, my health has seriously deteriorated and, under medical advice, I am not in a position now or in the near future to embark on an assignment of this nature. As in these circumstances I could not possibly do justice to the position, I am obliged in fairness to the community and to my health, and with deepest regret, to apprise you of this development.

'I pray that it may be given me in other ways in the future to serve Judaism and the Jewish people with full effectiveness. I send through you to the Board of the United Synagogue my best wishes and deep regrets.'[73]

The background to the drama—in patches, at least—was painted by Wolfson on his return from France, when he addressed an emergency meeting of the Chief Rabbinate consultative and advisory committee at his Great

Universal House offices. He told his colleagues that he had been in the south of France when, some three weeks earlier, Pnina Herzog had contacted him with the news that her husband was ill. He understood that, with rest, Dr Herzog would recover fairly quickly and suggested that they went to Switzerland to recuperate. He intimated that the appointment 'could be held over for two or three months to enable Dr Herzog to regain his strength.'

Mrs Herzog had travelled to the south of France especially to see him. He had heard nothing further until 2 September, when he received an urgent call from her asking him to come to see them in Geneva on the following Sunday, at which point the two letters were handed to him. Sir Isaac was deeply grieved and upset, and felt it was essential that a statement be made to the press as soon as possible, before the news was made public through other sources.

The committee 'noted and approved' the prepared statement and agreed that a press conference be held that morning to enable the United Synagogue secretary to speak directly with the media.[74] 'A serious deterioration of his health' was the reason given to the press for Herzog's decision to stand down.[75]

Not all in the media saw it that way. Anglo-Jewry's most seasoned observer, journalist Sam Goldsmith, commented that 'those who know Herzog well will assure us that his illness was genuine and that he needed a long time to recover completely. This may be so. But there was an element of doubt about his enthusiasm for the post—he did take a long time to make up his mind. And many Israelis did say that he would be much more useful to the Jewish people as a top Israel diplomat than as a top rabbi. Also, some Anglo-Jews had their doubts about the appointment. They did not question, of course, Herzog's knowledge or piety or suitability in any other way. But he did not look before the whole world like a Chief Rabbi. It was the image that was missing.

'All these considerations must have made their mark upon a sensitive and perceptive man like Herzog. Coupled with a serious illness and a prolonged and tedious convalescence, there was enough force to prompt a drastic decision.'[76]

The *Jewish Chronicle* declared that, 'as we mentioned when welcoming his appointment, Dr Herzog is "a stranger both to the scene and the calling," and as he attempted to familiarise himself with them, his anxieties understandably grew. He has now been compelled to take the course which he was inclined to take in May.'[77]

And, in a dispatch from its Tel Aviv correspondent, *The Times* asserted: 'While the rabbi's illness was patently not diplomatic, religious circles here believe that it was not the only reason for his decision. He has expressed qualms about his competence to handle the touchy situation of British Jewry.'[78]

Against an unfolding—if confusing—backdrop, an interested party was soon to confront Herzog himself with these very doubts.

CHAPTER SEVEN

'When I Return ...'

FOLLOWING HERZOG'S WITHDRAWAL, the wheels of the Chief Rabbinate Council were soon back in motion—although, as became evident, at a 'more leisurely'[1] pace. Informing its members of 'the new situation,' the United Synagogue gave notice of a meeting of the council on 3 October 1965, originally planned to finalise arrangements for the Chief Rabbi's installation.[2]

In advance of the meeting, the ministerial body, piqued at its exclusion from the consultative process, re-asserted its right to have a say in the appointment. In addition to presenting its own short-list of preferred candidates, naming St John's Wood's Solomon Goldman alongside Jakobovits and Rabinowitz, the ministers presented ameliorative proposals which the honorary officers agreed to consider.[3] A later approach from the Union of Anglo-Jewish Preachers urged Wolfson to follow the precedent of the 1913 and 1948 elections 'in enabling us to express our views during the selection process.'[4]

One of their number—Raymond Apple, of Hampstead—contended that unless the wider issues of the Chief Rabbinate were first submitted to 'courageous and radical rethinking,' neither the ministry nor the community 'could allow a new man to be imposed upon us.' And questioning whether, even within the Orthodox community, the job of spiritual leadership had not become 'too big for one man,' he proposed the establishment of a council of ministers of the United Hebrew Congregations, whose chairman—elected every five years—would bear the title of Chief Rabbi.[5]

Within weeks, the Council of United Synagogue Ministers appeared to have had second thoughts over its choice of candidates. At a private meeting embracing its wider constituency, notable opposition was voiced to Jakobovits, while considerable support emerged for a new name on the agenda—that of Alexander Altmann, whose 1948 candidacy had provoked spirited debate. The ministers' support came despite Altmann's advocacy, in the years after Brodie's election, of a synthesis between Jewish theology and outside sources as an additional dimension giving—as he (and Jacobs) put it—'greater spiritual depth' to Judaism, a view widely attacked in Orthodox circles as 'deviationist.'

While Rabinowitz and Goldman remained on the ministers' agenda, the latter disclaimed any interest, declaring unashamedly to the *Sunday Times* that he was 'not big enough' for the post, and stimulating speculation in the community that, as minister at St John's Wood (the Chief Rabbi's traditional place of worship), he might be embarrassed at having to share the synagogue with someone who had been his 'rival' in the election. All three names, however, were presented to Wolfson at his second meeting with the ministers' executive committee.[6]

No names were discussed when the Chief Rabbinate Council met in early October, its principal task being 'to take official cognisance of the vacancy which has occurred and to advise on the necessary steps to fill it.' While several members urged caution and advised a measured approach in the search for a successor, others argued that the longer the delay, the more difficult it might be to find suitable names to submit to the Conference.[7]

That the latter view prevailed was apparent when, in late November, 'without a single word of comment from the platform and virtually none from the floor,' the US council set the search process in motion by requesting its executive committee 'to confer at an early date.' Sir Isaac's lack of comment, the *Jewish Chronicle* suggested, 'strongly contrasted with the manner in which he moved the same resolution in June of last year, giving the impression that there was no need to hurry.'[8]

The Federation of Synagogues, meanwhile, having patched up its differences with the US during the election of Herzog,[9] signified its readiness to 'cooperate fully' in choosing his successor and in the upkeep of his office.[10] As a result, ten places—the same number as before—were allocated to its delegates at the Chief Rabbinate Conference scheduled for February 1966, although, it was reported, their attendance could not be taken for granted.

The dispute a year earlier had been settled, in part, by agreement to cooperate with the United Synagogue on a unified Beth Din and reorganised kashrut authority, neither of which had been implemented. The US had delayed the former scheme until after the election, while the latter had been thwarted by Sephardi opposition. Dismayed by this failure to carry out the original agreement, the Federation signified that it would review the situation before rejoining the electoral process.[11]

In the event, the ten places remained vacant when the Conference reconvened, the Federation having decided to absent itself following 'the United Synagogue's refusal to create a unified Beth Din on which we would be strongly represented.' Wolfson, in opening the proceedings, made no mention of the boycott, but confirmed provision for five Federation representatives on the selection committee.

The main topic at the meeting was a bid to abandon the age limit of prospective candidates, previously set at fifty—with a provision that, 'in an exceptionable case, it might be thought desirable to appoint someone older.' After a recount, the delegates decided by fifty-two votes to forty-six to retain the wording. Although no names were mentioned, the move was seen as an attempt to strengthen the chances of sixty-year-old Rabinowitz, with former US president Ewen Montagu contending that 'the only reason the revised age limit was inserted was as an excuse to hide behind should there be a need to exclude certain names.'[12]

By April, the US–Federation rift was complete. Following what it described as 'the United Synagogue's failure to ratify the agreement,' the Federation voted to establish its own Beth Din 'with immediate effect.' Addressing its council, the president, Morris Lederman, asserted that 'the spirit of co-operation and good will shown by US representatives seemed to have vanished into thin air once it became evident that there would be some considerable delay before a new Chief Rabbi was appointed.'

The agreement, he claimed, was to have been ratified in November, with the Federation taking 'the logical view' that it would be better for unification measures to become effective before the Chief Rabbi assumed office. The US, on the other hand, 'was satisfied that things should be left as they are, a situation we could not accept. It seems that its previous friendly attitude was based less on a desire for communal unity than on the Federation's promise of financial support of the Chief Rabbinate.'

But, said Lederman, this was 'no reflection on that great personality and man of vision, Sir Isaac Wolfson. With Sir Isaac at the helm, I still trust and hope that, despite the steps we have been obliged to take, there will be avenues for co-operation in the defence and furtherance of Torah-true Judaism.'[13]

Lederman's trust in Sir Isaac was not entirely misplaced. Within the month, the United Synagogue president was off to the United States, ostensibly on a business trip, but—wrote the Israeli religious weekly *Panim el Panim*, whose informed sources were close to Wolfson—'it was impossible to conceal from oneself that the principal "business" for which he was going was to persuade Rabbi Jakobovits to withdraw his refusal and accept the position of Chief Rabbi. "When I return from America," Sir Isaac had declared, "we shall be able to proceed with the election of a Chief Rabbi."'[14]

* * *

The last Sunday in June was destined to be a busy day for Wolfson. Back from the United States, but remaining tight-lipped, he fended off questions about the purpose of his visit, which continued to spark widespread speculation over whom he had seen.

Among the names mentioned was that of thirty-eight-year-old Norman Lamm, associate rabbi of the Jewish Center of New York, and widely described as 'a new contender for the Chief Rabbinate.' His chances, it was being suggested, were being rated as 'especially high should Dr Jakobovits again withhold his candidature,' and this had 'probably necessitated the approach to Rabbi Lamm, who could count on the support of those members of Sir Isaac's selection committee—and finally of the Chief Rabbinate Conference itself—who would have preferred Dr Jakobovits had he been available.'

Asked whether he had been approached and, if so, whether he considered himself as a candidate, Lamm replied: 'It would be no service to the office if I said that I had accepted or refused the offer. When the London selectors have made their choice, I shall be glad to give you a story.'[15]

Over Jakobovits' candidature, similar uncertainty hovered. While denying local reports that he had declined an offer, he added, cryptically: 'My intention has always been to remain here. But I can never say what pressures will be brought to bear.' American circles suggested that, during recent conversations with Wolfson, Jakobovits had been urged to offer his candidacy and had indicated his willingness to do so, provided he received a unanimous call. Such a possibility was seen as doubtful, however, in view of the 'substantial support' being shown for Rabinowitz.[16]

On the morning of the final selection-committee meeting, the US honorary officers held consultations with a joint delegation from the Preachers' Union and the US Council of Ministers, and, separately, with the London Beth Din. Wolfson told the ministers that the committee was left with 'only two names to be considered'—those of Rabinowitz, aged sixty, and Jakobovits, aged forty-five. 'Rabbi Lamm can be disregarded, as that gentleman is not prepared to leave his present post.'

Apart from the age gap, said Wolfson, the two remaining rabbis differed 'in many other ways, particularly in temperament.' If points were to be awarded for the qualities one should look for in the future Chief Rabbi, Dr Jakobovits would, he felt, 'win quite convincingly,' a view widely shared by those on the committee. 'If Rabbi Jakobovits can be convinced that he has a mission to perform in Anglo-Jewry, and that Anglo-Jewry itself wants and needs him, the committee will have achieved the task of obtaining the Chief Rabbi for which the community is undoubtedly waiting.'

Speaking on behalf of the Council of Ministers, Solomon Goldman described Rabinowitz as 'unpredictable—one never knows which way he will jump.' Of the two names mentioned, he said, they would prefer Jakobovits on account of his personality, 'a young man who would grow in the position and would work with his colleagues.' For the Preachers' Union, Isaac Livingstone thought it necessary to canvass its one hundred-plus members before a preference could be given.

Despite this view, the meeting ended with an agreed statement, which would be delivered that afternoon to the selection committee, that 'the representatives of the ministry, in their individual capacities, had expressed their opinion in favour of Rabbi Jakobovits.'[17]

The Beth Din's meeting with the honorary officers was of similar hue. Morris Swift opined that it was 'a pity that the position has been so lowered that Rabbi Dr Rabinowitz is a candidate.' His own service in the ministry, said Swift, had coincided with that of Rabinowitz, and he had known him since childhood. 'He would bring down the standard of the Chief Rabbi to a very low ebb. This is not a personal vendetta, but I know that he is persona non grata with the other ministers.'

Declaring that the Beth Din knew the pulse of the Orthodox rabbinate in both Britain and the Commonwealth, Abraham Rapoport and Meyer Steinberg confirmed Swift's view. 'I have nothing against Rabbi Rabinowitz,' said Rapoport, 'but I know he is persona non grata with Orthodox rabbis all over the world. As far as they are concerned, Rabbi Jakobovits is the best.'

Arye Leib Grossnass asserted that, in the Beth Din's opinion, the essential qualities for a Chief Rabbi were honesty and integrity. 'He must be a God-fearing person and devoid of evil. He must work in co-operation with the Beth Din and, from a religious and scholarly point of view, must not act irresponsibly or lose the trust of the dayanim.'[18]

While these meetings were taking place, questions of another nature were surfacing across the Atlantic. In discussions with Wolfson during his visit to New York, Jakobovits had suggested that any decision and publicity about his possible appointment be delayed until he had been able to establish whether 'conditions indispensable to my acceptance existed.' Wolfson and his colleagues, however, 'were evidently prepared to take the chance of extending the call to me without knowing what my response would be—whether, that is, I would succeed in securing the prior conditions of which I had apprised him.'[19] Enlarging on these concerns, on the eve of the crucial selection meeting, Jakobovits wrote to Norman Cohen:

> I had intended—and still intend, though now under somewhat changed circumstances—to visit London for a few days, primarily on a discreet 'peace mission.' I could not contemplate assuming the office in the existing climate of bitterness and sharp disunity, constantly exposed to campaigns of abuse, subversion and misrepresentation. I feel I can either resolve

the crisis now before I assume office, when I enjoy many distinct advantages, or I will be saddled with it for the rest of my life. Since I am not prepared to face the latter alternative, the complete success of my visit will determine my response, as I have made clear to Sir Isaac.

I realise that the odds are against me, and if I fail I will have no personal regrets. But I think there is some reasonable chance that, with skill, sincerity and some genuine gestures of good will and conciliation, I might succeed. What I have in mind is to secure a firm agreement for a modus vivendi with the opposition (I am thinking of the Jacobs-JC crowd, of course, not the Federation, which bothers me little) based on some tangible 'agreement to disagree,' within well-defined limits, in exchange for an assurance that the war on Orthodoxy and its institutions will be called off and that the office of the Chief Rabbi will be unconditionally respected, even if its jurisdiction and rulings may not always be recognised.

With this agreement may well go a thorough overhaul and modernisation of the functions of the Chief Rabbinate, with greater emphasis on opportunities for spiritual leadership in the intellectual sense (lectures, university visits, regular meetings with various professional groups, etc.) and less on purely ceremonial, administrative and judicial duties, which would be decentralised. I would, of course, work out a detailed outline of these proposals beforehand.

I have a feeling that both sides—and I include the Beth Din here—may by now be tired of the acrimonious and purely destructive conflict and look for an honourable way out by reconciliation. Once a young Chief Rabbi is appointed, the efforts either to crown Jacobs or to destroy the office must needs be abandoned, so that this may be a propitious moment to restore unity (especially if it were true, as Sir Isaac surmised, that Jacobs was on his way out of Britain).

Of course, there will have to be some give-and-take on a few matters of substance on both sides, but principally I think what is needed is to change the atmosphere, to restore trust and friendliness, and on my part to exchange the carefully built-up image of 'right-wing' militancy into the much truer likeness of 'enlightened Orthodoxy' in outlook, firmness in loyalty to halachic principles, moderation and personal tolerance in public relations, and a critically independent stance to both right and left extremism.[20]

Thus it was, with the situation still clouded in doubt, that Wolfson disregarded Jakobovits' request to delay the process, and, having notified the media of his colleagues' decision, telephoned New York with their unanimous invitation.[21]

Earlier that day, some twenty-five (out of thirty-seven) members of the selection committee had gathered in conclave at Woburn House, London—the Federation's five delegates being notable absentees—with the names of Rabinowitz, Jakobovits, and Lamm briefly before them. Advised that Lamm had declared himself unavailable, they then discussed the candidacy of Rabinowitz, whose two supporters were soon persuaded to withdraw his name. When these tidings reached Rabinowitz in Jerusalem, the former South African Chief Rabbi was quick to tell the emerging British Chief Rabbi: 'I always knew the better man would lose.'[22]

'The whole thing has burst upon me with the force of an avalanche,' Jakobovits declared on receiving the news. 'I need a breathing-space—and an opportunity to consult with some friends—before reaching a decision.'[23]

Having initially scheduled a gathering of the Chief Rabbinate Conference (or, in the event of Jakobovits' refusal, of the selection committee) for the following week, Wolfson was compelled to postpone the meeting until after the breathing-space expired. Paying the price for his precipitous action, he found himself drafting a letter to his colleagues which, on further reflection, he never dispatched:

> Before we dispersed on Sunday evening, I gave an undertaking either to call the Conference on Sunday next or, in its place, a further meeting of the committee. I now find that I was unduly optimistic, and perhaps a little unfair to the other party concerned, in trying to speed up the programme—though I still feel I was not unjustified in having attempted to do so.
>
> The gentleman whom we unanimously agreed I should approach has intimated his acceptance in principle, but very much desires a little more time in which to consider the whole matter from all angles before allowing the announcement to be made officially and in public. I have had two telephone conversations with him and I feel he is entitled to make this request, and in those circumstances I think we should consider holding the Conference to appoint him some time in September.

The national newspapers have, quite characteristically, 'jumped the gun,' and there is nothing we can do about that; but perhaps what they have done will not be to our disadvantage, and if we now await the required time—I believe I shall get his full and affirmative answer not later than by the end of July—we shall be able to proceed with the appointment as intended.

I also think on reflection, in the time that has elapsed since we were together, that it is perhaps better for all concerned that we do not bring pressure to bear for a hasty decision which might not be appropriate for an appointment to so high an office. In those circumstances, you will not be receiving a notice for a meeting of either the committee or the Conference this coming weekend, and I do hope you will understand.[24]

Within days, Jakobovits announced his visit to London, during which he planned to hold talks 'with various communal leaders' before reaching a decision. On the prospects of agreement with the parties concerned, to both the right and the left, he told the *Sunday Times*: 'I cannot imagine that anyone who knows me well, or knows my writings, would call me either unyielding or a fundamentalist. Broadly speaking, I should call myself a supporter of enlightened Orthodoxy. One requires a certain flexibility, especially in religious matters, where success lies in persuasion. One cannot persuade by rigidity.'[25]

'Even at this stage,' Jakobovits later admitted, 'I was still haunted by anxieties over the overwhelming responsibilities I was assuming. Amélie was even more fearful, especially when she recalled what had happened to the families of former incumbents. I consulted widely, turning to trusted leaders and friends in several countries, including the dayanim and leading rabbis in London, Rabbi Soloveitchik and others in New York, and Chief Rabbi Issar Yehudah Unterman in Israel. They all urged me to accept—mostly because they genuinely believed I would succeed, but in some cases, I suspect, because they wanted to avoid the selection of a less acceptable candidate.'[26]

Among the 'trusted leaders and friends' to whom he turned was Isidor Grunfeld, by then retired from the London Beth Din. 'Very much contrary to my personal ambitions and aspirations,' Jakobovits confided, 'it may be my fate to step into Herzog's unused shoes. The unique honour of this call is equalled only by its crushing burden, and I stand before an agonising decision in determining whether to give up my happy, peaceful and constructive life here in favour of an uncertain future.'[27]

Foremost among his other confidants was the original owner of the shoes, whose advice he sought before visiting London. 'No one realises better than you,' he told Herzog, 'what an agonising decision faces me, and I believe no one can help me more to make it. For this reason, I turn to you for counsel and assistance in the utmost confidence.

> I have made my acceptance dependent, above all, on succeeding in bringing about a reconciliation and some modus vivendi with the JC-Jacobs faction as an indispensable condition to communal unity and thus the discharge of my duties.
>
> If I succeed in my 'peace mission,' I may have rendered Anglo-Jewry a greater service before assuming office than I might ever have occasion to do later, and I will be confident that the gigantic burdens of the office are not entirely beyond my capacity to bear. If I fail and therefore decline the offer, I will have no personal regrets in continuing my present happy and peaceful life here.
>
> Now, in my considerations and efforts, I seek your invaluable information and help on these three points:
>
> 1. Were there any specific reasons, other than those publicised, which prompted you to withdraw? Obviously, having now to continue where you left off, it is of the most crucial importance to me to know precisely of any hurdles or disappointments you encountered after your acceptance, so that I may benefit from your experience and not find myself in a similar position afterwards.
>
> 2. I understand that you had already initiated some discreet discussions with the JC group. What terms of accommodation did they suggest to you, and how far were you able to reach an understanding with them in principle? I quite realise that there will have to be some give-and-take on a few matters of substance, but I think it is mainly a question of creating a new climate of good will and mutual trust. I am prepared to go a long way to achieve this, and once again your experience in this direction would be invaluable to me.
>
> 3. Above all, could you make some discreet approaches to these quarters with a view to building the necessary bridges for me? While I am busy putting out some other feelers, I think that no one could be more effective here than you. You know me well enough to be assured that I am not the 'right-wing extremist' they have made me out to be in the past. Unless I can correct this false image of militancy and inflex-

ibility in their mind and, through them, in the public mind, I cannot begin to win their and the community's confidence, and thus to restore respect for the office.

I realise, of course, the burden I am imposing on you in making these requests. My only justification for doing so is the public and historic interest at stake here, and my knowledge that you would feel more committed to this cause than anyone else.[28]

'The reasons for my withdrawal,' Herzog replied, 'are only those which were publicised. After my acceptance, I encountered only promises of co-operation.' Turning to the second and third points, he continued:

I had absolutely no discussions with the JC group. When my name was being discussed, the editor of the JC and the owner of the JC tried to dissuade me. Once I was nominated, they congratulated me; however, I had absolutely no contact with them on any matter of substance.

It had been my intention to ask the community for a cooling-off period of six months to a year, to enable me to study the problems on the spot and then to make my decision. I, too, felt that the first objective would have to be to attempt to create a climate of good will.

I will be happy to [make discreet approaches], but I have frankly a lack of technique at present, as I have not been in touch with anybody in London since my withdrawal. Let me, however, weigh up the matter and see what I can possibly do.

You realise that, in view of what has happened and in view of my present position, I cannot possibly be involved in internal matters of Anglo-Jewry. However, I wish to be of help and shall look out discreetly for appropriate opportunities. Rest assured that, with all my heart, I wish to help you.

I am not sure your idea of a 'peace mission' is a good one. If the various factions know that your acceptance may be dependent on the outcome of such a mission, they may put up obstacles in your way. Having received unanimous recommendation, I would think that the wisest course for you will be to accept without delay, while asking publicly for the co-operation of all sections of the community in the efforts you will make to restore peace.

You could add that you will require a little time to acquaint yourself with the problems at first hand, but that you will be frank with the community at the various stages of your study of the problems. You pray for guidance in uniting Anglo-Jewry in dedication to Judaism and to Klal Yisrael and you hope that all sections of the community will co-operate with you in facing up to the crucial problem of Jewish spiritual survival in our time.

Often, over the past year, I pondered the meaning of my experience. It has occurred to me that maybe I was the instrument of Providence in blunting the edge of crisis in Anglo-Jewry when it was reaching its crucial point. In public life, it is difficult to sustain momentum of crisis beyond a certain period. With my acceptance, the crisis subsided; with my withdrawal, the whole matter flagged. Surrounding your nomination, the tension was much less.

This, I believe, gives you opportunities which you could not have had a year ago. The question now is how to capitalise on the relative tranquility and to take up the position in good will. I believe that the basic sense of discipline and institutional attachment of Anglo-Jewry is in your favour. The spectre of schism is so great that you will have many avenues through which to work.

If, after a few years, you will find that the controversies are such that you cannot continue, you will always be able to withdraw, and you will surely find many other possibilities open to you. This thought, however, you should keep entirely to yourself and you should plunge into the matter without delay, as there is nothing to hope for from delay. I have the feeling that all sides will give you a year or so to chart your course. During this time, you will be able to assess the forces and find your way.[29]

Reinforcing this advice, Herzog wrote further on the eve of the visit: 'Again I would urge you not to give the impression of the promise of co-operation by the critics being a condition for acceptance. To my mind, your course should be as follows: (a) To meet with and hear the views of the various groupings. (b) To declare your acceptance, coupling it with a statement that the breach is deep indeed, but that maybe not all hope is lost for an ultimate narrowing of differences and peace, or at least a modicum of peaceful co-existence. (c) To appeal for time to study the situation and for co-operation from all factions during this period. (d) To appoint an advisory council to the Chief Rabbi of moderate people led, for example, by a man like Grunfeld, which should study the situation and make recommendations to you ...

'It is my general impression, though I cannot prove it, that the crisis in Anglo-Jewry has boiled over and that the community at large will resist any attempt in the future to revive it. The JC is by no means all-powerful and surely cannot be unaware of its failure. Moreover, there are other forces of no less consequence. And, in any event, you will have plenty of time and possibility for manoeuvre.'[30]

Herzog's assurance to Jakobovits that 'the reasons for my withdrawal are only those which were publicised' hid an underlying cause which became widely known only well after his death, some six years later. Having decided to accept the Chief Rabbinate, Herzog suffered—in the words of his biographer[31]—'a psychosomatic collapse ... He had made a decision and sincerely meant to carry it out, but he was mentally incapable of confronting it. He could not wholeheartedly renounce the political world and choose the rabbinical one. But if Yaacov was having second thoughts, he was unable to alter his decision. He had already resigned from his government posts, he was awaited in London, and his family was proud of his new status. Torn between opposites and unable to cope with the fateful choice, he collapsed.'

Pnina Herzog acknowledged the psychosomatic nature of her husband's collapse. 'It was a combination of his own inner struggles,' she said. 'Yaacov himself told Professor Zondek that the illness stemmed from his mental state.'[32] Herzog's brother, Chaim (Vivian), described the reaction as 'a tremendous inner conflict. Yaacov was very distressed at that time. Though he did finally accept the proposal from Britain, I'm not sure he was happy about it. He loved diplomatic work too much; he always wanted to be at the centre of things and was afraid to leave it. Perhaps his inner struggle about it made him fall ill.'[33]

* * *

Accompanied by his wife, Jakobovits reached London on 27 July and speedily began a series of consultations with a cross-section of leaders, including members of the Beth Din, Haham Solomon Gaon, and other prominent rabbis, the US honorary officers, and, at their request, the chairmen of the Reform and Liberal movements.

On his departure a week later, he declared: 'I was exceedingly pleased with my visit. I was received with great friendliness by all groups and individuals I have met here. I was ready to meet people from various spheres of the community in order to be able to measure up the local situation. I am now getting the feel of the temperaments.'[34]

Chapter Seven

Within days, he translated that 'feel' into words, in a lengthy memorandum to Wolfson and his colleagues:

> Your unanimous recommendation to call me to assume the spiritual leadership of British Jewry has honoured me with the most exalted rabbinical distinction as well as challenged me with the world's most exacting and commanding rabbinical responsibility. It has also placed me before the most agonising decision of my life.
>
> I owe it to you, who have selected me for this supreme office, to give you some explanations for my hesitation in confirming my acceptance:
>
> 1. To exchange the peace, security, happiness and freedom of my present position for the imponderables of an unknown future will involve a very heavy personal sacrifice which could not be compensated by any added wealth or fame of themselves.
>
> I presently enjoy all the comforts and honours any rabbi could wish for. I have no factions or dissension to contend with. I am a free man, accountable to no one except my conscience. I can say what I want, write what I wish, dress as I please, and lecture where I like. Whether inside or outside my congregation, my time is devoted exclusively to constructive and literary efforts.
>
> It will also not be easy to wrench myself and my family from our present congenial environment, particularly to transplant my children to a new soil probably offering them less educational and other facilities than they have here. Indeed, the two eldest of my six children would in all likelihood have to stay behind to complete their studies.
>
> 2. While I am fully aware of the unique and historic challenge the Chief Rabbinate would offer me, I am also all too conscious of my own limitations. This is no false modesty, but simply a questioning self-assessment in the light of the awesome responsibilities that would devolve on me in such a key position at this critical time in Jewish and human history.
>
> It should, therefore, not be unreasonable if, before I commit myself to such a gigantic task, I reassure myself that the challenge is not entirely beyond my capacities, by personal discussions with those on whose support the success of my work will largely depend. I want my London visit to convince

me that conditions exist for doing justice to my assignment.

3. Above all, I regard my ability to resolve the existing religious crisis in Anglo-Jewry as a crucial test of the community's confidence in my leadership and my own confidence in measuring up to the skills needed in the discharge of my duties.

I cannot work in a climate of continuous tension, nor under the pressure of abuse, subversion and misrepresentation. Communal peace, good will and unity are indispensable prerequisites to my success in the office, and therefore to my acceptance.

The dignity of the Chief Rabbinate, too, cannot be upheld in a community rent by ill-will and destructive conflicts. I am not prepared, or able, to preside over a constant succession of quarrels and hostilities in which the community will be reduced to a shambles, my office to a partisan battle headquarters, and my health to a wreck.

To sum up my conclusions, I deem it my ineluctable moral duty to heed your call and to dedicate all my energies to your challenge, provided the essential conditions for a successful incumbency, as listed below, can be secured.

A. *Resolving the Religious Crisis*
I believe I can assume that all parties to the recent conflict are by now thoroughly tired of the costly strife, disenchanted with the sterile results achieved, saddened by the bitterness and disunity which have disrupted the once-solid structure of the community, and anxious to find an honourable solution.

For my part, I am prepared to go a very long way in my quest for a lasting reconciliation, based on friendliness and mutual trust as well as on respect for our sacred traditions. Of course, I realise there will have to be some give-and-take on a few matters of substance, but primarily I think the situation calls for a new outlook and attitude on all sides, the creation of an atmosphere of good will, and an amicable 'agreement to disagree' within some well-defined limits.

It would be premature at this stage to spell out in detail the proposals for a formula I have in mind. Meanwhile, the following basic terms of an understanding should not be beyond reach or reason:

1. The 'Left wing' must agree
   (a) to respect the Chief Rabbinate as an institution which

is and will remain Orthodox, reflecting the religious loyalties, if not necessarily the views, of the overwhelming majority of religious Jews;

(b) to leave the determination and interpretation of Jewish law to duly qualified experts, and to oppose any incitement against their rulings by pressure groups, newspapers or especially individuals who themselves neither acknowledge nor practise the dictates of the halachah;

(c) to refrain from subversion, abuse and denigration directed at any established communal institution or its leaders; and

(d) to make the maximum positive contribution to the enrichment and unity of Jewish life.

2. The 'Right wing' must agree

(a) to look upon the Chief Rabbinate as serving to unite all segments of the community;

(b) to accept that dissent from tradition and authority is an inescapable fact of modern life, to be most effectively met by friendly persuasion and intelligent argument, not by denunciation and ostracism;

(c) to concentrate its energies on enhancing its own position and public respect, not on attacking others; and

(d) to work together with others in all areas that have no bearing on halachic considerations.

3. The Chief Rabbi must agree

(a) to revise the functions of the Chief Rabbinate (see Section B below) so that it will meet present-day needs and command the respect of the entire community;

(b) to promote good will and moderation without sacrifice of any principles he is appointed to defend;

(c) to seek common ground for joint enterprises among all factions, and not to limit his services to those who agree with him; and

(d) to endeavour to establish a modus vivendi with those who, while not submitting completely to the rabbinic jurisdiction of his office, are prepared morally, if not financially, to support it.

B. *Functions of the Chief Rabbinate*

The Chief Rabbinate, as a nineteenth-century institution with even far older roots, clearly requires some far-reaching modifications to meet the conditions and challenges of the present time. In its existing form, it was conceived nearly 100 years ago to provide the more or less homogeneous communities of an entire country with a single spiritual leader wielding rabbinic authority, while all other occupants of pulpits were invested merely with the status of ministers and preachers.

Since then, the Anglo-Jewish community has vastly grown in numbers and diversity, and this growth must be reflected in updating the functions both of the Chief Rabbinate and of the ministry. The manifold needs and trends of today can no longer be served by only one fully recognised rabbi.

While I must again defer detailed proposals on this reorganisation until I have thoroughly familiarised myself with local conditions, I may here present a general outline of the required changes as I see them.

1. The Chief Rabbi's foremost charge, claiming priority over ceremonial, administrative and juridical duties, must be the exercise of spiritual leadership. He must mobilise the community's religious and intellectual resources to make Judaism vibrant and relevant to the issues of our times. He must direct the interpretation of Jewish thought in contemporary terms, and he must stimulate an interest in Jewish living and thinking, especially among the youth and intellectuals.

He must frequently consult with his colleagues to evolve the most meaningful form of synagogue services, wedding ceremonies and other ministrations. At the same time, he is primarily responsible for strengthening the religious loyalties of the masses and for broadening their understanding of Judaism. He must also project a creative image of Jewish moral and religious teachings in the world at large.

Accordingly, a major part of his time should be devoted to regular meetings with rabbis and ministers, visits to Jewish student bodies at the universities, discussions with various professional groups, popular lectures, and literary activities.

He should also establish high-level contacts with the supreme rabbinical leaders in Israel, America and other countries to consult and pronounce on Jewish religious policies and moral attitudes of universal Jewish significance—an acute need so far entirely unmet.

These pursuits require much contemplation, a free mind, and a prior claim on his time.

I therefore propose reducing all other functions to a minimum. If congregations or organisations want the Chief Rabbi for lectures, conference addresses, consultations on religious direction, or even debates, they should be free to call on his services. But if they seek his presence for the opening of synagogues, the induction of ministers, the presiding at meetings or the arbitration of communal disputes, they may not find him so accessible. These duties must, in the main, be delegated to others.

2. This should be accomplished by a drastic diffusion of responsibilities. The function of the Beth Din, as the authoritative interpreters of halachah, including the administration of shechitah and kashrut, should be augmented by a Council of Rabbis and Ministers to assist the Chief Rabbi in the formulation of religious policies, directives and activities, and in the discharge of his responsibilities in other areas. Such a Council should be composed of ten to twenty members, serving in rotation for two to four years.

I also envisage setting up a 'Chief Rabbi's Cabinet' consisting of six rabbis and ministers appointed to take charge, respectively, of Jewish education, liaison with students, ceremonial functions, inter-faith contacts, inter-Jewish co-operation, and Israel affairs. To be effective and to contribute to raising the ministry's status and prospects of promotion, these services must be adequately compensated.

3. To command the respect and loyalty of all groups, and to be equally accessible to them, I believe the Chief Rabbi should have no political affiliations. He would, of course, lend his special support to religious organisations, whether political or not, but only as Chief Rabbi, not as a member or an honorary officer.

Likewise, the Chief Rabbi should make all reasonable efforts to keep his office outside and above communal controversies and organisational disputes. In part, this will inevitably be achieved by shifting the main burden of his functions from representational and administrative duties to the spiritual direction and instruction of the community.[35]

* * *

Jakobovits flew back to New York 'under a cloud of official silence,'[36] saying that he would decide whether to accept the position within a few days of his return. 'It would be presumptuous,' he added, 'to describe my visit as fruitful, since the result of the latest moves can be expected only in the long run. I know that I owe British Jewry an answer, but early publicity could prejudice my present inquiries.'

The official silence was broken within days when, 'with the deepest humility,' Jakobovits wrote to Wolfson: 'I can now inform you of my willingness to accept the historic challenge of the Chief Rabbinate of Great Britain and the Commonwealth, if your Council decide to offer me this supreme honour, together with the awesome responsibilities vested in this office, subject to the official ratification of the attached terms and conditions previously agreed upon between us.[37] Upon receiving your formal confirmation, I would be prepared to resign from my present position after six months' notice.

> You know how hard it has been for me to reach this fateful decision. The New World offered me and my family much happiness, contentment and opportunity for service. But I feel my moral duty to respond to your call is ineluctable.
>
> In this decision I have been influenced, in large measure, by the great friendliness, the sincere yearning for leadership, and the enthusiastic reaction to my policy proposals which I encountered in the numerous discussions with the leaders of the community during my recent encouraging visit to London. I am now convinced that, with dynamic, imaginative and tolerant leadership on my part, I can reasonably count on the unflinching support of the overwhelming majority of Anglo-Jewry, and on the respect and good will of the rest.
>
> Also decisive in my considerations was your extraordinary personal graciousness, combined with your magnanimity in securing the lay and material foundations [the proposed building of a Chief Rabbinate Centre, a personal gift from Isaac Wolfson and his brother, Charles][38] for raising the Chief Rabbinate into a distinguished and effective instrument of spiritual governance.
>
> I pray that the Almighty may find me worthy to be His principal public servant and spokesman in British Jewry. May He prosper our joint endeavours to inaugurate an era of communal glory and spiritual grandeur.[39]

Wolfson replied, 'with the greatest possible pleasure,' that he had put into motion the steps necessary for the Conference to be called on Sunday, 11 September—'when I am very confident that the proposal which I shall make as Chairman of the Committee vested with the task of selecting our future Spiritual Leader will be received with much gratification.

'You may be assured that the co-operation which you found manifested in London during your recent brief stay in our midst will become the pattern for the tenure of your office as Chief Rabbi, and that, with the overwhelming support of the spiritual and lay leaders assured to you, the future can only be of the brightest hue. With the blessing of the Almighty, we can look forward to an era which will stimulate and inspire the whole of the Anglo-Jewish community.'[40]

At the September gathering, attended by around one hundred of the two hundred and fifty nationwide delegates, Jakobovits' appointment was formally approved 'without dissent or discussion.'[41] When the Conference had met in June, Wolfson told his colleagues, he had refrained from giving his personal conclusions 'until I had heard the opinions of everybody present. It was my intention on that occasion to ensure that it was your committee who made the choice and that it could never again be said that the choice was mine, and that the committee had merely "rubber-stamped" my decision.'

He had been 'immensely heartened,' he added, by the fact that the committee's choice had been unanimous, and that it had coincided with the views expressed by the London Beth Din—acting as the Chief-Rabbinate-in-Commission—and by the representatives of the ministry.

Within the hour, by telephone, cable, and letter, Wolfson expressed his 'greatest possible pleasure' in informing Jakobovits of the Conference's decision. 'I now have the great honour,' he declared, 'to invite you to accept the appointment, the delegates having pledged themselves with unanimity to support you in all your undertakings.'[42]

'In accepting this supreme and historic charge to guide the spiritual destinies of a major segment of our people,' Jakobovits replied, 'I want solemnly to pledge to you, and through you to British Jewry, the enthusiastic dedication of all my energies, and of every resource of mind and heart I possess, to the successful discharge of my manifold duties and awesome responsibilities.

'In trying to vindicate the confidence and high hopes of countless Jews in the Commonwealth and beyond, I shall spare no effort in promoting the appreciation of traditional Judaism and in raising the stature of Anglo-Jewry as a harmonious and creative community worthily serving our people and its eternal faith, as well as enriching and ennobling British life in general.'[43]

In a second, more personal letter to Wolfson, Jakobovits noted that 'my decision, hard as it was, to heed your call was in large measure influenced, and made infinitely easier, by your personal graciousness and by my reassuring knowledge that at the head of the community stands a dynamic personality of your distinction, vision and religious stature. I rejoice in anticipating the privilege of working closely in the cause of Judaism with one of the outstanding men of our time.'[44]

Responding to both letters, Wolfson wrote: 'I feel confident that with your appointment Anglo-Jewry can now look forward to a new era, and one which will bring unity to the community, which has been long divided through lack of leadership.'[45]

* * *

Behind closed doors, in New York and London, another drama was beginning to unfold which, while remaining under wraps for several months, went some way towards explaining Jakobovits' statement that the Federation of Synagogues 'bothers me little.' In a BBC Hebrew-service broadcast the day after his appointment, he lost no time in referring to the divided community.

Of Louis Jacobs and his breakaway movement, the Chief Rabbi-designate declared: 'Dr Jacobs today leads a medium-sized congregation that calls itself Orthodox, but is regarded as heterodox by most Orthodox Jews. It is one of several independent synagogues in London and the provinces, and I believe it should not, as such, create any insuperable or intractable problems.'

However, said Jakobovits, 'the Federation of Synagogues is a different matter. It unites a number of London synagogues. It has never formally accepted or recognised the jurisdiction of the Chief Rabbi. Its non-recognition is nothing new and is used merely for partisan ends by those who want to see the hegemony of the Chief Rabbinate limited.'

For its part, the Federation anticipated Jakobovits' appointment with a strongly worded statement headed 'The first wrong step,' declaring that 'the United Synagogue's choice of the man who will be its "Chief Rabbi" is its own affair. We are not greatly exercised about who will be given the post, for whoever is elected will not have any mandate to represent or speak in the name of the whole of British Jewry.

'Not only will he be unable to speak for a number of *kehillot* in the metropolis—from the extreme right to the extreme left—but he will most certainly be unable to speak in the name of the second largest *kehillah*—the Federation of Synagogues. It can also be assumed that some provincial congregations will also refuse to recognise his jurisdiction.'[46]

Back in America, and reviewing afresh the ongoing divisions in Orthodox ranks, Jakobovits began forging links with the Federation's newly nominated Principal Rabbi, New York-based Eliezer Kirzner, and with the Sephardim's Solomon Gaon in London.

To the Haham, he wrote: 'The only effective path is to demonstrate the solidarity of the organisations—and especially the rabbinates—which really matter. I have little doubt that, once I assume my office, the tide will gradually turn, and the hegemony and overall unity of Orthodoxy will ultimately be restored. My problem is to halt and reverse the corroding influences in the meantime.

'To this end, it would be invaluable if you could issue some public statement declaring your delight and confidence in our eventual partnership, based on the intimate personal and official relations anticipated between us, and expressing your hopes for a new era of peace and understanding in the community, founded on Anglo-Jewry's two largest and oldest religious groups working harmoniously together through our two offices.'[47]

Jakobovits' approach to the Federation was in more circumspect terms. 'This letter,' he wrote in the first instance to Lederman, 'is addressed to you privately in a purely personal capacity, as between one man concerned with Orthodoxy and Anglo-Jewry and another, and in the strictest confidence. No one in "my camp" knows that I am writing to you, and for obvious reasons I would not wish anyone on your side to be informed of this correspondence for the time being.'

Expressing concern at the Federation's perceived attempts to undermine him, Jakobovits declared: 'Despite the recent friction, and the attacks on me and my new office, I have scrupulously avoided making any statement to decry or offend the Federation. Even the appointment of a rival "Chief Rabbi" did not provoke me to say anything against you.

'Rabbi Kirzner can confidently count on my friendship and co-operation. We are old friends from our past London days, and I revere him for his personal qualities, his great scholarship, and his advanced age. There is ample room in a community as large as London for him and for me—and for two or even more batei din—to work harmoniously together without anyone denigrating or interfering with the other, or seeking to minimise each other's position. *Halevai* [If only] we could import more rabbanim of Rabbi Kirzner's calibre.

'I appeal to you personally'—added Jakobovits to Lederman—'not to say or do anything to accentuate Orthodox differences, and thus to further sap its strength. Seek to restore good will and unity with all your power. Wait for precise formulae of co-operation, at least until I can be involved in the negotiations.

'I would be prepared, if you agree, to issue a joint statement with Rabbi Kirzner, or with you, declaring our confidence that all problems between us will be satisfactorily resolved, and our determination to strengthen Orthodoxy by closest co-operation. This will clear the air for constructive negotiations once I arrive in London.'[48]

The launch of this approach provoked extreme discomfort among Jakobovits' future paymasters in London. Writing in 'strict confidence' to Wolfson, he sketched the events that had led to his clandestine meetings with Lederman and Kirzner.

'With the growing deterioration in the Federation wrangle,' he confided, 'and the immense damage done to the image and interests of the Orthodox community as a consequence, I decided a few weeks ago to take the initiative in discreetly and privately contacting Mr Lederman, who has now visited me in strictest secrecy. As a result, I had today a three-hour meeting with Rabbi Kirzner, and I believe the agreement reached at the most friendly meeting will be a major breakthrough in restoring the unity of Anglo-Jewry.

'I have, in effect, agreed to extend full recognition to the Federation's Rabbinate and Beth Din in certain areas, while they have agreed to drop the title "Chief Rabbi," to desist from any further secession (as had been planned) in such fields as shechitah and matzot, and to recognise the spokesmanship and authority of my office in representing the community at large. We have also encouraged prospects for the Federation's representation on the Chief Rabbinate Council and for general harmonious co-operation in all other spheres of common interest.'[49]

Wolfson forwarded this letter to the Chief-Rabbinate-in Commission, whose secretary, Rabbi Maurice Rose, expressed dismay on their behalf. 'The Dayanim,' he wrote to Jakobovits, 'recognise the need for discussions in order to establish understanding and to create an atmosphere of good will. But they do not see the urgency of entering into arrangements with the Federation before all the considerations of policy affecting the future of the Kehillah and the Ecclesiastical Authorities are carefully debated ...

'The London Beth Din is one of the historic and vital institutions of Anglo-Jewry and, together with the other rabbinates, has helped to uphold and enhance the office of the Chief Rabbinate. No other rabbinate has been accorded the rights envisaged in your arrangements. No analogy can be drawn from the Rabbinate of the Union of Orthodox Hebrew Congregations because this Rabbinate was specifically set up to cater for the needs of the members of the Union.

'Once a Beth Din is set up with such rights as referred to in your letter, it will undermine the entire historic and traditional structure of the Chief Rabbinate and the Anglo-Jewish Community.'[50]

Writing to Silverman at the Chief Rabbinate Council, Jakobovits declared of the Federation: 'To my mind, it is an irritant or a divisive force only so long as there is friction, to be inflated and exploited by our detractors as a "breach of Orthodox solidarity." Once things are quiet, the Federation will resume its relative impotence and insignificance in the community at large as before, whatever formal concessions are made to them, and however large their names may appear on paper.'[51]

On the question of kashrut and matzot supervision, Jakobovits sought to reassure the US leaders that the Federation had agreed to respect previous arrangements. Silverman expressed 'much relief and elation' on reading this because, he wrote, 'rumours were becoming rife here in London as to what agreements you had reached with various rabbonim and others, and as we were unable to elicit any information from the President on the subject, my honorary officers were getting very restive indeed.'[52]

By December, however—as a telegram to Jakobovits made abundantly clear[53]—the US honorary officers were again 'most embarrassed and concerned about [reports of an] alleged agreement between yourself and Federation circulat[ing] in [the] London Jewish community.' They requested Jakobovits to advise Wolfson of his willingness to meet two of their representatives to clarify the situation, and Jakobovits immediately telephoned Silverman to arrange a secret visit to London.

Explaining their embarrassment and concern, Silverman told him that the honorary officers 'had become very perturbed at the fact that there was being bruited around in London a document, the contents of which none of us had seen and, therefore, had not the slightest idea. It was being stated quite openly that this was an agreement which had been entered into by yourself with Rabbi Kirzner, with the full knowledge and consent of our President …

'The honorary officers felt that, with all your other responsibilities, and being so far from the scene, it was manifestly unfair to expect you to be in possession of all the facts and information necessary to form a complete picture of the situation here.' At their meetings in London in early January, Silverman concluded, they 'looked forward to discussing these major problems in detail,' and meanwhile requested that 'no form of agreement should be entered into—even as between rabbis—where the implications are so far-reaching as to involve a new approach to communal administration.'[54]

A letter from the dayanim following Jakobovits' visit summed up the disquiet he had engendered in promoting the agreement. Written by Rose on behalf of the Beth Din, it began generously by expressing the dayanim's 'satisfaction with your persistent efforts to ensure harmony in the Orthodox community.

> They share fully your desire to secure the fullest co-operation and means of co-existence. They are indeed mindful of the value of conciliatory conversations and of the need for a spirit of trust, confidence and friendship. Such endeavours should help to create an atmosphere for constructive work

and strengthen the office of the Chief Rabbi, an office whose attributes the dayanim are most anxious to maintain and enhance.

The matters raised by you, however, are of such fundamental importance that the dayanim feel that they need most careful deliberation and consultation. The question of a unified Beth Din or of departmentalisation which you mentioned in the course of your conversations with the dayanim, and which is referred to in your proposed statement to the press, is one which should be discussed in all its aspects and implications before any definite arrangements and commitments are made. For this is, indeed, a basic issue, and any premature publicity would prejudice it.

After further and careful reflection, it is clear that its effects would change radically the very character, prestige and influence of the Beth Din, an institution which has been and remains, in the face of all hostile criticism, the mainstay of the religious life of the larger community of Anglo-Jewry. There are many other considerations, and it is felt that reference to them in press statements will be subject to misinterpretation, give an unwarranted and misleading importance to certain individuals, and prove harmful to future stability.

Shechitah and kashrut, in which field the Beth Din have at all times sought and enjoyed the co-operation of other rabbis and Rabbinates, is nevertheless, in the main, the responsibility and concern of the London Beth Din, who can justly claim credit for the high standard attained ... Altogether, it is safe to assume that appeasement of certain individuals of the community may well prove an encouragement and stimulus to other sections in Anglo-Jewry to indulge their ambitions of independence, influence and power.[55]

Despite this rap over the knuckles, Jakobovits continued to advance his negotiations with Kirzner. The result was the publication, on 25 January 1967, of an 'official agreement' signed by the two Chief Rabbis-in-waiting and termed 'An Understanding with the Rav Rashi-Elect of the Federation of Synagogues':

> Having recently been elected to assume the spiritual and rabbinic leadership of the two largest groups of Ashkenazi Congregations in Anglo-Jewry, we have had several meetings together to ensure the closest and most effective co-operation

between us upon our assumption of office in London.

Determined to promote the strength of, and respect for, traditional Judaism as our supreme goal, and resolved to eliminate all past frictions, we have agreed to commit ourselves personally to, and to obtain the fullest support for, the following understanding in principle:

(a) In matters affecting the representation of the Ashkenazi community at large, the Chief Rabbi of the United Hebrew Congregations of the British Commonwealth shall be recognised as its spokesman and authority, and he agrees to consult with the Rav Rashi of the Federation of Synagogues on policy decisions and public statements affecting also the Federation of Synagogues.

(b) Each will give full and unqualified recognition to the other's rabbinic rulings.

(c) Every endeavour will be made to combine the activities of our independent Batei Din (Ecclesiastical Courts) together with the Haham of the Spanish and Portuguese Congregation, by setting up a unified and departmentalised Beth Din.

(d) We are resolved to ensure and maintain the joint administration of Shechitah and Kashrut (including Matzot).

We will make every endeavour to extend our harmonious co-operation to all other areas of common concern, such as Jewish education. We also look forward to the eventual representation of the Federation of Synagogues on the Chief Rabbinate Council.

We realise that the succcss of each of us lies in a strong Orthodoxy, and each of us is profoundly interested in strengthening the other, fulfilling the Prophetic vision: 'Each shall help his neighbour, and everyone say to his brother: "Be of good courage."'

We are confident this understanding will help to restore the solidarity of Orthodox Judaisrn as a constructive force to inspire and uplift the Anglo-Jewish community.[56]

'This agreement,' Jakobovits told the *Jewish Chronicle*'s New York correspondent, 'brings the Chief Rabbinate and the Federation closer together than they have ever been in the past. Previously, there had never been any official recognition by either side of the other. This is now assured for the first time in Anglo-Jewish history. It is also, and perhaps more significantly, the first breakthrough in resolving the Anglo-Jewish crisis, reversing the process of disintegration which has embittered communal relations in the past few years.'

'I fully endorse this,' remarked Kirzner. 'This understanding is unprecedented in Anglo-Jewry and it may be a stepping-stone to enable other rabbinical leaders to realise that there is very little hope and very little future, if any, in isolationism. But in co-existence leading to co-operation, there is every hope for a successful future for Anglo-Jewry. And it may also help the lay leaders to see the example set for them and follow in the right direction.'[57]

Other rabbinical leaders—or one, at least—did realise the implications. Three weeks later, a second statement, signed by Gaon, Jakobovits, and Kirzner, declared that, 'in order to promote the unity of Anglo-Jewry and give added strength to the rule of Torah in our communal life, we agree in principle to make every endeavour to co-ordinate the functions of our Batei Din.'[58]

Reacting to the first of the statements, *The Observer* wrote: 'Jews in Britain, who have had no Chief Rabbi since Dr Israel Brodie retired in April 1965, may shortly have two ... The Federation of Synagogues, which has a long history of rivalry with the United Synagogue, has traditionally called its own leader Principal Rabbi, and has made at least token acknowledgement of the supreme authority of the Chief Rabbi, elected by the United Synagogue. But it has now decided to call its own leader Chief Rabbi—though the Hebrew term *Rav Rashi* may be used to avoid confusion.'[59]

On behalf of Britain's Liberal Jewish community, Sidney Brichto responded: "There are very substantial sections of Anglo-Jewry which, on principle, won't have one Chief Rabbi, still less two. Liberal synagogues, as only one example, do not believe in a religious hierarchy by appointment. All matters of religious policy are decided by a conference of rabbis in which the knowledge and vision of the individual rabbi, and not his office, determine the respect and authority he will win for himself. It is our firm conviction that the non-acceptance of any rabbi as "Chief" is in keeping with the religiously democratic spirit of the Jewish religion.'[60]

As for Jakobovits, he remarked to Rose on the morrow of the signing: 'Having at last reached the first significant milestone in our tortuous road to communal peace, I can only hope that it will last as long in days as the combined mileage of our half-a-dozen transatlantic telephone conversations.'[61]

He could indeed only hope, for he was soon to discover that it was not to be.

Immanuel Jakobovits (1967): 'Do not ask me to make Judaism easier or cheaper'

FROM THE PULPIT — V
Prophet, Priest and King

Address delivered by Dr Immanuel Jakobovits at his installation as Chief Rabbi of the United Hebrew Congregations of the British Commonwealth of Nations, St John's Wood Synagogue, London, 11 April 1967—1 Nisan 5727

'Trembling, I now pour forth speech from my heart. Wisdom I lack, how shall I start?'[1]

My dear brothers and sisters!

With these words from our exalted New Year liturgy, I inaugurate on this Rosh Chodesh Nisan, this 'New Year of the Months,'[2] my new life in the office to which you have called me, and the new era to which I am to call you.

No rabbi ever had more reason than I to say with our father Jacob, as he returned home after fleeing from his brother's fury, 'I am too small for all the favours and all the truth which Thou hast done to Thy servant'; and I might continue, adapting Jacob's words, 'for I once crossed with but a staff the water' of the English Channel, as a refugee fleeing from oppression, 'and now I am become two encampments,'[3] at home in two continents.

How fervent must be my praise of Him 'who is good and who does good' to me in thanksgiving for the supreme privilege of serving as Chief Rabbi the very country which once saved and sheltered me; for calling me to preside over the very Beth Din once graced by the inspired but all-too-brief service of my sainted Father; and for the honour, unique in the history of this office, of installation by the very leader who previously occupied it with such grace and dedication—my revered teacher and mentor, now for the second time inducting me into a Chief Rabbinical office. Only history will record the full measure of his achievement in consolidating the Torah forces at a time of exceptional stress. May he be granted 'length of days and years in pleasantness' and in further distinguished service to our faith and people.

---

1   First day Rosh Hashanah *shacharith* service. [All citations are as in the original text.]
2   Exodus 12:2.
3   Genesis 32:11.

I

On this resplendent occasion, usually witnessed but once in a generation, and before this august and uniquely representative assembly—covering the entire spectrum of the community like a colourful rainbow of peace after a storm—permit me to share with you some of the hopes and prayers stirring my heart, as well as a few thoughts agitating my mind on the future of Judaism and British Jewry as we consecrate our partnership.

The first day of Nisan, by an extraordinary coincidence of anniversaries, marks the beginnings of the three classic forms of Jewish leadership: prophecy, priesthood and kingship. On this day, in the first dated event in the history of prophecy, God told Moses and Aaron: 'This month shall be unto you the first of months,' proclaiming to the Children of Israel the dawn of freedom when time, the count of months, would belong to them and not to their Egyptian masters, as before.[4] On this day, a year later, the Tabernacle was completed[5] and the Jewish priesthood began to function. And on this day, 'the New Year of the Kings,'[6] the kings of Israel started to count the years of their reign.

In some respects, the rabbi today is heir to all three roles of leadership. Let me, then, outline my aims and responsibilities in this triple capacity as I see them.

'Who are the kings? These are the rabbis,' says the Talmud.[7] Ever since the lapse of temporal sovereignty, Judaism has invested rabbis with certain royal prerogatives in guiding the destinies of our people. They directed its thoughts, inspired its actions, initiated its great historical movements, and gave Jewish life its sense of destiny and moral purpose.

In this capacity, it will be my charge to help in directing the community's internal and external affairs, and to suffuse them with religious content.

I will seek to bring the influence of my office to bear on promoting world peace and the moral regeneration of society—our most urgent universal task; on alleviating the religious attrition and communal isolation of our Russian brethren—the most painful Jewish problem of our day; on cementing the bonds of our common heritage between Israel and the Diaspora—our most acute national problem; and on moving with prudence and caution in the uncharted territory of inter-faith understanding and co-operation—the most serious post-war challenge to religious statesmanship. Within our community, I will encourage friendliness in our relations, imagination and originality in our planning, and a constant search for dedicated talent and high idealism in

---

4 See Sforno, a.1.
5 Exodus 40:17.
6 Rosh Hashanah 1:1.
7 Though usually quoted in this form, the statement reads differently in the Talmud (Gittin 62a, based on Proverbs 8:15).

our communal work. I will use every available means of communication with the public in pursuit of my determination always to take the community into my confidence.

In particular, it will be among my major objectives to enhance the status of the Anglo-Jewish ministry. I realise that the intense concentration of rabbinical power and authority in the Chief Rabbinate is bound to stunt the growth of a dynamic ministry. In fashioning my office to meet the needs of our time, I will try to strike a judicious balance between excessive decentralisation, leading to religious chaos, and over-centralisation, stifling ambition and responsibility among ministers, reducing them to mere functionaries. Having myself risen from their ranks and once joined the brain-drain for bigger opportunities abroad, I know their frustrations. I would like our spiritual leaders to assume unquestioned spiritual command in their congregations, and increasingly to participate at the highest level in the direction of the community and its religious policies. Only thus will we attract our finest sons to a rabbinical vocation.

II

Secondly, I am charged to assume some principal functions of the ancient priesthood. Perhaps this gives a little sense to the curious reference to Britain's earlier Chief Rabbis as 'High Priests of the Jews.' Moses defined the tasks of the priests as: 'They shall teach Thy laws unto Jacob, and Thy Torah unto Israel; they shall put incense before Thee, and whole burnt-offerings upon Thine altar.'[8] Let me here, then, come to the heart of my responsibilities as teacher and guardian of Jewish law, coupled with the duty to make Judaism sweet as incense and also to exact sacrifices for it.

Far above all else will be my obligation to promote the study of the Torah.

I want to assure the inalienable birthright of every Jew to an adequate Jewish education. On this I stake the success of my ministry, for on this will depend Jewish survival. During the post-war period, Jewish education has made vast strides in many lands. There are today tens of thousands of Jewish children, even outside Israel, who master Hebrew fluently, to whom immortals like Isaiah and Rashi and Maimonides speak in familiar accents, who have completed several tractates of the Talmud before they leave school, and who freely consult the genius of Judaism for authentic answers to the social, moral and intellectual perplexities of our age. If Jewish education ends, instead of starts in earnest, at barmitzvah age, is it any wonder that the products are juvenile Jews, quite incompetent to assert their faith in an adult world, their love of Judaism too flimsy to resist the temptation of intermarriage and the al-

---

8   Deuteronomy 33:10. The first part of this verse begins and ends with the letters making up the name of my Father, and is inscribed on his tombstone.

lurements of pagan philosophies? Just imagine we were to stop our children's natural growth and their secular instruction at thirteen years of age; would they not become physical and intellectual cripples?

Wherein lies the glory of beautiful synagogues if tomorrow they will be empty monuments to our neglect? What is the profit of the finest kashrut supervision if kosher homes will continue to decline, and of all our Zionist work without committed Jews in the next generation?

In this emergency of appalling defections among our youth, our expenditure in money and energy on Jewish education represents our defence budget in the communal economy, and it must be given the highest priority over every other Jewish effort.

What Judaism is it I will teach and defend? It is the vibrant faith found in synagogues filled every week, and equally evident 'when you sit in your home and when you go about' your business, sanctifying life at work and at leisure, as a guide to professional ethics in public, and to sexual morality in private.

It is the Judaism which was never in step with the times; which was as much out of date when it preached the brotherhood of man in pagan antiquity as when our martyrs defied the enticing attractions of Hellenistic culture and the savage bigotry of the Middle Ages; the Judaism which will never be in accord with the times until the times are in accord with Judaism. But it is also the Judaism which is ever dynamic and creative, addressing its eternal message to each generation in terms of its needs and accents; the Judaism which produced the prophets in response to the challenge of immoral paganism; which evolved the Talmud as a reaction to our encounter with Greece and Rome and to our dispersion among the nations; and which created Jewish philosophy to articulate Jewish teachings in an age of scholasticism and theological speculation; the Judaism which will now have to project its teachings in terms of the scientific thinking and intellectual stirrings of our times.

It will be my priestly duty to offer you, as best I can, this Judaism, fragrant and refreshing like incense, to make it meaningful and attractive.

But in my priestly charge, I must also insist on sacrifices. Do not ask me to make Judaism easier or cheaper, to devaluate its worth to the soft currency of convenience. I can no more offer you a programme without toil and sacrifice than you can offer me a life of ease and leisure. There is no instant Torah, prepared in one or three hours a week of study and practice, no Judaism without tears, just as there is no creation without travail and no triumph without hardship. Remember always, a religion which demands nothing is worth nothing, and a community which sacrifices nothing merits nothing.

Let me here make this quite clear: I am resolved to preserve the Orthodox traditions of my office and the predominantly traditional character of our community. To borrow from the memorable words uttered, in Britain's finest hour, by the man to whom we all owe our lives and our freedom: I have not become Anglo-Jewry's First Minister in order to preside over the liquidation of British Judaism.

I will do my best to serve and unite all sections of the community, but I am not prepared to replace the Torah by an umbrella, either open or closed, as the symbol of my office. In any event, I anticipate fair weather rather than rain or hail, and we should not require any umbrellas.

For, in my priestly capacity, I also want to be among the disciples of Aaron in 'loving peace and pursuing peace.'[9] In my attitude to all my fellow-Jews, I will look to the example of the saintly Rabbi Kook's boundless 'love of Israel,' and of my revered Father's broad tolerance. In our free society, I cannot ensure that everyone will submit to my decisions, but I can aspire to earn respect for my convictions and for my right to make decisions as my conscience dictates. I cannot bend or compromise Jewish law which is not mine to make or unmake, but I can administer it with compassion and despatch.

To those whose faith in the Divine origin of the whole Torah is weak and who do not accept the discipline of Judaism as entrusted to me, may I say this in all solemnity: never forget the immense tragedy of our religious differences. Should your and our hearts not bleed with grief when we, your brothers and heirs to a common tradition, cannot worship in your synagogues, cannot eat in your homes, and sometimes cannot even marry your sons and daughters, because laws which we recognise as Divine and sacred have become meaningless to you, because what has united us for thousands of years now estranges you? I will never cease pleading with you to rediscover the thrills of traditional Jewish living and the awesome magnificence of our faith: the Divinity of the Torah, the truth of the prophets, the authority of the halachah, and the messianic vision of the future, born of hope and toil. Nor will I ever surrender my firm belief in the promise of our prophets that eventually the entire House of Israel will be reunited in the service of our Creator.

Meanwhile, it will be my privilege and my duty to do all within my power and authority to close the gaps within our people, and I appeal to all segments of the community for help in this vital effort. To this end, I pledge all the skills and resources I command, for God will hold me to account for the failings of any Jew I can influence, as well as for my own many shortcomings.

Nevertheless, I recognise dissent as an inescapable fact of Jewish life today. I will seek to befriend those who dissent, and to work with them in Jewish and general causes unaffected by our religious differences. After the devastating losses we have suffered by slaughter, repression and assimilation, every Jew's contribution to the enrichment of Jewish life is now more precious

---

9   Avoth 1:12.

than ever, and I will encourage all British Jews to give of their best to the common good.

III

Finally, I am summoned to provide the vision and inspiration of the prophet, whose mantle, according to the Talmud,[10] was bequeathed to the rabbis from the day the Temple was destroyed. Unlike the priests, who expected the people to come to them in the sanctuary, the prophets went out to the people to proclaim their message. I shall likewise seek out my brethren wherever they are. Those who do not visit me in the synagogue I will try to meet in their surroundings, speaking and debating with them wherever they allow me to appear, and writing to vindicate the Torah wherever it is challenged.

As successor to the prophets, the rabbi today must demonstrate the relevance of Judaism to the contemporary experience. He must also spiritualise the mechanics of Jewish observance, showing the moral grandeur of religious discipline, the stirring uplift of true prayer, and the holiness of lives daily consecrated to God's service.

He must interpret the interplay between faith and reality, between ritual and ethics, between Israel and the nations. He must make manifest the gap between the laws of nature and the moral law, between impersonal science complacently dealing with things as they are and personal religion impatiently dealing with things as they ought to be. He must demand commitment, denounce indifference, and ennoble the aim of life as a quest for living in the image of God instead of the selfish pursuit of happiness and personal success.

Living in the aftermath of the most turbulent age in the annals of man and of Israel, our generation faces a special challenge in matching our gigantic material strides with a commensurate spiritual advance. The past generation experienced unparalleled bloodshed, first in a world war of unprecedented proportions, then in the heinous Holocaust which claimed more Jewish lives than all the medieval massacres combined, and finally in the restoration of Jewish rule to Zion. Such an afflicted generation, however heroic, could not evince the capacities, the vision and peace of mind, to concentrate on spiritual endeavours, any more than King David, conqueror of Jerusalem, because he had spilt blood, could build the Temple.[11]

It is our assignment, blessed as we are with peace and prosperity, to complete the rebirth of Israel. As they restored the soil of Israel, we must restore the soul of Israel.

A generation ago, the Jewish problem was the survival of Jews. Today, it

---

10 Baba Bathra 12a.
11 II Chronicles 22:8.

is the survival of Judaism. A generation ago, one-third of our people was annihilated. Today, one-quarter of our people is forcibly denied the right to live as Jews, and at least another quarter wilfully abdicates the right to live as Jews, being just as ignorant about Judaism, just as estranged from the synagogue, from Jewish traditions and literature by choice as the Jews of Russia are by compulsion. Even in the most catastrophic periods of the Middle Ages, when the total number of Jews in the world exceeded scarcely one million, and when they were exposed to slaughter, oppression and destitution, no Jew ever worried about Jewish survival as we do now in this age of unequalled freedom, affluence, and opportunity. How passionately would our prophets indict our generation if we now failed to bestir ourselves to rebuilding our destroyed sanctuary, to invest Jewish existence with meaning, and to turn the martyrdom of the past into the consecration of the future.

In the broader arena of mankind's tortuous evolution, we have also just passed an age of unrivalled conquest and material advance.

In the process, life has become mechanised, and man the victim of his own inventive genius. Man today lives longer, he has more time through labour-saving gadgets and faster communications, and yet he pants, too short of breath for contemplation and spiritual pursuits, his moral sense blunted by the hunt for pleasure, his vision obscured by the glitter around him, and the temple within him crushed under the weight of his technocracy.

As history's religious pioneers and moral pathfinders, we are summoned to reassert our national purpose in ministering to our fellow-men as 'a kingdom of priests and a holy people.'

If we expect the world to take up our cause when we are in trouble, we must also be prepared to involve ourselves and our teachings in the travails of mankind.

IV

I pray that in the office I now assume, I may be granted a humble share in reorienting the aspirations of our people and our fellow-men towards these prophetic goals. I pray especially that Anglo-Jewry may occupy an honoured place within the world Jewish community in the fulfilment of these ideals.

In the past, British Jewry has enjoyed an enviable reputation for stability and service. From these isles radiated an example of communal solidarity and religious loyalty. From these isles went forth the great translations of our Jewish classics, casting our sacred Bible, Talmud, Midrash, and Zohar into new vessels of understanding from which all may drink. From these isles came aid and intervention for suffering Jews everywhere. And from these isles, through their genius and ours, issued the Balfour Declaration fifty years ago, title-deed to Israel's rebirth. As the principal survivor of the European catastrophe,

Anglo-Jewry must now assume an even more eminent position of leadership and responsibility.

In our shrinking and interdependent world, Anglo-Jewry can no more afford to be insular and self-contained than Britain can afford to withdraw from the rest of the world. We must share with, and contribute to, the Jewish experience of other communities. And we must consolidate our part in the upbuilding of the Land of Israel, by encouraging aliyah and by freely aiding the spiritual and material growth of Israel as a land flowing with the milk of Torah and the honey of prosperity.

I pray that I may always be worthy of your support, trust and friendship. I plead with our eminent dayanim, our learned rabbis and all my distinguished colleagues: uphold my hands on the right and on the left.[12] Thus will my arms be firm, the one as 'a mighty hand,' to defend 'the Law of Moses and Israel,' and the other as 'an outstretched arm,' to grasp with love those who stray or falter. I call upon our dedicated lay leaders, perhaps with a touch of homiletical licence: You take charge of our administrative wants, supply our material needs, and give me the freedom to devote myself to things of the spirit, as we share in equal parts, like Issachar and Zevulun, the efforts and rewards in building a flourishing Torah society.

I turn with special fondness to our youth, bright hope of our future, whom I am so delighted to see represented here for the first time in such numbers: Make me at home in your midst, stimulate me by your questions, rejoice me by your response, and humble me by your restless search for depth and meaning beneath the shifting sands of passing fads as you prepare yourselves to become tomorrow's guardians of yesterday's heritage.

To all my brothers and sisters in the far-flung dispersion of the Commonwealth, I say: Let us seize each other's hands across our distances to form the most wonderful family of communities cheerfully responding to Jewish history's greatest challenge in these exciting times.

Let us so acquit ourselves of our diverse tasks that no Jew will ever spurn his heritage, and that, as promised in the Torah, 'all the nations of the earth shall see that the name of the Lord is called upon us.'[13]

As for myself, what do I crave in this hour of destiny? Upon King Solomon's accession to his high office, he had a dream in which God said: 'Ask what I shall give you.' His response is my response: 'O grant to Thy humble servant an understanding heart to judge Thy people, to know between right and wrong.'[14]

I seek neither power nor authority, for no rabbi today can impose himself

---

12   Exodus 17:12.
13   Deuteronomy 28:10.
14   I Kings 3:5, 9.

upon unwilling people, or enjoy their respect without earning it. Rather do I seek the wisdom to judge and make the right decisions, the inspiration to guide and persuade, the mind to instruct, and the heart to comfort. I crave the ability to elicit understanding, not submission; to win partners, not subordinates.

We have now reached the end of the beginning. In responding to your call, I am sustained by a vision. In its fulfilment, I have abiding faith. And I desire you to come and share with me this vision, as I now impart it to you in the sight of Him Who is the Sovereign of us all:

My vision is that 'out of the cruel shall come the sweet.'[15]

My vision is that out of the age of monstrous depravity there arises the great vindication of the age-old Jewish faith in the brotherhood of man, now a more universal hope than ever before.

My vision is that out of the religious hatreds of the past, polluted by rivers of Jewish blood, there is born the great confrontation between Judaism and the world, an encounter not of theological parleys, but of the world religions—secure from bigotry within and missionary subversion without—attacking the common enemy of evil and godlessness, and acknowledging their debt to Judaism as the enduring fountainhead of all that has inspired moral progress in the human story.

My vision is that out of the age of soulless materialism and the blasphemy of 'God's death' there stirs the search for a higher morality transcending reason, a quest for the living God to replace the sham gods made to order by today's pseudo-theologians.

My vision is that out of our people's agony there is reborn Zion restored to its glory, radiating the Word of the Lord everywhere, and there prosper Jewish communities living in tranquillity and harmony with our fellow-citizens.

My vision is that out of Anglo-Jewry's past tribulations there emerges a happy, forward-looking community, confounding the defeatists and routing the strife-mongers, as a mighty fortress of our spiritual treasures.

And my vision is that out of the clash of opinions, and sparked by the eternal fire of the Torah, there are released the massive energies to raise us to the peak of achievement, towering majestically in a universal panorama of peace and basking in the everlasting sunshine of God's choicest blessings.

May God grant us, in the words of the first and chiefest rabbi consecrating the first sanctuary on this first of Nisan 3,500 years ago: 'May the Divine Presence rest upon the labour of our hands.'[16]

* * *

---

15 Judges 14:14.
16 Rashi, Exodus 39:43.

Induction address delivered by Emeritus Chief Rabbi Israel Brodie at the installation of Dr Immanuel Jakobovits as Chief Rabbi of the United Hebrew Congregations of the British Commonwealth of Nations, St John's Wood Synagogue, London, 11 April 1967–1 Nisan 5727

'And in thy glory, prosper, ride on in behalf of truth, humility and righteousness.'[17]

This is a unique and memorable hour. For the first time in the history of the British Chief Rabbinate, one who has occupied the high office of Chief Rabbi participates in the solemn service of the installation of his successor. This hour is for me further enhanced, and emotionally so, by reason of my personal association with Rabbi Dr Jakobovits in the formative and also decisive years of his distinguished career in the rabbinate. I experience something of the unmixed generous pride which, as our sages tell us and as many of us can confirm, a teacher has for the outstanding success of his pupil in the teacher's own field, or a fond father for his son's brilliant reputation.

I bless the Giver of all things, the God of the spirits of all flesh, for His goodness in sparing me to witness the appointment and elevation to his exalted office of a former student and colleague, known in the gates 'distinguished for the affirmative declaration of Law and Testimony.' I am particularly happy that the appointment of my successor has been greeted by our community and the general public with so large a measure of interest and good will and friendliness. I pray that our community, its leaders and members, will sustain and implement their present manifestation of support and encouragement in all his endeavours in their service and in the highest purposes of our Faith.

I am content in the knowledge that a successor has been chosen who, like his predecessors, will uphold with steadfastness and constancy the authority, the validity, the relevance of the Torah, Written and Oral. Fortified by his trust in Heaven and the stimulating meritorious example of his learned, pious, lovable, saintly father, I am confident he will bring to the discharge of the manifold and various duties of his office the gifts of personality, scholarship, vision, moral courage, and wide human sympathies with which he is conspicuously endowed.

The years in the rabbinate in this country, in Eire and the United States of America have witnessed his abilities as preacher, lecturer and author. He has brought an enriched, dynamic, practical experience to his newly enlarged area of activity which will give him ready access to the hearts and understanding of men and women, of young and old. Certain and firm in conviction, mature in the gift of exposition, he is equipped to teach, to guide, to redirect and fortify those of our time who walk about as if in darkness, the doubting and the

---

17 Psalms 45:5.

frustrated, the strayers and the discontented with the teachings and demands of our spiritual heritage. They will listen; many will respond when heart talks to heart.

In his endeavours to cope with his tasks and his hopes, he will, I know, be able to count on the loyalty and co-operation of learned and able colleagues—the distinguished dayanim, and of tried and dedicated rabbis and ministers who faithfully serve and guide their congregations in Britain and overseas. Over the years, a tradition of friendliness, mutual understanding and the pursuit of joint efforts in religious and communal causes has cemented the association of the Ashkenazi and Sephardi communities. I am prayerful that the spiritual leaders of the respective communities will maintain this cordial spirit of co-operation and continue in unison to magnify the Torah and make it glorious.

May the period of office of my dear successor be one in which peace will be completely restored in the world, and in which our own *kehillah* will advance in knowledge of the Torah and the service of the Creator. May it become an admired and enviable hegemony, distinguished spiritually, morally, and culturally. May the will to honest unity and animated harmony prevail in our midst.

May individual and corporate conduct reflect the joy and discipline of observance, ethical fastidiousness, sympathetic philanthropy, the love of our fellow Jews and of all men, the unwavering attachment to Israel's hope and consolation—all of which belong to the very substance of our Eternal Faith and way of life. May the young generation be taught of the Lord, gladdening our hearts with the hopes of a bright future such as is pictured by the prophet Isaiah: 'Jacob shall not be ashamed, neither shall his face now wax pale: when he seeth his children, the work of My hands, in the midst of him and that they sanctify My Name. Yea, they shall sanctify the Holy One of Jacob and shall stand in awe of the God of Israel. They also that err in spirit shall come to understanding, and they that murmur shall learn instruction.'[18]

CHARGE

And now, my beloved successor, it is with solemn joy that I am about to lead you to the pulpit from which you will deliver your *derashah* and message to this large representative assembly and to the community. May He who favoureth man with knowledge inspire the utterances of your lips to speak to minds and hearts with knowledge and compassion and according to the Divine Will.

Without fear, without stumbling, with courage and humble confidence, may your words influence for good all who may look to you for guidance. May Providence that hath been thy protection unto this day continue His bounte-

---

18 Isaiah 29:22-24.

ous grace. May He grant you, your dear wife and your children and all the members of your family many years of health, happiness and well-being. May He enlarge your powers of mind and heart to be equal to the responsible tasks which you will from this day undertake to the service of God and to the honour and purposeful continuity of the whole House of Israel.

May the Lord, God of Israel, prosper your way! In the battle for Torah and its abiding spiritual and moral values, go forth and, with all the opportunities of your eminent position, prosper, ride on in behalf of truth, in humility and with righteousness. Be strong and of good courage, and the Lord be with you always.

CHAPTER EIGHT

Natural Selection

THE JAKOBOVITS–KIRZNER 'understanding' began to unravel within months of its signing. Despite the Chief Rabbi's attendance at the installation of the 'Grand Rabbi and head of the religious tribunal of the Federation of Synagogues, hailing the unprecedented unity in the ranks of Orthodox Jewry,'[1] neither of their respective lay hierarchies supported the terms of the agreement. The kashrut and shechita operations of the two organisations intensified their competition; the rival batei din continued apace; and Kirzner's position at the Federation appeared ever-more precarious when, after barely twelve months, he returned to New York 'on grounds of ill-health.'[2]

While it later emerged that his appointment was 'terminated, by mutual consent,' at the time of his departure,[3] his 'official resignation' was revealed to the Federation council only in December 1969, a full year after he had left. Ruling out any discussion on the subject, Lederman stated that he had met with Kirzner in New York some six weeks earlier, when the Rav Rashi had 'asked to be released from his post.' No payments had been made to him since his brief stay in Britain.

Reports circulating in London indicated that if it were decided to fill the vacancy, the new incumbent might be styled not 'Rav Rashi'—Kirzner's own choice of title—'but something different, such as "Chief Rabbi."'[4] With the agreement of the Federation council, meanwhile, the head of its Beth Din, Michael Fisher, and the other dayanim carried out the Rav Rashi's duties.

Kirzner's resignation was said to have led to plans to co-opt Jakobovits in his place, but a lengthy dispute over an amendment to the Board of Deputies' constitution—conferring consultative status on the religious leaders of congregations not under the jurisdiction of the Chief Rabbi and the Haham (namely, the Reform and Liberals)—soured relations between the United Synagogue–Chief Rabbinate axis and those to the right, and scotched any further notion of Jakobovits as Principal Rabbi.[5]

Of his pact with Kirzner, he was later to write: 'The signed agreement provided for a working arrangement with the Chief Rabbi and the London Beth

Din to obviate rivalry and duplication; unfortunately, petty interests invalidated the accord. I was never unduly concerned with whether there were one, two or three kosher stamps on our products, except that it would involve an enormous extra cost to the community. The Federation could have contributed something invaluable to the community had they chosen fields like schools, adult education or leadership training. But by providing services adequately taken care of without them, they proved a vociferous and expensive anachronism.'[6]

Based on his own experiences with the Federation's leaders, and its historical record spanning several Chief Rabbinates, Jakobovits' contention that they 'bother me little' grew increasingly evident as the left-wing came to bother him more.[7] In the week before his agreement with Kirzner, he had penned a plea to the Progressives jointly to 'foreswear intolerance and personal acrimony in our relations.

> I can oppose 'heresy-hunts' looking for a deviant in every cupboard, and you can oppose 'heresy-hunts' in reverse, whereby every little incident of Orthodox zeal is inflated into a *cause célèbre* or a public scandal. We can generate good will and banish despondency, by confounding the prophets of doom who hold out, and preach, nothing but strife and disintegration for the community. We can jointly fight all attempts to sow subversion and secession breeding further disunity within Anglo-Jewry.
>
> Next, we can intelligently debate our differences, using light instead of heat in our arguments. In this way, we can raise from the dregs the intellectual level and public image of our community, and at the same time test our convictions by mature discussion rather than by the exchange of irrelevant abuse.
>
> We can work together in Jewish and general causes upon which our religious differences do not impinge, such as Jewish defence, Zionism, philanthropy and Jewish–Christian relations. We can also join with our fellow-citizens in the moral crusade against rampant evils. We can participate together in communal and national events, so long as they are not of a specifically religious character in form or locale, implying a mutual endorsement where there can be no mutual endorsement.
>
> Most importantly, we can explore ways and means to narrow our religious gap. I can make my synagogue services more attractive to the unfamiliar, and you can make yours

more traditional. We can search for formulae to put an end to the fearful havoc wrought by our conflicting definitions of divorce and conversion, whereby tragic marriage barriers are being raised between Jew and Jew, and whereby thousands of people are considered Jewish by some Jews and Gentile by all others.

These, and eventually other, bridges of understanding and co-operation can raise over the wide gulf at present separating us. But let me add this word of caution to prevent them from collapsing before they are even built. Do not force the pace of this historic evolution by looking for issues, challenges or head-on collisions. These developments must grow organically from the seeds of good will fertilised by time. Any act of provocation only leads to a reaction of antagonism and drives us further apart.[8]

In an interview with the *Sunday Times* before assuming office, Jakobovits had mentioned the possibility of a rapprochement with Jacobs. 'If he can see his way clear to accept the jurisdiction of the Chief Rabbinate,' he declared, 'the path to a reconciliation would be wide open.'[9] Responding the following week, in a letter to the *Jewish Chronicle*, Jacobs asked: 'What can "reconciliation" mean in this context? If it means that our group will engage in friendly dialogue with other groups in Anglo-Jewry, and work together with them for the many aims we all have in common, this is already happening; and where it is not, the remedy lies with Rabbi Jakobovits and his colleagues.'[10]

As the years turned, however, relations between Jakobovits and the Progressives and Masorti (the name by which Jacobs' movement came to be known) steadily worsened, despite covert attempts to steady the ship. At the core of the 'sectarian schism,' as Reform's Dow Marmur described it,[11] were differences over conversion, marriage and divorce which Jakobovits showed willingness to discuss while his own dayanim proved unflinchingly resistant. When the left-wing clamour threatened, in the Chief Rabbi's words, 'to sever the last ideological bonds of commitment that bound us together,' the collapse of his bridges of understanding was all but complete.

* * *

In October 1988, some eighteen months before Jakobovits was due to retire, the United Synagogue launched the search for his successor by announcing a meeting of the Chief Rabbinate Council, its first for more than five years. 'We are starting with an empty piece of paper,' stated US president Sidney Frosh. 'We have no particular candidate in mind, but he will have to be a man of learning and of stature—a man for this day.'[12] Jakobovits, expressing a similar view—'he should be a man who is in tune with the times'[13]—was said to be backing Emanuel Feldman, rabbi of Congregation Beth Jacob, Atlanta, and associate editor of Tradition, journal of the Rabbinical Council of America.

While no particular candidate may have occurred to Frosh, the wider community was awash with names. Jakobovits' nephew by marriage—London-born Reuven Bulka, of Ottawa's Congregation Machzikei Hadas—was 'brought over from Canada' that very week to deliver a lecture under United Synagogue auspices, and among others being mentioned were South African Chief Rabbi Cyril Harris, Jews' College principal Jonathan Sacks, and Irish Chief Rabbi Ephraim Mirvis.[14]

Discussing the Chief Rabbinate in an interview following his lecture, Bulka declared: 'I had not expected my visit to lead to a flush of electoral speculation. The position of Chief Rabbi offers the type of challenge one would not dismiss lightly. While it is something I have not given much thought to, it would obviously be a tremendous challenge. I cannot tell you how I would react if asked, because I haven't been asked, but just being mentioned as a possibility is itself a compliment.'

Placed by many—it was put to him—'within the "modern" band of the Orthodox spectrum,' Bulka dismissed the use of labels. 'We are almost getting to the point where you have to identify your standing not just in terms of right-wing, centrist or left-wing Orthodox, but whether you are eighty-nine degrees to the right, or eighty-six, or eighty-three. It has become a little absurd. My outlook is coloured by a desire to try to encompass the entirety of the community into all of my concerns, without getting into the question of whether this is rightist, leftist or centrist. This is essential Orthodoxy.'

Bulka added: 'The broad approach of institutions such as the United Synagogue, which tries to keep as many as it can within the Orthodox fold, is something I would certainly go along with. Action is needed on an international scale—a global strategy—to woo back the unaffiliated into the Jewish community. It's a scary thing: these are the ones who are probably in greatest danger of falling by the wayside, and it's our responsibility to make sure this does not happen.'[15]

The electoral process gathered pace when, some weeks later, the Chief Rabbinate Council established a thirty-six-strong committee, including five Federation representatives, to consider the duties and emoluments of the office, as well as the methods of selection and appointment. Significantly, Jews' College chairman Stanley Kalms was among those on the panel.[16]

By the following month, a seven-man 'sifting' committee—headed by Frosh and also comprising communal notables Michael Goldmeier, Gerald Jospe,

Victor Lucas, Aubrey Newman, Robert Rodrigues-Pereira, and Leslie Wagner—had drawn up a so-called 'Applicants' list,[17] subsequently reduced to 'Short-Lists I and II.' The names of twenty rabbis appeared in the preliminary list, some accompanied by their age at the outset and, potentially, on taking up office:

JONATHAN SACKS (41/43)	KENNETH HAIN
CYRIL HARRIS (53/55)	RAYMOND APPLE (53/55)
JEFFREY COHEN (49/51)	SHLOMO RISKIN
ALAN KIMCHE	MAURICE LAMM
CHANOCH EHRENTREU (56/58)	EMANUEL FELDMAN
ISAAC BERGER	REUVEN BULKA
NISSON SHULMAN (56/58)	MORDECHAI PIRON
ABNER WEISS (50/52)	SIMCHA KOOK
YISRAEL LAU	ELAZAR MUSKIN
AHARON LICHTENSTEIN	[−] SHECHTER (Yeshiva University)

Several of the rabbis were subsequently marked for 'elimination,' a few with comments alongside their names.[18] Bulka, Feldman, Sacks, Harris, and Lau (Tel Aviv's Chief Rabbi) remained on both short-lists, having seen off Hain ('Rabbi, Orach Chayim, Manhattan') and Kook ('Rabbi, Rehovot') from the first of the two. Weiss ('Rabbi, Beth Jacob Congregation, Los Angeles'), though not named on 'Short-List II,' was granted an interview at a later date.

Responding to an initial request from Frosh for nominations, Kalms proposed Sacks, 'having given a great deal of thought to this matter, particularly in view of our close association.' Sacks' nomination, he wrote, was based on 'two separate analyses':

> Firstly, does the candidate have sufficient technical qualifications for the appointment? Clearly, Rabbi Sacks has a high standard of learning, with perhaps a greater emphasis on Jewish philosophy rather than halachah, but certainly intellectually he is of top calibre in his profession and, indeed, in world Jewry. This view is shared by many distinguished authorities with whom I have discussed the matter either in my capacity as chairman of Jews' College or on a personal level.
>
> The second consideration is his personal suitability for the appointment, and here there is equally strong ground. Rabbi Sacks represents a model profile of the type of leadership we require. He has a first-class secular education; he is English; he is persona grata throughout the United Synagogue world, and this extends both to Lubavitch and to the less committed of

the Reform and Liberal movements. He is seen as a man who will keep open personal lines of communication.

There remains only the question of his personal capacity to deal with a complex and, at times, an onerous appointment. Provided he is not expected to slavishly imitate the present incumbent, I believe he will bring a quality of commitment and focus on contemporary issues which are perhaps more important today than the conventional pastoral problems.

Elaine, his wife, will be—provided she is also not subjected to comparison—a steadfast and firm influence. Her confidence over the last few years has substantially increased as Rabbi Sacks has become more widely involved in the community, and she is extensively prepared.

Thus I have no hesitation in nominating Rabbi Dr Jonathan Sacks as a candidate for the position of Chief Rabbi.[19]

Further support for Sacks reached Frosh from Wagner, vice-chancellor of the University of North London, who wrote: 'The major task of the new Chief Rabbi must be to be a bridge between the rabbinical leadership and the members of the United Synagogue. He must have the learning and intellectual clout to command the respect of the rabbinical leadership, and the lifestyle and appreciation of modern culture to enable him to communicate with the mass of US members.

'He must be able to look inwards to our own community, and outwards to the wider community, and he must have the verbal and linguistic skills to carry out that communication effectively. He must understand the special nature of the community and be in tune with its needs and, by his personal example and his leadership, bring our members to a more sympathetic appreciation of their heritage. To do all that, he must above all be an inclusivist rather than an exclusivist. The candidate who best fills that job description is Jonathan Sacks.'

Wagner stressed that 'an understanding of our community is vital, and the best understanding comes from having served here ... We have the best candidate right here, and we must have the self-confidence as a community to choose him because he is the best and not because we couldn't attract an overseas star.'[20]

Similarly emphasising the 'place of origin' of possible candidates in the light of historical experience—with alternate foreign- and native-born incumbents having set a 'pattern' for the Chief Rabbinate—Newman, author of a history of the United Synagogue, wrote to Frosh: 'The present Chief is foreign-born. I am not saying that we should for that reason go automatically for a native candidate, but that there are reasons for that sort of pattern.

'It means that we combine the experience of someone who comes into the community from outside, seeing the community and its problems with a fresh viewpoint, with that of someone who knows the community from inside and a very living understanding of what needs to be done. Had we nobody from Anglo-Jewry who could be considered suitable, we would have to look very carefully at an "outsider," but since there are at least two very good candidates known to be Anglo-Jewish, who have in their different ways considerable standing both inside and outside the community, I think we should be looking at them.'

Another point to consider, wrote Newman, was 'the fact that the Chief has two major roles, and that these in themselves have considerable impact upon the other issues we are to discuss on Sunday. He obviously has a representative role outside the community. He is important within it, not least in the ways in which he brings together all the various congregations in the country; but he is equally important to the non-Jewish world. Whoever we choose to recommend must be able to talk to the non-Jews and be a fitting person in that context.'[21]

As Newman had indicated, his remarks came on the eve of a meeting of the larger committee set to cover a range of issues. Coinciding with the meeting was a letter in the *Jewish Chronicle* from K. P. Barnett, of Hampstead, expressing regret—and clearly mirroring a wider consensus—that 'the committee chosen to select a successor is so wholly unrepresentative of our community.

'First,' wrote Barnett, 'the committee is all male. Even within the United Synagogue, every sane-minded constituent congregation now has a council of management which includes women members. This glaring omission is therefore as much regressive as it is insulting to at least half of our community.

'Secondly, no representation has been reserved for young people. Surely representatives under thirty-five ought to have been included, so as to ensure that the new Chief Rabbi will have some rapport with the very section of the community that will comprise his constituency for the greater part of his period in office.'

Foreshadowing a controversy that, in due course, was to cloud the campaign, Barnett called for the inclusion of both right-wing Orthodox and Progressive representatives on the committee, which 'might have gone some way to building bridges. Although Reform and Liberal Jews will naturally differ from the Chief Rabbinate on matters of halachah, there are nevertheless many areas in which the Chief Rabbinate is involved where there is common ground. And the absence of a representative of the rabbis and dayanim with whom the new Chief Rabbi will have to work so closely also appears insensitive.'[22]

While not enlarging the committee to include any of the representatives suggested, Frosh later made clear that the selectors had 'consulted with leading rabbonim in this country, in Israel and in the United States; with ladies of this community, including some from the provinces; with the executive committee of the US Rabbinical Council and the chairman of the Provincial Rabbinical Council; and, most importantly, with the dayanim of the London Beth Din and, of course, with the Chief Rabbi.'[23]

* * *

Kalms' letter supporting Sacks was one of several such endeavours to advance his candidacy. The most influential was his sponsorship of a London conference the following month, 'Traditional Alternatives: Orthodoxy and the Jewish Future,' addressing the relationship of Orthodoxy to modernity and secularisation, to the Jewish people as a whole, and to the State of Israel.[24] The symposium, Sacks acknowledged, owed its genesis to Kalms. 'It was his restless questioning that gave birth to the idea, and his support that has sustained it ever since. To him, I personally, and Jews' College collectively, owe a unique debt of friendship.'[25]

In his keynote address—underpinning Kalms' faith in his fitness for the post—Sacks asserted that, while Jews everywhere shared a common sense of destiny, 'the links between religious and secular, Orthodox and Reform, Israel and the diaspora, have grown increasingly fragile in the past few years, to the point where only crisis brings us together. Thus a formidable responsibility lies with Orthodoxy, a responsibility of leadership towards the entire Jewish people.

> Orthodoxy [said Sacks] has undergone a remarkable resurgence since the last century, when some people believed that its light would go out. But there is a long way to go to match the greatness of the past. The Orthodox world has been too occupied with the small details of ritual observance at the expense of larger issues.
>
> The laws of Torah are compassion and kindness and peace in the world. If Torah does not inspire even religious Jews, then irreligious Jews will not come closer to Torah. If it does not make women feel included, then we will have excluded them. If Torah is not allowed to speak with its true stature, then the rabbis and teachers we produce will not have their true stature.
>
> Our conference is not about right, left or centre, but about smallness or greatness. Will Orthodoxy see itself threatened by assimilation and secularisation? Will it retreat yet further into its protected enclaves, while the rest of the Jewish world falls to pieces? Will it build an ark for itself, like Noah, while the rest of the Jewish world drowns? Or will it see itself chal-

lenged by this unique moment to lead the Jewish world?

For that is the challenge. To make sure that every child has a Jewish education, as intellectually demanding and inspiring as the best secular education. To teach us how to be Jews in our secular involvement as well as in our private lives. To teach us what it is to create a society, in the *golah* and, especially, in *Eretz Yisrael*, based on compassion, justice and righteousness.[26]

Years later, Kalms looked back on this period with mixed emotions. 'Jonathan Sacks,' he recalled, 'was the rabbi at Golders Green Synagogue when we first met in 1979. I was a new honorary officer at Stanmore and I invited him home for some community talk. Our first conversation was sharp as I probed him for signs of fresh thinking, and I struck gold.

'Within a few weeks, we were friends and, for the next twelve years, we spoke, met or planned daily. It needed no insight to sense that the United Synagogue was heading towards the depths of decline. A traditional antagonism reigned between the lay leadership and their rabbis, employer/employee relations at their worst: the organisation was run with unrivalled inefficiency by a centralist administration and a stifling constitution and was bogged down in ideological battles that should have been ditched long ago.

> This was the background to Jonathan Sacks' preparation for office. He saw the challenges, the problems and the opportunities. He saw some of the limitations of office and, not unreasonably, underestimated them. The office is, in reality, an appointment of the United Synagogue and demands the good will of the right, centre and left to give it purpose and effect. A Chief Rabbi needs to be a trained navigator. But unburdened by a rabbinical family background, he saw integrity and reason around every corner.
>
> At the time, Lord Jakobovits was busy with changes which would increase the influence and reputation of the Chief Rabbinate. A man of deep self-confidence and rabbinic pedigree, with a unique home support system—Lady Jakobovits—he had the strength to break with the authoritarianism of his employers. Gathering around him substantial lay leaders from across the community, he formed the Jewish Educational Development Trust (JEDT) to reinvigorate Jewish education outside of the impoverished and bureaucratic hand of the United Synagogue.
>
> I was privileged to be the JEDT's first chairman and, later

on, chairman of Jews' College. We were a formidable team to inject some fresh thinking into Anglo-Jewish life, and one of our major sources of motivation was our hopes for the Chief Rabbi-to-be.

Jonathan Sacks hit the ground running. He became principal of Jews' College, and a coterie of new students started their career under his auspices. His years of preparation for his inevitable office were constructive. A prolific author, he proved an inspiring writer of manifestos, preaching his vision of an inclusivist Jewish society.

Our greatest success, perhaps, in establishing the eligibility of Jonathan Sacks as natural successor to Chief Rabbi Jakobovits was our first 'Traditional Alternatives' conference in 1989. It was an ambitious event—a full day of challenging seminars with world-famous participants—to set out an agenda for modern Orthodoxy.

Perhaps it was now that Rabbi Sacks should have heard the first early-warning sirens. Two of our guest speakers, Rabbi David Bleich and Rabbi Emanuel Feldman, would not share the platform with another important guest, Rabbi David Hartman[27]—and they don't come more kosher—for reasons which, to the middle ground, were distinctly uncomfortable. So Rabbi Hartman held forth from the floor of the conference with powerful and persuasive arguments for open dialogue among all Jews. Sacks and Hartman lifted their audience that day.[28]

Within a week of the conference, Cyril Harris and his wife, Ann, were in London for the engagement party of their son, Michael. The visit included a sermon by Harris at St John's Wood, where they spent a Shabbat as guests of the congregation.[29]

'We were to be in London for only a few days,' Ann Harris wrote in her diary.[30] 'Cyril was immediately approached by Sidney Frosh and Jonathan Lew [chief executive of the United Synagogue] and invited to a confidential meeting on the very morning of the party. They expressed doubts as to whether, if Rabbi Sacks were the most favoured candidate, he was suitable for the position, and they had a long discussion with Cyril on his ideas about how the job should be done.

'I was quite amazed when, later at the party, one or two influential people in the community, the most emphatic of whom was Lionel Swift,[31] expressed great delight at the prospect of Cyril's candidacy and indicated a firm view that he would return [as Chief Rabbi]. Victor Lucas[32] and Tony Grabiner[33] expressed their willingness to lobby support and did, in fact, begin to do so.'

Jews' College-ordained Harris had left Britain eighteen months earlier to take up his South African post, having served three congregations in London, as well as communal and educational bodies. At the time of his departure, he had asserted that he was 'not a contender' for the British Chief Rabbinate and that, 'after the initial five years of my South African contract, I hope that circumstances will allow me to continue in that position.'[34] His credentials, nevertheless, clearly marked him out for Anglo-Jewry's highest ecclesiastical office.

> Purely by chance [he was later to write], before I was appointed Chief Rabbi of South Africa, I had the opportunity of gaining experience in almost every branch of rabbinic endeavour: educational, welfare, managerial, communal—and even, on occasion, spiritual.
>
> Since the age of sixteen, I had been teaching Torah and giving *shiurim*. Always close to the youth movements, I was given the youth portfolio in Chief Rabbi Jakobovits' first 'cabinet.' A student leader in my college days, I was in 1956 elected vice-chairman of the Inter-University Jewish Federation, predecessor of the Union of Jewish Students, and I served as national director of the Hillel Foundation in the early 1970s.
>
> Acquaintance with the military was gained as senior Jewish chaplain to Her Majesty's forces. For several years, I was joint chairman of Mizrachi in Britain. I was active on the rabbinical council of the United Synagogue for two decades, on the committee and as secretary and as chairman. Quite often appearing on radio, I was taught a great deal by Michael Freedland, who successfully ran BBC Radio London's 'You Don't Have To Be Jewish' programme for many years.
>
> I think I have visited every hospital in London—those hospitals where I was Jewish chaplain many hundreds of times. I have been at the Middlesex Hospital, Mortimer Street, in London's West End, at all hours of the day and night. When a Jewish patient was dying, it was correctly expected that the chaplain would be at the bedside helping the patient, saying *tehillim* and consoling the family.
>
> Teenage, marital, and bereavement counselling was a regular occurrence. For a decade in the 1960s, I was chaplain at a maximum-security prison.
>
> Real depth of experience I cannot claim, but for one rea-

son or another I am able to claim range of experience. Also, the way things worked out, without knowing that I would ever become a chief rabbi, I had the good fortune in St John's Wood of being near to Chief Rabbi Lord Jakobovits. A mentor of rare quality, his staunch adherence to principle on all issues of moral well-being; his capacity, ably assisted by his energetic wife Amélie, to develop cordial and notable relationships with the highest in the land; and the finely-honed balance he always brought to bear in solving controversial issues were lessons of immense value that I picked up subconsciously, and which were to stand me in good stead.[35]

While a self-declared and vocal opponent of the Progressive left, Harris was regarded as a moderate within his own constituency, initiating 'reforms' in line with the times. 'Kenton,' he wrote of his first pulpit, 'had the distinction in the early 1960s of reviving the batmitzvah ceremony for girls. A feature of the pre-war years, this had unfortunately fallen away, with the result that most girls left cheder by the age of eleven—unlike their brothers, who had barmitzvah to look forward to.

> Encouraged by my dear friend Bent Melchior, later to become Chief Rabbi of Denmark, I introduced a special syllabus for girls in our Hebrew classes. It concentrated on the traditional basics of the Jewish home, the laws of kashrut and the preparation of Shabbat and the holy-days being given prominence. A working knowledge of the Siddur, especially becoming acquainted with the Shabbat-morning service, was included, and the history section concentrated on the women of the Bible.
>
> Our philosophy was quite simple. Judaism is a domestic religion, the home being even more important than the synagogue, and thus the education of Jewish girls in running it properly is vital to Jewish continuity. We went so far as to say that batmitzvah was as imperative as barmitzvah. The course proved very popular, and seventeen girls passed the first examination and participated in a Sunday-afternoon ceremony at which the synagogue was packed to capacity.
>
> For this innovation, we were attacked by almost every rabbi in London, the *bat chayil* (as it was then known) course and ceremony being denounced as 'not in accordance with Jewish tradition.' We hit back by pointing to our success in retaining the girls at cheder, and to how genuinely enthusias-

tic they were in becoming familiar with the domestic aspects of Judaism. Within five years, all the mainstream synagogues in London—and many beyond—were offering special classes for girls and conducting a variety of graduation ceremonies.[36]

One of Harris's earliest mentors was Louis Jacobs, an attachment that may have raised eyebrows during his later pursuits. 'Many teachers influenced me in important and diverse ways,' Harris recalled. 'Because I held a United Synagogue studentship, I was seconded while at Jews' College to various London shuls. The rabbi who was most encouraging to me was Dr Jacobs, and in 1957 I was attached to his New West End Synagogue. He went out of his way to help me, and whatever difference there may be regarding his approach towards Judaism, when it comes to *menschlichkeit*, he can teach his colleagues a thing or two.

'When I was in the rabbinical diploma class at Jews' College, Rabbi Koppel Kahana Kagan made an immediate impression. He was wonderfully lenient in his approach to halachah, continually reminding us that anyone could say "No," but it took a *talmid chacham* to find a way to say "Yes" within the parameters of the law. How he would have objected to the current trend of extreme Orthodoxy and its tendency to heap prohibition upon prohibition on an overburdened religious public ...

'I am the first to admit that my personality and approach are riddled with contradictions somewhat unusual in a Chief Rabbi. I am utterly traditional and at the same time like to think of myself as thoroughly modern. I am strictly Orthodox, yet liberal enough to work with Reform associates for the common good. I am intensely passionate—*oy*, am I passionate!—on all matters of principle, but I loathe fundamentalism and much prefer moderation.

'I deal in the main with absolutes, yet politically espouse the centre—well, just left of centre. I live in an inner world of concepts and ideals and constant spiritual reflection, yet I am equally at home watching my favourite soccer or cricket team. Whether such hybrid qualities are an advantage is debatable.'[37]

Whether they were to appeal to his interlocutors when, in the summer of 1989, he was screened for the Chief Rabbinate was equally debatable. By then, steps were well in hand for the sifting committee to interview him, Weiss, Sacks, and Bulka at private sessions in London; Feldman and Lau, meanwhile, had ruled themselves out of the contest.[38] Earlier that year, Weiss had visited Britain at the invitation of the US Rabbinical Council and had lectured and preached in Hampstead Garden Suburb and Edgware.[39] The committee were later summoned to meet him during a visit in September.[40]

Of Harris's interview the same week, his wife recalled: 'As a result of the conversation between Cyril, Sidney [Frosh] and Jonathan [Lew], Cyril was formally invited to come to London to meet the search committee.[41] This was arranged to coincide with the eightieth-birthday celebrations of Cyril's cousin, Solly [Rabbi Dr Solomon Goldman]. The cover worked well, as very few people knew or suspected the reason for the visit.

'To my surprise, I was asked to accompany Cyril, even to the interview, where I sat and merely observed the proceedings.[42] I was not asked to go into the room until half-way through. My overriding impression was one of extreme good humour, flowing conversation, interchange of ideas, bright and positive. I remember thinking: if they want someone with experience of every facet of communal life, they would be crazy not to take him. The discussions I heard concerned relationships with the Reform, the ultra-Orthodox, and other topics. Everyone parted amicably and positively.'[43]

At the end of his visit, Harris was reported to have 'leapt from the starting-block in the race for the British Chief Rabbinate,' having told Greater London Radio: 'I am highly flattered to be considered a candidate.' In his vision of the post, he said, 'the Chief Rabbi must, most importantly, return to the grass-roots, helping to revitalise Zionism and to prevent the "stiebelisation" of the young Orthodox, caused by Anglo-Jewry resting on its laurels.'[44]

Also in London that week was Yisrael Lau,[45] invited by the United Synagogue to launch the annual Kol Nidre appeal. Frosh, supporting Lau's call to diaspora Jewry 'to help bear Israel's burdens,' gave no hint of any interview with Tel Aviv's Chief Rabbi.

Bulka's discussions with Frosh were equally covert. As he recounts them,[46] 'I was in London a number of times during this period, and the conversations were discreet and often beat about the bush, although with a clear view as to where they were leading. At a very friendly meeting with the committee, I outlined my vision of the office and what my priorities would be. Of course I was interested in the Chief Rabbinate, as any responsible Jewish leader would be in a position that, arguably, could shape the face of Judaism possibly for generations.'

Of his connection with Jakobovits, Bulka recalls: 'The Chief Rabbi, my uncle, understandably did not get directly involved, nor did I directly involve him. That would have been unfair to him and to the process. And, as far as I know, he never intervened in the selection on my behalf.'

By this time, meanwhile, Jakobovits' relationship with Kalms had reached a low ebb as differences over Sacks—and other issues—began to emerge. 'It is a tragedy and sad reflection on rabbinical disharmony,' Kalms had written to the Chief Rabbi, 'that you never grasped his [Sacks'] talents and developed him into your heir-apparent. You must take more than half the blame for that ...

'We diverge because your selected path takes you in another direction. It is inevitable that there must be at some time a public expression of this split.

In so far as it is possible, and bearing in mind my style, I hope it will remain civilised.'[47]

'There should be no illusion,' Kalms told Jakobovits on another occasion, 'that a word here or a lunch there can settle differences. An olive-branch is not a panacea. Indeed, your dismissiveness of these differences is more fractious than a simple acceptance that we have a substantive disagreement about communal leadership.'[48]

Jakobovits replied: 'I am looking neither for "a panacea" nor to "settle differences." Sometimes the art is not to settle them but to live with them, perhaps even to recognise their legitimacy, certainly to tolerate opinions one does not share. As you know, this has always been my philosophy, whether on personal, human, political or even religious relationships.

'In our context, I do not seek surrender from my critics. I do not want them to abdicate their genuinely held views, nor to withhold their honest expression of them to me. I never expected even the best of friends "to defend my statements" when they had differing opinions. But what I do seek is a willingness to listen, an effort to understand and, if necessary, an agreement to disagree without the slightest effect on personal friendship and communal partnership ...

'On Jonathan S., I will not be so insensitive as to reverse the call for "taking more than half the blame." I share your disillusionment, as well as your acclaim, of his talents. He knows, even if you do not, that the failure to strike up proper bonds between us is certainly not due to any lack of trying on my part—and is definitely not a "reflection on rabbinical disharmony."

'As you well know, I for one do not think we are doing him any favours, or promoting his professional prospects, by supporting his every whim, however irrational—whether a sabbatical after two years' tenure, or agreeing to be his agent in dismissing Lieberman[49] (which costs me heavily to this day in exposure to ceaseless public slander), or support for his refusal to take over rabbinic responsibility for the Jews' College minyan—at an ongoing cost to the College and the community which cannot be calculated.

'In all these cases, my views firmly opposed yours, but out of friendship as well as respect for your chairmanship [of the College], I did not demur. But Jonathan, sadly, did not benefit, and missed out on any number of essential opportunities for development into an heir-apparent, which can only be gained the hard way.

'As you will confirm, I had even offered him regular experiences by delegation—at inductions, top-level representation, and other "development" occasions, but all to no avail. If you knew all the facts on this objectively, you would certainly revise and retract the relevant remarks in your last letter.'[50]

'It was unnecessary,' Kalms responded, 'for me to talk about responsibility for Jonathan in percentage terms. I certainly agree that I have been indulgent, perhaps excessively. You know I have a soft spot for rabbis—and you, of course, know their minds better and are much less simpatico.

'Maybe you subconsciously saw him as an intellectual competitor. Perhaps I was frightened of losing his unique talents to the community. A critic might say I bought his friendship and loyalty. I will be proved right or wrong within the next one or two years. But you, typically, asked me to retract without asking yourself some key questions. Why was your relationship a failure? Was it entirely Jonathan's fault? A little critical self-analysis is demanded.'[51]

In a separate dispute over Jews' College,[52] Kalms wrote to Jakobovits: 'At our meeting on Monday, you expressed two strong demands: that your views regarding the appointment of Head of Rabbinics at the College must prevail; and that, due to your lack of trust in me, I should resign from Jews' College and the JEDT. I totally rejected out-of-hand your request, which I considered to have been made without authority, to be improper, to be personally motivated, and of no merit.

'When I suggested an alternative, that you might equally consider resigning, you said it was impossible due to your binding contract with the United Synagogue. What about my inviolable *covenant* with a greater authority? Do you think your contract takes precedence over my covenant? In our discussion, you talked about your sacred duty to achieve your ends. I did not realise you had the exclusive franchise on sacred duty!'

Asking 'where goeth Jews' College?', Kalms wrote: 'The crucial challenges of the next decade must be faced. We have to reinvigorate the College with long-term objectives. We have shared much aggravation on this subject, so don't pretend we do not inhabit mainly common ground. We have agreed to disagree regarding Jonathan. The future plans must be by consensus, but that consensus must be viable—that is my responsibility.'

In a reference to Jakobovits' plans for his remaining period in office, outlined in a 5749 New Year message to Anglo-Jewry, Kalms declaimed: 'It was poor judgment on Rosh Hashanah, when inspiration and vision were needed, to express a personal time-scale. Leadership is not talking about one's own span; it makes no sense to reduce the dreams and ambitions of others merely to your own term of office. It is also dangerous, for an unrealistic time-scale, a shortening of discussion and forced precipitation towards an artificial date can be immensely damaging.'[53]

The Chief Rabbi retorted: 'It is demeaning as well as futile to continue the discussions and correspondence between us, and, under present circumstances, I will no longer be a party to them. I totally reject your doctored version of my "strong demands," together with most other charges and distortions in your vituperative letter.'[54]

Anxious to repair the 'present circumstances,' Kalms concluded his side of the exchange by assuring Jakobovits that 'my letter was intended to exorcise the issues of disagreement and open the door to discussions about the future of the organisations we lead. May I suggest that you read only the affectionate parts of my letter, under the heading "The Future," and see whether we can bring back our dialogue to both a pragmatic and a philosophical level.'[55]

Reciprocating Kalms' expressed desire to greet the imminent Simchat Torah as 'a period of real joy and, may I say, shalom,' Jakobovits replied: 'I, too, now look forward to a happy Simchat Torah—and, equally, to restoring our friendly partnership.'[56]

This, however, was wishful thinking. Before Simchat Torah came round again—indeed, in the very week that Weiss and Harris were being interviewed in London—Kalms resigned his chairmanship of the JEDT and Jews' College, claiming that he had 'been involved in communal leadership long enough.'[57]

* * *

Soon after his split with Kalms, Jakobovits was involved in another controversy that was to have a lasting impact on intra-communal relations. His 'bridges of understanding' had all but collapsed some years earlier, and by 1985 he was faced with an open revolt from the Progressive movements.

'To my colleagues,' wrote Tony Bayfield to Jakobovits, on behalf of the Council of Reform and Liberal Rabbis, 'the present climate appears to be one of growing hostility towards our section of the community. There are two key issues. How can anyone who is so publicly opposed to us still represent us? And how can we tolerate an increasing number of public statements with which we disagree, about which we have had no opportunity for prior consultation or discussion?

'I am now under considerable pressure to write to *The Times* and the BBC publicly stating that you no longer represent our section of the Jewish community. I am obviously very loathe to take such a step, which would have far-reaching consequences. I would very much like to have an opportunity of discussing the matter with you—if not personally, at least in a small and private gathering which can look with some degree of calmness before irrevocable public steps are taken.'[58]

No satisfactory result was forthcoming, and a fortnight later—writing in *Manna*, the journal of Reform's Sternberg Centre for Judaism—Bayfield cautioned Jakobovits that 'if he still claims to represent us and our independent friends, he must cease to lambast us as "dissidents" or "priests" of an alien religion. If he wishes to speak for us, then he must have some regard for our conscience and our sincere interpretation of Judaism. If he continues to choose to do the opposite, then the delicately balanced edifice at whose pinnacle he now stands will surely collapse.

'We are prepared to represent ourselves. We are strong enough to face the challenge, and from that position of strength we shall continue to build bridges. Are Sir Immanuel and his United Synagogue able to respond? Does the Chief Rabbi in name wish to remain the Chief Rabbi in reality?'[59]

Jakobovits' response came in a *Jewish Chronicle* interview, in which he emphasised the 'two functions' of his position. 'I am not only "chief" in the sense of being religious spokesman for the entire community, but I am also "rabbi." As a rabbi, I head an Orthodox establishment and I have my beliefs which I cannot sacrifice for the sake of good neighbourly relations.

'I believe the religious stability of the community will determine the future of the community more than our unity. Unity is a precious thing, an important thing. But even more important than a façade of unity where none exists is that we should convey to our children, and our children's children, loyalties and allegiances, beliefs and practices, which are the sole *raison d'être* of Jewish existence. I cannot compromise on that.'[60]

The pot simmered for several more years before boiling over on the eve of the Chief Rabbinical appointment, with a front-page statement in *The Times* from the Union of Liberal and Progressive Synagogues (ULPS):

> In view of the procedure now being implemented to appoint a successor to the present Chief Rabbi, we feel it important to clarify our own relationship to the Office of the Chief Rabbi.
>
> The Chief Rabbi of the United Hebrew Congregations of the British Commonwealth is elected by a committee appointed by the officers and council of the United Synagogue. All members of the committee are members of constituents of the United Synagogue and associated synagogues. No other synagogue body is formally consulted in the election of the Chief Rabbi.
>
> Accordingly, it is appropriate for us to say on behalf of the Union of Liberal and Progressive Synagogues that the Chief Rabbi to be elected has no authority over our own rabbis or lay people, nor does he represent us or speak on our behalf. Our community appoints its own rabbinic and lay representatives and spokespersons.
>
> This statement does not seek to detract from the status of the Chief Rabbi of the United Hebrew Congregations or his authority over his constituents, but only to reaffirm that the Jewish community is not monolithic but pluralistic in nature. In Judaism, as in other faiths, there is much diversity of belief

and practice, even though the common ground far exceeds the differences.

We make this statement before the forthcoming appointment to make it clear that our relationship to the Office of the Chief Rabbi is not dependent on the person who fills it. We will respect the view of the new appointee and seek to co-operate with him in our mutual efforts towards the strengthening of the Jewish community. We hope that he, too, will respect the differences between his views and ours, and that those differences will not be allowed to diminish co-operative endeavour in areas of common interests and objectives.[61]

Commenting on the statement, The Times' religious-affairs editor, Clifford Longley, wrote: 'Leaders of the Liberal Jewish community in Britain have decided to stop treating the office of Chief Rabbi as the titular head of all Britain's 300,000 Jews. After the retirement of Lord Jakobovits, they will regard his successor as the leader only of Orthodox Jews and will describe him as "Chief Rabbi of the United Hebrew Congregations."'[62]

The Reform movement speedily dissociated itself from the move, telling its rabbis and synagogue chairmen that it had rejected an approach from the ULPS to add its imprimatur to the statement. 'We took the view that to issue a declaration which stated only what everyone already knows would be interpreted as unnecessarily divisive and would tend to alienate those in the centre of the community who are concerned for its unity. At a joint meeting with the ULPS, we said that were an unacceptably "right-wing" rabbi to be appointed [as Chief Rabbi], that might be the time for a statement of the kind proposed. The present time was not appropriate.'[63]

In an unpublished letter to The Times, seeking to clarify its position, Reform's lay and rabbinical leaders wrote: 'Despite our doctrinal differences, the present Chief Rabbi has sought in a number of ways to foster greater unity in the community. We trust that whoever is appointed to succeed him will advance the work started by Lord Jakobovits, helping to bring greater harmony and common purpose to the whole of British Jewry.'[64]

Condemning the ULPS declaration, Board of Deputies president Lionel Kopelowitz stressed the Chief Rabbi's 'second role—a role which is not defined, but which is recognised both within and outside the Jewish community as being the public religious representative of British Jewry as a whole. This is a role which has worked to our advantage.

'I am firmly of the view that it is not in the communal interest for any group to take up a hard position at this stage, before a new Chief Rabbi has been appointed, to say whether they would or would not accept him in a representative capacity. The statement in yesterday's *Times* was ill-conceived and badly timed.'⁶⁵

Taking issue with Kopelowitz, the ULPS chairman, Harold Sanderson, questioned 'the validity of the "second role" you ascribe to the Chief Rabbi of the United Hebrew Congregations. He has never been recognised by either wing of the Progressive movement as the *religious* representative of the whole of the British Jewish community or the Commonwealth. It may have slipped your memory that the chairman of the Council of Reform and Liberal Rabbis has been our representative in this area for two decades. It is not our statement which has caused division, but your comments which have helped to mislead the Jewish community.'⁶⁶

Brushing this aside, Kopelowitz defended his comments as 'accurately reflecting the position of the Chief Rabbi, both as the religious authority of those congregations who recognise that authority, and as the public religious representative of the totality of British Jewry.' He told Sanderson: 'I have now had an opportunity of discussing this matter with your president, Lord Goodman, who has indicated to me that he saw the statement in draft, when it was shown to him by Rabbi Dr Sidney Brichto. Lord Goodman has assured me that he agreed to it "with great reluctance."'⁶⁷

The last published word on the subject came from ULPS director Rosita Rosenberg, commenting on a lecture given by Sacks days earlier in which he had warned that 'Jewish unity cannot be achieved quickly' and that 'there is a terribly widespread belief that unity lies just within our grasp.

> Divisions that have lasted for almost two centuries [said Sacks] are not going to be healed overnight. It is a mistake to see the Orthodox–Reform divide as the single problem confronting Jewry. Other deep divisions beset the Jewish world, and false expectations of finding quick solutions are bound to lead to frustration and disappointment.
>
> Each of us wants Jewish unity, but each of us wants it on our own terms. That is why the search for unity doesn't resolve the tensions in the Jewish world, but instead merely reproduces them. In fact, it does worse, because it leads us to believe that there is some resolution in sight, and that all it needs is good will, tolerance and dialogue to achieve it.
>
> Now, manifestly, that is not so. What divides Jews today is not misunderstanding but a deep, substantive set of conflicts about what it is to be a Jew. Instead, the art is to know where we are going and to move forward, if necessary, an inch at a time.

Pluralism is not an answer. Pluralism supposes that, somehow, all the different and conflicting things that Jews believe today can be accommodated within one universe. They can't. If pluralism means that we should grant equal legitimacy to every interpretation of Judaism, it is not there to be granted. Orthodox rabbis cannot be called on to legitimate non-halachic forms of Judaism.

There can be no dialogue if that means the kind of public, staged confrontation between Jews of different beliefs, because that kind of dialogue never moved anyone an inch closer together. Instead, all Jews should engage in a personal dialogue with Torah and the totality of Jewish history in critical self-questioning.[68]

'The wisdom of expressing just where we stand,' wrote Rosenberg in response, 'was amply borne out when we read the reported words of Rabbi Jonathan Sacks. If Rabbi Sacks, a leading candidate for Chief Rabbi, known as a moderate, can reject the possibility of a pluralistic religious Jewish society (one which exists satisfactorily in the USA, in the absence of a Chief Rabbi), how can anyone claim that there is a likelihood the new holder of the post could or would wish to speak satisfactorily for Progressive Jews?'[69]

* * *

Sacks' comments on pluralism were to be read in conjunction with similar references in the run-up to the appointment. In his bid to 'bind all Jews to one another,' he had frequently called on the community to observe the courtesies of civility and tolerance. 'It would be wrong,' he asserted in 1986, 'to say that today's Jewish religious circles are ones in which *lashon hara* [slander, calumny] occurs, is tolerated, passes without notice. Wrong because it would be the most perverse understatement.

> *Lashon hara*, far from being an occasional forgivable lapse, has become part of the very texture of a certain kind of Jewish life. We have evolved a culture, an apotheosis, of *lashon hara*. It has become almost impossible in certain circles to gain religious credence or acceptability without 'talking disparagingly' of someone. *Lashon hara* has become a ritual of initiation and group membership.
>
> Character assassination, condemnation, heresy-hunting, baseless denigration, the rush to judgment on a spider's-

web of gossip: these have become the normal conversational modalities in at least some Jewish groups, not least those to whom the *Mishnah Berurah* and its author, the Chafetz Chaim, are held in esteem.

In such a culture, words are not words but weapons; stature is measured by the exhaustiveness of one's condemnations; verbal terrorism reigns. The violence done to Jewish law and values is insane and obscene. This the Chafetz Chaim saw, understood and said. Few listened.

No reader of Jewish news, no observer of religious life over these past few years, can have failed to recognise this escalating culture of condemnation ... It has even penetrated, sadly, to the normally judicious ranks of mainstream Anglo-Jewish Orthodoxy, where attacks have begun to be heard on the so-called 'Right'—the yeshivah and Chasidic worlds.

It would be a tragedy indeed if the mainstream were to cut itself off from the energies, enthusiasm and sheer flow of Torah that come from these worlds. That the mainstream has a wider constituency and a different challenge to face in maintaining the allegiance of its members should not need to be defended by denigrating others.[70]

'The most urgent task of Orthodoxy in modernity,' Sacks wrote later, 'is to think a way forward to recovering the substantive reality of *Knesset Yisrael*, the Jewish people as a single entity standing before God ...

'If Orthodoxy is to act responsibly toward the whole Jewish world and not simply toward its own immediate constituency, there are deep dilemmas to be faced about its relationship with secular and non-Orthodox Jews. It cannot embrace pluralism, the view that a secular or non-halachic reading of tradition is legitimate. But it cannot withdraw altogether into segregation without abdicating the responsibilities of religious leadership.'[71]

'"Argument for the sake of Heaven,"' Sacks asserted on the eve of Traditional Alternatives, 'does not imply pluralism. But it does imply a willingness to engage in reasoned dialogue with views with which one disagrees.'[72] And, at the conference itself: 'If Torah is, God forbid, ideologised, politicised, used to delegitimate other Jews who also care for Torah, then it will bring not peace but conflict to the world.'[73]

Months later, he declared: 'The religious voice that has sounded loudest, and most often, has been that of one group of Jews denouncing the faith and practice of another. Who benefits? Neither Jews nor Judaism. No movement was ever given strength by castigating the rest of the Jewish world as heretics, on the one hand, and fanatics, on the other. We need not be religious pluralists in order to treat other Jews with respect. In the end, we must realise that there is more at stake than institutional rivalries. There is the honour of Judaism itself which must, if it is to command respect, speak with a voice that transcends the politics and personalities of its human representatives. We must never use the language of our enemies in speaking of other Jews.'[74]

'Institutional rivalries' came to the fore even as Sacks was decrying them when, not to be outdone by previous elections, and 'on the advice of its rabbis,' the Federation of Synagogues pulled out of the election. 'The Federation,' announced its president, Arnold Cohen, 'wishes to keep its independence and could not work under a constitution where it would have to accept the authority of the Chief Rabbi.'

Addressing the US council in the wake of the boycott, Frosh described the move as 'not unexpected, though very disappointing.' But, he added, 'the door is still open.'[75]

Several weeks later, Chanoch Ehrentreu, head of the London Beth Din, visited South Africa with his wife and was feted, on the evening of his arrival, by the Harrises and the Johannesburg dayanim. During the evening, Ann Harris later recorded,[76] Victor Lucas phoned from London.

'Cyril was able to speak to him only after the guests had gone. The call was to warn him that the Sacks camp was in the ascendancy and that Cyril should be wary because a deal had apparently been struck with the dayanim regarding the future management of the London Beth Din. Victor's advice was to withdraw from the contest, but Cyril decided not to do so, having telephoned Jonathan Lew and been assured that the competition was still open.

'The dayan's visit went well and he seemed very impressed by Cyril's handling of his position in South Africa. We talked it all over and came to the conclusion that, as Jonathan and Linda Lew would shortly be holidaying in South Africa and spending some time with us, this would be a good opportunity to discuss the position face to face.'

After a sifting committee meeting in early December, Harris heard that neither of the 'two major contenders'—himself and Sacks—had commanded the support of a majority and that 'the committee has decided to look further.' Lew (with his wife) arrived in South Africa towards the end of the month, expressing support for Harris and telling him that he [Lew] had been instrumental in forestalling any adverse recommendation at the earlier meeting.

Visiting Israel days later, the Harrises encountered a delegation from the Board of Deputies, led by Kopelowitz and joint vice-president Israel Finestein,[77] and received an assurance that 'the [Chief Rabbinate] decision is still open.' They also met other 'men of standing and influence' who expressed 'open support for Cyril,' although none appeared willing to provide a platform for him while in London for the wedding of their son.[78]

Kopelowitz recalls that the deputies' visit concluded with a farewell dinner 'at which I invited Chief Rabbi and Mrs Harris to be our guests and to sit at my table. As I entered the room, Judge Finestein and his wife requested that I allow the Harrises to sit at their table, saying "They are our close and very special friends." I did not object: Judge Finestein was a member of the Chief Rabbinate Conference committee, and Cyril Harris regarded his gesture in a very positive way.'[79]

During the last week in January, Frosh announced that the identity of the new Chief Rabbi would likely be known 'by early April.' His seven-man team were 'sifting through the short-list and will soon come up with a name.' Popular speculation held that Sacks and Harris were 'well in the running' and that visits by Lau and Bulka 'have also kept the grapevine busy. But, as yet, there is clearly no firm favourite.'[80]

On 28 January, Ann Harris travelled to London for the wedding, leaving her husband—delayed by official duties—to follow a week later. 'When he arrived,' she wrote in her diary, 'he received no courtesy whatever—no phone calls from anyone except Victor Lucas. He could only assume that his presence was no longer required by the formal establishment.

'Over the period of Michael's wedding, we were thrown in the path of almost all those taking part in the game. There were two distinct camps—supporters who felt helpless and horrified by what was happening, or who did not realise that matters had progressed so far, and establishment people who had made up their minds in favour of Sacks and either ignored us totally or offered pretence friendship.

'The situation annoyed me so much that I decided to try to find an impartial opinion as to whether to advise Cyril to withdraw. In the end, I confided in Lionel Swift. During a lengthy telephone conversation, he expressed the view that Cyril should not withdraw and that he was a suitable candidate, given his enormous communal experience and expertise.

'Finally, the day before leaving England on 19 February, Cyril decided to withdraw and face the more exciting challenges South Africa had to offer, rather than be a candidate without the full and honest support of either the lay leadership or his rabbinical colleagues.'[81]

Decades later, describing this decision, Kopelowitz stated: 'On 18 February, Prime Minister Margaret Thatcher addressed the monthly meeting of the Board of Deputies, where—at my invitation—Chief Rabbi and Mrs Harris were also present and where I presented them to Mrs Thatcher. During the subsequent lunch, Rabbi Harris advised me that he had withdrawn his name from the Chief Rabbinical contest, explaining that South African State President F. W. de

Klerk had just released Nelson Mandela from prison and there were exciting challenges to be faced back home.'[82]

In the week of Harris's departure, supporters of Sacks were said to be 'looking for a clear signal that he has triumphed. While the search-committee members are still counselling caution and warning of possible last-minute hitches, the mood in the Sacks camp is one of suppressed excitement following the news that Chief Rabbi Cyril Harris, of South Africa, has withdrawn.

'In a terse statement to the *Jewish Chronicle* on Sunday, immediately before returning to his post in Johannesburg, he said he no longer wished to be considered a candidate. Friends say that his decision resulted from his appreciation that developments in South Africa demanded continuity in senior Jewish leadership, as well as his assessment that he could not command a majority in the selection committee.'

The paper reported that 'the search committee did not reach its recommendation easily. One member, Victor Lucas, a former United Synagogue president, was known to favour Rabbi Harris, and the other members were rarely of one mind.

'While Rabbi Sacks was always regarded as the prime contender, advice was heaped in on the search committee suggesting, variously, that his lack of an extensive yeshivah background and advocacy of centrist Orthodoxy would put him at a disadvantage with the right-wing; that he was insufficiently experienced in Anglo-Jewish politics to withstand pressures which surround the Chief Rabbinate; or, quite simply, that he was too young (he is forty-one) to command his rabbis.

'At the end of the day, however, it seems that the search committee—which never seriously considered suggestions that Lord Jakobovits should stay on after seventy—could produce no combination of teacher, scholar and public personality of the standing to challenge Rabbi Sacks for Anglo-Jewry's prime spiritual post.'[83]

Reminiscing years later, Kalms—the kingmaker in the process—put it this way: 'It was really a case of natural selection, helped by my Traditional Alternatives seminar that established in the community's mind the likely next Chief Rabbi—which was, of course, the purpose of the conference. In any case, there was hardly any competition—Rabbi Harris[84] and Rabbi Bulka—so it was really no contest. The United Synagogue held several inconsequential meetings, pretending to be searching for candidates, but at the end of the day Jonathan Sacks was the only credible choice.

'As far as his personal relationship with me was concerned, at that time he stood on the platform of inclusivism, aiming to bring the left and right together by finding common ground. As things turned out, this was a failure and, in many ways, a disaster for the community, but the facts on that are on the record.'[85]

Chapter Eight

* * *

Addressing the Chief Rabbinate Conference committee on the last Sunday in February, Frosh revealed that, during their search over the previous year, the sifting team had had 'correspondence from all over the country, offering advice and endorsing support for more than one rabbi.' Suggested candidates had been located in Britain, Israel, the United States, Canada, Australia, and South Africa, ranging from communal rabbis and dayanim to heads of yeshivot and academics. It had soon become clear, however, that 'if at all possible, the new Chief Rabbi should be an Englishman, or at least conversant with the Anglo-Jewish scene.'

'On Sunday, 11 February,' Frosh told his colleagues, 'the sifting committee met with Dayan Ehrentreu and Dayan Berger, of the London Beth Din, in order to seek their perception of the essential qualities necessary for the position of Chief Rabbi and Av Beth Din and, at the same time, their view of the credentials and suitability of the two leading personalities, Rabbis Harris and Sacks. The dayanim indicated that both were acceptable to them, but that they had a stronger preference for Rabbi Sacks.' A similar preference, said Frosh, had earlier been expressed by the executive committee of the US Rabbinical Council.

'After the dayanim left our meeting, and after considerable discussion, it was unanimously agreed that a recommendation go forward to the Chief Rabbinate Conference that a call be issued to Rabbi Sacks. Two days later, a deputation comprising Victor Lucas, Leslie Wagner and myself, accompanied by Jonathan Lew, called upon Rabbi Sacks and his wife. We indicated that we were prepared to recommend the call on the understanding that he would disengage himself as speedily as possible from his present posts.

'It was left to Rabbi Sacks to consider the matter and to advise me within a few days whether he would accept the call. He met with me after Shabbat of last week and said that he would be honoured to accept the call and the high responsibilities of leadership that went with it.

'It was his wish, however, that prior to his installation he would spend a period of intensive study in Israel under the tutelage of *gedolim*, during which, along with such study, he would be able to familiarise himself with the work of the Chief Rabbinate and batei din in Israel; this would, he believed, enhance the authority of the office. He would also spend time with Chief Rabbi Lord Jakobovits and the dayanim of the London Beth Din to apprise himself of the general and particular problems currently facing the Anglo-Jewish community.'[86]

Frosh later told the *Jewish Chronicle*: 'This has been no compromise appointment. He is the best man for the job—an intellectual, a communicator, and a unifier. In my view, this is the most prestigious Chief Rabbinate in the diaspora. That is why the selection took so long. It was never going to be anyone's sinecure.'

Agreeing that Sacks' age had been an important factor, Frosh added: 'We must have a young approach. Rabbi Sacks is a person who can relate to the wide spread of the community, particularly young people, helping them to become more committed to Judaism. He is one of the new breed of Jewish intellectuals, well qualified to deal with contemporary issues in both the Jewish and the wider context.'[87]

Following the committee's meeting, Frosh phoned Bulka to advise him of their decision. In a letter the following day, Bulka wrote: 'As I mentioned to you over the phone, it was an honour to be considered for the prestigious post of Chief Rabbi, and it was certainly a pleasure to meet you, to get to know you, and to have a chance to meet prominent members of the Anglo-Jewish community during my recent visit there.

'Congratulations on your choice of Rabbi Dr Jonathan Sacks as your new Chief Rabbi. I hope that during his tenure he will provide the leadership and guidance that you anticipate, to enhance the Anglo-Jewish community in the crucial period ahead. As I mentioned, I should like to maintain close contact with the Anglo-Jewish community and be available for lectures and other opportunities of shared experiences.'[88]

'I feel honoured and privileged,' said Sacks of his nomination; 'my family and I are very excited. My Chief Rabbinate will aim to heal some of the rifts that divide the community. It will encourage debate and will not shy away from communicating Jewish values to the wider community. I am determined, as far as possible, to emphasise what unites Jews and to encourage an atmosphere of mutual respect. But there can be no compromise in matters of halachah. There are no short cuts.'[89]

The appointment was formally ratified at a gathering of the Chief Rabbinate Conference on the first day of April, when its two hundred delegates voted unanimously to rubber-stamp the call.[90] Despite his earlier reservations, Jakobovits greeted the outcome 'with particular delight.' Rabbi Sacks' record of leadership and scholarship, he affirmed, 'provides every promise of a richly blessed incumbency.'[91]

Jonathan Sacks (1991): 'We must reach out to every Jew with open arms'

FROM THE PULPIT — VI
A Decade of Jewish Renewal

Address delivered by Rabbi Dr Jonathan Sacks on his installation as Chief Rabbi of the United Hebrew Congregations of the Commonwealth, St John's Wood Synagogue, London, 1 September 1991–22 Elul 5751

I have had more than a year to contemplate this moment, but the closer it has come, the more overwhelmed I have been. The greatest leader the Jewish people has ever known, Moses, trembled when he contemplated the burden of leadership, and said *mi anochi*,[1] 'Who am I?' What then shall I say, who until the age of twenty-five never even dreamed of becoming a rabbi, let alone a Chief Rabbi? Thirteen years ago, almost exactly to the day, I began a journey as rabbi of the Golders Green Synagogue, and today, on my barmitzvah in the rabbinate, you have bestowed on me the honour of one of the great positions of leadership in the Jewish world. Now, as then, I am determined never to rely on my own merits. Instead, I pray to God, in the words of King Solomon, for a *lev shome'a lishpot et amcha*, a listening and discerning heart, attentive to the needs of His community and ever obedient to His word. *Ana avdah dekudsha brikh hu:* I am a servant of the Holy One, blessed be He. No Jew can say less; no Jew can aspire to more.

Let me begin by paying tribute to my distinguished predecessor, Lord Jakobovits. Here in this pulpit, nearly a quarter-century ago, he spoke at his own installation of the three crowns of rabbinic leadership: the crowns of kingship, priesthood and Torah. Since then, no one has done more to raise those crowns to their proper glory: kingship, in addressing and securing the admiration of the wider public, recognised in his elevation to the peerage and the award of the Templeton Prize; priesthood, in his great work for Jewish education; and Torah, in his adoption of the mantle of the prophets as the voice of Jewish ethics in confused times. Lord Jakobovits, you have raised the standing of the Chief Rabbinate in both Jewish and non-Jewish eyes; and for you and Lady Jakobovits, may your years of retirement be as long and as creative as your years of office.

---

1   [Hebrew transliteration throughout as in original text.]

At this emotional moment, let me express my thanks to those in whose merit I stand here today: to my teachers, especially to Rabbi Nachum Rabinovitch, from whom I learned that love of Torah and moral courage go hand-in-hand; to the distinguished dayanim of our Beth Din, for their constant encouragement and advice; to my revered colleagues in the rabbinate, without whom I could not hope to achieve what must be achieved in the coming years; and to all those with whom I had the privilege of working at Jews' College, and in the Golders Green and Marble Arch synagogues—true friends who made each of those experiences memorable.

Above all, my heart goes out today to my family. Elaine and I married young, and little did she know then where this strange journey of ours would one day lead. But she has been with me every inch of the way, as have our children, Joshua, Dina, and Gila, giving strength and support and love. Most of all on this day of days, I thank my parents, who gave me a *yiddisher neshomo*, a Jewish soul, and who made me realise that the greatest love parents can have for a child is to want him always to grow. To you all, I pray that I may be worthy of your hopes.

I want today to set out the direction of my Chief Rabbinate, and to share with you the vision that lies behind it. Let me begin with the vision. Time and again this past year, as I sat in Jerusalem, breathing its inspiration, one saying came into my mind, the saying of one of the great heroes of Judaism, Akavia ben Mehalalel. He said: *histakel bishloshah devarim v'ein atah ba lidei averah*—Reflect on three things and you will not transgress, go wrong, lose your way. *Da me'ayin bata*—know from where you came; *ule'an atah holekh*—and where you are going; *v'lifnei mi atah atid liten din v'cheshbon*—and know before Whom you will have to give an account.

Akavia was suggesting something daring and fundamental. We can go wrong as individuals or as a people, not necessarily because we were driven by malice, but simply because of a failure of imagination. For a moment we lived for the moment; and we forgot what the past should have taught us, what the future consequences would be, and we forgot that there is always an accounting, a moral price to pay. We can go astray simply because of a failure of imagination. A failure of *historical* imagination: we forgot where we came from. A failure of *prophetic* imagination: we forgot where we were travelling to. Or a failure of *spiritual* imagination: we forgot before Whom we stand. Akavia spoke of individuals. But I want today to apply his three great questions to the Jewish people as a whole, because it is there that my vision belongs.

How does Jewish history begin? With a journey. *Lech lecha*, 'get thee out.' The very first words of God to Abraham set him on a journey, *el ha'aretz asher areka*, towards a land, *v'escha l'goi gadol*, towards nationhood, *va'avarechecha va'agadla shemecha vehyeh berakhah*, towards being blessed and a blessing unto others. The whole of the Torah from Genesis to Deuteronomy is the story of that journey. But what happens?

And here we come to a mystery which haunts the whole of Jewish existence. The story the Torah tells about Israel begins with the journey of Abraham to the land. But by the time it ends, his children still have not arrived. The book of Devarim ends with Moses on the mountain looking down on Israel from afar, but still not having crossed the Jordan. *Me'ayin bata ule'an atah holech*, Where have the children of Israel come from, and to what are they going? From a small family to a great nation. From exile to a land. From slavery to freedom. The five books of Moses tell that story. What they do not tell is what happened when Israel finally arrived.

We are an ancient people, older than almost any other. We have seen one civilisation after another rise to power and then decline and fall. But in almost 4,000 years of our history, only three times have we stood on the brink of our destination. Only three times have we been a great nation, with freedom and a land. Once, in the days of Joshua. A second time when Cyrus of Persia gave the Babylonian exiles permission to return. And the third time, today. The whole of Jewish history has been a journey to those three moments. What happened when we arrived?

On the first occasion, Israel fell apart. There was the period of the judges, when *ish hayashar b'enav ya'aseh*, each person did what was right in his own eyes. Then, after only three kings—Saul, David, and Solomon—the country split into two, with the ultimate loss of eighty per cent of the people of Israel, the lost ten tribes. Those who remained were too few and weak to overcome the might of Babylon. And so the first Temple was destroyed, the first arrival failed.

On the second occasion, Israel fell apart. Under Ezra and Nehemiah, they renewed the covenant. But then they succumbed to Hellenisation, what we would today call assimilation. There were fierce divisions within Jewry, even at times civil war. It was, said the rabbis, a time of *sinat chinam*, of groundless hatred between Jew and Jew. And by the time Vespasian and Titus marched on Jerusalem, Jews were too disunited to resist. And so the second Temple was destroyed, the second arrival failed.

And at that moment a great question-mark was raised over the Jewish people. We have an unparalleled capacity to travel hopefully. Abraham, Isaac, Jacob, Moses, all of them spent their lives travelling in hope. But do we have the capacity to arrive? That is the single most crucial question facing Jewry today. Because, for only the third time in the annals of our people, we stand as Moses stood at the end of his life: within sight of the destination to which the whole of Jewish history has been a journey.

For nearly 2,000 years of exile, we longed for freedom. We have it now. We prayed for a land. We have it now. We prayed to stand within thy gates,

O Jerusalem. We have it now. We prayed for the ingathering of exiles from the four corners of the world. We have it now. Nothing stands between us and the realisation of the greatest dream ever dreamed by our grandparents, or theirs, all the way back to Abraham: to be a *mamlechet kohanim v'goi kadosh*, a people dedicated to God in freedom and sovereignty. We stand at the threshold of millennial longings. And only one thing stands in our way: a failure of imagination. Of historical imagination, remembering where we came from. Of prophetic imagination, remembering where we are travelling to. Or of spiritual imagination, remembering before Whom we stand.

Consider this. For 2,000 years, we were the people of the book. No nation has ever cherished Jewish learning, education, as did we. Against every other civilisation, Jews said education is not for an elite but *morashah kehillat ya'akov*, the heritage of every Jew. It is not just for the young, but *chayenu v'orech yamenu*, it is our whole lives and the length of our days. Only one people ever predicated its very survival not on might or power, but on a book: education is the link that binds the generations.

And today? Despite the great advances in Anglo-Jewish education, how many of our children have been to a Jewish school? How many of them can understand Hebrew, the one language that connects us to the Jewish people? How many of them carry on studying about Judaism beyond the age of twelve or thirteen, perhaps the earliest age that it begins to make sense? How often do we study a Jewish book?

Or consider this. Since the time of Abraham and Sarah, if there was one thing Jews guarded as the very fulcrum of their survival it was the family. What did they pray for more than anything else? For children to carry on the covenant. When the prophets rose to the climax of religious passion, how did they describe the relationship between God and Israel? In the language of the family. *Bni bechori yisrael*. We are God's children, and He is our father. *V'erastich li l'olam*. We are God's betrothed, and He is our beloved. The family was where Jews learned who they were, where they came from, and where they were going to. The family was where Jews learned to love. The family was the crucible of Jewish survival.

Today, we know that in Anglo-Jewry there are too few synagogue marriages. Divorce has become an epidemic. Non-marriages, mixed marriages and broken marriages have become not the rare exception but the rule. How can we, almost within a single generation, have taken perhaps the Torah's greatest single contribution to human happiness and simply thrown it away?

Or consider this. For the last 1,800 years, Jews were scattered across every country of the globe, from Babylon to Birmingham, from Buenos Aires to Berditchev. And yet they knew, and their neighbours knew, that they were an extended family, a single nation, *yeshno am echad m'fuzar umeforad bein ha'amim*.

Though they were dispersed, they were united: by a common past, a common hope, and a common faith. They knew where they had come from, where they were going to, and before Whom they stood. Though they had no land, they were one people.

And today: we have a land, but are we one people? We are more deeply divided than at almost any time in our history. Israel is divided. We in the diaspora are divided. A few years ago, Jewish thinkers asked the question: Will there be one Jewish people in the year 2000? Today, there are already many prepared to give the answer 'No.' These are fundamental rifts which threaten the very integrity of Jewry as *am echad*, a single people.

The Jewish people has lost its way. For generations, we travelled hopefully; but do we now have the courage to arrive? For generations, we prayed; but can we live with the answer to our prayers? We survived slavery; but can we handle freedom? We have eaten the bread of affliction; but can we handle affluence? We learned to live with Israel as a dream; can we live with Israel as a reality?

Can it be that on the very brink of the fulfilment of the hopes of generations, our strength of will might desert us at the last moment yet again? It cannot be. The first failure brought us an exile of seventy years. The second failure brought us an exile of 1,870 years. There can be no third failure.

In this fifty-eighth century, Jewish time, Jews have passed through the Shoah, the greatest human tragedy ever to befall our people; and the rebirth of the State of Israel, our greatest collective miracle in 2,000 years. In Israel during the Gulf War, I could not believe what was happening, that even through the missiles and the danger, Russian and Ethiopian Jews kept on coming; and I knew that, though Jews had said these words for thousands of years, it was our generation that had been privileged to see them come true: *im yihyeh nidachacha bizkei hashamayim*, 'Though you are scattered to the ends of the world, from there the Lord your God will gather you and bring you back.' And within the last two weeks, we have witnessed Soviet Communism, one of the greatest attempts ever made to eliminate God, Judaism, and the biblical value of individual freedom, bring upon itself its own destruction. Can any of us believe that we live in ordinary times?

A Jewish writer once said: 'The number of Jews in the world is smaller than a small statistical error in the Chinese census. Yet ... big things seem to happen around us and to us.' This century, things have happened to us, for evil and for good, so big that they have no precedent since the days of the Bible; and they summon us to greatness. I pray: let our imagination not fail us now.

We must work together to renew the Jewish world. For nearly 2,000 years, we travelled in hope; and now, on the brink of arrival, let us not lose our way. We have suffered from complacency and religious under-achievement. We have injured ourselves by divisions and petty rivalries. A section of our community is slowly drifting away. We are losing our most precious possessions—Jewish identity; the Jewish family; above all, our commitment to the Torah which inspired generations to lead lives of holiness and moral beauty. Are we, who once heard the call of destiny, deaf to it now? Are we, who taught the world that religious faith is a journey from slavery to freedom, unable to cope with the challenges of freedom? God forbid. We have lost our prophetic vision. But we, who live at this momentous time, can recover it together.

Because *me'ayin bata*? Where did we come from? From a hundred generations of Jews who suffered because of their faith and people, yet remained loyal to both. *L'an atah holekh*? Where are we going to? To the day when, living our faith in freedom and pride, *v'ra'u kol amei ha'aretz ki sham hashem nikra alecha*, 'all the nations of the earth shall see that we are called by the name of God.' *V'lifnei mi atah atid liten din v'cheshbon*? And to Whom are we responsible? To God, and to all the generations of Jews who came before us and prayed for what we have; and to all those generations yet unborn whose Jewish fate is in our hands.

I was sitting one Shabbat afternoon watching children playing in the streets of Jerusalem. There was a stillness and a peace which exists only on Shabbat in Jerusalem as the sun begins to set and the houses turn red and gold. And then I remembered how, almost 2,000 years ago, Rabban Gamliel and Rabbi Elazar ben Azariah and Rabbi Yehoshua had seen this city in ruins and they wept. But Rabbi Akiva, that giant of faith, said: One day Zechariah's prophecy will come true. 'Old men and women will once again sit in the streets of Jerusalem ... *urechovot ha'ir yimalu yeladim viyladot mesachakim birchovoteha*, and the streets of the city will be filled with children playing.' And I thought, *ribbono shel olam*, how long we waited; how many exiles, expulsions, persecutions and pogroms we endured; but we never lost that vision.

And here was Israel, the oldest of lands, renewed; here was Jerusalem, the oldest of cities, made new again; here were Jewish children giving an ancient faith new life. I understood as never before what the rabbis meant when they said that, when God gave us the Torah, *chayei olam nata b'tochenu*, He planted everlasting life in our midst. And at that moment I knew what it was I had come to Jerusalem to learn. That in each generation the *Shechinah*, the Divine Presence, rests with those who take our old faith and make it new again. It rested with the builders of Israel; with the builders of yeshivot and Jewish schools; with those who lived not for the moment but for the sake of future generations of Jewish children. It is they who gave us, as a people, new life.

And I no longer doubted what I had to do in Anglo-Jewry. I had to begin by calling on you to join with me in creating a Decade of Jewish Renewal. Let us cease to be a community whose institutions and attitudes are growing old. Let us start this day, and for the next ten years, a process of working together to build a community where Jewish children can stand proud and free, knowing where they came from, where they are going to, and before Whom they stand.

I call on you to join with me in renewing our *ahavat yisrael*, our categorical commitment to the love of every Jew. We must reach out to every Jew with open arms and an open heart. If we must disagree, and sometimes we must, let us do so with love and dignity and respect. We can prove the Torah's greatness only by inspiration, not by negation. We are a divided community. But let us work to lessen those divisions by coming closer to one another and to God. We have suffered enough from anti-Semitism. Let us practise philo-Semitism. We have suffered enough from assaults of others. Let us never inflict them on ourselves.

Help me to renew *ahavat torah*: a love of the way of life which is our one claim to distinctiveness as a people; and, above all, a love of learning. Let us renew Jewish learning at every level, formal and informal, child and adult, in every context and every form. There is no more radical idea than *v'dibarta bam*,'You shall speak words of Torah, when you sit in your house and when you walk on the way, when you lie down and when you rise up.' That we should never stop learning. That we should continually grow. That we should serve God not only with our hearts, but also with our minds. The greatest single renewal of Anglo-Jewry will come about if we make learning the heritage of every Jew.

Help me to renew *ahavat hashem*, love of God, Who brought the Jewish people into being and lifted us above the shifting winds of history to make us an eternal people. We have become secularised. There are times when we believe that Jews can survive without beliefs, as an ethnic group sustained on nostalgia. But faith is not a luxury we can live without. It is the air we breathe. If we can speak to God in prayer; if we can give to God through charity or service to the community; if we can create in our private lives a home for the Divine Presence, and in our public lives a *kiddush hashem*, a sanctification of God's name, we gain that one sense without which there can be no human happiness: that, in this fleeting transitory span of years, we did something great. We walked in *derekh hashem*, the path of God.

Let us renew our contribution to British society. Here in this country we love, we have found freedom, tolerance and respect for our traditions. Britain was and is a moral giant among nations; and we must play our full part in carrying it forward as a caring and compassionate society. As Jews, we must care about the environment, about social, medical and business ethics, and about the image of God in our fellow human being, Jew and non-Jew alike.

Let us renew our attachment to the land and State of Israel. For there, in the land where we were born as a people, we have been reborn as a people. Because of Israel, after 2,000 years Jews have taken up their destiny once again as a sovereign people. Because of Israel, there is some place that every Jew whose life or liberty is threatened can call home. Because of Israel, Jewish learning flourishes as never before, and as nowhere else. Without sidestepping any of the dilemmas Israel faces, let our love for it be unequivocal, and our attachment to its people unbreakable.

A Decade of Jewish Renewal: Let me be quite clear what I mean. I do not mean that I have a personal programme which I am determined to impose on the community with or against its will. That is not how I understand leadership. I want to encourage leadership in others; to be a catalyst for creativity; to open closed doors and let in the fresh air of initiative and imagination. I want to start a process that will gather momentum over time. I want to listen to and involve everyone willing to work with me in three great areas—leadership, education, and spirituality.

And so I call, first and foremost, to our rabbis: my colleagues. Let us lead from the front. Let us be driven by our calling to reach out, bring close, enthuse and inspire. If there is only one great leader in Anglo-Jewry and it is the Chief Rabbi, I will have failed. Because my greatest ambition is not my success but your success.

I call to our educators: let us see how we can make the whole of Anglo-Jewish education greater than the sum of its constituent parts. Let us see how we can bring the school, the synagogue and the Jewish home closer so that they reinforce one another.

I call to our lay leaders: let us work together to plan, not for today or even tomorrow, but for the next generation. Let us start now to recruit the leaders of ten and twenty years' time. Let us be less cautious, less insular, less afraid of experiment and open debate.

Above all, I call to every member of Anglo-Jewry to join with me in the task of renewing this great community. I cannot, nor will I ever try to, lead alone. I call not for your appreciation but for your participation. I will succeed only if you will join the ranks of the doers. I call on every group in the community to begin this year the process of defining objectives and constructing plans. Let us become joint architects of the Anglo-Jewish future.

A Decade of Renewal: I choose the word 'renewal' carefully. Judaism recognises not *shinui* but *chiddush*, not change but revitalisation. And if we do not renew our institutions, they will die the slow death of increasing irrelevance. There is more than one way of building a shul, or conducting a service, or teaching Torah, or constructing a communal institution. Every year, Rosh Hashanah tells us that we are living now, not a century ago. We must search out a hundred new ways of letting prayer speak to our souls, learning to our minds and mitzvot to our lives; and if they fail, we must search for the hundred-and-first way. Our community has been immeasurably enriched in recent years by yeshivot, Chasidic groups, outreach movements, new ventures in adult and informal education. I see in each of these developments a priceless source of spiritual energy; and I want, above all, to liberate spiritual energy so that Judaism lives as if it were given new this day.

What, then, should we hope to achieve?

An Anglo-Jewry in which we reach out in love and with respect to every Jew.

An Anglo-Jewry in which we do not pretend that all is right with our community so long as there are groups who feel neglected; and there *are* groups who feel neglected: women, the young, intellectuals, the less well-off, the provinces, the small communities.

An Anglo-Jewry in which Judaism challenges us at the highest levels of our minds, hearts and souls.

An Anglo-Jewry in which we praise the successes of others, because we are not threatened but enlarged by the many ways of serving God.

An Anglo-Jewry in which, precisely as committed Jews, we make a distinctive contribution to Britain as a compassionate society.

An Anglo-Jewry in which we bring all our powers of leadership, creativity and energy to the service of God.

An Anglo-Jewry in which we are never afraid to grow as Jews.

An Anglo-Jewry of open doors, open hearts and open minds, open to the love of God, Torah and the Jewish people.

A small agenda. Can it be done? *Ein hakadosh barukh hu ba betyrunia im beriyotav.* God never sets us tasks that cannot be done. Never for one moment believe that it cannot be done.

You have given me, as Chief Rabbi, one precious gift above all: the gift of time. One of my great predecessors, of blessed memory, once said: 'Chief Rabbis never retire, and only very rarely die.' Well: all men are mortal, and nowadays Chief Rabbis retire as well. And yet, since 1845, there have been only five Chief Rabbis, and I am the sixth. You have given me the mandate to build for the future. What I cannot achieve one year, I will work for the next. I recognise the problems. We are a declining and ageing community. We are in the midst of a recession. We must work with limited resources. There are in our community attitudes and divisions which will take a long time to change. I approach my task with open eyes. I will make mistakes, but I will learn from them. I will have failures, but I will try again, another way, another time. But I will never give up or relax or despair. And if it is not ours to complete the task, neither are we free to desist from it.

Together, we have great things to do. For this is a rare and special moment in the history of the Jewish people. Only twice before in our long life as a people have we had the chance to practise Judaism in freedom and against the background of a sovereign State of Israel. For 2,000 years we prayed for it to come again, and now that it has, we must not fail the challenge of this *et ratson*, this window of opportunity. We will not fail. Because *haba letaher mesayin oso*, because God helps those who turn towards Him; and never does He allow those who seek Him to fail. We will succeed because *ein bererah*: this time, there is no choice but to succeed.

Let us work together to plan and create a Decade of Renewal of Jewish leadership, education and spirituality. And may God, who will not forsake His people, cause His spirit to rest in the work of our hands.

* * *

Induction address delivered by Emeritus Chief Rabbi Lord Jakobovits at the installation of Rabbi Dr Jonathan Sacks as Chief Rabbi of the United Hebrew Congregations of the Commonwealth, St John's Wood Synagogue, London, 1 September 1991–22 Elul 5751

'Be strong, be strong, and let us be strong together.' This call reverberates with emotion within our synagogues everywhere whenever we conclude the reading of one of the Five Books of Moses. The words are a reference to the first installation charge in history when Moses told Joshua, his successor, *chazak ve'ematz*—'Be strong and of good courage.' It was both the end and the beginning of a new era. For me, too, this is a double event.

At this momentous hour in my life, when I conclude twenty-four and a half years in the highest office this community or, indeed, any community can confer, and inaugurate the new epoch by installing my successor, my heart is filled to overflowing with the three essential constituents of prayer: First, *shevach*—praise to the Almighty for the infinite blessings of life, for myself and my family, and for His divine deliverance from all undue trouble and sorrow; second, *hoda'ya*—thanksgiving for a wonderful community which has given me loyalty, affection and opportunities enjoyed by few other rabbis; and third, *bakasha*—'petition,' pleading that my distinguished successor, too, may enjoy these blessings at least in equal measure; that he likewise may in due course look back without regrets, echoing the words recorded in the Yom Kippur machzor on the High Priest emerging safely from his supreme service in the Temple on the holiest day of the year: 'And the High Priest would make a feast for his friends, as he entered in peace and came out in peace, without mishap,' after making atonement for his people in the Holy of Holies.

As I fleetingly reflect on the experiences of my four illustrious predecessors over the past century and a half, I have particular cause to render thanks. For they faced greater internal strife and tribulations than I ever had to endure. Under Dr Hertz, lasting communal splits occurred with the foundation of the

Adath and, at the opposite pole, of the Liberal congregations. Moreover, he was locked in bitter conflicts with his lay leaders, when, in a letter to The Times, he denounced their opposition to the Balfour Declaration, and later, when the president of the United Synagogue countermanded the Chief Rabbi's instructions to his ministers to protest against the British White Paper on Palestine. His successor, Rabbi Israel Brodie, faced a major rebellion which threatened to break up his office, as well as the cohesion of the community altogether.

As this year happens to be the one-hundredth anniversary of the installation of Chief Rabbi Hermann Adler, it is appropriate to recall that already the Adlers witnessed major challenges to communal unity, with the breakaway to the right of the Federation and the Machzikei Hadath, and of the Reform to the left. By comparison, I can say of myself that I went in and I went out without hurt, and I have reason to turn this day into a feast, a *yomtov* of very special thanksgiving.

The thanksgiving is increased by a particular joy. During this final year in office, concluding today, two new Jewish day-schools have been approved, while another opened earlier this year, already operating with such singular success. I refer to Immanuel College, so magnanimously named in my honour. These three schools will almost exactly complete the educational development programme for new schools announced some twenty years ago. Much remains to be done, but for much we have reason to rejoice and be profoundly thankful.

As I now address you for the last time as 'my community,' I want you to share these feelings with me. Together, we have gone through some of the most convulsive times in history—the Six-Day War, with the exultant return of Jerusalem undivided to Jewish sovereignty; the Yom Kippur War and the thrilling exodus of Soviet and Ethiopian Jews to Israel; the collapse of Communism; the reunification of Germany; and the Gulf War—all events of cataclysmic proportions from which we have emerged, by the grace of God, as a stronger community, a better-educated community, a more committed community than has ever inhabited these shores, since Jews resettled here in 1656.

I now turn with affection to my dear and revered successor. If you were to pose the questions, 'How can I, as the newly installed Chief Rabbi, triumph over the lurking dangers, pitfalls and challenges, how can I assert myself to leave the distinctive mark of my leadership upon this great community, and how can I be certain that I will enter *b'li pega*, without mishap, and emerge without mishap, to celebrate a *yomtov* at the end of my career?', then the two words *chazak ve'ematz*, addressed to Joshua, say it all: 'Be strong and of good courage.'

Our sages in the Talmud interpreted this phrase to have two distinct meanings: *chazak batorah ve'ematz bema'asim tovim*, 'Be strong in Torah, and courageous in good deeds.' In your new exalted office, your first task will be to preserve the Torah, to keep intact our traditions, to interpret Jewish teachings as you find and understand them. *Chazak*—for this 'be strong!' If you will sometimes encounter enormous pressures, to bend a little here, to modify there; if some will seek to subject you to their dictates, telling you what you may say and what you may do, then 'be strong.'

In matters of principle and conviction, resist at all costs, assert your freedom of action and of speech to ensure that you are never deflected from what you deem to be right. Thus you will be respected. Your task will be, above all, to become, as our illustrious predecessor, Chief Rabbi Hertz, said of his charge in his installation address in 1913, 'Defender of the Faith.' His biography, written some thirty years later by Philip Paneth to mark his seventieth birthday, was entitled 'Guardian of the Law.'

Secondly, *ve'ematz*, 'be of good courage,' *bema'asim tovim*, regarding good deeds in the community. Anglo-Jewry has a peculiar penchant for self-denigration. It delights in running itself down, stressing failings, magnifying scandals, while ignoring or belittling successes and achievements. A community that does not believe in itself cannot flourish. It will not attract its best sons and daughters to community service—for who wants to invest in failure?

Ve'ematz—'be of good courage.' Highlight *ma'asim tovim*, the many wonderful good deeds to be found in the community, and confound the prophets of doom. Generate courage through self-esteem, and success through confidence. Through such good courage, Joshua managed to conquer the Promised Land, and through such indomitable courage, this great community under your leadership will prosper spiritually.

I recall that on one of my last visits in Jerusalem to Rabbi Abramsky, of sainted memory—one of the greatest Torah sages ever to have graced our shores—he showed me the passage in the first chapter of Joshua: 'Be strong and of good courage, for you shall cause this people to inherit the Land which I swore to their fathers to give to them.' Then it states: 'Only be strong and very courageous to observe, and to do according to all the law which Moses My servant commanded you.' You see, commented Dayan Abramsky, 'for the conquest of the Land, you need to be "strong and of good courage"; but for the conquest of the Torah, you require to be "strong and very courageous."'

After 2,000 years of exile, and the catastrophe of the Holocaust, our generation has two supreme priorities: to consolidate our national rebirth in the Land of Israel given to our Fathers; and to restore our people to its timeless assignment given at Sinai. Of these two, said the dayan, the second is the more difficult and demands even greater courage.

This is indeed manifest in our time. Harder still than to generate concern to advance peace with security is the even greater challenge to excite Jews the world over to resume our destiny as a 'light unto the nations,' as spiritual pathfinders and moral pioneers, fulfilling the purpose for which we wondrously survived all our tribulations over the millennia. We, the rabbis, must help to restore the balance between the yearning for our physical homeland and the commitment to our spiritual heritage, as commanded to Joshua.

My dear colleague, you enter this venerable office with a higher public profile than any of your predecessors. Your notable achievements, in reviving the fortunes of Jews' College, in blazing new trails through your Traditional Alternatives, and in winning fame and acclaim through your outstanding Reith lectures—all these testify to the exceptional endowments you bring to this high office, and the good will within and beyond the community on which you can count for support and response to your leadership.

Sustained by your wife, your parents and family, and your many friends, may you be blessed with robust health and the gift of wisdom to write a new volume, a *shirah chadashah*, to the glory of our community and our people, earning the reverence for our faith by this promise of Moses when he laid down his office: 'And all the peoples of the earth shall see that the Name of the Lord is called upon you, and they shall have respect for you.'

Notes

PREFACE

1. *Jewish Chronicle*, 3 February 2012, 40. Earlier notices (1844 and 1912) had taken the form of announcements in various news columns rather than as paid advertisements.
2. Jennifer Lipman, *Jewish Chronicle* website, 14 December 2010. Days later, former JC editor Geoffrey Paul wrote: 'Do we really need another Chief Rabbi? An Av Beth Din with impressive halachic qualifications and an approachable personality could perform for the United Synagogue all the rabbinical and communal duties it might require. After all, the USA has managed perfectly well without a Chief Rabbi ... Doing without would save the United Synagogue housing, salary, expenses, office, staff and pension—a not inconsiderable argument for not appointing another Chief Rabbi at a time of national economic retrenchment. It would also save the unsavoury jockeying and squabbling which a Chief Rabbinical contest would provoke' (*Jewish Chronicle*, 17 December 2010, 3). Commenting earlier in the year, a leading article in the paper declared: 'The conversation about the future of the Chief Rabbinate must not be ducked ... The community must discuss now whether it wishes to continue with the post in its current form, to limit or expand it, or to abolish it altogether. This must not be left until Lord Sacks stands down, but tackled now, while we can still make considered decisions' ('After Sacks,' ibid., 12 March 2010, 36).
3. 'How to succeed in picking a Chief Rabbi successor in Britain,' Alex Weisler, Jewish Telegraphic Agency, 15 November 2011. Pack's remark, with an eye on UK employment and immigration law, related to the possibility of an overseas appointee. He later told the Jewish Telegraphic Agency: '[Rabbi Sacks] will maintain his charismatic presence as a Jewish leader in the House of Lords and on the public stage. This gives us the luxury of being able to look for somebody who can devote a bit more time to matters within the [Modern Orthodox] congregations. Do we have an appetite just to maintain the status quo and push it along for, say, another twenty years, or do we recognise that demographics change and there are different forces and pressures, that there is scope to do things differently? I think that when we are looking at candidates, we will be looking at people who will have come up with a vision on how they'd like to do the job which is refreshing and new' (Dianna Cahn, 'With Sacks retiring, British Jews mixed on relevancy of Chief Rabbi,' 16 April 2012).
4. Simon Rocker, 'The tightrope awaiting the next Chief Rabbi,' *Jewish Chronicle*, 31 December 2010, 19.
5. Former United Synagogue president Elkan Levy disputes this description. In his essay, 'The Next Chief Rabbi,' a brief account of past British Chief Rabbis (*The Jewish Year Book 2012* [London and Portland, OR: Vallentine Mitchell, 2012], 34-43), he writes: 'Jakobovits was due to retire in 1990, and shortly before that the presi-

dent of the United Synagogue again contravened [sic] a selection committee of which (after a contested election) I was a member ... The committee created two sub-groups, one to consider names that had been put forward (and there were a large number of them) and the other to consider financial matters. There was no kingmaker. In the end, there was a short-list of four names and the unanimous choice was Rabbi Dr Jonathan Sacks.'

6   In the event, as in past contests, rabbis did not have a seat on the selection panel, although Dayan Menachem Gelley, of the London Beth Din, and Rabbi Baruch Davis, chairman of the Rabbinical Council of the United Synagogue, acted as advisers. Well into the process, a poll of United Synagogue and regional Orthodox rabbis, conducted by the *Jewish Chronicle* (8 June 2012, 1), suggested that no candidate was ahead of the pack. Five of the twenty rabbis canvassed were undecided, two were unwilling to declare a preference, one hoped Lord Sacks would stay on 'for a few more years,' and one believed there should be no Chief Rabbi at all. Four favoured the eventual choice, Finchley's Ephraim Mirvis, whose candidacy had earlier been mooted in 1988 (see Chapter Eight, 222).

7   *Jewish Chronicle*, 27 May 2011, 2.

8   Rabbi Yitzchak Schochet, 'Prejudice against Chabad is the glue that binds the US,' ibid., 16 March 2012, 33. Anticipating by some considerable time the election of a successor to Sacks, Elkan Levy told this writer (26 August 2008): 'The Chief Rabbinate needs some credibility within the wider Anglo-Jewish community, and only someone from the United Synagogue centre would be broadly acceptable.'

9   Leading article, *Jewish Chronicle*, 12 August 2011, 3.

10 Ibid., 19 August 2011, 20.

11 'Position Specification: Role and Responsibilities.' Application Pack for Chief Rabbi of the United Hebrew Congregations of the UK and Commonwealth (London: Office of the Chief Rabbi, February 2012).

12 *A Few Words Addressed to the Committee for the Election of a Chief Rabbi of England, and to the Electors at Large* (London: Brain & Payne, 1844), 3, 11.

13 Leading article, *Voice of Jacob*, 9 December 1842, 74.

14 Hermann Adler, 'The Ideal Jewish Pastor: An Installation Sermon,' preached at the Great Synagogue, London, 23 June 1891.

15 From a letter written by Hermann Adler to his family, dated erev Rosh Chodesh Adar, 29 Shevat 5671 (27 February 1911), reproduced in the *Jewish Chronicle*, 21 July 1911, 18.

16 *Jewish Chronicle*, 19 January 1912, 24.

17 'Memorandum by the members of the Beth Din, London (Court of the Chief Rabbi) on the forthcoming election of the Chief Rabbi of the United Hebrew Congregations of the British Empire in succession to the late Dr J. H. Hertz,' 28 March 1946, LMA/ACC/2712/15/2040.

18 Minutes of meeting of delegates to the Chief Rabbinate Conference, Woburn House, London, 30 May 1948, LMA/ACC/2712/15/2122.

19 'Memorandum by the members of the Beth Din, London,' op. cit.

20 See, for example, Benjamin J. Elton, *Britain's Chief Rabbis and the Religious Character of Anglo-Jewry, 1880–1970* (Manchester University Press, 2009).

21 'About the London Beth Din (Court of the Chief Rabbi),' United Synagogue web-

site, 2012. On Abramsky's influence, see Meir Persoff, *Faith Against Reason: Religious Reform and the British Chief Rabbinate, 1840–1990* (London and Portland, OR: Vallentine Mitchell, 2008), 237-240, 252-253, 287-288; and Meir Persoff, *Another Way, Another Time: Religious Inclusivism and the Sacks Chief Rabbinate* (Boston: Academic Studies Press, 2010), 39-41. See also Aaron Sorasky, *Melech Beyofyo* [*A King In His Glory*], Vol. I (Jerusalem: privately published, 2004), 318-340, 393-410; and Miri Freud-Kandel, *Orthodox Judaism in Britain Since 1913: An Ideology Forsaken* (London and Portland, OR: Vallentine Mitchell, 2006), 88-104.
22 See *Faith Against Reason*, 89-98, 380-390, and Todd M. Endelman's introduction, xxv-xxxi; and *Another Way, Another Time*, 33-44, 295-315. See also Keith Kahn-Harris and Ben Gidley, *Turbulent Times: The British Jewish Community Today* (London and New York: Continuum, 2010), 15-37, 94-116; and Freud-Kandel, op. cit., 1-22.
23 *Jewish Chronicle*, 24 January 1890, 13-14.
24 As discussed by Stephen Sharot in 'Religious Change in Native Orthodoxy in London, 1870–1914: Rabbinate and Clergy,' *Jewish Journal of Sociology* (London) 15, no. 2 (December 1973), 168, 171.
25 Norman Cohen, 'Non-Religious Factors in the Emergence of the Chief Rabbinate,' in *Transactions of the Jewish Historical Society of England* (London) 21 (1968), 304-313.
26 Barry A. Kosmin, 'Localism and Pluralism in British Jewry, 1900–80,' in *Transactions of the Jewish Historical Society of England* (London) 28 (1982), 113.
27 Immanuel Jakobovits, 'An Analysis of Religious Versus Secularist Trends in Anglo-Jewry,' in *Jewish Life in Britain, 1962–1977*, ed. Sonia L. Lipman and Vivian D. Lipman (New York and London: K. G. Saur, 1981), 40-41.
28 *A Community of Communities: Report of the Commission on Representation of the Interests of the British Jewish Community* (London: Institute for Jewish Policy Research, 31 March 2000), 1.
29 Lord Kalms to this writer, 20 February 2012. See also *Another Way, Another Time*, 1-2, 270-271; and Michael Freedland's interview with Kalms ('I made Sacks Chief Rabbi, but he's been a huge failure'), *Jewish Chronicle*, 14 October 2011, 12-13, in which the one-time 'kingmaker' depicted the quest for Sacks' successor as 'a worthless search for a pretty unimportant post,' and added: 'Chief Rabbi? Big deal. Who the hell cares?' On Kalms' support for Sacks in the run-up to the 1990 appointment, see Chapter Eight below.
30 London and Portland, OR: Vallentine Mitchell, 2002.

CHAPTER ONE

1 *Voice of Jacob*, 4 February 1842, 76.
2 Title-page of *The Axe Laid to the Root, or Ignorance and Superstition Evident in the Character of the Rev. Solomon Hirschell, Major Rabbi, commonly called The High Priest of the Jews of England* (London: L. Alexander, 1808).
3 James Picciotto, *Sketches of Anglo-Jewish History*, revised and ed., Israel Finestein (London: Soncino Press, 1955), 367. Italics as in original text.
4 Moses Margoliouth, *The History of the Jews in Great Britain*, Vol. III (London: Richard

Bentley, 1851), 78-85.
5   *Voice of Jacob*, 11 November 1842, 60-61.
6   Ibid., 22 December 1843, 56.
7   Ibid., 25 November 1842, 65.
8   Leading article, ibid., 9 December 1842, 74.
9   Ibid.
10 Ibid., 23 December 1842, 84.
11 *Report of the Committee Appointed for the Selection of Candidates for the Office of Chief Rabbi, With an Appendix Containing Abstracts of Testimonials, Etc.* (London: John Wertheimer and Co., 1884).
12 *Voice of Jacob*, 3 February 1843, 111-112.
13 Arthur Barnett, *The Western Synagogue Through Two Centuries, 1761–1961* (London: Vallentine Mitchell, 1961), 190. Although this report, conveyed by means of a letter in the *Voice of Jacob* signed 'A Member of the Western Synagogue,' was otherwise anonymous (the writer having supplied his name to the paper, undertaken to substantiate his charges, and 'refused further to modify or withdraw any of them'), Barnett 'hazards a guess' that the informant 'was none other than Nathan Defries, a former Honorary Reader to the Congregation and, about this time, its Overseer; and from the nature of the contents of this letter when compared with several other *obiter dicta* of this individual during the exciting period of the Reform agitation, it would not be unjustifiable to draw this inference' (ibid., 188).
14 With effect from the 1891 election, the provision 'without the consent of the Committee of the Congregation to which such person shall belong' was removed from this clause, the outcome of resolutions adopted at the preceding Chief Rabbinate Conference.
15 *Voice of Jacob*, 3 March 1843, 121-122.
16 On Raphael Meldola, see Albert M. Hyamson, *The Sephardim of England* (London: Spanish and Portuguese Jews' Congregation, 1951), 224-239. Meldola's son David, the Sephardi Av Beth Din, was a co-signatory with Hirschell of the 1842 *cherem*. After Raphael Meldola's death, no Haham was appointed for thirty-eight years, until in 1866 the Haham of Naples, thirty-year-old Benjamin Artom, took up the post. He held office, however, for barely twelve years, dying suddenly on 6 January 1879, after a few hours' illness, while on a visit to Brighton.
17 *Voice of Jacob*, 17 March 1843, 132-133
18 Ibid., 16 February 1844, 84.
19 Ibid., 19 January 1844, 68.
20 Ibid., 16 February 1844, 84.
21 Ibid., 20 April 1844, 130.
22 Ibid., 19 July 1844, 185.
23 *Report of the Committee*, op. cit.
24 *Voice of Jacob*, 16 August 1844, 201.
25 Having earlier referred to 'the tribute paid to Dr Hirschfeld's literary labours in our vol. ii, pp. 63 and 80,' the paper here made similar reference to Hirsch's 'papers on the "Vocation of Judaism," in our vol. ii, and to various other extracts from his writings dispersed elsewhere.'
26 *Voice of Jacob*, 13 September 1844, 228.

27 Elias Davis ('By order'), 20 September 5605–1844, LMA/ACC/2805/01/02/002/001. Appended to the letter was an indication that 'Offers of support addressed to me, 14 and 15 Aldgate High Street, will be gratefully received, and meet with immediate attention.'
28 'Address,' LMA/ACC/2805/01/02/002/001.
29 *Voice of Jacob*, 4 October 1844, 1-2.
30 Later confirmed in the *Jewish Chronicle and Working Man's Friend*, 6 December 1844, 45.
31 *Voice of Jacob*, 11 October 1844, 11.
32 *Jewish Chronicle and Working Man's Friend*, 18 October 1844, 3-5.
33 Ibid., 1 November 1844, 12-13.
34 'While not explicitly endorsing the standpoint of the Reform movement, the *Jewish Chronicle* defended the right to publish differing points of view. Notwithstanding the fact that it advocated the strengthening of Jewish religious life and Jewish education, it was generally felt that the new Jewish paper was going to be more broad-minded than its competitor' (David Cesarani, *The Jewish Chronicle and Anglo-Jewry, 1841–1991* [Cambridge: Cambridge University Press, 1994], 16).
35 *Voice of Jacob*, 15 November 1844, 35.
36 Ibid., 29 November 1844, 45.
37 *Jewish Chronicle and Working Man's Friend*, 22 November 1844, 39.
38 *Voice of Jacob*, 29 November 1844, 45.
39 Ibid., 6 December 1844, 53-54.
40 *Jewish Chronicle and Working Man's Friend*, 6 December 1844, 45.
41 *Voice of Jacob*, 6 December 1844, 53-54.
42 H. D. Schmidt, 'Chief Rabbi Nathan Marcus Adler: Jewish Educator from Germany,' in *Leo Baeck Institute Year Book*, VII (London: East and West Library, 1962), 294; M. Friedländer, 'The Late Chief Rabbi Dr N. M. Adler,' in *Jewish Quarterly Review* 2 (July 1890), 375; Eugene C. Black, 'The Anglicization of Orthodoxy: The Adlers,' in *Profiles in Diversity*, ed. Frances Malino and David Sorkin (Detroit: Wayne State University Press, 1998), 296.
43 *Voice of Jacob*, 18 July 1845, 199.
44 *Jewish Chronicle*, 19 April 1850, 218. In 1889, the paper—in its column 'Notes of the Week'—carried the following (possibly apocryphal) item: 'In connection with the death of HRH the Duchess of Cambridge, we may recall an interesting circumstance at the time—more than half a century ago—when the personal union between the Kingdoms of Great Britain and Hanover was still existing, and the late Duke of Cambridge, husband of the lady just deceased, filled the office of Governor-General of Hanover. The Duchess was dangerously ill—it was in 1833, just before the birth of the Duchess of Teck—and the doctors had declared human aid unavailing. The then Chief Rabbi of Hanover, the Rev Dr Nathan Marcus Adler, summoned his flock to the synagogue to offer up fervent prayers for the Royal patient. The Duke afterwards forwarded to Dr Adler a letter of thanks, accompanied by a purse containing one-hundred Friedrichs d'or. The Chief Rabbi respectfully returned the money to the Duke, with the request that it should be distributed to the poor of the city. When the Duke subsequently returned to London on the accession of the Queen, he was able to render a signal service to Dr Adler. When he heard of the death of Dr Solomon Hirschell, the Chief Rabbi, and that the heads

of the London Jewish community were looking out for a successor to the Chief Rabbinate, the Duke immediately placed himself in communication with them; in fact, he drove at once to Baron Lionel de Rothschild, who was then one of the Wardens of the Great Synagogue, and called his attention to Dr Adler as a man whom he highly respected and esteemed and who was no doubt well qualified to fill the position of Chief Rabbi of England with much distinction. The result is well known to our readers' (*Jewish Chronicle*, 12 April 1889, 5).

45 The Hebrew document was formulated by M. S. Keyser 'to the satisfaction of the [Chief Rabbinical] executive committee, by whom severally it was attested in the usual way' (*Voice of Jacob*, 14 February 1845, 97). Well before this letter appeared in print, the paper commented (20 December 1844, 62): 'The circumstances that our Chief Rabbi is a Cohen—a lineal descendant of Aaron and of the order of the priesthood—will be regarded by many who have manifested an interest in this election as one of its most interesting features. The Holy Scriptures make direct and important reference to the vocation of the Cohen, in times of doubt or difficulty. See Deuteronomy xvii:8, and especially Malachi ii:7'—the quotation included by Keyser in the invitation to Adler.

46 'With greatest respect, your obedient servant, Dr N. Adler,' Hanover, to Samuel Helbert Ellis, Keppel Street, Russell Square, London, 18 December 5605, received 25 December 1844; Jewish Museum, London.

47 Adler to Ellis, 6 January 5605, received 14 January 1845; Jewish Museum, London.

48 Adler's reply, in Hebrew with English translation, and dated 22 Shevat 5605 A. M. [19 January 1845], was published and circulated as a two-page pamphlet by the Committee Appointed for the Selection of Candidates for the Office of Chief Rabbi (London, 1845). It was translated, at Ellis's behest, by Louis Cohen, a nephew and confidant of Sir Moses Montefiore and the father of Lionel Louis Cohen, principal co-founder in 1870—with Sir Anthony de Rothschild—of the United Synagogue.

49 On Moses Montefiore (1784–1885), see S. and V. D. Lipman, eds., *The Century of Moses Montefiore* (Littman Library of Jewish Civilization, Jewish Historical Society of England, and Oxford University Press, 1985); L. Loewe, ed., *Diaries of Sir Moses and Lady Montefiore* (London, 1890; facsimile edition, introduced by Raphael Loewe (London: Littman Library of Jewish Civilization, JHSE, and Jewish Museum, 1983); Israel Finestein, 'Sir Moses Montefiore: A Modern Appreciation,' in *Scenes and Personalities in Anglo-Jewry, 1800–2000* (London: Vallentine Mitchell, 2002), 164-177; *Jewish Chronicle* Supplement, 31 July 1885.

50 *Voice of Jacob*, 18 July 1845, 198.

51 Ibid., 199. Montefiore was accompanied by Sir A. de Rothschild, S. H. Ellis, I. Foligno, H. de Castro, I. I. Brandon, H. Hyams, I. M. Montefiore, H. Guedalla, I. Barned, H. H. Cohen, J. Salmon, J. Levy, S. Cohen, L. Cohen, and I. H. Helbert.

CHAPTER TWO

1. Nathan Adler (Dr) to Chairman and Executive Committee of the United Synagogue, 13 October 5640 [1879]. LMA/ACC/2805/01/02/002/001.
2. Commenting on these provisions, Aubrey Newman writes in *The United Synagogue 1870–1970* (London, Henley and Boston: Routledge & Kegan Paul, 1977), 90: 'In 1879, there was no suggestion that there should be a new Chief Rabbi. Dr Nathan Marcus Adler was still Chief; there was no age limit; and there could be no suggestion of an enforced retirement. On the other hand, he was far from well, and so permission was given to him to "relegate" some of his duties to his son, Hermann. Various conditions were laid down, however, by the honorary officers of the United Synagogue. The Chief Rabbi had expressed a desire to move from Finsbury Square to the "extreme West or North-West of London"; the honorary officers pointed out that the removal of the office of the Chief Rabbi "would be not only a personal loss, but a grievance ... The Communal life of the Congregation is intimately bound up with the personality of the Chief Rabbi, who must be readily accessible to every member of his flock ... If, acting under medical advice, Dr Adler should be obliged to remove from the City, it is imperative that the Office should still be within, or immediately contiguous to, the City, and that his Delegate shall be in regular attendance thereat." Nor did the honorary officers intend to permit the Chief to "relegate" a full range of duties, laying down the five functions which they would permit him to pass on.'
3. Clauses two, three, and four of the *Report of the Executive Committee*, signed by Lionel L. Cohen, chairman, to the United Synagogue Council, Central Synagogue Chambers, London, 4 November 1879, LMA/ACC/2805/01/02/002/001.
4. 'Nathan's youngest child by Henrietta Worms was born on the 29th May, 1839, and owes his name "Hermann," as his second cousin Baron H. de Worms does that of "Henry," to their common ancestor Hirsch Worms' (*Jewish Chronicle*, 5 June 1891, 10). 'Baron Henry de Worms, MP [later Lord Pirbright], was a warden at the Central Synagogue from 1879 to 1881. At the end of one year of office, he consented to his re-election on condition that Mr Frederick Davis should remain as his colleague. The pressure of his parliamentary duties was the cause of his resignation in 1881' (The Rev Michael Adler, *History of the Central Synagogue, 1855–1905* [London: Office of the *Jewish Chronicle*, 1905], 23). Despite the pressures, de Worms served as a vice-president of the United Synagogue during the same period (1880–1882), having been treasurer in 1872.
5. *Jewish Chronicle*, 7 November 1879, 7.
6. Nathaniel Mayer de Rothschild (1840–1915), known as 'Natty,' was the eldest son of Baron Lionel de Rothschild, grandson of Nathan Mayer Rothschild (after whom he was named), and great-grandson of Mayer Amschel Rothschild, founder of the banking dynasty. He became the second Baronet de Rothschild after the death, in 1876, of his uncle Anthony Nathan de Rothschild, who had no male heir, and in 1885 became Baron Rothschild, of Tring in the County of Hertford. He was vice-president of the United Synagogue 1876–1879, thereafter serving as president until his death, when he was succeeded by his brother, Leopold (1845–1917).

7   LMA/ACC/2805/01/02/002/001.
8   *Jewish Chronicle*, 14 November 1879, 4.
9   Ibid., 24 January 1890, 8.
10 Hermann Adler, Marcus N. Adler, Elkan Adler, Mrs Henry Solomon and Mrs Marcus Schapp, all of whom had been at the Chief Rabbi's bedside since the previous Thursday.
11 *Jewish Chronicle*, 24 January 1890, 6. 'For the last twelve years or so,' wrote the paper eighteen months later, 'Dr [Hermann] Adler has practically had to bear the burden of the Chief Rabbinate of the British Empire. That he has done so efficiently and with dignity is evidenced by the unanimity of the public, who recognised in him the only possible candidate fit to bear his father's mantle on his shoulders. The late Dr Adler specially trained his son to be his successor, and though in his will he did not express any hope that his community would give effect to his heart's desire, he gives the choice of his Rabbinical library to "my son Hermann, in consideration of his having chosen the vocation of Rabbi and having filled to my satisfaction the arduous duties of my delegate"' (ibid., 5 June 1891, 10).
12 Hermann Adler, 'The Ideal Jewish Pastor: An Installation Sermon,' preached at the Great Synagogue, London, 23 June 1891. Reproduced in full following this chapter.
13 A. Schischa, 'Hermann Adler, Yeshivah Bachur, Prague, 1860–1862,' in *Remember the Days: Essays in Honour of Cecil Roth*, ed. John M. Shaftesley (London: Jewish Historical Society of England, 1966), 258.
14 Raymond Apple, 'Hermann Adler: Chief Rabbi,' in *Noblesse Oblige: Essays in Honour of David Kessler, OBE*, ed. Alan D. Crown (London: Vallentine Mitchell, 1998), 128.
15 *Jewish Chronicle*, 6 June 1891, 10.
16 Born in Warsaw in 1831, Abrahams graduated from University College, London, and succeeded Louis Loewe as principal (then known as headmaster) of Jews' College in 1858, combining the post with those of dayan and acting Haham. He died five years later, leaving a widow and six young children, many of whom were to attain prominence in the community.
17 Kalisch held this post from 1848 to 1853, before being engaged as tutor and literary adviser to the Rothschild family. Born in Treptow, Pomerania in 1828, he died in Derbyshire, England in 1885.
18 At the invitation of a wealthy relative, Asher, a German educationist and philosopher (1818–1890), spent some years in London, where he studied English at a private school and subsequently taught. He later held positions in the Jewish community and became tutor to Nathan Adler's children. On returning to Germany, he gained his doctorate of philosophy at Berlin University and thereafter wrote widely.
19 Apple, op. cit., 128. Schischa (op. cit., 241) writes: 'These good and dedicated men imparted to the young and very bright scholar not just a mechanical, dry knowledge of Jewish lore. They implanted in him a love for "learning"; they imbued him with the enjoyment of the "*Blatt Gemoreh*." This love for learning which Hermann Adler showed as a youngster he fully enjoyed until his last days.' Schischa adds: 'This information is based on a typescript biographical sketch compiled after his death, I think, by his daughter Miss Nettie [Henrietta] Adler.' Apple ascribes it to

'some notes he [Adler] compiled about himself, probably at the time of his election as Chief Rabbi.'
20 These positions included the presidency of Aria College and the Jewish Historical Society of England, and the vice-presidency of the Jewish Religious Education Board and the Anglo-Jewish Association.
21 Olga Somech Phillips and Hyman A. Simons, *The History of the Bayswater Synagogue 1863–1963* (London: privately published, 1963), 17.
22 Eugene C. Black, 'The Anglicization of Orthodoxy: The Adlers,' in *Profiles in Diversity: Jews in a Changing Europe*, ed. Frances Malino and David Sorkin (Detroit: Wayne State University Press, 1998), 312.
23 Hermann Adler, *The Ideal Jewish Pastor*.
24 Moses Gaster, *History of the Ancient Synagogue of the Spanish and Portuguese Jews* (London: privately published, 1901), 178.
25 *Voice of Jacob*, 29 August 1845, 229.
26 *Jewish Chronicle*, 25 February 1848, 441, in a leading article, 'The Modern Farce, Entitled "Excommunication."'
27 James Picciotto, *Sketches of Anglo-Jewish History*, revised and ed., Israel Finestein (London: Soncino Press, 1955), 378-379.
28 'History of the Reform Movement,' in *Supplement to the Jewish Chronicle*, 29 January 1892, 20.
29 *Jewish Chronicle*, 25 April 1890, 9.
30 C. Russell and H. S. Lewis, *The Jew in London: A Study of Racial Character and Present-Day Conditions* (London: 1900), 97, cited in Todd M. Endelman, *The Jews in Britain, 1656–2000* (Berkeley: University of California Press, 2002), 176; and in Stephen Sharot, 'Native Jewry and the Religious Anglicisation of Immigrants in London, 1870–1905,' in *Jewish Journal of Sociology* (London) 16, no. 1 (June 1974), 47.
31 As described by V. D. Lipman in *A History of the Jews in Britain Since 1858* (New York: Holmes & Meier, 1990), 94.
32 *Hamelitz* (St Petersburg and Odessa), 28, no. 287 (30 December 1888); *Hamaggid* (Lyck, Berlin, Cracow and London), 33, no. 1 (3 January 1889).
33 On the founding of the Machzike Hadath, see *A Fortress in Anglo-Jewry: The Story of the Machzike Hadath* (London: Shapiro, Vallentine & Co., 5713–1953), 5-46, by Werner's grandson, Bernard Homa; and Albert M. Hyamson, *The London Board for Shechita, 1804–1954* (London: Henry F. Thompson & Co., for the London Board for Shechita, 1954), 45-48. Homa writes (*A Fortress*, 6): 'Dr Hermann Adler was a lesser scholar and authority [than his father] and was far less able to withstand the growing encroachments on traditional Jewish practice that were constantly being demanded and made. There can be no doubt that Anglo-Jewry was fast moving towards religious decadence when it was sharply awakened from its spiritual somnolence by the influx of thousands of Jewish refugees from Russia, Poland and Romania which began about 1880.'
34 At a preliminary meeting of the *chevras*, held on 6 November 1887, it was agreed to call the new organisation the Federation of Minor Synagogues, and to proceed to elect a Board of Delegates. The word 'Minor' was deleted from the title soon afterwards.
35 Joseph E. Blank, *The Minutes of the Federation of Synagogues: A Twenty-Five Years' Review*

(London: E. W. Rabbinowicz, 5673–1912), 14. Blank was appointed secretary of the Federation on 4 December 1887, at the first meeting of its Board of Delegates; he remained in office until 1925. Also elected at the meeting were Lord Rothschild, president; Samuel Montagu, MP, vice-president (in effect, and also known as, acting president); and H. Landau and I. Weber, treasurers. The next meeting of the Board, on 16 January 1888, was the one and only time that Rothschild presided (Blank, op. cit., 15-16).

36 Minutes of the United Synagogue council, 18 February 1890; *Jewish Chronicle*, 21 February 1890, 8-9.

37 Lerner, the rabbi of Wurzheim in Elsass (Alsace), remained with the Federation until his election, four years later, to the Chief Rabbinate of Altona and Schleswig-Holstein. Among others who applied for the Federation post was the Rev Moses Hyamson (Blank, op. cit., 21), later a member of the London Beth Din and a candidate in the 1913 Chief Rabbinical election.

38 The appointment of a Minister for the Federation was proposed by Montagu in a letter to his Board (6 November 1889), stipulating that the successful candidate 'be a Talmudical Scholar, well versed in Jewish Laws, orthodoxy to be vouched for by our Ecclesiastical Authorities; in religious matters he must be under the jurisdiction of Dr Adler.' In Clause 1a of its draft constitution (6 November 1887), the Federation had set out 'to provide or render available to its members the additional Services of Jewish Ministers, such Ministers to be the medium between the Federated Synagogues and the established Ecclesiastical Authorities of the Spanish and Portuguese Congregation and of the United Synagogue.' This was modified 'to make clear that that any minister or dayan appointed would have to be "certified as holding orthodox opinions by the Ecclesiastical Authorities"—that is, in appointing its own spiritual leaders, the Federation would acknowledge the primacy of the Chief Rabbi and would not establish a religious authority in opposition to him' (Geoffrey Alderman, *The Federation of Synagogues, 1887–1987* [London: Federation of Synagogues, 1987], 20-21; see also Blank, op. cit., 14-15). The title 'Chief Minister' of the Federation—who would, according to the newly ennobled Lord Swaythling (letter dated 26 July 1907), 'co-operate in all orthodox movements acceptable to our Board'—was a later appellation and implemented only with the appointment of Rabbi Dr Maier Jung, of Hungary, inducted into office at the Philpot Street Synagogue on 16 June 1912.

39 Noting that Lerner's appointment coincided with the preparations for the Chief Rabbinate election, Julius Jung, a later secretary of the Federation, writes (*Champions of Orthodoxy* [London: G. J. George & Co., 1974], 13): 'Shortly before the two elections, the naïve suggestion had been put forward to make one appointment only—namely, by the United Synagogue. Such a decision, it was claimed, would assure complete harmony in the religious field between the two synagogal bodies and avoid any rivalry, which every well-wisher of the community would deplore ... The suggestion, if adopted, would have succeeded merely in retarding the growth of the Federation of Synagogues in favour of the United—a thought then most dear to many an English-born Jew. The suggestion was naturally ignored by the Federation.'

40 *Jewish Chronicle*, 25 January 1889, 8; 3 January 1890, 7. On the controversy sur-

rounding the East End Scheme, see Daniel Gutwein, *The Divided Elite: Economics, Politics and Anglo-Jewry, 1882–1917* (Leiden, New York and Cologne: E.J. Brill, 1992), 224-232, 243-271.

41 London-born Philip Magnus (1842–1933) served as an assistant minister at the West London Synagogue from 1866 to 1880, when he left the clergy to become organising secretary and director of the City and Guilds of London Institute. He was MP for the University of London from 1906 to 1922, was knighted in 1886, and became a baronet in 1917. Magnus was among leading members of the Reform movement who opposed changes to the liturgy and format of the Sabbath-morning service, contending that they were 'in direct conflict with the traditional Jewish ritual' and would, if adopted, 'have the effect of widening the breach that divides the Berkeley Street congregation from other Jewish synagogues—the breach which, during seventy years, has been growing less and less and, in the near future, might have been expected to be completely bridged' (*To the Members of the West London Synagogue*, 26 October 1910, reprinted in the *Jewish Chronicle*, 4 November 1910, 8-9). When the changes were later adopted, Magnus asserted that 'the service would be so distasteful to him that he would have to retire from the synagogue altogether' (*Jewish Chronicle*, 3 February 1911, 18).

42 Ibid., 9 May 1890, 9.

43 Ibid., 25 April 1890, 9.

44 An Ashkenazi by birth and a native of Romania, Moses Gaster (1856–1939) studied at Bucharest and Leipzig universities before attending the Rabbinical Seminary at Breslau. On arriving in Britain in 1885, he taught Graeco-Slavonic literature at Oxford University, and was appointed Haham ('Chief Rabbi') of the Spanish and Portuguese Jews' Congregation two years later. 'Gaster was a man of strong character, accustomed to express his opinions on a variety of subjects, with vehemence, and not always submissive to criticism, no matter from what direction it came. He was, above all, a personality, whom no one could overlook, no matter in what milieu he found himself' (Albert M. Hyamson, *The Sephardim of England* [London: Spanish and Portuguese Jews' Congregation, 1951], 362-363).

45 *Jewish Chronicle*, 9 May 1890, 10.

46 Ibid., 23 May 1890, 6.

47 Ibid., 13 June 1890, 11.

48 Ibid., 27 June 1890, 15-17.

49 Ibid., 25 July 1890, 20.

50 Ibid.

51 Ibid., 20 June 1890, 13.

52 Quoted in Newman, op. cit., 91-92.

53 Clause 8 of the United Synagogue *Deed of Foundation and Trust*, 13 January 1871.

54 Additionally, in the early years of Hermann Adler's delegacy (1879–1883), Montagu had served as chairman of the United Synagogue's building committee.

55 Minutes of the Federation of Synagogues, 2 March 1890 (Blank, op. cit., 43).

56 *Jewish Chronicle*, 7 March 1890, 16. When this issue came to the fore in the subsequent negotiations, Montagu and Rothschild were of like mind, the former declaring that it was 'absolutely necessary that Dr Adler [who had yet to be nominated, let alone elected] should reside within at least walking distance of the East End …

so that he might be easily accessible to those who desired to seek his advice and to ask such questions as related to their religious life.' Rothschild averred that he was 'always of the opinion that the Chief Rabbi should reside in the East End, and the importance of this was forcibly brought home to him last year when he heard the Bishop of Bedford say to Dr Hermann Adler: "How can you know anything of the condition of your people in the East End when you do not live among them?" When he heard that, he resolved that he would leave no stone unturned, nor spare any effort, to have the residence of the Chief Rabbi among the bulk of the Jews of the East End' (ibid., 25 July 1890, 20). As events transpired, Adler made clear that he had accepted an informal offer of the appointment 'on the clear understanding that, in Lord Rothschild's words, "You are to have a residence in the City, but you may sleep and live wherever you like"' (Newman, op. cit., 93).
57 *Jewish Chronicle*, 25 July 1890, 19.
58 See Chapter One, note 14, on the change to this clause compared to the 1844 election.
59 *Jewish Chronicle*, 6 February 1891, 6.
60 Ibid., 20 February 1891, 12.
61 P. Ornstein, secretary of the United Synagogue, to delegates, 21 May 5651–1891, LMA/ACC/2712/15/0136/B. 'I have to point out,' Ornstein wrote in his summons to the gathering, 'that the object of the Meeting is confined to the election of the Chief Rabbi, as the powers, duties and emoluments of the office have already been settled.' Following the election, in letters to the presidents of congregations contributing to the maintenance of the office of Chief Rabbi, Ornstein wrote, inter alia: 'You are aware that the salary of the Chief Rabbi has been fixed at £2,000 per annum, and that the United Synagogue has consequently incurred a heavy addition to its already overburdened expenditure' (4 June 5651–1891, ibid.).
62 That the clouds had far from dispersed over the East End Scheme was demonstrated by the escalation of the controversy in the ensuing eight years, before the project's demise in 1899 (see Gutwein, op. cit., 266-271).
63 *Jewish Chronicle*, 5 June 1891, 9-10.

CHAPTER THREE

1 Extract from a letter written by Hermann Adler to his family, dated erev Rosh Chodesh Adar, 29 Shevat 5671 (27 February 1911). Reproducing the extract, the *Jewish Chronicle* (21 July 1911, 18) commented that it was 'remarkable that the Chief Rabbi based the Communal Charge, which was written in February, upon a text [Numbers 27:16-17] from the *sidrah* [Torah portion, *Pinchas*] for last Shabbat.'
2 Joseph E. Blank, *The Minutes of the Federation of Synagogues: A Twenty-Five Years' Review* (London: E. W. Rabbinowicz, 5673–1912), 73-74.
3 United Synagogue memorandum of the meeting, June 1910, quoted by Aubrey Newman in *The United Synagogue 1870–1970* (London, Henley, and Boston: Routledge & Kegan Paul, 1977), 95-96.
4 US secretary P. Ornstein to presidents of affiliated synagogues, and to 'all the con-

gregations outside the United Synagogue who acknowledge the Chief Rabbi as their Spiritual Chief,' 19 July 5671–1911, LMA/ACC/2712/15/0136/B.
5 *Jewish Chronicle*, 7 March 1902, 13.
6 'Installation into the Office of Dayan,' preached at the Great Synagogue, London, on 13 May 1902, in the Rev M. Hyamson, *The Oral Law and Other Sermons* (London: David Nutt, 1910), 139.
7 *Jewish Chronicle*, 4 August 1911, 15
8 Blank, op. cit., 72-73.
9 *Memorandum Re Chief Rabbinate Conference* (London: United Synagogue, January 5672–1912), 1-2.
10 LMA/ACC/2712/01/143; *Jewish Chronicle*, 5 January 1912, 21-22; 12 January 1912, 24-25.
11 *Jewish Chronicle*, 12 January 1912, 25-26.
12 Asher Feldman to the Revs J. F. Stern and S. Levy, ibid., 8 January 1912, 26.
13 *Chief Rabbinate Conference: Report of Sub-Committee Appointed at the Meeting of the Delegates on 14th January 1912*, Appendix A and Appendix B, 7-9, LMA/ACC/2712/01/143.
14 Letter dated 15 February 1912, from Rabbi S. I. Hillman (Glasgow), honorary secretary, Association for Furthering Traditional Judaism in Great Britain, to P. Ornstein, secretary, United Synagogue, minuting the Chief Rabbinate sub-committee meeting with delegates, LMA/ACC/2712/01/143.
15 Louis Samuel Montagu (1869–1927) succeeded to the title on the death of his father in January 1911. Educated at Clifton College, Bristol, he became head of the family banking business and married Gladys Goldsmid, a member of the Goldsmith and Rothschild banking families. Their eldest son, Ewen, was a later president of the United Synagogue. Of the second Lord Swaythling, Geoffrey Alderman writes (*The Federation of Synagogues, 1887–1987* [London: 1987] 42): 'In retrospect, it is clear that the decision of the Federation's executive committee, on 28 February 1911, to elect Louis Samuel Montagu as the Federation's second president was a mistake. At the time, the decision seemed entirely natural and was taken as a formality ... a succession which Samuel Montagu had specifically requested. The increasingly independent posture of the Federation, more especially in relation to the United Synagogue, demanded that, if possible, the office of president be given to a peer of the realm, the equal of the head of the House of Rothschild; significantly, Louis Montagu became at once "president," not "acting president," as his father had been ... However, Louis Montagu was not the man that his father had been and did not share his father's religious outlook. It is a remarkable fact that the staunch piety of Samuel Montagu seems to have repelled rather than to have attracted his children. Two of his daughters, Marian and Lilian [Lily], were founders of Liberal Judaisrn, "the objects of which [he declared in his will] I strongly disapprove" ... Like many of his generation of Anglo-Jewish leaders, Louis regarded the Zionist movement of Theodor Herzl as a profound danger to the safety and standing of the Anglo-Jewish community.' Alderman adds (*Modern British Jewry* [Oxford: Clarendon Press, 1992 and 1998], 201-202): 'Louis wore his orthodoxy lightly while conducting a campaign of slander and libel against the immigrants with whom his father had identified so closely.'

16 Federation of Synagogues to United Synagogue, 23 November 1911, in Blank, op. cit., 74-75.
17 *Jewish Chronicle*, 19 January 1912, 24-28.
18 Blank, op. cit., 75-77.
19 *Jewish Chronicle*, 3 May 1912, 20.
20 Swaything to meeting of the Federation Board, 30 April 1912, *Jewish Chronicle*, 3 May 1912, 24.
21 Ibid., 20-23.
22 Ibid., 7 April 1911, 22.
23 The details first appeared in an interview Hertz gave to the *Jewish Morning Journal*, New York, and subsequently reported in the *Jewish Chronicle* (16 August 1912, 11).
24 Born in Leghorn (Livorno), Rabbi Sabato Morais (1823–1897), the guiding force behind the Jewish Theological Seminary, was briefly assistant chazan, and then teacher, of the Spanish and Portuguese Congregation in London before occupying the pulpit of the Mikve Israel Synagogue in Philadelphia. 'Though his ministry covered the period of greatest activity in the adaptation of Judaism in America to changed conditions, he, as the advocate of Orthodox Judaism, withstood every appeal in behalf of ritualistic innovations and departures from traditional practice, winning the esteem of his opponents in consistency and integrity' (Cyrus L. Sulzberger, *Jewish Encyclopedia*, Vol. VIII [New York: Funk & Wagnalls, 1925], 680). Hertz was to say of Morais: 'All around him [in America] were so-called rabbis who were fanatically advocating the tearing up of Jewish life by the roots. To all this treason and revolution in religion, Sabato Morais was the lifelong foe. Like Elijah, he for a long time stood alone; but he never lost courage. He at last succeeded in rallying all the forces that stood for historic continuity of Jewish life in America and called into existence the Jewish Theological Seminary. There, under his faithful guidance, and later under the guidance of Solomon Schechter, hundreds of Jewish teachers of religion have been trained who have definitely stemmed the advance of religious radicalism in American congregations' (J. H. Hertz, 'Divided Counsels,' in *Sermons, Addresses and Studies*, Vol. I [London: Soncino Press, 1938], 224-225). Following the establishment of the Seminary, Morais was appointed president of the faculty and professor of Bible, holding both posts until his death.
25 *Jewish Chronicle*, 3 May 1912, 23.
26 *On the Sanctification and Desecration of God's Name* (based on Leviticus 22:32 in the weekly Torah portion), preached at the Great Synagogue, London, 4 May 1912.
27 'Rabbi Dr Hertz at the Bayswater Synagogue,' *Jewish Chronicle*, 17 May 1912, 19.
28 Leviticus 25:10.
29 *Jewish Chronicle*, 3 May 1912, 23. The letter appeared immediately above the report of Hertz's visit to London.
30 Ornstein to Chief Rabbinate Conference delegates, 19 June 1912, LMA/ACC/2712/01/143.
31 *Jewish Chronicle*, 21 February 1913, 26.
32 No reasons were evident, either in the minutes of the meeting or later, for Daiches' rejection. Preceding the vote of the Electoral College on 16 February 1913, Jessel did, however, refer to the lack of success of other candidates, despite having said that 'I am not going to discuss what led us to reject the other names' (ibid., 27).

33 Ibid.
34 Chief Rabbinate Conference Selection Committee, 23 June 1912, LMA/ACC/2712/01/143.
35 Bernard Drachman, *The Unfailing Light: Memoirs of an American Rabbi* (New York: Rabbinical Council of America, 1948), 291-292.
36 Ibid., 294.
37 Ibid., 295.
38 Leading article, *Jewish Chronicle*, 25 October 1912, 8.
39 Ibid., 1 November 1912, 15.
40 Drachman, op. cit., 299-300, 302.
41 *Jewish Express*, 29 and 30 October 1912, *Jewish Journal*, 29 October 1912, cited in the *Jewish Chronicle*, 1 November 1912, 15. The quotations were translated from the original Yiddish.
42 Drachman, op. cit., 307.
43 Ibid., 313.
44 Ibid., 316.
45 Meeting of US Honorary Officers, 2 December 1912, LMA/ACC/2712/01/143.
46 *Jewish Chronicle*, 20 December 1912, 17.
47 See below for further details on this subject, particularly in relation to Hyamson.
48 Meeting of Chief Rabbinate Selection Committee, 12 January 1913, LMA/ACC/2712/01/143.
49 *Jewish Chronicle*, 17 January 1913, 9.
50 Ibid., 7 February 1913, 30.
51 Ibid.
52 Jessel to United Synagogue council, 13 January 1913, accompanying invitation (24 January 5673–1913) to meeting of delegates on 16 February, LMA/ACC/2712/15/0136/B.
53 Invitation to meeting of delegates, ibid.
54 On 'Schechter's Seminary,' by Mel Scult, see *Tradition Renewed: A History of the Jewish Theological Seminary of America*, Vol. I, ed. Jack Wertheimer (New York: Jewish Theological Seminary of America, 1997), 45-102.
55 Schechter to Jessel, 31 January 1913, *Jewish Chronicle*, 14 February 1913, 13. Referring to this letter, Harvey Meirovich observes (*A Vindication of Judaism: The Polemics of the Hertz Pentateuch* [New York and Jerusalem: Jewish Theological Seminary of America, 1998], 195): 'Initially, Schechter indicated that he did not want the letter published, but apparently he changed his mind after receiving an urgent telegram urging him to do so from Lord Rothschild and Mr Jessel.' Scult (op. cit., 95) mentions that Cyrus Adler, later president of the JTS, also supported Hertz in a letter to Schechter dated 15 August 1912. Of Schechter's 'ambivalent' relationship with Drachman, Scult writes (ibid., 64): 'During the early months of Schechter's administration, the question of whether or not to retain Drachman was constantly under discussion ... For the time being, Drachman's position was secure. According to his own account, he was popular with the students, but this conflicts with Schechter's report to the Seminary board in May 1907 that his "teaching does not come up to the modern standards and this is instinctively felt by the students." In 1908, the board decided to ask for Drachrnan's resignation and gave reasons of

economy.' For Drachman's account of this deteriorating relationship, and a comment by his son, Julian (who edited his autobiography), see Drachman, op. cit., 259-261.
56 Schechter to Jessel, 5 August 1912, JTS Library Archives, Schechter Papers, Correspondence 101-103, Box 3, quoted in Meirovich, op. cit., 195, and in Scult, op. cit., 64. In his speech to the delegates, Jessel described Schechter's 1913 letter as 'confirming a testimonial previously given' (*Jewish Chronicle*, 21 February 1913, 28).
57 'The Chief Rabbinate,' Petition to The Right Honourable The Lord Rothschild, P.C., G.C.V.O., President of the United Synagogue, 12 February 1913, LMA/ACC/2712/15/0137/B.
58 'The Chief Rabbinate,' 7 February 1913, ibid.
59 Memorandum accompanying the protest, pointing out that 4,200 copies of the letter were sent out in all, ibid.
60 Described as 'privately communicated' and quoted in Newman, op. cit., 100-101.
61 Drachman, op. cit., 301.
62 *Jewish Chronicle*, 14 February 1913, 13-14.
63 During his lengthy address to the delegates, Jessel mentioned the disputed role of Lord Milner, the British High Commissioner for Southern Africa and Governor of Cape Colony, in connection with Hertz's nomination. 'It is said,' remarked Jessel, 'that he [Hertz] came to us introduced by Lord Milner ... The statement is without foundation. He was not introduced by Lord Milner. A statement has appeared in the *Standard* in reference to Lord Milner, and I shall read to you what Lord Milner said about him [Hertz] in a private communication obtained by Lord Rothschild unsolicited by Dr Hertz. It was a private letter, but in consequence of that statement in the *Standard*, communicated by someone who heard it confidentially— and had no right to communicate it—Lord Rothschild communicated with Lord Milner and obtained his permission to read the letter to the Conference.' Jessel later read out the letter (dated 14 June 1912), in the following terms: 'My Dear Lord Rothschild,—I knew Dr Hertz quite well in South Africa. I have heard him speak in public several times, and have had many conversations with him. He is certainly a remarkably able man, and a most eloquent speaker. He also gave me personally the impression of great sincerity, and of being "a good fellow." His reputation, as far as I was acquainted with it, stood high. Personally, as far as I am able to judge of such a matter, I should say that he was well fitted by character and capacity for even so important a position as that of Chief Rabbi.' Commenting on the letter, Jessel told the delegates: 'That is the testimonial of a man who knows England, and knows the position occupied by Dr Adler.' *Jewish Chronicle*, 21 February 1913, 26, 28-29.
64 Ibid., 26.
65 Ibid., 27-28.
66 Drachman, op. cit., 317.
67 *Jewish Chronicle*, 21 February 1913, 28.
68 Ibid., 31.
69 Ibid., 32-33.
70 Rothschild to Hertz, 19 February 5673–1913, LMA/ACC/2712/15/0137/B.
71 Hertz to Rothschild, 5 Adar Sheni–14 March 5673, ibid.

72 Jewish Chronicle, 21 February 1913, 24.
73 Leading article, 'The Chief Rabbi-Elect,' ibid., 13.
74 The Installation Sermon of The Very Rev Dr Joseph Herman Hertz, Chief Rabbi of the United Hebrew Congregations of the British Empire, preached at the Great Synagogue, London, 14 April 5673–1913. Reproduced in full following this chapter.
75 Jewish Chronicle, 4 April 1913, 20.
76 Cable from C. Joshua Epstein (president) and Julius J. Dukas (treasurer), Congregation Orach Chayim, to the Jewish Chronicle, 7 May 1913. Announcing Hyamson's appointment, the paper declared (9 May 1913, 10): 'The good wishes of the whole community in this country will be accorded Dr Hyamson in the new sphere of his activity, and regret will be general at the loss of his services which will thus be sustained.'
77 At one point, Hyamson had stated that 'if, God forbid, the presidency of the Seminary should be offered to me, I could not accept it' (Ira Robinson, in *Tradition Renewed*, 124-125). Hyamson held the chair in Codes until his appointment as professor emeritus in 1940, nine years before his death. A vice-president of the Union of Orthodox Jewish Congregations of America, he translated *Hovot Halevavot* (*Duties of the Heart*), by the eleventh-century Spanish philosopher Bahya ibn Pakuda, and *Sefer Hamadah* from Maimonides' *Mishneh Torah*.
78 On this period in Drachman's and Hertz's careers, see Drachman, op. cit., 184-185.
79 Ibid., 318.

CHAPTER FOUR

1 The New West End Synagogue, London, where on 18 October 1919 Hertz delivered this sermon, *Traditional Judaism: An Appeal for the Jewish War Memorial* (London: Williams, Lea & Co., 1919; reprinted, abridged and amended as 'Religion and Life,' in *Sermons, Addresses and Studies*, Vol. I [London: Soncino Press, 1938], 288-293).
2 Hertz to Aaron Blashki, a potential backer for his commentary on the Chumash, in Harvey Meirovich, *A Vindication of Judaism: The Polemics of the Hertz Pentateuch* (New York and Jerusalem: Jewish Theological Seminary of America, 1998), 23.
3 Prefatory note to J. H. Hertz, *Affirmations of Judaism* (London: Oxford University Press, 1927), 7.
4 See Michael Leigh, 'Reform Judaism in Britain, 1840–1970,' in *Reform Judaism*, ed., Dow Marmur (London: Reform Synagogues of Great Britain, 1973), 36; Anne J. Kershen and Jonathan A. Romain, *Tradition and Change: A History of Reform Judaism in Britain, 1840–1995* (London: Vallentine Mitchell, 1995), 97; and Lawrence Rigal and Rosita Rosenberg, *Liberal Judaism: The First Hundred Years* (London: Liberal Judaism, 2004), 60-62.
5 Jewish Chronicle, 23 July 1926, 5.
6 Ibid., 28 June 1940, 1.
7 'Recall to the Synagogue – I,' delivered at the United Synagogue Conference, Woburn House, London, 25 July 1940, in J. H. Hertz, *Early and Late: Addresses, Messages, and Papers* (Hindhead, Surrey: Soncino Press, 1943), 153-159.

8   Hertz to honorary officers of the United Synagogue, 9 April 1945 (Papers of Chief Rabbi J. H. Hertz, MS 175, Hartley Library, Southampton University). The broadside against 'priestly dictatorship' had been aimed at Hertz by the US honorary officers following a dispute at the Finchley Synagogue, London, when (14 March 1945) they accused him of 'capriciousness' and of seeking 'to assume dictatorship and to rule the community by coercion.' Fuller accounts of these disputes appear in this writer's *Faith Against Reason: Religious Reform and the British Chief Rabbinate, 1840–1990* (London: Vallentine Mitchell, 2008), chapters 8-13, from which the above passages are adapted.
9   *Jewish Chronicle*, 18 January 1946, 1.
10 J. H. Hertz, preface to the first edition, *The Pentateuch and Haftorahs* (London: Oxford University Press, 1936), vii.
11 Aubrey Newman, *Chief Rabbi Dr Joseph H. Hertz*, lecture delivered at the Adolph Tuck Hall, Woburn House, London, 25 September 1972 (London: United Synagogue, 1972), 20-22.
12 *Jewish Chronicle*, 18 January 1946, 15.
13 Kopul Rosen, 'Foreword,' in *Essays and Addresses in Memory of the Very Rev Dr Joseph Herman Hertz*, ed., Wolf Gottlieb (London: Mizrachi Federation of Great Britain and Ireland, 1947), i-ii. In a brief preface, Gottlieb observed: 'This volume … was originally prepared for publication shortly after [Hertz's] death … A series of unforeseen circumstances has delayed the publication until now, on the eve of the second anniversary of his lamented death,' Tevet 5708–December 1947, ibid., iii.
14 Alexander Altmann, 'Memorial Address delivered at the Great Synagogue, Manchester,' 3 February 1946, ibid., 3.
15 Isidor Grunfeld, address at the memorial service of the United Synagogue, Golders Green Synagogue, London, 23 January 1946, ibid., 21.
16 Robert Waley Cohen, 'President's Address,' meeting of the United Synagogue and District Synagogues Councils, and of representatives of the Affiliated and Associated Synagogues, Adolph Tuck Hall, London, 16 January 1946, in *Joseph Herman Hertz, 1872–1946: In Memoriam*, ed. Isidore Epstein (London: Soncino Press, 1947), 43-44.
17 Report of executive committee, Chief Rabbinate Conference, 2 March 1948, United Synagogue, London, 2.
18 Aaron Wright, 'Principal Rabbi of the Federation of Synagogues,' in *Memories of Kopul Rosen*, ed. Cyril Domb (London: privately published [Carmel College, Wallingford, Berkshire], 1970), 78-80.
19 Leading article, *Jewish Chronicle*, 18 January 1946, 10.
20 Philip Goldberg to US honorary officers, 17 January 5706–1946, LMA/ACC/2712/15/2040.
21 Robert Waley Cohen to US wardens and officers, 23 January 5706–1946, ibid.
22 On Lazarus, see Raymond Apple, *Harris M. Lazarus—The Beloved Dayan*, Jerusalem, 2011.
23 Robert Waley Cohen to US honorary officers and elders, and others, 1 February 1946, LMA/ACC/2712/15/2040.
24 'Memorandum by the members of the Beth Din, London (Court of the Chief Rabbi) on the forthcoming election of the Chief Rabbi of the United Hebrew Congregations of the British Empire in succession to the late Dr J. H. Hertz,' 28

March 1946, ibid.
25 Ibid.
26 Robert Waley Cohen, Southampton Lodge, Fitzroy Park, N.6, to The Very Rev the Chief Rabbi, Dr I. Herzog, M.A., Palestine, 1 April 1946, ibid.
27 Yitzchak Isaac Halevy Herzog, M.A., D.Litt., Chief Rabbi of the Holy Land, Jerusalem, to Sir Robert Waley Cohen, London, 28 April 1946, ibid. The letter concluded: 'It is good to hear that you are in good health and spirits, and that the Almighty is giving you strength to continue your great public service. With kind regards and reiterated thanks.' Herzog had opened his letter with a reference to the United Synagogue as 'that noble and fundamental institution of Anglo-Jewry.'
28 For Temkin's reminiscences of their relationship, see his 'Orthodoxy With Moderation: A Sketch of Joseph Herman Hertz,' in *Judaism*, No. 95, Vol. 24/3, summer 1975 (New York: American Jewish Congress), 278-295.
29 Anglo-Jewish Association to United Synagogue, 10 May 1946, LMA/ACC/2712/15/2040. The AJA headquarters were in Woburn House, Upper Woburn Place, London, where the United Synagogue offices were also situated.
30 'Sir Robert's report of his interview with the Rabbi at 12 noon, Friday, 21st June, 1946, seen & approved by Sir R.,' ibid.
31 Note dated 16 July 1946, attached to minutes of United Synagogue honorary officers' meeting, 22 July 1946, ibid. This proposal was curious, in view of the apparent deletion of Brodie's name from the original list.
32 John M. Shaftesley, 'Israel Brodie, Chief Rabbi: A Biographical Sketch,' in *Essays presented to Chief Rabbi Israel Brodie on the Occasion of his Seventieth Birthday*, ed. H. J. Zimmels, J. Rabbinowitz, and I. Finestein (London: Jews' College Publications and Soncino Press, 1967), xvi. An affectionate portrait by the Rev Arthur Saul Super—'Israel Brodie: Chief Rabbi'—also appeared in the *Jewish Monthly* (London) 2, no. 3 (June 1948). Brodie's childhood, wrote Super, 'was passed in the traditional Jewish, happy home atmosphere. His parents were of modest means [Aaron Brodie was a commercial traveller] and brought up their children on strictly orthodox lines, with a love of the intelligent practice of the commandments and with a complete sense of unity with the whole of Israel, "Klal Yisroel." There was nothing cold or ritually formal about the Brodie household' (134). See also Raymond Apple, *Rabbi Israel Brodie—Seventy-Five Years Later* (Sydney: 1998), and *Rabbi Brodie and the Australian Ministry* (Sydney: 1980).
33 Minutes of US honorary officers' meeting, 22 July 1946, LMA/ACC/2712/15/2040. Ordained at the Jewish Theological Seminary of America, Louis Finkelstein (1895–1991) was a talmudic and halachic authority and a trail-blazing Conservative in its modern Jewish connotation (though the United Synagogue president appears to have been unaware of this). He joined the JTA faculty in 1920 as a teacher in Talmud, later became professor of theology, and was successively appointed provost, president, chancellor, and chancellor emeritus. At the time of their 1946 interviews with Waley Cohen, Harry Freedman (1901–1982) was rabbi of the Melbourne Hebrew Congregation, South Yarro, and head of the Melbourne Beth Din; Israel Porush (1908–1991) was chief minister of the Great Synagogue, Sydney, and chairman of the city's Beth Din; and Israel Abrahams (1903–1973) was Chief Rabbi of the Cape Town Hebrew Congregations. All three had held posts

in the British rabbinate. Porush's name appeared on the shortlist of candidates in the 1965–1966 election, although he wrote in his synagogue journal that many in Australia considered a British Chief Rabbi to be an anachronism and that Australia was ready for its own Chief Rabbi. He subsequently became the Chief Rabbi's representative in Australia (*Jewish Chronicle*, 31 May 1991, 14).

34 Otto M. Schiff (1875–1952) was a leading communal worker and philanthropist in British Jewry who played an acclaimed role on behalf of Jewish refugees in both world wars. He was described by Waley Cohen in his letter to Wyzanski as 'our mutual friend.'

35 In the original copy of Wyzanski's letter, this sentence is heavily underlined in pencil (presumably by Waley Cohen) and the word 'quite' is underscored three times.

36 Charles E. Wyzanski, Jr., District Judge, United States Court, Boston 9, to Robert Waley Cohen, Esq., London, 28 October 1946, LMA/ACC/2712/15/2041.

37 In July 1945, a Federation search committee—following a decision by its general council and executive to fill the post of religious head left vacant by the death of Rabbi Dr Maier Jung in 1921—consulted Hertz, Abramsky, Herzog, Rabbi Meir Berlin (Bar-Ilan) of Jerusalem and its own rabbinical council with a view to securing a suitable candidate. The committee reported that 'there was only one man who could combine all the necessary qualities, Rabbi J. B. Soloveitchik, of Boston, USA. But he was unwilling to accept the post ... However, on the recommendation of Dr Hertz, the Federation secured the services of the then Communal Rabbi of Glasgow, Kopul Rosen' (Geoffrey Alderman, *The Federation of Synagogues* [London: Federation of Synagogues, 1987], 72). After Herzog's death in 1959, Soloveitchik declined an invitation to become Ashkenazi Chief Rabbi of Israel.

38 Aaron Wright, op. cit., 74-75.

39 Shaftesley writes (op. cit., xxi): '[Brodie] was a member of the New West End Synagogue Service League and as such he became one of the Managers of the Stepney Boys' Club. While he was here, he had the good fortune to meet another of the managers, a Miss Fanny Levine, who was a teacher at the Stepney Jewish Schools, and this was the lady whom he married in 1946.' Super (op. cit., 139) adds: 'In person, the Chief Rabbi is of middle height, inclined somewhat to be an *embonpoint* over which Mrs Brodie, his charming and talented wife, watches with affectionate, tolerant but firm control.'

40 'In 1940,' wrote Cyril Domb ('A Biographical Sketch,' in *Memories of Kopul Rosen*, 15), 'he [Rosen] was married to Bella Cohen, elder daughter of a Cardiff communal leader, M. J. Cohen. His marriage was outstandingly successful and he continually referred in his personal diaries (kept while he was away on extensive tours abroad) to his good fortune in having been blessed with such a suitable companion and such a happy and integrated family life. In a touching letter written to his father-in-law shortly before his death, he pays the following tribute: "I do not believe ... that there can be many couples who have known such a deep love and sense of partnership as we have known. I am called the founder of Carmel, but the real truth is that I am the co-founder; Bella is at least an equal partner. Had we not been united by the deepest of bonds, we could not have faced all our problems together and triumphed."'

41 Minutes of meeting of US honorary officers, 16 December 1946, LMA/ACC/2712/15/2041.

42 Minutes of informal sub-committee meeting, 19 January 1947, ibid.
43 Harris M. Lazarus to Sir Robert Waley Cohen, 20 January 1947–5707, ibid.
44 Such sentiments were echoed by a Special Correspondent in the *Jewish Chronicle* (14 March 1947, 11), who wrote that 'if the interregnum has had one peculiar characteristic, it has been the lack of public discussion of the issues connected with the filling of the vacancy. This circumstance contrasts sharply with the wordy controversies which broke out immediately after the death of previous Chief Rabbis and continued until, and, in some cases, after, the election of their successors. But of late an impatience at the lack of any overt action towards appointing a successor has been noticeable.'
45 Rev Isaac Livingstone, honorary secretary, Union of Anglo-Jewish Preachers, to A. H. Silverman, secretary, United Synagogue, 12 February 1947, LMA/ACC/2712/15/2041.
46 Preamble to Part I of the 'Report of the Executive Committee, Chief Rabbinate Conference, for the Meeting of the Council, 9 March 1948' (London: United Synagogue, 2 March 1948), 1.
47 *Jewish Chronicle*, 7 March 1947, 5.
48 Leading article, ibid., 14 March 1947, 10.

CHAPTER FIVE

1 Moravian-born Leo Jung (1892–1987) was educated at Vienna University and at the Hildesheimer Rabbinical Seminary in Berlin, as well as at Geissen University, where he pursued doctoral studies on 'The Concept of God in Anglo-Saxon Philosophy.' During 1916–1919, he gained bachelor and master degrees at Cambridge University, and while in Britain received three rabbinical ordinations. His first pulpit was at Congregation Knesset Israel in Cleveland, Ohio, and in 1922 he became spiritual leader of the New York Jewish Center, where he remained for fifty years.
2 On Abrahams, see previous chapter.
3 'The only persons who could form the Electoral College,' Waley Cohen told the delegation, 'were the lay leaders of the Community, in whom the responsibility for the conduct of the affairs of the Community was vested. He felt sure that the Ministers would appreciate that no such responsibility rested on them, and therefore he could not possibly see any way in which they could either be consulted again or play any part in the election.'
4 'Note of interview between Sir Robert Waley Cohen, K.B.E., and Mr Frank Rossdale, Esq., B.A., LL.B, with Rev I. Livingstone, Rev Dr M. Lew, Rev Arthur Barnett and Rev I. M. Fabricant,' 19 March 1947, LMA/ACC/2712/15/2041.
5 Jack Levine to Sir Robert Waley Cohen, K.B.E., 28 March 1947, LMA/ACC/2712/15/2042.
6 'Memorandum to Sir Robert Waley Cohen, K.B.E., together with a list of names and congregations of the rabbis who signed,' March 1947, ibid.
7 'Interview between Sir Robert Waley Cohen, Dayan Abramsky, Dayan Grunfeld

and Dayan Swift, with Mr A. H. Silverman (Secretary),' 27 March 1947, LMA/ACC/2712/15/2041.
8 'Note of interview between Sir Robert Waley Cohen, K.B.E., and deputation of rabbonim,' 2 April 1947, LMA/ACC/2712/15/2042.
9 Waley Cohen to Rosen, 1 April 1947, ibid.
10 Rosen to Waley Cohen, 3 April 1947–5707, ibid.
11 Rosen to Waley Cohen, 7 April 1947–5707, ibid.
12 A draft of this letter carries the following alternative sentence: 'Once these gentlemen descend into the arena generally associated with rather low political propaganda, they naturally lose control of the situation, and a most unsatisfactory campaign is bound to result' (ibid).
13 Waley Cohen to Rosen, 10 April 1947, ibid.
14 Rosen to Waley Cohen, 21 April 1947, ibid.
15 Expanding on this statement, Cymerman wrote: 'We feel that the information upon which you have based your letter has come from persons who are deliberately distorting and falsifying the position for their own propaganda ends. We regret to note that this unpleasantness arose solely from a breach of confidence on the part of Rabbi [Binyamin Beinish] Atlas of Glasgow, who sought fit to speak to Mr Levine about a confidential talk which took place in his house. We are reluctantly compelled to point out that Rabbi Atlas refused to sign the memorandum for rather a strange reason. He maintained that no orthodox Rabbi should have any truck with the institution of the Chief Rabbinate, and that the Chief Rabbinate should be discontinued.' In an unconnected reference to Atlas, Rabbi Dr Ari Z. Zivotofsky writes (*Jewish Action* [Fall 5767–2006]): 'In 1941, Rabbi Yechezkel Abramsky supported Rabbi Binyamin Beinish Atlas, of Glasgow, in rejecting the butchers' request to sell hindquarters.' The reference appeared in an article entitled 'What's the truth about … *nikkur achoraim*,' the act of rendering the hindquarters of an animal fit for kosher consumption. Four years later, some of the protagonists in the Chief Rabbinical election battle found themselves sharing a platform, when Kopul Rosen, as Communal Rabbi of Glasgow, presided over a local Sabbath Observance Organisation meeting at which the speakers included Abramsky and Grunfeld, and Atlas as honorary secretary of the Glasgow Beth Din (*Jewish Chronicle*, 26 January 1945, 12).
16 Cymerman to Waley Cohen, 16 April 1947, LMA/ACC/2712/15/2042.
17 Waley Cohen to Cymerman, 22 April 1947, ibid.
18 Minutes of meeting of US honorary officers, 31 March 1947, LMA/ACC/2712/15/2041.
19 'Text of Speech delivered by Mr Aaron Wright to the General Council of the Federation of Synagogues on Tuesday, 18 April 1947,' LMA/ACC/2712/15/2121.
20 'Statement by the Honorary Officers of the United Synagogue to the Members of the Council,' 23 April 1947, ibid. The two statements elicited an ongoing correspondence in the *Jewish Chronicle* from supporters of both sides.
21 'The Chief Rabbinate,' J. H. Taylor to Sir Robert Waley Cohen, KBE, 29 April 1947, LMA/ACC/2712/15/2042.
22 I. Livingstone to the President of the United Synagogue, 6 May 1947, ibid.
23 Minutes of meeting of US honorary officers, 12 June 1947, ibid.

24 Minutes of meeting of informal sub-committee, 20 July 1947, ibid.
25 Minutes of meeting of informal sub-committee, 8 September 1947, LMA/ACC/2712/15/2043.
26 Report of executive committee, Chief Rabbinate Conference, 2 March 1948, United Synagogue, London, 1.
27 Minutes of Chief Rabbinate Conference, 9 November 1947, LMA/ACC/2712/11/40.
28 The committee comprised twelve United Synagogue representatives, five from the Federation, seven from the provinces, and one from the Dominions.
29 Report of executive committee, Chief Rabbinate Conference, 2 March 1948, United Synagogue, London, 2.
30 Julius Jung to A. H. Silverman, 13 January 1948, LMA/ACC/2712/15/2122.
31 This last sentence is included in some versions of the statement (ibid.), but appears to have been deleted from the submitted memorandum.
32 'Statement of the Federation of Synagogues concerning the duties and privileges attaching to the Office of the Chief Rabbi,' ibid.
33 Report of executive committee, Chief Rabbinate Conference, 2 March 1948, United Synagogue, London, 2-3.
34 Alfred H. Silverman to members of the committee, 26 January 1948, LMA/ACC/2712/11/40. The letter stated: 'I confirm that on the instructions of the Chairman, the following telegram was despatched to you today: "Executive Committee of Federation decided and notified us that they refuse participate Chief Rabbinate unless United Synagogue and all others accept their memorandum 13 January substituting Beth Din authority for that of Chief Rabbi. Consultation last night failed modify this decision. Therefore urgently important Committee meet next Sunday First February 10.30 a.m. Woburn House to consider situation created. ROBERT WALEY COHEN." In view of the extremely serious turn which events have now taken, I am to request you to make every possible effort to attend without fail.'
35 Minutes of Chief Rabbinate Conference, 22 February 1948, LMA/ACC/2712/11/40.
36 Clause 14(b) of 'duties, privileges and conditions attaching to the Office of Chief Rabbi.'
37 Report to Chief Rabbinate Conference, 22 February 1948, ibid. Report of executive committee, Chief Rabbinate Conference, 2 March 1948, United Synagogue, London, 4, 10. The Conference also voted to set up a committee of twenty-two members 'to consider the question of Voting Rights and the steps to be taken to select and appoint a Chief Rabbi.'
38 Minutes of Chief Rabbinate Conference committee, 21 March 1948.
39 In this connection, see note 43 below.
40 'Sir Robert's statement at Chief Rabbinate committee meeting,' 21 March 1948, LMA/ACC/2712/15/2122.
41 'Statement by the Chairman, Sir Robert Waley Cohen, KBE, to a strictly private meeting of bodies and congregations in the London area contributing to the maintenance of the Office of Chief Rabbi,' 5 April 1948, ibid.
42 Many years later, in relation to the 'full and unqualified support' he had expressed

for Brodie, Wright disclosed that 'shortly before the election, Kopul came to see me and advised me and those associated with me to support the candidature of Rabbi Brodie. In this, he showed grace and wisdom. At the great gathering in May 1948, it was my privilege to support the nomination of Rabbi Brodie.' Asking 'what was the likelihood of Kopul being a successful candidate for the Chief Rabbinate?', Wright wrote: 'He had many great and commanding qualities, but he was criticised for being too young, a fault too easily remedied. His scholarship had not yet matured. But what counted heavily against him was that his determination of character was too obvious. Other candidates may have been as strong, but this strength of character was held in reserve, as later events established' (Aaron Wright, 'Principal Rabbi of the Federation of Synagogues,' in *Memories of Kopul Rosen*, ed. Cyril Domb [London: privately published, Carmel College, 1970], 81). Rosen resigned as Principal Rabbi of the Federation of Synagogues in late 1948 on establishing Carmel College, the boarding school of which he remained principal until his death in 1962. David Stamler, Carmel's vice-principal and later headmaster, described Rosen's days at the Federation as 'rarely satisfying or happy ones. The whole concept and scope of the organisation was, for him, claustrophobic and restricting ... Repeatedly, and as late as 1961, whenever he discussed the question of a return to communal life, he stated that, however attractive this might sound and however imperative the call might be, he had only to think back to his life in the Federation for the idea to lose all its attractions' (David Stamler, 'Kopul at Carmel,' in ibid., 99).

43 Waley Cohen to Moss, 8 April 1948, LMA/ACC/2712/15/2046. To appease Moss regarding Altmann's future, the US president wrote: 'I do not like to formulate by myself any more detailed methods of carrying out the plan I personally envisage until we have had an opportunity of consulting those who would be responsible for making the appointment which I should like to see him [Altmann] hold. I do not think any financial difficulty would arise and I entirely agree with your view that the salary would have to be advanced to meet the higher cost of living in London. There are plenty of precedents for this, the most authoritative being that of the University Grants Committee in the scale of salaries for Professors and Lecturers at Universities.' Waley Cohen's 'plan' was not revealed, but after the Chief Rabbinical election, Altmann continued to pursue his scholarly studies, which led him in 1953 to found and direct the Institute of Jewish Studies, which at the time was an independent institution. There he edited the *Journal of Jewish Studies* and *Scripta Judaica* and wrote his work (co-authored with Samuel M. Stern), *Isaac Israeli: A Neo-Platonic Philosopher of the Early Tenth Century*. After securing the future of the Institute by bringing it under the auspices of University College, London, he left Britain in 1959, aged fifty-three, to join the faculty of Brandeis University at Waltham, Massachusetts, serving as Philip W. Lown Professor of Jewish Philosophy and History of Ideas until his appointment as professor emeritus and subsequent retirement in 1976. Following two years as a visiting professor at Harvard and at the Hebrew University of Jerusalem, he served, until his death in 1987, as an Associate at the Harvard University Center for Jewish Studies.

44 Chief Rabbinate Conference committee minutes, 18 April 1948, LMA/ACC/2712/15/2046; 'Report of the committee appointed at the meeting of delegates

on 22 February 1948' (18 April 1948–5708), 1-2, LMA/ACC/2712/15/2121.
45 Minutes of meeting of delegates to the Chief Rabbinate Conference, Woburn House, London, 30 May 1948, LMA/ACC/2712/15/2122.
46 Ibid.
47 Waley Cohen to Brodie, 30 May 1948, LMA/ACC/2712/15/2048.
48 Brodie to Waley Cohen, 31 May 1948, ibid.
49 *Jewish Chronicle*, 19 March 1948, 1.
50 'Fettering a Chief Rabbi,' leading article, ibid., 10.
51 Aubrey Newman, *The United Synagogue, 1870–1970* (London, Henley, and Boston: Routledge & Kegan Paul, 1977), 182.
52 John M. Shaftesley, 'Israel Brodie, Chief Rabbi: A Biographical Sketch,' in *Essays presented to Chief Rabbi Israel Brodie on the Occasion of his Seventieth Birthday*, ed. H. J. Zimmels, J. Rabbinowitz, and I. Finestein (London: Jews' College Publications, and Soncino Press, 1967), xxix.
53 Lazarus to Waley Cohen, 29 June 1948–5708, LMA/ACC/2712/15/2048.
54 Waley Cohen to Lazarus, 30 June 1948, ibid.
55 Daphne Cudmore, Private Secretary, War Office, to Sir Robert Waley Cohen, 4 June 1948, LMA/ACC/2712/15/2049.

CHAPTER SIX

1 After studying as a teenager at Manchester Yeshivah, Jacobs (1920–2006) joined the newly founded Gateshead kollel, where his 'teacher *par excellence*,' as he put it (*Helping With Inquiries: An Autobiography* [London: Vallentine Mitchell, 1989], 59), was its founder, Rabbi Eliyahu Eliezer Dessler. He later received *semichah* from Rabbi Moshe Yitzchak Segal (assisted by Rabbis Baruch Steinberg, Raphael Margolies and Isaac Lerner) and Rabbi Moshe Rivkin. His first rabbinical post was as assistant to Rabbi Dr Eliyahu Munk at the Golders Green Beth Hamedrash, London, before joining the Manchester Central Synagogue in 1947. For a detailed study of Jacobs' transition from *Torah lishmah* to Biblical Criticism, see Elliot Joe Cosgrove, *Teyku: The Insoluble Contradictions in the Life and Thought of Louis Jacobs* (PhD dissertation, University of Chicago, 2008).
2 The first and second 'Jacobs Affairs' are comprehensively discussed in Miri J. Freud-Kandel, *Orthodox Judaism in Britain Since 1913* (London: Vallentine Mitchell, 2006), 123-157; Benjamin J. Elton, *Britain's Chief Rabbis and the Religious Character of Anglo-Jewry, 1880–1970* (Manchester University Press, 2010); and Meir Persoff, *Faith Against Reason: Religious Reform and the British Chief Rabbinate 1840–1990* (London: Vallentine Mitchell, 2008), 283-317. A Conservative viewpoint is supplied by Sefton Temkin, 'A Crisis in Anglo-Jewry,' in *Conservative Judaism* 18, no. 1 (fall 1963), 18-34; an Orthodox perspective by Norman Cohen, 'The Religious Crisis in Anglo-Jewry,' in *Tradition* 8, no. 2 (1966), 40-57; and a Reform overview by Ignaz Maybaum, 'The Jacobs Affair,' in *Quest* 1 (September 1965), 80-83. Jacobs provides detailed discussions in 'Reflections on a Controversy,' in *Quest* 1:4-5; the Epilogue to *We Have Reason to Believe*, third edition (London: Vallentine Mitchell,

1965), 138-151; the 'Retrospect' to the fifth edition (2004), viii-xvi; *Helping With Inquiries* (London: Vallentine Mitchell, 1989), 134-222; and *Beyond Reasonable Doubt* (London: Littman Library of Jewish Civilization, 1999), 1-30. On the twenty-fifth anniversary of the Jews' College controversy, he examined 'its contemporary relevance and long-term repercussions' in 'For the Sake of Heaven' (*Jewish Chronicle*, 19 December 1986, 22-23). A *Jewish Chronicle* insider's view is in William Frankel, *Tea With Einstein And Other Memories* (London: Halban, in association with the European Jewish Publication Society, 2006), 157-171.

3   *Jewish Chronicle*, 22 December 1961, 10.
4   Ibid., 5 January 1962, 8.
5   Ibid., 11 May 1962, 10.
6   Immanuel Jakobovits, 'Fragments from an unpublished autobiography,' in Meir Persoff, *Immanuel Jakobovits: a Prophet in Israel* (London: Vallentine Mitchell, 2002), 114.
7   Cohen to Jakobovits, 23 February 1962, Jakobovits Papers, London.
8   'Fragments,' op. cit., 114-115.
9   Jakobovits to Cohen, 15 February 1962, Jakobovits Papers, London.
10 Ewen Montagu (1901–1985), a grandson of the first Lord Swaythling, was elected president of the United Synagogue in 1954, resigned in 1961 over policy differences, was re-elected weeks later, and resigned again the following year, at the height of the Jacobs Affair. Isaac Wolfson (1897–1991) became the first head of the United Synagogue to emerge from the strictly Orthodox wave of East European immigration a generation earlier. Managing director of Great Universal Stores, he was an outstanding philanthropist, both within and outside the Jewish community.
11 Jakobovits to Cohen, 24 May 1962, Jakobovits Papers, London.
12 'Fragments,' op. cit., 115. The London visit was accompanied by a report in the *Jewish Observer and Middle East Review* (30 November 1962, 9), entitled 'Rabbinical Contender': 'The open season is beginning for contenders for the Chief Rabbinate of the United Hebrew Congregations of the British Commonwealth of Nations. The Chief Rabbi will be seventy in 1965 and has announced that he will retire then. There is clearly no self-evident successor in the field, so prospective candidates are beginning the tilling process fairly early. My New York correspondent tells me that the Rabbi of the Fifth Avenue Synagogue, and former Chief Rabbi of Ireland, Immanuel Jakobovits, has made no bones about his intention to project himself back into the Anglo-Jewish scene. His sojourn in America has convinced the Rabbi that, while graven images were a wickedness in the eyes of the Lord, the projection of a rabbinical image was an essential part of good public and ecclesiastical relations in the age of the New Frontier. For some time, in fact, experts in this field have noted the increasing appearances of the Jakobovits image in the press, and I was not surprised, therefore, that Dr Jakobovits' arrival in this country as the guest of the Jewish Agency and the Mizrachi should have been heralded by a loyal accompaniment of image-projection of this orthodox rabbi who wants to synthesise modernity and orthodoxy.' *The Jewish Review* (14 November 1962, 4) preceded the lecture tour by a profile, headed 'Immanuel Jakobovits: *Baruch Haba* [Welcome!],' written by N.C. [Norman Cohen] and remarking that 'the

fortnight that he is spending in Great Britain as the guest of the Jewish Agency Torah department will enable him to help in bringing 1962 to a more successful conclusion, religiously speaking, than at one time seemed likely. The last months have witnessed a remarkable change in the balance of power in the community, and the gain has been entirely that of orthodoxy. But this will avail nothing unless religious revival goes hand in hand with communal leadership. The Old Paths [Hermann Adler's description of 'Traditional Judaism'] remain, despite all efforts to obliterate them, and it is now high time to show that they still possess an attraction and a validity shared by no others.'

13 'The unanimous election of Sir Isaac Wolfson to the presidency of the United Synagogue,' commented the *Jewish Chronicle* (7 December 1962, 24), 'marks a turning-point in the evolution of the Anglo-Jewish community and is bound to have its repercussions in many aspects of our religious and synagogal life ... The late Chief Rabbi [Hertz] liked to refer to the "broad umbrella" of the United Synagogue. Today there is a tendency to fear only the thrusting extremist minority and to satisfy them at the cost of the loss of interest of the greater numbers who dissent from this view but are not militant. The damaging result may not immediately be apparent, but it is more than the United Synagogue can afford in the long run. The new president can, by his determination, understanding and force of character, give a fresh lead to the community. The fact that Sir Isaac's own observance is beyond question may, we hope, strengthen his hand. This is the great challenge and the great role which lies before him. The good wishes of all sections of the community will attend him in the pursuit of this endeavour.'

14 Jakobovits, along with Rabbi Joseph Soloveitchik, was among those whose help and advice Brodie (and the London Beth Din) sought during the New West End rebellion. 'While normally I would not like to involve Rabbis of other communities in an issue which is domestic,' Brodie told Jakobovits, 'the publicity which has been given to the whole matter in the general press and on radio outside the United Kingdom does make it necessary for spiritual leaders of the stature of Rabbi Soloveitchik to make a pronouncement.' Brodie added that he had 'been considerably helped by the attitude of the Honorary Officers of the United Synagogue, who have loyally maintained the authority and dignity of my Office' (Brodie to Jakobovits, 30 April 1964–5724, Jakobovits Papers, London). Brodie gave a full account of his stand on the New West End issue to a gathering of rabbis and ministers at the Adolph Tuck Hall, London, on 5 May 1964 (later published by the Office of the Chief Rabbi), preceded by a similar statement from Wolfson (also published) to a special meeting of the United Synagogue council on 23 April 1964.

15 *Jewish Chronicle*, 12 June 1964, 1, 14.

16 Meeting of the Chief Rabbinate Conference, 12 July 1964, Jakobovits Papers, London.

17 'Leisurely search for next Chief Rabbi,' *Jewish Chronicle*, 8 January 1965, 12. In a statement on the dispute, the Federation's president, Morris Lederman, noted that its participation in the appointment 'is on the understanding that the following conditions are fulfilled: 1. That the London Beth Din and the Federation Rabbinate shall continue to exist independently, but the Chief Rabbi shall be the head of

both bodies. Ecclesiastical authority in the Greater London area shall be shared by the London Beth Din and the Rabbinate of the Federation of Synagogues working in conjunction, under the chairmanship of the new Chief Rabbi. 2. That a meeting shall be convened shortly after the appointment of the Chief Rabbi between the Chief Rabbi, the chairman of the Federation Rabbinate, and the presidents of the United Synagogue and the Federation of Synagogues, to consider how the work of the ecclesiastical administration should be allocated between the London Beth Din and the Federation Rabbinate. 3. That the Federation of Synagogues reserves the right to be free from the obligation to accept a decision of the Chief Rabbi if it differs from a decision of its own Rabbinate' ('Mr Lederman's Statement,' 7 February 1965, LMA/ACC/2712/15/01/128).

Presenting an account of the dispute in relation to these conditions, the Chief Rabbinate Conference committee later reported: 'The Committee first met on 18 October 1964, when the representatives of the Federation of Synagogues did not attend. The Committee had before it the document originally circulated with the agenda on 3 July 1964, to the delegates to the Conference, and on the suggestion of the chairman each section of the document was dealt with in detail. Before coming to a final decision as to its report to the Conference, the chairman was asked to use his endeavours to secure the attendance of the representatives of the Federation of Synagogues at the next meeting of the Committee, when it was hoped that it would be possible to settle the report now being presented. The Committee met again on 7 February 1965, and the representatives of the Federation of Synagogues attended. The Committee then considered the draft of its report and, after several amendments had been agreed, reached Section (d) dealing with "The relationship with the Chief Rabbinate of the Congregations supporting his Office." It appearing to the Committee from the debate that ensued that the delicate negotiations necessary to effect reconciliation between the views of the leaders of the United Synagogue delegation and those of the Federation of Synagogues delegation would be somewhat hampered in so large a body as the Committee, it was decided to appoint a sub-committee consisting of three representatives of the United Synagogue and three representatives of the Federation of Synagogues, under the chairmanship of Councillor S. Davies, of Manchester, to see whether such a reconciliation could be effected. It was also agreed that if happily a large measure of unanimity could be achieved, then the effect of such agreement should be incorporated in the report to be presented to the Conference. The sub-committee met on 9 February 1965, and reached complete agreement. It is with great pleasure, therefore, that the Committee now reports that the Federation of Synagogues have intimated their intention to participate fully in the election of a new Chief Rabbi, in the recognition of his authority, and in the maintenance of his Office, and thus it might be fairly claimed that the Traditional Orthodox Congregations of the British Commonwealth of Nations are solidly behind the appointment of the new Chief Rabbi' ('Report of the executive committee of the United Synagogue,' 30 May 1965–5725, for the meeting of the US council on 14 June 1965).

18 *The Irish Times*, Dublin, 8 June 1964.
19 Ivan Yates, *The Observer*, 7 June 1964. An earlier version of the report on the same

day, speedily corrected, related the Soloveitchik remarks to Jakobovits. The reference to Jacobs was subsequently deleted.
20 *Jewish Chronicle*, 21 May 1965, 14. An earlier list, prepared for a meeting of the Conference committee on 16 May 1965, included the names of Rabbi Dr Solomon Brown (Leeds) and Rabbi Oscar Fasman (United States). This document was described as 'not a list of candidates' and included the caveat: 'Most of the names listed have been put forward by various persons in response to the Chairman's general invitation for anyone interested to do so. The information set out has been gleaned from various sources, but full facts have not always been available and, in some cases, have for obvious reasons not been sought,' LMA/ACC/2712/15/01/128.
21 Rabbi Dr Emanuel Rackman, Assistant to the President, Yeshiva University, to the *Jewish Chronicle*, 18 June 1965, 6.
22 'Chief Rabbi from U.S.?', *Daily Express*, London, 22 March 1965.
23 'Chief Rabbi Candidate No. 1,' ibid., 24 March 1965.
24 'Search for a Rabbi,' *The Observer*, London, 21 March 1965.
25 *Jewish Chronicle*, 12 February 1965, 12.
26 Ibid., 26 March 1965, 12.
27 Immanuel Jakobovits, 'My Decision and our Challenge,' address to the Fifth Avenue Synagogue, New York, 13 April 1965, Jakobovits Papers, London.
28 German-born Elie Munk (1900–1981), rabbi of the Synagogue de la Rue Cadet (Adas Yereim) in Paris, studied at the Hildesheimer rabbinical seminary in Berlin, and in 1926 gained his doctorate in philosophy from the city's university. A prolific writer and scholar, he was the author of the classic, *The World of Prayer*. His daughter Amélie, Lady Jakobovits, died in 2010.
29 Jakobovits to Cohen, erev Shabbat '*Rav Lachem*' (*Devarim*) 5724 (17 July 1964), Jakobovits Papers, London.
30 Jakobovits to Cohen, 17 January 1965, ibid.
31 'My Decision and our Challenge,' op. cit.
32 Of the project's abortive end, Chaim Bermant notes: 'When it came to the point, the promised funds were not forthcoming' (*Lord Jakobovits: The Authorized Biography of the Chief Rabbi* [London: Weidenfeld and Nicolson, 1990], 65). Gloria Tessler writes (*Amélie: The Story of Lady Jakobovits* [London and Portland, OR: Vallentine Mitchell, 1999], 174): 'Jakobovits had a dream to extend the Fifth Avenue Synagogue, which now had a worldwide reputation, by adding a centre of Jewish ethical teachings, which would include medical, business, marriage and consumer ethics, but the membership was less than enthusiastic. They told him that he had created for them exactly what they wanted. They demanded no more; they had no interest in opening another dimension of Jewish life, for which there was also no offer of financial support. While Amélie privately criticised the membership for their short-sightedness, she realised later what she could not see then—that their objections opened her husband's mind to other offers, including the chance to look very seriously at the invitation from Sir Isaac Wolfson to become Chief Rabbi of the United Hebrew Congregations of Great Britain and the Commonwealth in succession to retiring Chief Rabbi Israel Brodie.'
33 Jakobovits to Wolfson, 14 April 1965, Jakobovits Papers, London.

34 *Jewish Chronicle*, 13 November 1964, 13. Michael Bar-Zohar writes (*Yaacov Herzog: A Biography* [London: Halban, 2005], 258): 'Early rumours about the surprising idea of inviting Yaacov Herzog to be Britain's Chief Rabbi reached Israel in the autumn of 1964. At first, Yaacov did not react, and at his express wish the Jewish press in Britain avoided mentioning it.'
35 Bermant, op. cit., 116. 'For his mother,' Bar-Zohar writes of Sarah Herzog (op. cit., 259), 'this would have been the realisation of her fondest dream, Yaacov's place at the pinnacle of the rabbinical world. The author of the initiative, Sir Isaac Wolfson, was a friend of hers and of her family, and she received his suggestion with pride and joy.'
36 Bar-Zohar, ibid.
37 'Fragments,' op. cit., 116.
38 *Daily Express*, 3 April 1965.
39 *Daily Mail*, 5 April 1965.
40 *Jewish Chronicle*, 14 May 1965, 16.
41 Born in Kul, Lithuania, Yosef Shlomo Kahaneman (1886–1969) became rabbi of Ponevezh in 1919 and opened a number of yeshivot there. He emigrated to Palestine in 1940 and built Kiryat Ha'Yeshivah ('Town of the Yeshivah') in Bnei Brak, becoming a leading member of Agudat Israel's Council of Torah Sages. His commendation of Yaacov Herzog acknowledged the family's strong commitment to Torah Judaism and was in line with Kahaneman's support for the State of Israel, in contrast to the anti-Zionism of many of his charedi colleagues.
42 An influential figure in United Synagogue circles, Edmund de Rothschild (1916–2009) was a son of Lionel Nathan de Rothschild and played a key role in the Association of Jewish Ex-Servicemen and Women, of which he was president.
43 Edmund de Rothschild to Sir Isaac Wolfson, Bart., 4 May 1965, LMA/ACC/2712/15/01/128.
44 de Rothschild to Herzog, 4 May 1965, ibid.
45 On the question of an interregnum, Dayan Isaac Jacob (Yitzchok Yaacov) Weiss and Dayan Isaac Golditch, of the Manchester Beth Din, wrote to Wolfson: 'Apart from the undesirability of the Chief Rabbi being forced to go at this particular psychological moment, there exist other reasons for his remaining in office until a successor is appointed. An interregnum will inevitably paralyse Anglo-Jewry at the top. Appointing another man as Acting Chief Rabbi in the place of Rabbi Brodie would be a personal affront to the present holder of the high office who is, by the grace of G-d, not incapacitated or disabled in any way, and who is equipped by his experience to remain at the helm of Anglo-Jewry, whose trust and confidence he has earned and retained. To replace him by an untried and temporary stand-in is uncalled-for and would inevitably be interpreted as an expression of no-confidence in a man who has not deserved such an indignity at the hands of Anglo-Jewry' (Weiss and Golditch to Wolfson, 13 May 1965, ibid). Wolfson replied: 'I am afraid that you are probably not aware that we are precluded from acting on the suggestion so earnestly set out in your letter. I did, however, bring the matter up again at a meeting of the Chief Rabbinate Council as recently as Sunday evening last, and that meeting confirmed what I had related. Please believe me when I say that my colleagues and I have so arranged matters

that no possible affront will be offered to Rabbi Brodie or, indeed, that we would even think of replacing him in the interregnum with, as you say, "an untried and temporary stand-in." Above all, I am fortified in my decision, and those of the Chief Rabbinate Council, by the entirely spontaneous and characteristic gesture of the Chief Rabbi in offering to be of any assistance that might in any circumstances be required after his official retirement on 31st of this month' (ibid.).

46 Israel Brodie to Jacob Herzog, 3 May 1965, ibid.
47 Press release, Chief Rabbinate Conference committee, 16 May 1965, ibid.
48 *Jewish Chronicle*, 21 May 1965, 1.
49 Ibid., 1, 14.
50 Nahum Goldmann interview, Herzog memorial publication, 1973, quoted in Bar-Zohar, op. cit., 259-260.
51 Golda Meir interview, Herzog memorial publication, 1973, quoted in ibid., 260.
52 Golda Meir, *My Life* (London: Weidenfeld & Nicolson, 1975; Futura, 1976), 346.
53 Wolfson to Herzog, 17 May 1965, LMA/ACC/2712/15/01/128.
54 'Report of the delegation sent to wait upon Rabbi Jacob Herzog in Jerusalem, 24 May 1965,' ibid.
55 Bar-Zohar writes (op. cit., 261): 'Yaacov's mother was ecstatic. "She dearly wanted him to accept,' said Shira Herzog [Yaacov's elder daughter]. 'It would have continued the dynasty. She didn't have to pressure him—she was inside him."'
56 *Jewish Chronicle*, 28 May 1965, 1, 18.
57 Herzog to Rabbis Myer Berman, Benjamin Gelles, Maurice Landy, Abraham Melinek and Maurice Unterman, 28 May 1965, LMA/ACC/2712/15/01/128.
58 *Daily Express*, 25 May 1965.
59 'Statement of the President to the Chief Rabbinate Conference,' 30 May 1965, LMA/ACC/2712/15/01/129.
60 *Jewish Chronicle*, 28 May 1965, 7.
61 Rabbi Sidney Brichto to Yaacov Herzog on his appointment as Chief Rabbi, 1 June 1965, Brichto Papers, London.
62 Herzog to Brichto, June 1965, ibid.
63 Immanuel Jakobovits, *If Only My People...: Zionism In My Life* (London: Weidenfeld and Nicolson, 1984), 18.
64 Jakobovits to Cohen, 14 June 1965, Jakobovits Papers, London. The ellipsis appears in the original text.
65 Herzog to Jakobovits, undated, ibid.
66 Wolfson to Herzog, 30 May 1965–28 Iyar 5725, LMA/ACC/2712/15/01/128.
67 Wolfson to the dayanim of the Beth Din of London, 31 May 1965–29 Iyar 5725, ibid. On behalf of his colleagues, Dayan Arye Leib Grossnass replied affirmatively, adding: 'May we take this occasion to congratulate you on the unanimous appointment of Rabbi Dr Yaacov Herzog as Chief Rabbi. It is our sincere prayer that Divine blessing will rest upon him and that all our efforts for the maintenance and strengthening of Judaism will be crowned with success' (Grossnass to Wolfson, 31 May 1965–29 Iyar 5725, ibid).
68 *Jewish Chronicle*, 28 May 1965, 15.
69 Ibid., 4 June 1965, 6. John Shaftesley, a former editor of the *Jewish Chronicle*, wrote of this passage: 'There are ironic echoes in the farewell comment of some of his

[Brodie's] fiercest critics'; and of the reference to 'a raging conflict which tore the community asunder': 'The hyperbole in this statement may be disregarded' ('Israel Brodie, Chief Rabbi: A Biographical Sketch,' in *Essays Presented to Chief Rabbi Israel Brodie on the Occasion of his Seventieth Birthday*, ed. H. J. Zimmels, J. Rabbinowitz, I. Finestein, Jews' College Publications, New Series, No. 3 [London: Soncino Press, 1967], xxxviii).

70 *Jewish Chronicle*, 27 August 1965, 1, 13.
71 LMA/ACC/2712/15/01/128. Heavily underscored 'DRAFT—NOT SENT,' this letter from US secretary Alfred Silverman was addressed to the presidents of the congregations participating in the Chief Rabbinate Conference. It also noted that, 'from 6 September 1965, the office of the Chief Rabbi is situated at Adler House, Tavistock Square, London WC1.' Rabbi Maurice Rose, secretary to the Chief Rabbi's office, explained (*Jewish Chronicle*, 27 August 1965, 1, 13) that the official residence in Hamilton Terrace, St John's Wood—which had hitherto housed the office—was 'being renovated in preparation for the arrival of the new occupant. As the new Chief Rabbi and Mrs Herzog have two daughters, they will need the whole house for their own use.' Pnina Herzog was in London a few weeks earlier (ibid., 10 September 1965, 15) 'to discuss and supervise the arrangements for the renovation, reconstruction and refurbishing which had been ordered by Sir Isaac and was to cost some £20,000.'
72 Dr Hermann Zondek, Maimon Street, Jerusalem, to Sir Isaac Wolfson, Bt., 31 August 1965, LMA/ACC/2712/15/01/128. Alfred Silverman replied: 'I am asked by Sir Isaac Wolfson to acknowledge receipt of your letter of 31 August concerning the health of her husband which was handed to him by Mrs Herzog. Needless to say, your letter, together with the letter from Rabbi Herzog relinquishing the position of Chief Rabbi of the United Hebrew Congregations of the British Commonwealth of Nations, to which he was appointed in May last, has been received with considerable dismay and much regret by Sir Isaac and his colleagues here in London' (Silverman to Zondek, 7 September 1965, ibid).
73 Yaacov Herzog to Sir Isaac Wolfson, Bt., 3 September 1965, ibid.
74 Minutes of special meeting at Great Universal House, 7 September 1965, attended by Sir Isaac Wolfson (in the chair), A. Woolf, S. S. Levin, M. Lederman, Cllr. S. Davies, with A. H. Silverman and W. Norwood in attendance, ibid.
75 Press release, Chief Rabbinate Council, 7 September 1965, ibid.
76 S.J. Goldsmith, 'In Search of a Chief Rabbi,' Jewish Telegraphic Agency, 8 September 1965.
77 *Jewish Chronicle*, 10 September 1965, 6.
78 *The Times*, 8 September 1965, 1.

CHAPTER SEVEN

1 As described by the *Jewish Chronicle*, 8 October 1965, 1.
2 Alfred H. Silverman, secretary, to members of the Chief Rabbinate Council, 7 September 1965, LMA/ACC/2712/15/01/128. Within hours of the press con-

ference in London, and with his ear close to the ground, the *Daily Express*'s Israel correspondent, Roland Flamini—one of the first to have tipped Herzog for the post—reported that Rabbi Louis Rabinowitz, 'the No. 2 choice, is a pessimistic candidate.' Claiming, despite his earlier pronouncement, that he had 'no ambition to become Chief Rabbi,' Rabinowitz told Flamini: 'I have come to the conclusion that I am too independent-minded for Anglo-Jewry. I have always had the attitude that a leader should lead. I certainly would not accept the post in which the Chief Rabbi was a showpiece representative.' In any event, he added, 'I regard the chance of a unanimous call from Britain's Jews as an impossible case. I never had any great hopes of becoming Chief Rabbi of Britain, but I was willing to be considered because friends wanted me to. I think Anglo-Jewry will look elsewhere. My personal view is that the man for the post is Rabbi Jakobovits of New York. He is well equipped for it and is a personable chap' (*Daily Express*, 9 September 1965).

3   *Jewish Chronicle*, 24 September 1965, 10.
4   Isaac Livingstone, honorary secretary, Union of Anglo-Jewish Preachers, to Silverman, 16 February 1966, LMA/ACC/2712/15/1/159.
5   Raymond Apple, *If There Is No Vision, The People Perishes*, sermon delivered at Hampstead Synagogue, London, on Shabbat Ki Teitzei, 11 September 1965. 'If the Chief Rabbinate is so much akin to the leadership of the Churches,' Apple declared, 'in what other "Church" have the ministers absolutely no say in the selection of their chief? And is the ministry in this country so poor, so negligible and so ineffective that not one minister in the whole of Britain is worth considering as Chief Rabbi? Must one go abroad, or enter another profession, to find scope to show one's talents?' Melbourne-born Apple (b. 1935) gained *semichah* from Jews' College and was minister at the Bayswater and Hampstead Synagogues (1960–1972) before returning to Australia to become senior rabbi of the Great Synagogue, Sydney, and dayan and registrar of the Sydney Beth Din. He retired to Jerusalem in 2006. His valedictory sermon, *In Farewell To Hampstead* (Yom Kippur 5733–18 September 1972, later published), expanded on his views of the United Synagogue ministry and the wider Anglo-Jewish community.
6   *Jewish Chronicle*, 22 October 1965, 11.
7   Ibid., 8 October 1965, 1, 40.
8   'No rush to find a Chief Rabbi,' ibid., 19 November 1965, .1.
9   See previous chapter, note 17.
10 *Jewish Chronicle*, 24 September 1965, 12.
11 Ibid., 11 February 1966, 11.
12 Ibid., 25 February 1966, 11.
13 Ibid., 22 April 1966, 11.
14 'I Have a Rabbi,' *Panim el Panim*, Jerusalem, 27 May 1966.
15 *Jewish Chronicle*, 24 June 1966, 1, 23.
16 Ibid., 23.
17 'Meeting between the honorary officers of the United Synagogue and representatives of the Union of Anglo-Jewish Preachers and the Council of Ministers of the United Synagogue,' 26 June 1966, LMA/ACC/2712/15/1/159.
18 'Meeting between the honorary officers of the United Synagogue and the dayanim of the London Beth Din,' 26 June 1966, ibid.

19 Jakobovits to Cohen, 24 June 1966, Jakobovits Papers, London.
20 Ibid.
21 Jakobovits' immediate response was a Western Union telegram to Wolfson: 'Profoundly honored by your call. However, as previously agreed with you, I cannot confirm acceptance until I am satisfied after projected London visit that communal peace and unity firmly assured. Little patience now may save many heartaches later for all' (Jakobovits to Wolfson, 26 June 1966, ibid).
22 Immanuel Jakobovits, *If Only My People...: Zionism In My Life* (London: Weidenfeld and Nicolson, 1984), 19.
23 *Jewish Chronicle*, 1 July 1966, 1, 12.
24 Sir Isaac Wolfson, chairman, to members of the selection committee, 27 June 1966 (marked '<u>DRAFT—NOT SENT</u>'), LMA/ACC/2712/15/1/159.
25 *Sunday Times*, 3 July 1966.
26 'Fragments,' op. cit., 118.
27 Jakobovits to Grunfeld, 3 July 1966, Jakobovits Papers, London.
28 Jakobovits to Herzog, 1 July 1966, ibid.
29 Herzog to Jakobovits, 7 July 1966, ibid.
30 Herzog to Jakobovits, handwritten from the Hôtel du Rhône, Geneva, 17 July 1966, ibid. After Jakobovits' consultations in Britain, Herzog wrote: 'I was very pleased to read of your basically positive impressions of London and feel that you have started off very well ... I certainly agree with you as to the need for an effective yeshivah high school and college school programme in England on the American lines and do not think that such an idea is beyond achievement' (Herzog to Jakobovits, 27 September 1966, ibid). Reflecting on this episode, years later, Jakobovits commented: 'I thought that [Herzog's] London appointment, surprising as it was, might restore the respect for the office after the denigration it had suffered for many years. Even in retrospect, I felt that his acceptance helped to break the back of the pro-Jacobs campaign. I was later to be the beneficiary of this, but meanwhile was relieved that his appointment had taken the pressure and the focus of attention off me' ('Fragments,' op. cit., 116).
31 Bar-Zohar, op. cit., 261-262.
32 Pnina Herzog to Michael Bar-Zohar, ibid., 262.
33 Ibid., 262. Detailing Herzog's progress following his withdrawal from the Chief Rabbinate, and after several months' convalescence in Switzerland away from his daughters (then aged twelve and ten), Bar-Zohar concludes: 'Towards the end of the winter, while still recuperating in Geneva, Yaacov received a surprising offer from the Prime Minister to become his political adviser. Eshkol also hinted that in a few months' time, when Teddy Kollek left, Yaacov would succeed him in the post of director of the Prime Minister's office. And that is what happened ... He wrote about it to his brother Vivian before leaving Geneva. "Vivian helped him a good deal in those days," said Vivian's wife, Aura. "Vivian saw that he was in distress, that he didn't want to discuss the matter with his mother, and the only person left to him was Vivian ... I knew that Vivian wrote to Wolfson and tried to calm the storm in London when Yaacov turned down the position. Vivian used his connection with Wolfson to help Yaacov discreetly, and didn't mention it to a soul"' (Aura Herzog to Bar-Zohar, ibid., 265). Herzog died on 6 March 1972, aged fifty.

Bar-Zohar (348-349) records his final weeks, following a visit to Canada: 'He was exhausted and aching. He returned ill, and his doctor thought he had a bad case of flu. In fact, he must have been struck by some unidentified virus ... "In the middle of the night, we heard a thump," Shira [Herzog] recalled. "He'd got out of bed and probably stumbled and fell. Later they found that he had suffered a haemorrhage in his head, near the brain" ... He lay in bed for three months, and it is doubtful if he recognised the members of the family around his bed. Once he stirred and mumbled something about the Jews of Russia, about opening the gates for Jewish immigration from the USSR. That was the last time they heard him speak.' For several weeks, his brother later recalled (Chaim Herzog, *Living History: A Memoir*, London: Phoenix, 1998, 184, 251), 'he struggled for life, but it was clear he was dying ... No one knows exactly what happened to Yaacov. We knew he had a stroke and we knew he fell, but it was never determined which had come first. All we know was the result: a haemorrhage, a coma, and then death at the tragically young age of fifty.' In a tribute to him, former Israeli President (1963–1973) Shneur Zalman Shazar wrote (Misha Louvish, ed., *A People that Dwells Alone: Speeches and Writings of Yaacov Herzog*, London: Weidenfeld and Nicolson, 1975, 11): 'I was a close witness to his perplexities when he was offered the Chief Rabbinate of Great Britain and he was faced with the choice of which comes first – even from the point of view of Israel itself – the post of Chief Rabbi in the greatest Jewish capital in Europe, or the leadership of the Prime Minister's Office? I said to myself at the time: who else among the Jewish people has ever been confronted with a choice of this kind? For he was truly fitted, in talent, knowledge and innermost being, to fulfil either of the two functions – so distant from each other – with the same measure of complete success.' Of Herzog, Professor Sir Isaiah Berlin eulogised (ibid., 14): 'His life and his death seem to me to possess the heroic quality of a man who gives all that he is and has to the cause that absorbs him entirely. This cause was Judaism in all its aspects – religious and secular, historical and contemporary, personal and political. Above all, it was embodied in the State of Israel, which for him (as for many of us) was the spirit of Judaism in its most real historical incarnation. For it he laid down his life.'

34 *Jewish Chronicle*, 5 August 1966, 1, 12.
35 Jakobovits, 'Your Call and My Response,' memorandum to the members of the Chief Rabbinate Committee, later extracted in *Prelude to Service*, a selection of statements, letters and interviews by Jakobovits prior to his installation (London: Office of the Chief Rabbi, II Adar 5727–April 1967). The original typewritten text, which includes confidential sections of a personal nature, is in the Jakobovits Papers, London.
36 'Dr Jakobovits likely to accept,' *Jewish Chronicle*, 5 August 1966, 1, 12.
37 'The attached terms and conditions' were contained in the final sections of the memorandum sent to the Chief Rabbinate Committee following Jakobovits' visit to London, covering—among other topics—the Chief Rabbi's emoluments, his public-relations team, and his assumption of office (Jakobovits Papers, London).
38 In the event, the Chief Rabbinate Centre was not built, it being reported in due course that an appropriate site never became available close to the Chief Rabbi's official residence in St John's Wood. The Wolfson brothers had also

agreed to establish an endowment for the maintenance of the Centre, planned to house the Chief Rabbinate office and library, as well as a beth hamedrash and meeting-rooms (*Jewish Chronicle*, 2 September 1966, 1). Soon after Jakobovits' appointment, Silverman wrote to him that, at the annual meeting of the Chief Rabbinate Council, 'Sir Isaac outlined his and Mr Charles's plans for the new Centre and we were rather excited because, on Friday last, a property came on to the market which would be absolutely ideal—site value only for the purpose we have in mind. The matter is now in the hands of the Wolfsons and I am waiting to hear further from them.' In a postscript, he added: 'Sir Isaac, before leaving for America, has instructed me to see if I can purchase the site and I am about to enter into the rather delicate negotiations in connection with this matter' (Silverman to Jakobovits, 23 November 1966, Jakobovits Papers, London). Early in 1967, Silverman told Jakobovits that 'the planning department of Westminster Council have turned down our application for the site in Abbey Road. The reasons for doing so will follow in a few days' time. Meanwhile, I have had to instruct the agents to seek other properties or sites, and we shall do our best to find something else—though Westminster's reaction is not a favourable one. We shall probably have to see the planning people and find out what it is they take exception to, but this, however, we can do only when their reasons are set out on paper' (Silverman to Jakobovits, 26 January 1967, ibid.).

39 Jakobovits to Wolfson, 9 August 1966, ibid., and LMA/ACC/2712/15/1/159. In a personal letter to Wolfson (1 September 1966, Jakobovits Papers, London), Jakobovits wrote: 'Let me tell you how greatly I was cheered and moved by your wonderful letter in response to mine of August 9. You could not have chosen nobler words, nor written with greater beauty and felicity, to express your hopes, prayers and assurances. I will always cherish your letter among my most prized possessions. I wished you could share with me some of the great bounty of felicitations which already reach me from all over the world. They all bespeak the happy confidence with which they view the future of Anglo-Jewry, crediting me with more statesmanship and inspiration of leadership than I can ever deserve. Especially touching have been the numerous communications from friends and communal leaders who know me from my ministrations and lectures in this country, including the most enthusiastic letters from Conservative and Reform quarters.'
40 Wolfson to Jakobovits, 15 August 1966, Jakobovits Papers, London.
41 *Jewish Chronicle*, 16 September 1966, 1.
42 Wolfson to Jakobovits, 11 September 1966, LMA/ACC/2712/15/1/159.
43 Jakobovits to Wolfson, 18 September 1966, Jakobovits Papers, London.
44 'Personal,' Jakobovits to Wolfson, 18 September 1966, ibid.
45 Wolfson added: 'I have no doubt that the pledge which you make to dedicate all your energies and resources of mind and heart to serving the position to which you have been appointed will be carried out with dignity and efficiency' (Wolfson to Jakobovits, 23 September 1966, ibid.).
46 *Jewish Chronicle*, 16 September 1966, 14.
47 Jakobovits to Gaon, 25 September 1966, Jakobovits Papers, London.
48 Jakobovits to Lederman, 27 September 1966, ibid.

49 Jakobovits to Wolfson, 13 October 1966, ibid.
50 Rabbi A.M. Rose, secretary, Office of the Chief Rabbi, to Jakobovits, 19 October 1966–5 Cheshvan, 5727, ibid.
51 Jakobovits to Silverman, 13 November 1966, ibid.
52 Silverman to Jakobovits, 23 November 1966, ibid.
53 US honorary officers to Jakobovits, Western Union telegram, 7 December 1966, ibid.
54 Silverman to Jakobovits, 13 December 1966, ibid.
55 Rose to Chief Rabbi Dr I. Jakobovits, 26 January 1967, ibid. A postscript adds: 'The Dayanim decided to send you this letter on which they agreed last Monday, 23 January.'
56 'An Understanding with the Rav Rashi-Elect of the Federation of Synagogues,' signed by Immanuel Jakobovits and Eliezer Kirzner, Office of the Chief Rabbi, London, 25 January 1967, ibid.
57 'Chief Rabbis' plans for Anglo-Jewry,' interview with Richard Yaffe, New York, *Jewish Chronicle*, 17 February 1967, 16.
58 'Statement by the Chief Rabbi-Elect, the Rav Rashi-Elect, and the Haham,' Office of the Chief Rabbi, London, 14 February 1967, Jakobovits Papers, London.
59 Donald Trelford, 'Jews may get 2 Chief Rabbis,' *The Observer*, London, 29 January 1967. Similar reports appeared in other British national newspapers, including the *Daily Telegraph* and *The Guardian* (27 January 1967) and the *Daily Mail* (27 and 30 January 1967).
60 Sidney Brichto, executive vice-president, Union of Liberal and Progressive Synagogues, to *The Observer*, 12 February 1967.
61 Jakobovits to Rose, 26 January 1967, Jakobovits Papers, London.

CHAPTER EIGHT

1 Jewish Telegraphic Agency, 10 September 1967.
2 'Rav Rashi ill,' *Jewish Chronicle*, 22 November 1968, 1. The report stated: 'Rabbi Dr Eliezer Kirzner, Rav Rashi of the Federation of Synagogues, is undergoing hospital tests in New York for an internal ailment. Dr Kirzner went to America in September for a holiday. Our New York correspondent cabled this week that Dr Kirzner was unlikely to return to England in the immediate future. But Mr Morris Lederman, president of the Federation, said on Wednesday that he looked forward to his return "at an early date."'
3 Geoffrey Alderman, *The Federation of Synagogues, 1887–1987* (London: Federation of Synagogues, 1987), 111.
4 *Jewish Chronicle*, 19 December 1969, 15.
5 Alderman writes (op. cit., 111-112): 'The resignation of Dr Kirzner led to the resurrection and further discussion of the old plan to give the post of Principal Rabbi to the Chief Rabbi. But these discussions, which had by March 1971 resulted in an exchange of memoranda with Dr Jakobovits, were overtaken by two separate developments [the Board of Deputies crisis, and the Federation's

establishment of a separate kashrut authority] ... and undoubtedly made the leadership of the Federation less enthusiastic than they might otherwise have been about elevating him to the office of Principal Rabbi.'
6   Jakobovits, 'Trouble and Tradition,' *Jewish Chronicle*, 25 September 1992, 26.
7   In his initial letter to Lederman (27 September 1966), noting that 'I gather you are aggrieved over my failure to meet with Federation representatives during my visit to London last summer,' Jakobovits wrote in mitigation: 'The true reason is simply that I had to limit my requests for meetings to persons and bodies that would come under my official jurisdiction ... All other official groups or representatives I met at their request, such as leaders of the Board of Deputies and even of the Reform and Liberal congregations.'
8   Jakobovits to the editor of *Pointer*, journal of the Union and Liberal and Progressive Synagogues, 20 January 1967 (Jakobovits Papers, London). The letter was published in *Pointer* 2, no. 3 (spring 1967), 4, alongside a lengthy response from ULPS executive vice-president Sidney Brichto, who wrote: 'The editor showed me your letter before publication, and I was delighted by its forthrightness and candour. It should set a pattern for the oral and written exchanges between Orthodox and Progressive Jews. It indicates the way in which we should, to use your own words, "intelligently debate our differences, using light instead of heat"' (ibid., 5). The same issue (9-11) included an article by S. D. Temkin on 'The Chief Rabbinate in England.'
9   *Sunday Times*, 26 March 1967.
10 *Jewish Chronicle*, 31 March 1967, 12.
11 Ibid., 28 February 1975, 6.
12 Ibid., 28 October 1988, 1.
13 'Jewish World,' Greater London Radio, 24 September 1989.
14 *Jewish Chronicle*, 28 October 1988, 1. On the 2012 appointment of Mirvis as Sacks' successor, see ibid., 21 December 2012, 1, 4-5, 22-23.
15 Simon Rocker, ibid., 4 November 1988, 11. Bulka's lecture marked the 500th anniversary of Rabbi Joseph Caro, compiler of the Shulchan Aruch. Described in reports as 'a possible successor to Lord Jakobovits as Chief Rabbi,' Bulka also addressed the Cockfosters and North Southgate community on 'The Pleasure Principle in Judaism' (ibid., 18 November 1988, 'London Extra,' 2).
16 *Jewish Chronicle*, 20 January 1989, 1.
17 Dated February 1989, LMA/ACC/2712/11/9/15. The handwritten list, in block capitals, is believed to have been compiled by United Synagogue chief executive Jonathan Lew (Leslie Wagner in conversation with this writer, 4 March 2012). The term 'Applicants' is as employed in the list.
18 LMA/ACC/2712/11/9/15.
19 Stanley Kalms to Sidney Frosh, 24 April 1989, ibid.
20 Leslie Wagner to Sidney Frosh, 14 April 1989, ibid.
21 Aubrey Newman to Sidney Frosh, 30 April 1989, ibid.
22 K. P. Barnett, 'Choice of new Chief Rabbi,' *Jewish Chronicle*, 12 May 1989, 27.
23 Sidney Frosh, 'Statement to the Chief Rabbinate Conference committee,' February 1990, LMA/ACC/2712/11/9/15.
24 As outlined by Sacks in *Orthodoxy Confronts Modernity* (New York and London: Ktav

in association with Jews' College, 1991), vii.
25 Jonathan Sacks, *Traditional Alternatives: Orthodoxy and the Future of the Jewish People* (London: Jews' College Publications, 1989), i.
26 *Jewish Chronicle*, 26 May, 1989, 8.
27 As founder and director of Jerusalem's Shalom Hartman Institute (named after his father), the Yeshiva University-trained Hartman (b. 1931) espoused a pluralistic approach to Judaism and Israeli society. His views led some to align him with the right wing of Conservative Judaism, hence the rebuff he received from Bleich and Feldman.
28 Stanley Kalms, 'On the Right Track: The Chief Rabbi's First Ten Years,' *Jewish Chronicle*, 31 August, 2001, 28-29.
29 'Rabbi Returns,' ibid., 26 May 1989, 'London Extra,' 2.
30 Ann Harris, March 1990, communicated to this writer, 21 July 2011.
31 Lionel Swift, QC (1931–2011), son of Rabbi Harris Swift, was an adviser to the Chief Rabbinate and the London Beth Din. A long-time warden of the Central Synagogue, he played a prominent role in peace negotiations between the United Synagogue and the Progressive movements (see Meir Persoff, *Another Way, Another Time: Religious Inclusivism and the Sacks Chief Rabbinate* [Boston: Academic Studies Press, 2010], 130-136).
32 Victor Lucas (1916–1997) was president of the United Synagogue from 1994–1998, and a former treasurer and vice-president of the Board of Deputies. On his death, the *Jewish Chronicle* wrote (16 May 1997, 23): 'He acquired a deep-rooted and self-conscious attachment to the traditions of the United Synagogue. He did not regard them as conflicting with the habits of the Judaism of his boyhood [in London's Bethnal Green], but as supplementing—even protecting—them, in a new age, by a dose of English order, good sense, and discipline ... He was anxious to enhance the role and status of the rabbis, whom he viewed as vital to the progress of the US. Encouraging them to act and be heard on communal issues, he perceived that old-style lay paternalism had had its day ... He attached importance to the example of Anglo-Jewry to other Jewish communities. In later years, he was troubled by what he saw as the growth of sectarianism, religio-political infighting, the limited vision of some leading spokesmen, and a decline in the quality of leadership.'
33 Anthony Grabiner, QC (b. 1945), now Lord Grabiner of Aldwych, was a congregant of Harris's at the St John's Wood Synagogue and, at the time, a Crown Court Recorder. He has advised the Chief Rabbinate on a number of Jewish legal issues, including pre-nuptial agreements.
34 Cyril Harris to Hyam Corney, 'The new Chief Rabbi,' *Jewish Chronicle*, 15 January 1988, 29. Corney commented: 'A contender [for the British Chief Rabbinate] he may not be, but one cannot escape the feeling that, were he to be approached, he would be tempted to consider accepting.'
35 Cyril Harris, *For Heaven's Sake* (London and Portland, OR: Vallentine Mitchell, 2000), 41-42.
36 Ibid., 25-27.
37 Ibid., 12-13, 52.
38 Sidney Frosh, 'Statement to the Chief Rabbinate Conference committee,' February

1990, LMA/ACC/2712/11/9/15. Speaking from Israel, Lau later told the *Jewish Chronicle* (23 February 1990, 1): 'My future is here. All my eight children live in this country with their children, and I have an extremely challenging job to do which I took on only a relatively short time ago.'

39 *Jewish Chronicle*, 20 January 1989, 30, 37; 17 February 1989, 30. Weiss's public lecture at Hampstead Garden Suburb (26 January 1989) was entitled 'Love, the Jewish Way: Interpersonal Relationships and the Jewish Tradition.'

40 'Rabbi Abner Weiss, the Rabbi of Beth Jacob Synagogue of Beverley Hills, Los Angeles, will be in London on Monday, 4 September. Arrangements have been made for him to meet with the small sub-committee at 4.30 that afternoon, in the third-floor Committee Room at Woburn House,' Jonathan Lew to Gerald Jospe, Michael Goldmeier, Aubrey Newman, Leslie Wagner, Robert Rodrigues-Pereira, and Victor Lucas, 17 August 1989, LMA/ACC/2712/11/9/15. In the summer of 2000, Weiss returned to Britain to head Jews' College—by then renamed the London School of Jewish Studies—and to occupy the pulpit at Marble Arch. Eighteen months later, he quit both posts, 'worn out,' he said, 'by the imperilled college's financial woes and frustrated with the Orthodox establishment.' The underlying reasons for his resignations were contained in a *Jewish Chronicle* report (22 February 2002, 1) and in an interview with Simon Rocker ('Sad departure,' ibid., 15 March 2002, 32).

41 'Rabbi and Mrs Cyril Harris will be in London on Thursday, 7 September 1989, and the chairman [Sidney Frosh] has asked if you would join him here at Woburn House at 4 p.m. to meet with them,' Lew to sub-committee members, 19 July 1989, LMA/ACC/2712/11/9/15. During this period, the members of the committee also interviewed Sacks, the only one of the short-listed candidates resident in Britain (Leslie Wagner in conversation with this writer, 4 March 2012).

42 In the course of the 2012 selection process, Ann Harris wrote (*Jewish Chronicle*, 17 February 2012, 2): 'The inclusion of a meeting with the wives of candidates for the post of British Chief Rabbi raises some conflicting points of interest. While a formal interview by the selection committee of someone who is not to be employed would be totally unacceptable, an informal discussion relating to the position of the Chief Rabbi's wife in the community may well prove beneficial. An honest airing of the issues involved on both sides would allow the committee to examine the perceptions and expectations surrounding the incumbent and permit each rabbi's wife to bring out into the open any apprehension she may have about a possible future communal role.'

43 Ann Harris, March 1990, communicated to this writer, 21 July 2011. Of the Goldman occasion, the *Jewish Chronicle* reported ('London Extra,' 15 September 1989, 2): 'Two Chief Rabbis were present at the eightieth-birthday celebrations of St John's Wood emeritus rabbi, Dr Solomon Goldman, minister at the synagogue for twenty-six years. Dr Goldman flew in from Netanya, Israel, where he has retired, with his wife Sadie, for the special occasion. Among those present were Lord Jakobovits and the Chief Rabbi of South Africa, Rabbi Cyril Harris, formerly minister at St John's Wood.'

44 'Harris: "If I was Chief Rabbi,"' *Jewish Chronicle*, 15 September 1989, 7.

45 'Appealing rabbi,' ibid.

46 Bulka to this writer, 4 and 28 July 2011.

47 Stanley Kalms to Immanuel Jakobovits, 9 May 1988, Jakobovits Papers, London.
48 Kalms to Jakobovits, 15 June 1988, ibid.
49 A reference to the dismissal of Rabbi Simche Bunim Lieberman from the faculty of Jews' College (discussed in *Another Way, Another Time*, 15-21).
50 Jakobovits to Kalms, 17 June 1988, Jakobovits Papers, London. Expanding on his view of Sacks' preparation for higher office, Jakobovits later told the Israeli writer Michael Shashar (*Lord Jakobovits in Conversation* [London and Portland, OR: Vallentine Mitchell, 2000], 74-75): '[Sacks] is extremely talented, a brilliant speaker and quick with a pen … His approach and relations with the community are good. On the other hand, he sometimes encounters difficulties in his relations with other rabbis. This is because he never was a pulpit rabbi with responsibility over a congregation and its members, nor did he rise up from the ranks of the rabbinate.' Amélie Jakobovits provided a perceptive view of Sacks in Gloria Tessler, *Amélie: The Story of Lady Jakobovits* (London and Portland, OR: Vallentine Mitchell, 1999), 270, 281-285.
51 Kalms to Jakobovits, 18 July 1988, Jakobovits Papers, London.
52 *Another Way, Another Time*, 18-20, 25-26.
53 Kalms to Jakobovits, 28 September 1988, Jakobovits Papers, London. Kalms concluded: 'I am sending a private copy of this letter to a few selected friends as I think it ought to be on record.'
54 Jakobovits to Kalms, 29 September 1988, ibid.
55 Kalms to Jakobovits, 30 September 1988, ibid.
56 Jakobovits to Kalms, 30 September 1988, ibid.
57 *Jewish Chronicle*, 1 September 1989, 1.
58 Tony Bayfield, Council of Reform and Liberal Rabbis, to Jakobovits, 7 January 1985, Brichto Papers, London.
59 Leading article, 'Future leadership of Anglo-Jewry: No Representation Without Toleration,' *Manna*, February 1985, 3.
60 'Avoiding the Collision,' *Jewish Chronicle*, 8 February 1985, 18-19.
61 Harold Sanderson and Rosita Rosenberg, 'Statement on the Appointment of the Chief Rabbi of the United Hebrew Congregation,' Union of Liberal and Progressive Synagogues, London, 14 December 1989, Brichto Papers, London. Sanderson was the chairman, and Rosenberg the director, of the ULPS. Outlining the background to the statement, Rosenberg and her co-author, Lawrence Rigal, later wrote (*Liberal Judaism: The First Hundred Years* [London: Liberal Judaism, 2004], 172): 'In 1989, when [Lord Jakobovits'] retirement was announced, the ULPS approached the United Synagogue to inquire whether there was any intention of consulting Progressive Jewish movements in the selection process for a successor. As was to be expected, a refusal was forthcoming. Accordingly, in December 1989, the statement was issued.'
62 Clifford Longley, 'Liberal Jews will not back Chief Rabbi,' *The Times*, 16 December 1989, 1.
63 Raymond Goldman, executive director, Reform Synagogues of Great Britain, re: ULPS Statement on the Chief Rabbinate, 28 December 1989, Brichto Papers, London.
64 Marcus H. Bower, chairman, Reform Synagogues of Great Britain, and Rabbi

Simon Franses, chairman, RSGB Assembly of Rabbis, to the editor of *The Times*, 19 December 1989, ibid. This unpublished letter, slightly modified, was also released as a press statement (ibid.).
65 Statement by the president, Dr Lionel Kopelowitz, to meeting of the Board of Deputies, 17 December 1989, ibid.
66 Harold Sanderson to Lionel Kopelowitz, 27 December 1989, ibid.
67 Kopelowitz to Sanderson, 4 January 1990, ibid.
68 '"No quick route to unity," says Sacks,' *Jewish Chronicle*, 29 December 1989, 5.
69 Rosita Rosenberg, 'Whose Chief?' ibid., 12 January 1990, 22.
70 Editorial, *L'Eylah*, No. 21, Pesach 5746–April 1986, editor-in-chief, Jonathan Sacks (London: Office of the Chief Rabbi and Jews' College), 2.
71 Jonathan Sacks, *Tradition in an Untraditional Age* (London: Vallentine Mitchell, 1990), 133. The book is dedicated to Louis Mintz—'tireless fighter for the cause of Jewish unity'—who was instrumental in the sale of the redundant St John's Wood (United) Synagogue building to Louis Jacobs' New London Synagogue in 1964.
72 *Jewish Chronicle*, 19 May 1989, 29.
73 Ibid., 26 May 1989, 8.
74 Jonathan Sacks, 'The Way Forward,' in ibid., 29 September 1989, 73.
75 Ibid., 15 September 1989, 1.
76 Ann Harris, March 1990, communicated to this writer, 21 July 2011.
77 Judge Israel Finestein (1921–2009) lived in St John's Wood and was a member of Harris's former congregation. In 1991, he succeeded Kopelowitz as president of the Board of Deputies, on which he was then the longest-serving member, and was also on the council of the United Synagogue and of Jews' College, where Sacks had served as principal since 1984.
78 Ann Harris, March 1990, communicated to this writer, 21 July 2011.
79 Lionel Kopelowitz in conversation with this writer, 10 September 2012. Of Finestein's involvement, Ann Harris wrote in her diary: 'After the Board of Deputies' dinner, I found myself with a chance to speak to Shmul [Finestein's moniker] privately. On reflection, I think I made a mistake in so doing. At the time, it seemed like an opportunity to tell someone with influence and authority how concerning it was that Cyril was not getting a fair hearing in the UK. There appeared to be no one who would tell the selection committee what a great job he was doing as Chief Rabbi in South Africa, since no one seemed to have made an effort to ascertain what his level of success was. To my horror, Shmul remained silent and backed away from me as soon as he decently could. He was obviously extremely embarrassed and not in the least interested in what I had to say.'
80 Simon Rocker, *Jewish Chronicle*, 2 February 1990, 6.
81 Ann Harris, March 1990, communicated to this writer, 21 July 2011.
82 Lionel Kopelowitz in conversation with this writer, 10 September 2012. Many years after her diary account, Ann Harris wrote (January 2001): 'With hindsight, of course, South Africa has been the better option. Although there are now very many political and economic difficulties in and outside the community, Cyril's reputation of being "the right man in the right place at the right time," and of

performing superbly, is assured. I would never trust the British Jewish community again, and I am sure that that is one of Cyril's reasons not to return—nor even to retire—there.' Glasgow-born Harris died in September 2005, months after his retirement, in Hermanus, near Cape Town, aged sixty-eight.

83 'Final hurdle for Sacks,' *Jewish Chronicle*, 22 February 1990, 1, 48.
84 Linking Kalms to Harris in its obituary of the former South African Chief Rabbi, the *Jewish Chronicle* wrote (16 September 2005, 30): '[Harris's] induction speech at St John's Wood summed up his creed—"Tranquillity must not be obtained at the expense of valued principles." His attacks, whether on the halachic eligibility of nursery-school pupils or on leaders of the Liberal and Reform movements, led Jews' College chairman Stanley Kalms to issue a warning against "ranting sermons."'
85 Lord Kalms to this writer, 20 February 2012. Commenting on Sacks' incumbency, former United Synagogue president Elkan Levy stated: 'Externally, Sacks' record as Chief Rabbi is superb, having raised the prestige of the Chief Rabbinate, Anglo-Jewry and himself to great heights in the eyes of the gentile world. Within the Jewish community, however, his record is not good, partly because he fails to understand how his statements and actions impact on ordinary people, and partly because he lacks the courage and drive to take a stand on anything in which he really believes. He lacks the backbone to make a decision and stick to it, and this is glaringly obvious behind his public presence and the glamour of his speeches' (Levy to this writer, 26 August 2008).
86 Sidney Frosh, 'Statement to the Chief Rabbinate Conference committee,' 25 February 1990, LMA/ACC/2712/11/9/15.
87 'Appointment "not a compromise,"' *Jewish Chronicle*, 2 March 1990, 6.
88 Reuven P. Bulka to Sidney Frosh, 27 February 1990. Bulka later told this writer (28 July 2011): 'My children were happy at the decision, because they were wary of my being so far away from them. There have been many fulfillments here in Ottawa, so regret is not appropriate. But I have sometimes wondered what it would have been like.'
89 'Sacks to stress unity,' *Jewish Chronicle*, 2 March 1990, 6.
90 Jonathan M. Lew to members of the Chief Rabbinate Conference, 9 March 1990–12 Adar 5750, with 'Memorandum: The privileges, duties and conditions of the Office of the Chief Rabbi of the United Hebrew Congregations of the Commonwealth and the establishment of a Chief Rabbinate Council,' 26 February 1990, LMA/ACC/2712/11/9/15.
91 'It's Sacks—official,' *Jewish Chronicle*, 6 April 1990, 48.

Bibliography

A Friend of Truth, *A Few Words Addressed to the Committee for the Election of a Chief Rabbi of England, and to the Electors at Large*, London: Brain & Payne, 1844.

A Selection of Prayers, Psalms and Other Scriptural Passages and Hymns for Use at the Services of the Jewish Religious Union, London; second, revised edition, London: Wertheimer, Lea & Co., 5664–1903.

A Special Correspondent, 'The British Chief Rabbinate' in *The Jewish Monthly*, No. 2, May 1947, Anglo-Jewish Association, London.

Abramsky, Yechezkel, *Address at the Installation of Rabbi I. Jakobovits*, London: United Synagogue, 1947.

Act for confirming a Scheme of the Charity Commissioners for the Jewish United Synagogues [33 & 34 Vict., Ch. cxvi], 14 July 1870.

Addresses Delivered at the Services of the Jewish Religious Union During the First Session, 1902–03, London: Brimley Johnson, 1904.

Adler, Elkan Nathan, London, Phildaelphia: Jewish Publication Society of America, 1930.

Adler, Hermann, 'A Menace to Judaism,' in *Jewish Chronicle*, 8 October 1909.

Adler, Hermann, 'In Memory of the Late Sir Moses Montefiore,' in *Anglo-Jewish Memories and Other Sermons*, George Routledge and Sons, London, 1909.

Adler, Hermann, 'It is Time to Work for the Lord,' in *Jewish Chronicle*, 5 November 1909.

Adler, Hermann, 'The Chief Rabbis of England,' in *Papers Read at the Anglo-Jewish Historical Exhibition, Royal Albert Hall, London, 1887*, Office of the Jewish Chronicle, London, 1888.

Adler, Hermann, 'The Passing of the Late Chief Rabbi, Nathan Adler,' in *Anglo-Jewish Memories and Other Sermons*, London: George Routledge and Sons, 1909.

Adler, Hermann, *Anglo-Jewish Memories and Other Sermons*, London: Routledge, 1909.

Adler, Hermann, *The Jews During the Victorian Era*, London: Alfred J. Isaacs & Sons, 5657–1897.

Adler, Hermann, *The Old Paths*, London: Wertheimer, Lea & Co., 1902.

Adler, Hermann, *The Ritual: The Reply of the Chief Rabbi*, London: Wertheimer, Lea & Co., 1892.

Adler, Marcus N., *The Adler Family*, Office of the Jewish Chronicle, London, 1909; reprinted, expanded and translated into Hebrew, Yitzhak Kaufmann, Israel: Bnei Berak, 1993.

Adler, Michael, *History of the Central Synagogue, 1855–1905*, Office of the Jewish Chronicle, London, 1905.

Adler, N. M., 'The Reciprocal Duties of a Pastor and his Flock,' 1829, in '*Antrittsrede in Oldenburg*,' Sulamith, Vol. VII, 1824–1833, ed. David Frankel, Dessau, 1833.

Adler, N. M., 'Traditional Will,' in *Ethical Wills: A Modern Jewish Treasury*, ed. Jack Riemer and Nathaniel Stampfer, New York: Schocken Books, 1983.

Adler, N. M., *Abschiedspredight in Hannover*, Hanover, 1845.

Adler, N. M., *Laws and Regulations for all the Synagogues in the British Empire*, London: John Wertheimer and Co., 5607–1847.

Adler, N. M., *Solomon's Judgment: A Picture of Israel*, London: Wertheimer and Co., 1854.

Adler, N. M., *The Bonds of Brotherhood*, London: J. Wertheimer and Co., 1849.

Adler, N. M., *The Jewish Faith*, London: Effingham Wilson, 5608–1848.

Adler, N. M., *The Second Days of the Festivals*, London: Trübner and Co., 5628–1868.

Alderman, Geoffrey, 'Foreword,' in Meir Persoff, *Another Way, Another Time: Religious Inclusivism and the Sacks Chief Rabbinate*, Boston: Academic Studies Press, 2010.

Alderman, Geoffrey, 'The British Chief Rabbinate: A Most Peculiar Practice,' in *European Judaism*, vol. 23, no. 2, 1990.

Alderman, Geoffrey, *Anglo-Jewry: A Suitable Case For Treatment*, Egham: Royal Holloway & Bedford New College, 1990.

Alderman, Geoffrey, *British Jewry: Religious Pluralism and Public Identity*, Judentum und Moderne in Frankreich und Italien Internationaler Kongress, Universität Münster, 1996.

Alderman, Geoffrey, *Modern British Jewry*, Oxford: Clarendon Press, 1992; revised edition, 1998.

Alderman, Geoffrey, *The Federation of Synagogues, 1887–1987*, London: Federation of Synagogues, 1987.

Apple, Raymond, 'Hermann Adler: Chief Rabbi,' in *Noblesse Oblige: Essays in Honour of David Kessler, OBE*, ed., Alan D. Crown, London: Vallentine Mitchell, 1998.

Apple, Raymond, *Harris M. Lazarus—The Beloved Dayan*, Jerusalem, 2011

Apple, Raymond, *In Farewell to Hampstead*, London: Hampstead Synagogue, 1972.

Apple, Raymond, *Rabbi Brodie and the Australian Ministry*, Sydney, 1980.

Apple, Raymond, *Rabbi Israel Brodie—Seventy-Five Years Later*, Sydney, 1998.

Apple, Raymond, *The Hampstead Synagogue 1892–1967*, London: Vallentine Mitchell, 1967.

Asaria, Zwi, 'Samson Raphael Hirsch's Wirken im Lande Niedersachsen,' in *Udim: Zeitschrift der Rabbinerkonferenz in der Bundesrepublik Deutschland*, Heft I., Frankfurt, 5731–1970.

Baggini, Julian, 'My Philosophy: Jonathan Sacks,' *The Philosophers' Magazine*, no. 44, London: Philosophy Press, March 2009.

Barnett, Arthur, *The Western Synagogue Through Two Centuries, 1761–1961*, London: Vallentine Mitchell, 1961.

Barnett, Lionel D., *El Libro de los Acuerdos*, Oxford: Oxford University Press, 1931.

Bar-Zohar, Michael, *Yaacov Herzog: A Biography*, London: Halban, 2005.

Bayme, Steven, 'Claude Montefiore, Lily Montagu and the Origins of the Jewish Religious Union,' in *Transactions of the Jewish Historical Society of England*, Vol. XXVII, 1978–1980, London, 1981.

Bentwich, Norman, *Claude Montefiore and His Tutor in Rabbinics: Founders of Liberal and Conservative Judaism*, University of Southampton, 1966.

Bermant, Chaim, 'The Rabbi's Rabbi,' in *Jewish Chronicle*, 5 November 1999.

Bermant, Chaim, *London's East End: Point of Arrival*, New York: Macmillan, 1975.

Bermant, Chaim, *Lord Jakobovits: The Authorized Biography of the Chief Rabbi*, London: Weidenfeld and Nicolson, 1990.

Bermant, Chaim, *The Cousinhood: The Anglo-Jewish Gentry*, London: Eyre & Spottiswoode, 1971.

Bermant, Chaim, *Troubled Eden: An Anatomy of British Jewry*, New York: Basic Books, 1970.

Black, Eugene C., 'The Anglicization of Orthodoxy: The Adlers,' in *Profiles in Diversity*, ed. Frances Malino and David Sorkin, Detroit: Wayne State University Press, 1998.

Black, Eugene C., *The Social Politics of Anglo-Jewry 1880–1920*, Oxford: Blackwell, 1988.

Blank, Joseph E., *The Minutes of the Federation of Synagogues: A Twenty-Five Years' Review*, London: E. W. Rabbinowicz, 5673–1912.

Bornstein, Abba, and Homa, Bernard, *Tell It In Gath: British Jewry and Clause 43, The Inside Story*, privately published, London, 1972.

Breuer, Isaac, 'Samson Raphael Hirsch,' in *Jewish Leaders, 1750–1940*, ed. Leo Jung, New York: Bloch Publishing Company, 5714–1953.

Breuer, Mordechai, 'Samson Raphael Hirsch,' in *Guardians of our Heritage, 1724–1953*, ed. Leo Jung, New York: Bloch Publishing Company, 1958.

Brichto, Sidney, 'Halachah with Humility,' in *Jewish Chronicle*, 2 October 1987.

Brichto, Sidney, 'What is wrong with the Chief Rabbinate?', in *Liberal Jewish Monthly*, London: Union of Liberal and Progressive Judaism, May 1965.

Brodie, Israel, 'Historical Judaism: Challenge To Our Times,' in *A Word in Season: Addresses and Sermons, 1948–1958*, London: Vallentine Mitchell, 1959.

Brodie, Israel, 'Jews' College Centenary,' in *A Word in Season: Addresses and Sermons, 1948–1958*, London: Vallentine Mitchell, 1959.

Brodie, Israel, 'Opening Address, First Conference of European Rabbis,' in *The Strength of My Heart*, London: G. J. George & Co., 1969.

Brodie, Israel, 'Opening Address,' in *Addresses Given at the Ninth Conference of Anglo-Jewish Preachers*, London: Standing Committee, 1951.

Brodie, Israel, 'The Chief Rabbinate,' in *Jewish Chronicle Tercentenary Supplement*, 27 January 1956.

Brodie, Israel, *Statement by the Very Rev the Chief Rabbi, Dr Israel Brodie*, London: United Synagogue, 1964.

Brodie, Israel, *The Strength of My Heart: Sermons and Addresses 1948–1965*, London: G. J. George & Co., for the Israel Brodie Publications Committee, 1969.

Brook, Stephen, *The Club: The Jews of Modern Britain*, London: Constable, 1989.

Bulka, Reuven, *The Coming Cataclysm: The Orthodox–Reform Rift and the Future of the Jewish People*, New York: Mosaic Press, 1984.

Bye Laws of the Constituent Synagogues, London: United Synagogue, 1881.

Bye-Laws of the Constituent Synagogues, London: United Synagogue, 1936.

Carlebach, Julius, 'The Impact of German Jews on Anglo-Jewry–Orthodoxy, 1850–1950,' in *Second Chance: Two Centuries of German-Speaking Jews in the United Kingdom*, ed. Werner E. Mosse, Julius Carlebach, Gerhard Hirschfeld, Aubrey Newman, Arnold Paucker, Peter Pulzer, J. C. B. Mohr, Tubingen: Paul Siebeck, 1991.

Cesarani, David, 'The Transformation of Communal Authority in Anglo-Jewry, 1914–1940,' in *The Making of Modern Anglo-Jewry*, ed. David Cesarani, Oxford: Basil Blackwell, 1990.

Cesarani, David, *The Jewish Chronicle and Anglo-Jewry, 1841–1991*, Cambridge: Cambridge University Press, 1994.

Clark, Michael, *Albion and Jerusalem: The Anglo-Jewish Community in the Post-Emancipation Era, 1858–1887*, Oxford: Oxford University Press, 2009.

Cohen, Arthur, 'The Structure of Anglo-Jewry Today,' in *Three Centuries of Anglo-Jewish History*, ed. V. D. Lipman, Cambridge: W. Heffer & Sons, for the Jewish Historical Society of England, 1961.

Cohen, Jeffrey M., ed., *Dear Chief Rabbi: From the Correspondence of Chief Rabbi Immanuel Jakobovits on Matters of Jewish Law, Ethics and Contemporary Issues, 1980–1990*, New Jersey: Ktav, 1995.

Cohen, Jeffrey M., *Issues of the Day: A Modern-Orthodox View*, Stanmore: Gnesia Publications, 1999.

Cohen, Norman [N.C.], 'Immanuel Jakobovits: *Baruch Haba*,' *Jewish Review*, 14 November 1962.

Cohen, Norman, 'Non-Religious Factors in the Emergence of the Chief Rabbinate,' in *Transactions of the Jewish Historical Society of England*, Vol. XXI, London, 1968.

Cohen, Norman, 'The Religious Crisis in Anglo-Jewry,' in *Tradition*, Vol. 8, No. 2, ed. Walter S. Wurzburger, New York: Rabbinical Council of America, 1966.

Cohen, Stuart A., *English Zionists and British Jews: The Communal Politics of Anglo-Jewry, 1895–1920*, Princeton: Princeton University Press, 1982.

Cosgrove, Elliot Joe, *Teyku: The Insoluble Contradictions in the Life and Thought of Louis Jacobs*, PhD dissertation, University of Chicago, 2008.

Cowen, Anne, ed., *New London Synagogue: The First Twenty Years*, London: New London Synagogue, 1984.

Cowen, Philip, *Memories of an American Jew*, New York: International Press, 1932.

Creative Judaism: Some Aims And Objects, London: Society for the Study of Jewish Theology, 1963.

Death of Sir Moses Montefiore: Supplement to the Jewish Chronicle, 31 July 1885.

Diner, Hasia, 'Like the Antelope and the Badger,' in *Tradition Renewed: A History of the Jewish Theological Seminary*, Vol. I, ed. Jack Wertheimer, New York: Jewish Theological Seminary of America, 1997.

Domb, Cyril, 'A Biographical Sketch,' in *Memories of Kopul Rosen*, ed. Cyril Domb, privately published (Carmel College, Wallingford, Berkshire), 1970.

Domb, Cyril, 'Dayan Yechezkel Abramsky: A Centenary Tribute,' in *L'Eylah*, No. 23, Pesach 5747, London: Office of the Chief Rabbi and Jews' College, April 1987.

Drachman, Bernard, *The Unfailing Light: Memoirs of an American Rabbi*, New York: Rabbinical Council of America, 1948.

Duschinsky, Charles, *The Rabbinate of the Great Synagogue, London, from 1756–1842*, Oxford University Press, 1921.

Ehrmann, Salomon, 'Rabbi S. R. Hirsch as a Pioneer of Judaism in Eretz Yisroel and in the Diaspora,' in *Ateret Zvi: Rabbi Dr Isaac Breuer Jubilee Volume*, New York: Feldheim, 1962.

Ellenson, David, *After Emancipation: Jewish Religious Responses to Modernity*, Cincinnati: Hebrew Union College Press, 2004.

Ellenson, David, *Rabbi Ezriel Hildesheimer and the Creation of a Modern Jewish Orthodoxy*, Tuscaloosa and London: University of Alabama Press, 1990.

Elton, Benjamin J., 'Did the Chief Rabbinate move to the right? A case study— the mixed choirs controversies, 1880–1986,' in *Jewish Historical Studies*, Vol. 39, Jewish Historical Society of England, 2004.

Elton, Benjamin J., *Britain's Chief Rabbis and the Religious Character of Anglo-Jewry, 1880– 1970*, Manchester: Manchester University Press, 2010.

Emanuel, Charles H. L., *A Century and a Half of Jewish History: Extracted from the Minute Books of the London Committee of Deputies of the British Jews*, London: George

Routledge & Sons, 1910.

Endelman, Todd M., 'Communal Solidarity Among the Jewish Elite of Victorian London,' in *Victorian Studies* 28:3, Bloomington: Indiana University Press, 2002.

Endelman, Todd M., 'Introduction,' in Meir Persoff, *Faith Against Reason: Religious Reform and the British Chief Rabbinate, 1840–1990*, London and Portland, OR: Vallentine Mitchell, 2008.

Endelman, Todd M., 'Practices of a Low Anthropologic Level: A Shechitah Controversy of the 1950s,' in *Food in the Migrant Experience*, ed. Anne J. Kershen, Farnham: Ashgate Publishing, 2002.

Endelman, Todd M., 'The Englishness of Jewish Modernity in England,' in *Toward Modernity: The European Jewish Model*, ed. Jacob Katz, New Brunswick and Oxford: Transaction Books, 1987.

Endelman, Todd M., *British Jewry and the Jewish Historiographical Mainstream*, Parkes Institute for the Study of Jewish/non-Jewish Relations, Southampton, 2008.

Endelman, Todd M., *Radical Assimilation in English Jewish History, 1656–1945*, Bloomington: Indiana University Press, 1990.

Endelman, Todd M., *The Jews of Britain 1656 to 2000*, Berkeley, Los Angeles, and London: University of California Press, 2002.

Endelman, Todd M., *The Jews of Georgian England 1714–1830: Tradition and Change in a Liberal Society*, Ann Arbor: University of Michigan Press, 1999.

Englander, David, ed., *A Documentary History of Jewish Immigrants in Britain, 1840–1920*, London: Leicester University Press, 1994.

Englander, David, 'Anglicised not Anglican: Jews and Judaism in Victorian Britain,' in *Religion in Victorian Britain—I. Traditions*, ed. Gerald Parsons, Manchester: Manchester University Press and the Open University, 1988.

Englander, David, 'Integrated But Insecure: A Portrait of Anglo-Jewry at the Close of the Twentieth Century,' in *The Growth of Religious Diversity: Britain From 1945, Vol. I. — Traditions*, ed. Gerald Parsons, London: Routledge, in association with the Open University, 1993.

Epstein, Isidore, *Jewish Faith in Action*, ed. Philip Ginsbury, London: Jews' College Publications, 1995.

Facts and Fallacies about Liberal Judaism, London: Union of Liberal and Progressive Synagogues, 1961; revised and reprinted, 1972.

Feldman, David, *Englishmen and Jews: Social Relations and Political Culture, 1840–1914*, New Haven and London: Yale University Press, 1994.

Finestein, Israel, 'Joseph Frederick Stern, 1865–1934: Aspects of a Gifted Anomaly,' in *The Jewish East End, 1840-1939*, ed. Aubrey Newman, Jewish

Historical Society of England, 1981; reprinted in Israel Finestein, *Jewish Society in Victorian England*, London: Vallentine Mitchell, 1993.

Finestein, Israel, 'Sir Moses Montefiore: A Modern Appreciation,' in *Scenes and Personalities in Anglo-Jewry, 1800–2000*, London: Vallentine Mitchell, 2002.

Finestein, Israel, 'The Anglo-Jewish Revolt of 1853,' in the *Jewish Quarterly*, 26, 1978–79; reprinted in *Jewish Society in Victorian England*, London: Vallentine Mitchell, 1993.

Finestein, Israel, 'The Jews and English Marriage Law,' in the *Jewish Journal of Sociology* 8, 1964; reprinted in Israel Finestein, *Jewish Society in Victorian England*, London: Vallentine Mitchell, 1993.

Finestein, Israel, *A Short History of Anglo-Jewry*, London: Lincolns-Prager, for the World Jewish Congress British Section, 1957.

Finestein, Israel, *Anglo-Jewry in Changing Times*, London: Vallentine Mitchell, 1999.

Finestein, Israel, *Jewish Society in Victorian England*, London: Vallentine Mitchell, 1993.

Finestein, Israel, *Scenes and Personalities in Anglo-Jewry, 1800–2000*, London: Vallentine Mitchell, 2002.

Fishman, William J., *East End 1888*, London: Duckworth, 1988.

Fishman, William J., *East End Jewish Radicals, 1875–1914*, London: Duckworth, 1975.

Frankel, Jonathan, and Steven J. Zipperstein, eds., *Assimilation and Community: The Jews in Nineteenth-Century Europe*, Cambridge: Cambridge University Press, 1992.

Frankel, William, *Tea With Einstein And Other Memories*, London: Halban, in association with the European Jewish Publication Society, 2006.

Freedland, Michael, 'I made Sacks Chief Rabbi, but he's been a huge failure' (interview with Lord Kalms), *Jewish Chronicle*, 14 October 2011.

Freedman, Maurice, ed., *A Minority in Britain: Social Studies of the Anglo-Jewish Community*, London: Vallentine Mitchell, 1955.

Freud-Kandel, Miri J., *Orthodox Judaism in Britain Since 1913*, London: Vallentine Mitchell, 2006.

Friedländer, M., 'The Late Chief Rabbi Dr N. M. Adler,' in *Jewish Quarterly Review*, II, London, July 1890.

Frosh, Sidney, 'Clause 74 And All That,' in *Hamesilah* [The Path], Pesach 5745, London: United Synagogue, 1985.

Gaon, Solomon, 'The Contribution of the English Sephardim to Anglo-Jewry,' in *Studies in the Cultural Life of the Jews in England*, ed. Dov Noy and Issachar Ben-Ami, Jerusalem: Hebrew University Magnes Press, 1975.

Gartner, Lloyd P., *Simche Bunim Lieberman*, address to the Jewish Historical Society of England, Israel branch, 2010.

Gartner, Lloyd P., The Jewish Immigrant in England, 1870–1914, London: George Allen and Unwin, 1960.

Gaster, Moses, History of the Ancient Synagogue of the Spanish and Portuguese Jews, privately published, London, 1901.

Gavron, Daniel, 'Montefiore: Man or Myth?' in Jewish Chronicle, 13 October 1989.

Goldberg, David J., and Edward Kessler, eds., Aspects of Liberal Judaism, London: Vallentine Mitchell, 2004.

Goldschmidt-Lehmann, Ruth P., 'Nathan Marcus Adler: A Bibliography,' in Studies in Judaica, Karaitica and Islamica: Presented to Leon Nemoy on his Eightieth Birthday, Ramat Gan: Bar-Ilan University Press, 1982.

Gollancz, Hermann, 'Cohesion or Decadence,' in Fifty Years After: Sermons And Addresses Setting Forth The Teachings and Spirit of Judaism (Third Series), London: Oxford University Press, 1924.

Gollancz, Hermann, 'Halt!' in Sermons and Addresses, Second Series, London: Chapman & Hall, 1916.

Gollancz, Hermann, 'Jews' College—Then and Now,' in Sermons and Addresses Setting Forth the Teachings and Spirit of Judaism (Second Series), London: Chapman & Hall, 1916.

Gollancz, Hermann, 'Religious Neglect and Apostasy: The Other Side of the Picture,' in Sermons and Addresses, London: Myers & Co., 1909.

Gollancz, Hermann, 'Rev Professor D. W. Marks,' in Fifty Years After: Sermons and Addresses Setting Forth the Teachings and Spirit of Judaism (Third Series), London: Humphrey Milford, Oxford University Press, 1924.

Gollancz, Hermann, 'The Moderate Jew,' in Sermons and Addresses Setting Forth the Teachings and Spirit of Judaism (Second Series), London: Chapman & Hall, 1916.

Gollancz, Hermann, Sermons and Addresses Setting Forth the Teachings and Spirit of Judaism (Second Series), London: Chapman & Hall, 1916.

Gollancz, Hermann, Sermons and Addresses Setting Forth the Teachings and Spirit of Judaism (Third Series), London: Oxford University Press, 1924.

Gottlieb, Wolf, ed., Essays and Addresses in Memory of the Very Rev Dr Joseph Herman Hertz, London: Mizrachi Federation of Great Britain and Ireland, 1947.

Gould, Julius, and Shaul Esh, eds., Jewish Life in Modern Britain, London: Routledge & Kegan Paul, 1964.

Green, A. A., Sermons, London: Martin Hopkinson, 1935.

Grunfeld, I., Three Generations: The Influence of Samson Raphael Hirsch on Jewish Life and Thought, London: Jewish Post Publications, 1958.

Gutwein, Daniel, The Divided Elite: Economics, Politics and Anglo-Jewry, 1882–1917, Leiden: E. J. Brill, 1992.

Harris, Cyril, *For Heaven's Sake*, London and Portland, OR: Vallentine Mitchell, 2000.

Harris, Isidore, *Jews' College Jubilee Volume*, London: Luzac, 1906.

Heinemann, Isaac, 'Samson Raphael Hirsch: The Formative Years of the Leader of Modern Orthodoxy,' in *Historia Judaica*, XIII:1, ed. Guido Kisch, New York, 1951.

Heinemann, Isaac, 'Supplementary Remarks,' in *Historia Judaica*, X:2, ed. Guido Kisch, New York, 1948.

Henriques, Robert, *Sir Robert Waley Cohen, 1877–1952*, London: Secker & Warburg, 1966.

Hertz, J. H., 'Divided Counsels,' in *Sermons, Addresses and Studies*, Vol. I, London: Soncino Press, 1938.

Hertz, J. H., 'Graduation Address,' in *Early and Late: Addresses, Messages and Papers*, Hindhead, Surrey: Soncino Press, 1943.

Hertz, J. H., 'Inaugural Sermon,' Congregation Orach Chayim, New York, 13 January 1912, in Hertz, *Early and Late*.

Hertz, J. H., 'Installation Address,' in *Souvenir of the Decennial Celebration of the Witwatersrand Old Hebrew Congregation and of the Public Reception of the Rev Dr Joseph Herman Hertz, 16 November, 1898*, Johannesburg: M. J. Wood & Co, for the Council of the Congregation, 1898.

Hertz, J. H., 'Opening address at the Conference of Anglo-Jewish Preachers,' in *Sermons, Addresses and Studies*, Vol. II, London: Soncino Press, 1938.

Hertz, J. H., 'Recall to the Synagogue,' I and II, in Hertz, *Early and Late*.

Hertz, J. H., 'Reconstruction,' in *Sermons, Addresses and Studies*, Vol. I, London: Soncino Press, 1938.

Hertz, J. H., 'The "Strange Fire" of Schism,' in *Sermons, Addresses and Studies*, Vol. I, London: Soncino Press, 1938.

Hertz, J. H., 'The Holiness of Home,' in *Affirmations of Judaism*, London: Oxford University Press, 1927.

Hertz, J. H., 'The New Paths: Whither Do They Lead,' in *Affirmations of Judaism*, London: Oxford University Press, 1927; reprinted, London: Edward Goldston, 1946.

Hertz, J. H., *Affirmations of Judaism*, London: Oxford University Press, 1927.

Hertz, J. H., *Early and Late: Addresses, Messages, and Papers*, Hindhead: Soncino Press, 1943.

Hertz, J. H., *The Pentateuch and Haftorahs*, London: Oxford University Press, 1936.

Hertz, J. H., *Traditional Judaism: An Appeal for the Jewish War Memorial*, London: Williams, Lea & Co., 1919; reprinted (abridged and amended) as 'Religion and Life,' in *Sermons, Addresses and Studies*, Vol. I, London: Soncino Press, 1938.

Herzog, Yaacov, *A People That Dwells Alone: Speeches and Writings of Yaacov Herzog*, London: Weidenfeld & Nicolson, 1975.

Hirsch, S. A., 'Jewish Philosophy of Religion and Samson Raphael Hirsch,' in

Jewish Quarterly Review, London, January 1890.

Hochman, Joseph, 'The Chief Rabbi and the Ministry,' in Jewish Review, Vol. IV, No. 23, January–February 1914, ed. Norman Bentwich and Joseph Hochman, London: George Routledge and Sons, 1914.

Hochman, Joseph, 'The Chief Rabbinate,' in Jewish Review, Vol. III, No. 17, January 1913, ed. Norman Bentwich and Joseph Hochman, London: George Routledge and Sons, 1913.

Homa, Bernard, A Fortress in Anglo-Jewry: The Story of the Machzike Hadath, London: Shapiro, Vallentine & Co., 5713–1953.

Homa, Bernard, Footprints on the Sands of Time, Charfield: Beaver Press, 1990.

Homa, Bernard, Orthodoxy in Anglo-Jewry, 1880–1940, London: Jewish Historical Society of England, 1969.

Hyamson, Albert M., Jews' College, London, 1855–1955, London: Jews' College, 1955.

Hyamson, Albert M., The Sephardim of England, London: Spanish and Portuguese Jews' Congregation, 1951.

Hyamson, Moses, 'Installation into the Office of Dayan,' in The Oral Law and Other Sermons, London: David Nutt, 1910.

Hyamson, Moses, and Oswald John Simon, 'Authority and Dogma in Judaism,' in Jewish Quarterly Review, Vol. 5, ed. I. Abrahams and C. G. Montefiore, London: D. Nutt, 1893.

Installation of Chief Rabbi: Supplement to the Jewish Chronicle, 26 June 1891.

Jacobs, Gerald, 'Who'd want to be Chief Rabbi?' in New Statesman, 27 June 1997.

Jacobs, Louis, 'For the Sake of Heaven,' in Jewish Chronicle, 19 December 1986.

Jacobs, Louis, 'Four Rabbinic Positions in Anglo-Jewry,' in The Jewish Year Book 2000, ed. Stephen W. Massil, London: Vallentine Mitchell, in association with the Jewish Chronicle, 2000.

Jacobs, Louis, 'Reflections on a Controversy,' in Quest 1, ed. Jonathan Stone, London: Paul Hamlyn, 1965.

Jacobs, Louis, A Tree of Life: Diversity, Flexibility, and Creativity in Jewish Law, London: Oxford University Press for the Littman Library of Jewish Civilization, 1984.

Jacobs, Louis, Beyond Reasonable Doubt, London: Littman Library of Jewish Civilization, 1999.

Jacobs, Louis, Helping With Inquiries: An Autobiography, London: Vallentine Mitchell, 1989.

Jacobs, Louis, Induction Sermon, New West End Synagogue, London: Henry G. Morris &

Co., for the New West End Synagogue, 1954.

Jacobs, Louis, *Principles of the Jewish Faith: An Analytical Study*, London: Vallentine Mitchell, 1964.

Jacobs, Louis, *We Have Reason to Believe*, London: Vallentine Mitchell, 1957; second edition, 1962; third edition, 1965; fourth revised edition, 1995; fifth edition, with a new Introduction by William Frankel, and a new Retrospect by the author, 2004.

Jacobs, Louis, *What We Stand For*, London: Blackfriars Press for New London Synagogue, 1964.

Jakobovits, Immanuel, 'Avoiding the Collision,' in *Jewish Chronicle*, 8 February 1985.

Jakobovits, Immanuel, 'Division and Diversion,' in *Jewish Chronicle*, 26 February 1971.

Jakobovits, Immanuel, 'Fragments From An Unpublished Autobiography,' in Meir Persoff, *Immanuel Jakobovits: a Prophet in Israel*, London: Vallentine Mitchell, 2002.

Jakobovits, Immanuel, 'Modern Trends in Orthodoxy,' in *Encounter: Essays on Torah and Modern Life*, ed. H. Chaim Schimmel and Aryeh Carmell, Association of Orthodox Jewish Scientists, London; Jerusalem and New York: Feldheim, 1989.

Jakobovits, Immanuel, 'SOS: The Way We Live Now,' in *Jewish Chronicle*, 10 October 1986.

Jakobovits, Immanuel, 'The Changing Face of British Jewry: The Quiet Revolution,' in *Jewish Chronicle*, 9 November 1984.

Jakobovits, Immanuel, 'The Evolution of the British Rabbinate Since 1845: Its Past Impact and Future Challenges,' in *The Timely and The Timeless*, London: Vallentine Mitchell, 1977.

Jakobovits, Immanuel, 'The Influence of the Yeshivah on the Jewish Public,' in *HaChaim*, London: Tree of Life College, 1940.

Jakobovits, Immanuel, 'Torah im Derech Eretz Today,' in *L'Eylah*, New Year issue, 5746–1985, London: Office of the Chief Rabbi and Jews' College.

Jakobovits, Immanuel, 'Trouble and Tradition,' in *Jewish Chronicle*, 25 September 1992.

Jakobovits, Immanuel, 'Who is a Jew? New Questions, New Passions,' in *Jewish Chronicle*, 7 December 1984.

Jakobovits, Immanuel, *A Collection of Essays and Articles by the Chief Rabbi, Prepared for the Traditional Alternatives Symposium*, London: Jews' College, 1989.

Jakobovits, Immanuel, *Driving Forward*, United Synagogue, London 26 Ellul 5730–27 September 1970, London: Office of the Chief Rabbi, 1970.

Jakobovits, Immanuel, *If Only My People: Zionism in My Life*, London: Weidenfeld and Nicolson, 1984.

Jakobovits, Immanuel, *Journal of a Rabbi*, New York: Living Books, 1966.

Jakobovits, Immanuel, *Looking Ahead*, London: United Synagogue, 1967, second edition, 1968.

Jakobovits, Immanuel, *Memorandum on Synagogue Services*, London: Office of the Chief Rabbi, June 1971.

Jakobovits, Immanuel, *Milestones and Millstones: Centenary of the United Synagogue, 15 Tammuz, 5730–19 July 1970*, London: Office of the Chief Rabbi, 1970.

Jakobovits, Immanuel, *Moving Ahead: A Review and a Preview—A New Year Message from the Chief Rabbi to the Leadership of Anglo-Jewry*, London: Office of the Chief Rabbi, Ellul 5728–September 1968.

Jakobovits, Immanuel, *New Priorities on the Orthodox Agenda*, London: Office of the Chief Rabbi, 1989.

Jakobovits, Immanuel, *Prelude to Service*, London: Office of the Chief Rabbi, 1967.

Jakobovits, Immanuel, *Preserving The Oneness Of The Jewish People: Orthodox–Progressive divisions and discussions on marriage, divorce and conversion—can a permanent schism be averted?* London: Office of the Chief Rabbi, 1988.

Jakobovits, Immanuel, *Rabbinical Tasks in the Present Era*, London: Conference of European Rabbis, 1958.

Jakobovits, Immanuel, *Samson Raphael Hirsch: A Reappraisal of his Teachings and Influence in the Light of our Times*, London: Office of the Chief Rabbi, 1971.

Jakobovits, Immanuel, *The Timely and The Timeless*, London: Vallentine Mitchell, 1977.

Japhet, Seemy, 'The Secession from the Frankfurt Jewish Community Under Samson Raphael Hirsch,' in *Historia Judaica*, X:2, ed. Guido Kisch, New York, 1948.

Joint Celebration of the Seventy-Fifth Anniversary of Jews' College; the Seventieth Anniversary of the Jewish Religious Education Board; and the Sixtieth Anniversary of the United Synagogue, 23–24 March, 1931, London: Oxford University Press, 1931.

Joseph Herman Hertz, 1872–1946: In Memoriam, London: Soncino Press, 1947.

Joseph, Morris, *Judaism as Creed and Faith*, London: Macmillan & Co., 1903.

Joseph, Morris, *The Ideal in Judaism and Other Sermons Preached During 1890–91–92*, London: David Nutt, 1893.

Jubilee of the Reform Congregation: Supplement to the Jewish Chronicle, 29 January 1892.

Jung, Julius, 'Rabbi Dr Mayer Lerner,' in *Champions of Orthodoxy*, privately published, London, 1974.

Jung, Julius, 'Rabbi Maier Tsevi Jung,' in *Champions of Orthodoxy*, privately published, London, 1974.

Jung, Julius, 'Samuel Montagu,' in *Champions of Orthodoxy*, privately published, London, 1974.

Kahn-Harris, Keith, and Gidley, Ben, *Turbulent Times: The British Jewish Community Today*, London and New York: Continuum, 2010.

Kalms, Stanley (chairman), *A Time for Change: United Synagogue Review*, London: Stanley Kalms Foundation, 1992.

Kalms, Stanley, 'On the Right Track: The Chief Rabbi's First Ten Years,' *Jewish Chronicle*, 31 August, 2001.

Katz, David S., *The Jews in the History of England, 1485–1850*, Oxford: Clarendon Press, 1994.

Katz, Jacob, *A House Divided*, Hanover and London: Brandeis University Press, 1998.

Katz, Steven T., ed., *Interpreters of Judaism in the Late Twentieth Century*, Washington: B'nai B'rith, 1993.

Kershen, Anne J., ed., *RSGB/ULPS: 150 Years of Progressive Judaism in Britain, 1840–1990*, London: London Museum of Jewish Life, 1990.

Kershen, Anne J., and Jonathan A. Romain, *Tradition and Change: A History of Reform Judaism in Britain, 1840–1995*, London: Vallentine Mitchell, 1995.

Kessler, Edward, *A Reader of Early Liberal Judaism*, London: Vallentine Mitchell, 2004.

Klugman, Eliyahu Meir, *Rabbi Samson Raphael Hirsch*, New York: Mesorah Publications, 1996.

Kosmin, Barry A., 'Localism and Pluralism in British Jewry, 1900–80,' in *Transactions of the Jewish Historical Society of England*, Vol. XXVIII, London, 1982.

Kurzweil, Zvi E., 'Samson Raphael Hirsch: Educationist and Thinker,' in *Tradition* vol. 2, no. 2, ed. Norman Lamm, New York: Rabbinical Council of America, 1960.

Kushner, Tony, ed., *The Jewish Heritage in British History: Englishness & Jewishness*, London: Frank Cass, 1992.

Langdon, Harold S., 'The Place of Reform in Anglo-Jewry Today,' in *A Genuine Search*, ed. Dow Marmur, London: Reform Synagogues of Great Britain, 1979.

Laski, Neville, *The Laws and Charities of the Spanish and Portuguese Jews' Congregation of London*, London: Cresset Press, 1952.

Laws of the Congregation of the Great Synagogue, Duke's Place, London, London: Wertheimer and Co., 5623–1863.

Lehmann, Ruth P., 'Hermann Adler: A Bibliography of his Published Works,' in *Studies in the Cultural Life of the Jews in England*, ed. Dov Noy and Issachar Ben-Ami, Jerusalem: Hebrew University Magnes Press, 1975.

Lehrman, S. M., 'A Spiritual Warrior,' in *Essays and Addresses in Memory of the Very Rev Dr Joseph Herman Hertz*, ed. Wolf Gottlieb, London: Mizrachi Federation of Great Britain and Ireland, 1947.

Leigh, Michael, 'Reform Judaism in Britain, 1840–1970,' in *Reform Judaism*, ed. Dow Marmur, London: Reform Synagogues of Great Britain, 1973.

Lerner, Isaac, 'The Attitude to Halachah of the Progressive Movements: Can they be considered a kehillah kedoshah?' in L'Eylah, Vol. I, No. 10, autumn 5741, ed. A. Melinek, London: Office of the Chief Rabbi, 1981.

Levin, Salmond S. (ed.), *A Century of Anglo-Jewish Life, 1870–1970*, London: United Synagogue, 1971.

Levine, Ephraim, *The History of the New West End Synagogue, 1879–1929*, Aldershot: John Drew, 1929.

Levine, Howard I., 'Enduring and Transitory Elements in the Philosophy of Samson Raphael Hirsch,' in *Tradition*, Vol. 5, No. 2, ed. Walter S. Wurzburger, New York: Rabbinical Council of America, 1963.

Levy, Arnold, *The Story of Gateshead Yeshivah*, Taunton: Wessex Press, 1952.

Levy, Elkan, 'The Next Chief Rabbi,' in *The Jewish Year Book 2012*, London and Portland, OR: Vallentine Mitchell, 2012.

Levy, Elkan, *The New West End Synagogue, 1879–2004*, London, 2004.

Levy, Isaac, *Historic Judaism Versus Liberal Judaism*, London: United Synagogue, 1949.

Liberles, Robert, 'The Origins of the Jewish Reform Movement in England,' in *AJSreview*, Vol. I, Cambridge, MA: Association for Jewish Studies, 1976

Liberles, Robert, *Religious Conflict in Social Context*, Westport: Greenwood Press, 1985.

Lipkin, Goodman, 'Nathan Marcus Adler,' in *The Jewish Encyclopedia*, Vol. I, New York and London: Funk and Wagnalls Company, 1925.

Lipman, S., and V. D. Lipman, eds., *The Century of Moses Montefiore*, London: Littman Library of Jewish Civilization, Jewish Historical Society of England and Oxford University Press, 1985.

Lipman, Sonia L., and Lipman, Vivian D., *Jewish Life in Britain, 1962–1977*, New York: H. G. Saur, 1981.

Lipman, V. D., *A History of the Jews in Britain Since 1858*, New York: Holmes & Meier, 1990.

Lipman, V. D., *Social History of the Jews in England, 1850–1950*, London: Watts & Co., 1954.

Lipman, V. D., *Three Centuries of Anglo-Jewish History*, London: W. Heffer & Sons for the Jewish Historical Society of England, 1961.

Lipman, Vivian D., 'The Anglo-Jewish Community in Victorian Society,' in *Studies in the Cultural Life of the Jews in England*, ed. Dov Noy and Issachar Ben-Ami, Jerusalem: Hebrew University Magnes Press, 1975.

Livingstone, I., *The Union of Anglo-Jewish Preachers: A Retrospect*, London: Union of Anglo-Jewish Preachers, 1949.

Loewe, L., ed., *Diaries of Sir Moses and Lady Montefiore*, London, 1890; facsimile edition, introduced by Raphael Loewe, London: Littman Library of Jewish Civilization, Jewish Historical Society, and Jewish Museum, 1983.

Malino, Frances, and David Sorkin, eds., *Profiles in Diversity: Jews in a Changing Europe, 1750–1870*, Detroit: Wayne State University Press, 1998.

Margoliouth, Moses, *The History of the Jews in Great Britain*, London: Richard Bentley, 1851.

Marks, D. W., ed., *Forms of Prayer, used in the West London Synagogue of British Jews, with an English Translation. Volume I — Daily and Sabbath Prayers*, London: Wertheimer and Co., 1841.

Marks, D. W., 'Discourse Delivered at the Consecration of the West London Synagogue of British Jews, Thursday, 27 January, 5602 [1842],' in *Sermons Preached on Various Occasions at the West London Synagogue of British Jews*, Vol. I, London: R. Groombridge and Sons, 5611–1851.

Marks, D. W., 'On the Revelation at Sinai, and the Perpetuity and Immutability of the Mosaic Law,' in *Sermons Preached on Various Occasions at the West London Synagogue of British Jews*, Vol. I, London: R. Groombridge and Sons, 5611–1851.

Marks, D. W., 'The Law of Moses, the Great End of Revelation,' in *Sermons Preached on Various Occasions at the West London Synagogue of British Jews, Margaret Street, Cavendish Square*, Vol. II, London: A. W. Bennett, P. Valentine, 5622–1862.

Marks, D. W., 'The Synagogue and the Organ,' in *Sermons Preached on Various Occasions at the West London Synagogue of British Jews, Margaret Street, Cavendish Square*, Vol. II, London: A. W. Bennett, P. Valentine, 5622–1862.

Marmur, Dow, ed., *A Genuine Search: God, Torah, Israel—A Reform Perspective*, London: Reform Synagogues of Great Britain, 1979.

Marmur, Dow, ed., *Reform Judaism*, London: Reform Synagogues of Great Britain, 1973.

Maybaum, Ignaz, 'The Jacobs Affair,' in *Quest 1*, ed. Jonathan Stone, London: Paul Hamlyn, 1965.

Maybaum, Ignaz, *The Office of a Chief Rabbi* (Judaism Today—A Series Edited by Rabbi Dr Ignaz Maybaum), London: Reform Synagogues of Great Britain, 1964.

McLeod, Hugh, 'Why did Orthodoxy remain dominant in Britain?' in *Two Nations: British and German Jews in Comparative Perspective*, ed. Michael Brenner, Rainer Liedtke, and David Rechter, Tübingen: Mohr Siebeck, 1999.

Meir, Golda, *My Life*, London: Weidenfeld & Nicolson, 1975; reprinted, London: Futura, 1976.

Meirovich, Harvey, *A Vindication of Judaism: The Polemics of the Hertz Pentateuch*, New York and Jerusalem: Jewish Theological Seminary of America, 1998.

Meyer, Michael A., 'Jewish Religious Reform in Germany and Britain,' in *Two Nations: British and German Jews in Comparative Perspective*, ed. Michael Brenner, Rainer Liedtke and David Rechter, Tübingen: Mohr Siebeck, 1999.

Meyer, Michael A., *German-Jewish History in Modern Times*, New York: Columbia University Press, 1977.

Meyer, Michael A., *Response to Modernity: A History of the Reform Movement in Judaism*, New York and Oxford: Oxford University Press, 1988.

Mills, John, *The British Jews*, London: Houlston & Stoneman, 1853.

Montagu, Lily H., 'The Spiritual Possibilities in Judaism Today,' in *Jewish Quarterly Review*, Vol. XI, January 1899, ed. I. Abrahams and C. G. Montefiore, New York: Macmillan & Co.

Montagu, Lily H., *Samuel Montagu, First Baron Swaythling*, London: Truslove & Hanson, n. d. [1913].

Montefiore, Claude G., 'Religious Differences and Religious Agreements,' in *Truth in Religion, and Other Sermons Delivered at the Services of the Jewish Religious Union*, New York: Macmillan, 1906.

Montefiore, Claude G., 'The Jewish Religious Union: Its Principles and its Future,' in *Jewish Chronicle*, 15 October 1909.

Montefiore, Claude G., *Is There a Middle Way?* London: Jewish Religious Union, 1920.

Montefiore, Claude G., *Outlines of Liberal Judaism for the Use of Parents and Teachers*, first edition, London: Macmillan & Co., 1912; second edition, 1923.

Montefiore, Claude G., *Truth in Religion and Other Sermons*, London: Macmillan & Co., 1906.

Moor, James R. (ed.), *Religion in Victorian Britain—III. Sources*, Manchester: Manchester University Press-Open University, 1988.

Mudie-Smith, Richard, *The Religious Life of London*, London: Hodder and Stoughton, 1904.

Nathan, David, 'David Nathan Talks With Chief Rabbi Jakobovits,' in *Jewish Chronicle*, 6 January 1978.

Nathan, David, 'The Mystique of Survival: Interview with Chief Rabbi Sir Immanuel Jakobovits,' in *Jewish Chronicle*, 17 April 1987.

Newman, Aubrey, ed., *Provincial Jewry in Victorian Britain: Papers for a Conference at University College, London, Convened by the Jewish Historical Society of England, London, 6 July 1975*, London: Jewish Historical Society of London, 1975.

Newman, Aubrey, rapporteur, *Migration and Settlement: Proceedings of the Anglo-American Jewish Historical Conference*, London: Jewish Historical Society of England, 1971.

Newman, Aubrey, 'The Chief Rabbinate and the Provinces, 1840–1914,' in *Tradition and Transition: Essays Presented to Chief Rabbi Sir Immanuel Jakobovits to Celebrate Twenty Years in Office*, ed. Jonathan Sacks, London: Jews' College Publications, 1986.

Newman, Aubrey, 'The Chief Rabbinate,' in *Provincial Jewry in Victorian Britain*, London: Jewish Historical Society of England, 1975.

Newman, Aubrey, *Chief Rabbi Dr Joseph H. Hertz*, London: United Synagogue, 1972.

Newman, Aubrey, *The Board of Deputies of British Jews, 1760–1985*, London: Vallentine Mitchell, 1987.

Newman, Aubrey, *The United Synagogue, 1870–1970*, London: Routledge & Kegan Paul, 1976.

Paneth, Philip, *Guardian of the Law: The Chief Rabbi, Dr J. H. Hertz*, London: Allied Book Club, 1940.

Parsons, Gerald (ed.), *Religion in Victorian Britain—I. Traditions*, Manchester: Manchester University Press and Open University, 1988.

Pearl, Chaim, 'About "Chief Rabbis,"' in *Jewish Spectator*, New York, January 1967.

Persoff, Meir, 'Anti-Jacobs society to disband,' in *Jewish Chronicle*, 19 March 1971.

Persoff, Meir, 'Communal history was born in a succah,' in *Jewish Chronicle*, 11 September 1970.

Persoff, Meir, 'Learning lessons from our history,' in *Jewish Chronicle*, 28 January 2000.

Persoff, Meir, 'Stubborn resistance to change,' interview with Chief Rabbi Dr Immanuel Jakobovits, in *Jewish Chronicle*, 27 June 1969.

Persoff, Meir, 'The kind of rabbi we need now,' interviews with Rabbi Dr Nachum Rabinovitch and Salmond S. Levin, in *Jewish Chronicle*, 16 March 1973.

Persoff, Meir, 'When yesterday meets tomorrow,' interview with Chief Rabbi Dr Immanuel Jakobovits, in *Jewish Chronicle*, 21 July 1967.

Persoff, Meir, *Another Way, Another Time: Religious Inclusivism and the Sacks Chief Rabbinate*, Boston: Academic Studies Press, 2010.

Persoff, Meir, *Faith Against Reason: Religious Reform and the British Chief Rabbinate, 1840–1990*, London and Portland, OR: Vallentine Mitchell, 2008.

Persoff, Meir, *Immanuel Jakobovits: a Prophet in Israel*, London: Vallentine Mitchell, 2002.

Petuchowski, Jakob J., *Points of View*, London: Reform Synagogues of Great Britain, 1970.

Philipson, David, *The Reform Movement in Judaism*, New York: Macmillan, 1907; revised and updated, 1931.

Phillips, Olga Somech, and Hyman A. Simons, *The History of the Bayswater Synagogue 1863–1963*, privately published, London, 1963.

Picciotto, James, *Sketches of Anglo-Jewish History*, revised and ed., Israel Finestein, London: Soncino Press, 1955.

Rabinowitz, Louis, 'The Status of the Ministry,' in *The Jewish Monthly*, Vol. 4, No. 9, London: Anglo-Jewish Association, December 1950.

Recorded Minutes of the First Meeting of Elected Members of the Vestry of the United Synagogue, London, 11 January, 1871; and Deed of Foundation and Trust, signed, sealed and delivered by Sir Anthony de Rothschild, Baronet; Lionel Louis Cohen; Sampson Lucas; Solomon Schloss; and Assur Henry Moses, in the presence of Algernon E. Sydney, Solicitor, 46 Finsbury Circus, London, EC, 13 January, 1871.

Reif, Stefan C., *Judaism and Hebrew Prayer: New Perspectives on Jewish Liturgical History*, Cambridge: Cambridge University Press, 1993.

Report of the Committee Appointed for the Selection of Candidates for the Office of Chief Rabbi, With an Appendix Containing Abstracts of Testimonials, Etc., London: John Wertheimer and Co., London, 1844.

Report on the Sabbath Reading of the Scriptures in a Triennial Cycle, London: New West End Synagogue, Wertheimer Lea & Co., 1913.

Rigal, Lawrence, and Rosenberg, Rosita, *Liberal Judaism: The First Hundred Years*, London: Liberal Judaism-Union of Liberal and Progressive Synagogues, 2004.

Rocker, Simon, 'The tightrope awaiting the next Chief Rabbi,' *Jewish Chronicle*, 31 December 2010.

Romain, Jonathan A., 'The Establishment of the Reform Beth Din in 1948: A Barometer of Religious Trends in Anglo-Jewry,' in *Jewish Historical Studies*, Volume XXXIII, 1992–1994, London: Jewish Historical Society of England, 1995.

Romain, Jonathan A., *Faith & Practice: A Guide to Reform Judaism Today*, London: Reform Synagogues of Great Britain, 1991.

Romain, Jonathan A., *The Reform Beth Din: The Formation and Development of the Rabbinical Court of the Reform Synagogues of Great Britain, 1935–1965*, unpublished PhD thesis, University of Leicester, 1990.

Roth, Cecil, 'Britain's Three Chief Rabbis,' in *Jewish Leaders (1750–1940)*, ed. Leo Jung, New York: Bloch Publishers, 5714-1953.

Roth, Cecil, 'The Collapse of English Jewry,' in *The Jewish Monthly*, No. 4, London: Anglo-Jewish Association, 1947.

Roth, Cecil, *A History of the Jews in England*, London: Oxford University Press, 1941; reprinted, London: John Trotter, 1989.

Roth, Cecil, *Archives of the United Synagogue: Report and Catalogue*, London: United Synagogue, 1930.

Roth, Cecil, *History of the Great Synagogue, 1690–1940*, London: Edward Goldston & Son, 1950.

Roth, Cecil, *Records of the Western Synagogue, 1761–1932*, London: Edward Goldston, 1932.

Roth, Cecil, *The Federation of Synagogues, 1912–1937*, London, 5698-1937.

Roth, Cecil, *The Jewish Chronicle 1841–1941: A Century of Newspaper History*, London: Jewish Chronicle, 1949.

Roth, Cecil, *The Rise of Provincial Jewry*, London: The Jewish Monthly, 1950.

Rubinstein, W. D., *A History of the Jews in the English-Speaking World: Great Britain*, Houndsmills, Basingstoke: Macmillan, 1996.

Sacks, Jonathan, ed., *Orthodoxy Confronts Modernity*, New Jersey: Ktav, in association with Jews' College, London, 1991.

Sacks, Jonathan, ed., *Tradition and Transition: Essays Presented to Chief Rabbi Sir Immanuel Jakobovits to Celebrate Twenty Years in Office*, London: Jews' College Publications, 1986.

Sacks, Jonathan, 'A close-knit academic community, with a clear sense of its role. Reflections of a semichah candidate,' *Jewish Chronicle*, Jews' College Supplement, 3 September, 1976.

Sacks, Jonathan, 'Jews' College in Crisis: Commitment to the Community,' *Jewish Chronicle*, 30 November 1979.

Sacks, Jonathan, 'Jews' College: the way ahead. A story of self-discovery,' *Jewish Chronicle*, 26 October 1984.

Sacks, Jonathan, 'Prologue,' in Meir Persoff, *Immanuel Jakobovits: a Prophet in Israel*, London and Portland, OR: Vallentine Mitchell, 2002.

Sacks, Jonathan, 'The Origin of Torah,' *Jewish Chronicle*, 2 November 1984.

Sacks, Jonathan, 'The Role of Women in Judaism,' in *Man, Woman, and Priesthood*, ed. Peter Moore, London: SPCK, 1978.

Sacks, Jonathan, *A Time For Renewal: A Rabbinic Response to the Kalms Report, 'A Time For Change,'* London: Office of the Chief Rabbi, 1992.

Sacks, Jonathan, *Community of Faith*, London: Peter Halban, 1995.

Sacks, Jonathan, *One People? Tradition, Modernity, and Jewish Unity*, London: Littman Library of Jewish Civilization, 1993.

Sacks, Jonathan, *Tradition in an Untraditional Age: Essays on Modern Jewish Thought*, London: Vallentine Mitchell, 1990.

Sacks, Jonathan, *Traditional Alternatives: Orthodoxy and the Future of the Jewish People*, London: Jews' College Publications, 1989; published in the United States as *Arguments for the Sake of Heaven*, New Jersey: Jason Aronson, 1995.

Salaman, Redcliffe N., *Whither Lucien Wolf's Anglo-Jewish Community? — The Lucien Wolf Memorial Lecture, 1953*, London: Jewish Historical Society of England, 1954.

Salbstein, M. C. N., *The Emancipation of the Jews in Britain*, London: Littman Library of Jewish Civilization, 1982.

Salomon, Sidney, *The Jews of Britain*, London: Hutchinson, 1938.

Schimmel, H. Chaim, and Aryeh Carmell, eds., *Encounter: Essays on Torah and Modern Life*, New York: Association of Orthodox Jewish Scientists-Feldheim, 1989.

Schischa, A., 'Hermann Adler, Yeshivah Bachur, Prague, 1860–1862,' in *Remember* the Days: Essays in Honour of Cecil Roth, ed. John M. Shaftesley, London: Jewish Historical Society of England, 1966.

Schmidt, H. D., 'Chief Rabbi Nathan Marcus Adler: Jewish Educator from Germany,' in Leo Baeck Institute Year Book, VII, London: East and West Library, 1962.

Schwab, Hermann, 'A Champion of Orthodoxy (ii),' in The Jewish Monthly, Vol. IV, No. 3, London: Anglo-Jewish Association, June 1950.

Schwab, Hermann, The History of Orthodox Jewry in Germany, London: Mitre Press, 1950.

Scult, Mel, 'Schechter's Seminary,' in Tradition Renewed: A History of the Jewish Theological Seminary of America, Vol. I, ed. Jack Wertheimer, New York: Jewish Theological Seminary of America, 1997.

Seltzer, Robert M., Jewish People, Jewish Thought, New York: Macmillan, 1980.

Shaftesley, John M., ed., Remember the Days: Essays in Honour of Cecil Roth, London: Jewish Historical Society of England, 1966.

Shaftesley, John M., 'Israel Brodie, Chief Rabbi: A Biographical Sketch,' in Essays Presented to Chief Rabbi Israel Brodie on the Occasion of his Seventieth Birthday, ed. H. J. Zimmels, J. Rabbinowitz, and I. Finestein, Jews' College Publications, New Series, No. 3, London: Soncino Press, 1967.

Shaftesley, John M., 'Religious Controversies,' in A Century of Anglo-Jewish Life, 1870–1970, ed. Salmond S. Levin, London: United Synagogue, 1971.

Sharot, Stephen, 'Native Jewry and the Religious Anglicisation of Immigrants in London, 1870–1905,' in Jewish Journal of Sociology, Vol. XVI, No. 1, London: William Heinemann, June 1974.

Sharot, Stephen, 'Reform and Liberal Judaism in London, 1840–1940,' in Jewish Social Studies, Vol. XLI, New York: Conference on Jewish Social Studies, 1979.

Sharot, Stephen, 'Religious Change in Native Orthodoxy in London, 1870–1914: The Synagogue Service,' in Jewish Journal of Sociology, Vol. XV, No. 1, London: William Heinemann, June 1973.

Sharot, Stephen, 'Religious Change in Native Orthodoxy in London, 1870–1914: Rabbinate and Clergy,' in Jewish Journal of Sociology, Vol. XV, No. 2, London: William Heinemann, December 1973.

Sharot, Stephen, 'Secularisation, Judaism and Anglo-Jewry,' in A Sociological Yearbook of Religion in Britain, Vol. IV, ed. M. Hill, London: SCM Press, 1971.

Shashar, Michael, Lord Jakobovits in Conversation, London: Vallentine Mitchell, 2000.

Shewzik, B., A Grievous Mourning: A sermon in memory of the late Chief Rabbi, Rev Dr Nathan M. Adler, London: E. W. Rabbinowicz, 5650–1890.

Simmons, Vivian G., The Path of Life: A Study of the Background, Faith and Practice of Liberal Judaism, London: Vallentine Mitchell, 1961.

Simon, Maurice, Jewish Religious Conflicts, London: Hutchinson, 1950.

Simons, Hyman A., Forty Years a Chief Rabbi: The Life and Times of Solomon Hirschell, London: Robson Books, 1980.

Singer, Simeon, *The Literary Remains of the Rev Simeon Singer*, ed. Israel Abrahams, London: Routledge, 1908.

Singer, Steven, *Chief Rabbi Nathan Marcus Adler: Major Problems in His Career*, unpublished MA thesis, Bernard Revel Graduate School, Yeshiva University, New York, 1974.

Singer, Steven, *Orthodox Judaism in Early Victorian London, 1840–1858*, unpublished PhD thesis, Bernard Revel Graduate School, Yeshiva University, New York, 1981.

Sorasky, Aaron, 'The Life and Times of Rabbenu Yechezkel Abramsky,' in *Emunah: Pathways in Contemporary Jewish Thought*, No. 2, Tel Ganim, Israel: Kollel Tal Torah, January 1990.

Sorasky, Aaron, *Melech Beyofyo* [*A King In His Glory*], Vols. I and II, published privately, Jerusalem, 2004.

Super, Arthur Saul, 'Israel Brodie—Chief Rabbi,' in *The Jewish Monthly*, Vol. 2, No. 3, London: Anglo-Jewish Association, June 1948.

Susser, Bernard, 'Statistical Accounts of all the Congregations in the British Empire, 5606–1845,' in Aubrey Newman, ed., *Provincial Jewry in Victorian Britain*, London: Jewish Historical Society of England, 1975.

Taylor, Derek, *British Chief Rabbis, 1664–2006*, London: Vallentine Mitchell, 2006.

Temkin, Sefton, 'A Crisis in Anglo-Jewry,' in *Conservative Judaism*, Vol. XVIII, No. 1, ed. Samuel H. Dresner, New York: Rabbinical Assembly, 1963.

Temkin, Sefton, 'Orthodoxy With Moderation: A Sketch of Joseph Herman Hertz,' in *Judaism*, Vol. 24, No. 3, New York: American Jewish Congress, 1975.

Tessler, Gloria, *Amélie: The Story of Lady Jakobovits*, London: Vallentine Mitchell, 1999.

The Celebration of the Chief Rabbi's Silver Jubilee, London: Chief Rabbi Presentation Committee, 1938.

Trepp, Leo, *Die Oldenburger Jüdenschaft*, Oldenburg: Heinz Holzberg Verlag, 1973.

Unna Josef, 'Nathan Hacohen Adler,' in *Guardians of our Heritage*, ed. Leo Jung, New York: Bloch Publishing House, 1958.

Vallely, Paul, 'Jonathan Sacks: Defender of the Faith,' *The Independent*, London, 8 September 2001.

Waterman, Stanley, and Barry Kosmin, *British Jewry in the Eighties*, London: Board of Deputies of British Jews, 1986.

Webber, Jonathan, ed., *Jewish Identities in the New Europe*, London: Littman Library of Jewish Civilization, 1994.

Wertheimer, Jack, ed., *Tradition Renewed: A History of the Jewish Theological Seminary of America*, New York: Jewish Theological Seminary of America, 1997.

Wiesel, Elie, 'Foreword,' in Meir Persoff, *Immanuel Jakobovits: a Prophet in Israel*, London and Portland, OR: Vallentine Mitchell, 2002.

Williams, Bill, *The Making of Manchester Jewry, 1740–1875*, Manchester University Press, 1976.

Wolf, Lucien, 'The Queen's Jewry, 1837–1897,' in *Young Israel*, June and July, 1897; reprinted in *Essays in Jewish History*, ed. Cecil Roth, London: Jewish Historical Society of England, 1934.

Wolf, Lucien, *Essays in Jewish History*, London: Jewish Historical Society of England, 1934.

Wolfson, Isaac, *Statement by the President of the United Synagogue*, London: United Synagogue, 1964.

Wolkind, Jack, *London and its Jewish Community*, London: West Central Counselling and Community Research, 1985.

Wright, Aaron, 'Principal Rabbi of the Federation of Synagogues,' in *Memories of Kopul Rosen*, ed. Cyril Domb, privately published (Carmel College, Wallingford, Berkshire), 1970.

Zolti, Bezalel, 'The "Man Of Freedom" Of Our Generation,' in *Sefer Zikaron [Memorial Volume to Rabbi Yechezkel Abramsky]*, ed. Joseph Buchsbaum and Abraham Halevy Sher, Jerusalem: Moriah, 5738–1978.

London Metropolitan Archives (40 Northampton Road, London EC1R 0HB) houses the papers of, among other institutions, the Board of Deputies of British Jews (ACC/3121), United Synagogue (ACC/2712), Office of the Chief Rabbi (ACC/2805), London Beth Din (ACC/3400), Kashrus Commission (ACC/2980), Federation of Synagogues (ACC/2893), Western Synagogue (ACC/2911), Liberal Jewish Synagogue (ACC/3529), West London Synagogue

(ACC/2886), Westminster Synagogue (LMA/4071), London School of Jewish Studies, formerly Jews' College (LMA/4180), Jewish Memorial Council (ACC/2999).

The Archive and Manuscript Collections of the Hartley Library, University of Southampton (Highfield, Southampton SO9 5NH), include the papers of C. J. Goldsmid-Montefiore (MS 108), Lord Swaythling (MS 117), Selig Brodetsky (MS 119), Michael Adler (MS 125), Laski family (MS 134), West London Synagogue (MS 140), Bernard Homa (MS 141), London Board of Shechita (MS 142), P. Goldberg (MS 148), New London Synagogue (MS 149), Machzike Hadath Congregation (MS 151), Cecil Roth (MS 156), Jewish Religious Education Board (MS 157), H. F. Reinhart (MS 171), J. H. Hertz (MS 175), Solomon Schonfeld (MS 183), Adolf Büchler (MS 186), Salis Daiches (MS 189), Victor Schonfeld (MS 192), Israel Brodie (MS 206), Jewish Chronicle (MS 225), J. M. Shaftesley (MS 230), V. D. Lipman (MS 245), Van der Zyl family (MS 297).

The Special Collections of the Mocatta Library at University College London (140 Hampstead Road, London NW1 2BX) include books, manuscripts and papers of Frederic David Mocatta, Hermann Gollancz, Israel Abrahams, Lucien Wolf, Moses Montefiore and Moses Gaster.

The Archives in the Special Collection of the Jewish Theological Seminary of America Library (3080 Broadway at 122nd Street, New York, NY 10027-4649) contain personal papers of Nathan Marcus Adler (boxes 5-1 to 5-4), Hermann Adler (3-1 to 3-3) and Marcus Nathan Adler (4-1). Earlier and later Adler material is in boxes 1 and 2; papers relating to Morris Joseph, Albert H. Jessel and Albert M. Hyamson are in box 3; to Moses Montefiore, Judith, Lady Montefiore, Claude G. Montefiore, Cecil Roth and Redcliffe Nathan Salaman, in box 4; to Isidore Spielmann, in box 5. Boxes 6 to 17 include a wealth of material from organisations across the Anglo-Jewish spectrum.

Index

Abawicz, Meir, 125
Abertillery, 93
Abrahams, Barnett, 43, 267
Abrahams, Israel, 121, 129-130, 278
Abrahams, Joseph, 81, 91
Abrahams, M., 86
Abramsky, Yechezkel Alter, xviii-xix, 115, 125, 132, 137, 258, 279, 281
Act of Parliament, 1870 (United Synagogues, 33 & 34 Vict.), 45
Adas Yereim (Synagogue de la Rue Cadet, Paris), 288
Adath Yeshurun Synagogue (Syracuse), 77
Adler, Cyrus, 274
Adler, Elkan, 267
Adler, Hermann, xviii, 41, 43-44, 50, 52, 56-57, 59, 66, 69-70, 79-80, 86, 93, 95, 105, 125, 257, 266-268, 271, 275
Adler, Marcus N., 267
Adler, Michael, 86, 266
Adler, Nathan Marcus, xvii, xix-xxi, 14-15, 17-18, 20-23, 26-27, 29, 40-41, 44-45, 106, 264
Adler, Nettie (Henrietta), 267
Adlerism, 66
Aldgate, 67
Altmann, Alexander, 110, 124, 137, 140 seq., 146-148, 180, 283
Altona, 12, 269

America (United States of), xvi, 82-83, 91, 93, 106, 166, 195, 216
Amsterdam, 12
Anglican Church, xx, 45, 292
Anglo-American Commission, 118
Anglo-Jewish Association, 119, 268, 278
Anglo-Jewry, xi-xiii, xix-xx, 44, 52, 80, 104, 119, 127, 166, 173, 176, 189, 195, 198, 203, 213-215, 254, 255, 302
Anti-Semitism, 106, 119, 155, 253
Apple, Raymond, 180, 223, 292
Archbishop of Canterbury, xx
Aria College, 268
Army Chaplains' Corps, 121
Artom, Benjamin, 263
Arye of Rotterdam, 1
Asher, David, 43, 267
Association for Furthering Traditional Judaism in Great Britain, 71
Atlanta, 222
Atlas, Binyamin Beinish, 281
Auerbach, B., 7, 14, 16, 18
Australia, 121, 160, 162-163, 292, 279
Austria, 91

Balfour Declaration, 213, 257
Balliol College (Oxford), 120
Barned, I., 265
Barnett, A.S., 3

Barnett, Arthur, 129, 263
Barnett, K.P., 225
Bat chayil (batmitzvah) ceremony, 230
Bayfield, Tony (Anthony), 235
Bayswater Synagogue, 43, 56, 57, 79, 81-82, 292
Bentwich, Herbert, 90
Bergen-Belsen, 155
Berger, Isaac, 223, 244
Berlin, 4, 12, 17, 121, 124
Berlin (Bar-Ilan), Meir, 279
Berlin, Isaiah, 294
Berman, Myer, 290
Beth Jacob Congregation, 222
Bethnal Green, 298
Bevis Marks Synagogue, 1, 11, 51
Biblical Criticism, 284
Birmingham, 15, 20, 43, 71, 82, 148
Bishop of Bedford, 271
Blank, Joseph, 67, 269
Blashki, Aaron, 276
Bleich, David, 228, 298
Bloch, S., 71
B'nai B'rith, 177
Board of Deputies, xxi, 3, 27, 46, 49, 107, 219, 237, 242, 297-298, 301
Board of Guardians, 46
Board of Shechita, 41, 46
Boston, 121
Bournemouth, 148
Bower, Marcus H., 301
Brandeis University, 283
Brandon, I.I., 265
Bremen, 81
Breslau, 270
Brichto, Sidney, 205, 238, 297
Bridges of Understanding (Jakobovits), xxi, 221, 235

Brighton, 15, 43, 45, 129, 148
Brisk, 125
Bristol, 15, 20
British Broadcasting Corporation (BBC), 235
British Empire, xii, 6, 47-48, 70, 82, 88, 107, 113, 117, 129, 142, 147-148, 214
British School of Jewish Learning, 106
Brodie, Aaron, 120
Brodie, Fanny, 124, 279
Brodie, Israel, xxi, 116, 120, 123 seq., 129 seq., 140, 147 seq., 160, 162, 167 seq., 170, 257, 278, 283, 286, 289-290
Brodie, Sheina, 120
Brown, Solomon, 288
Bryanstone Street (Sephardi) Congregation, 51
Bucharest, 270
Bulka, Reuven, 222-223, 231-232, 242-243, 245, 297, 302
Burton Street Congregation, 14

Cambridge, Duchess of, 264
Cambridge, Duke of (Prince Adolphus Frederick), 23, 264
Canada, 294
Cape Town, 278, 302
Cardiff, 279
Carmel College, 279, 283
Caro, Joseph, 297
Casper, Bernard Moses, 162
Castro, Hananel de, 44, 265
Central Synagogue, 42
Chafetz Chaim, 240
Chatham, 15
Cherem (excommunication), 1, 3, 11, 19, 44, 263, 268
Chevros Bnai Yisroel, 46

Chief Rabbi's Cabinet, 196
Chief Rabbi's Fund, 52, 54-55, 73-74
Chief Rabbinate Centre, 197, 294-295
Chief Rabbinate Conference, 69, 72, 75, 79, 86, 111, 142, 162, 174, 181, 186, 244-245
Chief Rabbinate-in-Commission, 177, 198, 201
Cohen Louis, 265
Cohen, Arnold, 241
Cohen, Benjamin, 56
Cohen, H.H., 265
Cohen, Isaac (Ireland), 162
Cohen, Isaac (London), 11
Cohen, Jeffrey, 223
Cohen, Lionel L., 42, 109, 265
Cohen, Norman, xx, 160, 164 seq., 176, 184, 286
Cohen, S., 265
Cohen, Shear Yashuv, 162
Coleman, Shalom, 162
Conference of Jewish Ministers, 70, 86
Conservative Judaism, 88, 96, 111, 278, 298
Consultative and Advisory Committee, 145-146, 149
Corney, Hyam, 298
Council of Reform and Liberal Rabbis, 235, 238
Cudmore, Daphne, 284
Cymerman, J.H., 131 seq., 281

Daiches, Samuel, 81, 273
Daily Express, 163, 169, 174, 292
Dallas, 120
Dalston Synagogue, 79
Darmstadt, 7
Davies, Frederick, 266

Davies, Samuel, 172, 287
Davis, Baruch, 261
Davis, Benn, 42
Davis, Elias, 17, 264
Davis, Felix, 72 seq., 77, 91, 94
Davis, Noah, 55
Decade of Jewish Renewal, 252, 254, 256
Deed of Foundation and Trust (United Synagogue), 52, 70, 114, 143, 162
Defries, Nathan, 263
Delegate Chief Rabbi, 41, 44, 67, 74, 114, 154, 289
Denmark, 91, 230
Dessler, Eliyahu Eliezer, 284
Divine Revelation (*Torah min hashamayim*), 115, 160, 211
Drachman, Beatrice, 82, 85, 88
Drachman, Bernard, 80 seq., 85, 90, 96, 274-275
Drachman, Julian, 275
Dublin, 15, 287
Dukas, Julius J., 276

East End (of London), 46, 53-54, 56, 67-69, 84, 94, 266, 270-271
East End Scheme, 46, 52, 56, 270-271
Edgware Synagogue, 231
Edinburgh, 15, 148
Education, 2, 11, 16, 31, 34-36, 43, 62-63, 84, 102-103, 106, 139, 196, 209-210, 227, 230, 250, 254, 257
Ehrentreu, Chanoch, 223, 241, 244
Eichholz, Alfred, 89
Elias (Rabbi), Elyas le Evesk, 62
Ellis, Samuel Helbert, 12, 21, 23-24, 265

Emanuel, G.J., 86
Emden, 7
Emoluments, Chief Rabbinical, 9-10, 53-55, 69, 117, 125-126, 137, 142, 162, 222, 271, 294
Epstein, C. Joshua, 276
Epstein, Isidore, 160
Erlangen, 17
Eshkol, Levi, 169-170, 293
Etner, C.I., 133
Etz Chaim Yeshivah, 123, 125, 169
Europe, xix, 1, 14, 91
Europe, Nazi-occupied, 110, 213
European Jewry, xviii, 115

Fabricant, Isaac, 129
Falmouth, 15
Fasman, Oscar, 288
Federation of Synagogues, 45-46, 49 seq., 66, 69, 73 seq., 110, seq., 123, 130 seq., 142 seq., 162, 181, 199, 203, 241, 269, 283
Federation of Synagogues Beth Din, 143, 145, 182, 200-201, 203-204, 217, 220, 287, 296
Feldman, A., 67, 70-71
Feldman, Emanuel, 222-223, 228, 231, 298
Fifth Avenue Synagogue, 160, 165-167, 285, 288
Finchley Synagogue, xvii, 261, 277
Finestein, Israel, 241-242, 301
Finkel, L.G., 125
Finkelstein, Louis, 121, 278
First World War, 106
Fisher, M., 131, 219
Foligno, I., 265
France, xvi, 91, 178-179
Frankel, William, 285
Frankfurt, 12

Franses, Simon, 301
Freedland, Michael, 229, 262
Freedman, Harry, 121, 278
Freund, Samuel, 43
Friend of Truth, xvii
Frosh, Sidney, 221 seq., 228, 231 seq., 241 seq.
Frumkin, L., 67
Functions, Chief Rabbinical, xvii, 5, 10-12, 31 seq., 41, 61-62, 69-71, 77, 88, 113, 115, 127, 131-132, 143, 148-150, 192 seq., 207 seq., 223-224, 254-255, 261, 271

Gaon, Solomon, 171, 191, 199-200, 205
Garnethill Synagogue, 130
Gaster, Moses, 49, 270
Gateshead Yeshivah, 160, 284
Gee, George M., 172
Gelles, Benjamin, 290
Gelley, Menachem, 261
Geneva, 179
George III, 23
Germany, 91
Giessen, 17, 280
Glasgow, 15, 130, 134-135, 148, 281, 302
Gold, Raphael, 120
Goldberg, Philip, 114
Golders Green Beth Hamedrash, 284
Golders Green Synagogue, 129, 227, 247-248
Golditch, Isaac, 289
Goldman, Sadie, 299
Goldman, Solomon, 180-181, 183, 232, 299
Goldmann, Nahum, 172, 290
Goldmeier, Michael, 222, 299

Goldsmid, Colonel A.F., 104
Goldsmid, Gladys, 272
Goldsmid, Julian, 43, 49, 51
Goldsmith, Sam, 179
Gollancz, Hermann, 79, 81
Goodman, Lord (Arnold), 238
Gottlieb, Wolf, 277
Grabiner, Anthony, 229, 298
Great Synagogue (Duke's Place, London), 1, 8, 10, 12, 15, 20, 29, 55, 59, 79, 82, 96, 99, 153
Great Synagogue (Sydney), 292
Greater London Radio, 232
Green, A.A., 86
Grossnass, Arye Leib, 184, 290
Grunfeld, Isidor, 111, 115-116, 132, 187, 191
Guedalla, Haim, 44, 265
Gulf War, 257

Hain, Kenneth, 223
Haliva, A., 3
Hall, Viscount (George Henry), 119
Hambro' Synagogue, 15, 55
Hamburg, 12
Hammersmith, 60
Hampstead, 60
Hampstead Garden Suburb Synagogue, 129, 231, 299
Hampstead Synagogue, 79, 292
Hanover, 7, 12, 15, 23, 43, 264
Hanoverian Government, 23
Hardman, Leslie, 171
Harris, Ann, 228, 241-242, 299, 301
Harris, Cyril, 222-223, 228 seq., 235, 241 seq., 244, 302
Harris, Isidore, 50
Harris, Michael, 228, 242
Hartman, David, 228, 298

Harvard University, 283
Hebrew University of Jerusalem, 283
Hechal Shlomo, 172
Helbert, I.H., 265
Henry, Charles, 89
Hertz, Joseph Herman, xviii, xxi, 77 seq., 81, 85 seq., 95, 99, 106 seq., 111-113, 121, 126, 149, 153, 256, 258, 275, 279, 286
Hertz, Rose (née Freed), 110
Herzl, Theodor, 272
Herzog, Aura, 293-294
Herzog, Chaim (Vivian), 191, 293-294
Herzog, Isaac, 116, 118 seq., 120-121, 170, 278-279
Herzog, Joel Leib, 116
Herzog, Pnina, 169, 172, 179, 191, 291
Herzog, Sarah, 168, 289-290
Herzog, Shira, 290, 294
Herzog, Yaacov (Jacob), xvii, 162 seq., 168, 174, 177 seq., 187 seq., 289-290, 293-294
Hildesheimer Rabbinical Seminary, 124, 280, 288
Hillel Foundation, 229
Hillman, Samuel, 169, 272
Hirsch, Samson Raphael, 7, 14, 16, 18-20, 22, 46, 263
Hirsch, Zvi, 1
Hirschell, Solomon, xvii, 1, 3-4, 6, 264
Hirschfeld, Hirsch, 7, 14, 16-18, 20-22, 263
Hochhauser, Simon, xx
Holland, 91
Holocaust, xviii
House of Lords, 260
Hurwitz, Alter, 140

Hyams, H., 265
Hyamson, Moses, 67-68, 70, 80-81, 85, 93 seq., 269, 276

Immanuel College, 257
Immigration, xviii, xx, 44-46, 78, 155, 268
Inclusivism, xxi, 45, 224, 228, 243, 255
Institute for Jewish Policy Research, xxi
Inter-University Jewish Federation, 229
Ipswich, 15
Ireland, 116, 162, 216, 285
Irish Times, 162
Israel, xvi, 166, 173-174, 195, 212, 214, 226, 244, 251, 253-255, 289
Israel Ministry of Foreign Affairs, 169
Italy, 91

Jacob, Presbyter of the Jews, 62
Jacobs (Jakobovits), Joseph, 176
Jacobs Affairs, 162, 176, 284, 285
Jacobs, Louis, 160 seq., 180, 185, 188, 199, 221, 231, 284, 288, 293
Jaffe, Maurice, 172
Jakobovits, Amélie, 187, 227, 230, 247, 288, 300
Jakobovits, Immanuel, xiii, xx, 160 seq., 176, 180 seq., 187, 191, 197 seq., 207, 219 seq., 222, 227 seq., 232 seq., 236, 243 seq., 247, 285-286, 292-293, 295
Jakobovits, Julius, 115, 142
Japhet, Seemy, 89
Jersey, 15

Jerusalem, 173, 252
Jessel, Albert, 68, 74, 76-77, 81, 85, 87 seq., 273
Jewish Agency Torah Department, 161, 286
Jewish Center of New York, 183
Jewish Chronicle, xvi, 17-19, 22, 72, 85, 87, 90, 95, 108, 110, 113, 125, 150, 176, 178-179, 189, 191, 236
Jewish Educational Development Trust, 227, 234-235
Jewish Express, 84
Jewish Historical Society of England, 268
Jewish Journal, 84
Jewish Observer and Middle East Review, 285
Jewish Religious Education Board, 268
Jewish Religious Union, 45
Jewish Review, 285
Jewish Theological Seminary (New York), 77, 87, 96, 110, 121, 273-274, 276, 278
Jewish War Memorial, 106-107
Jews' College, xv, 43, 81, 120-121, 125, 160, 222, 226, 228, 231, 233-235, 248, 259, 267, 285, 302
Johannesburg, 77-78, 243
Joseph, Aaron, 25
Jospe, Gerald, 222, 299
Jung, Julius, 142, 269
Jung, Leo, 129-130, 280
Jung, Maier, 269, 279
Jurisdiction, Chief Rabbinical, 6, 8, 12, 27, 45, 47 seq., 53, 64, 69-71, 74-75, 138, 143 seq., 182, 199, 204-205, 221, 235 seq.

Kagan, Koppel Kahana, 231
Kahaneman, Yosef Shlomo (Ponevezher Rav), 169, 289
Kalisch, Marcus, 43, 267
Kalms, Stanley, xv, xxi, 222-223, 226 seq., 232 seq., 243, 262, 302
Kenton Synagogue, 230
Keyser, M.S., 265
Kimche, Alan, 223
King John, 62
Kirzner, Eliezer, 199 seq., 219, 296
Kisch, B., 89
Klal Yisrael, 174, 176, 190, 278
Kleiner, Mark, 172
Klerk, F.W. de, 243
Knesset Israel Congregation (Cleveland, Ohio), 280
Kollek, Teddy, 293
Kook, Abraham Isaac, 116, 211
Kook, Simcha, 223
Kopelowitz, Lionel, 237-238, 241-242, 301
Krotoschin, 1

Lainer, J., 133
Lamm, Maurice, 223
Lamm, Norman, 163, 183, 186
Landa, M.J., 93-94
Landau, Hermann, 56, 74, 76, 269
Landy, Harry, 172
Landy, Maurice, 290
Lashon hara (slander, calumny), 239
Lau, Yisrael, 223, 231-232, 242, 299
Lazarus, Emma, 103
Lazarus, Harris, 114, 125, 150, 153-154
Lazarus, Josephine, 103
Lederman, Morris, 172, 182, 200 seq., 219, 286-287, 296-297

Leeds, 82, 140, 148
Leipzig, 4, 43, 270
Lerner, Isaac, 284
Lerner, Mayer, 46, 269
Lesser, Ernest, 89
Levine, Jack, 130, 281
Levy, A., 3
Levy, Elkan, 260-261, 302
Levy, J., 265
Levy, J., 3
Levy, S., 71, 86
Lew, Jonathan, 228, 231, 241, 297, 299
Lew, Linda, 241
Lew, Myer, 129
Lewisham, 60
Liberal Jewish Synagogue, 104
Liberal Judaism, xx-xxi, 45, 66, 106-108, 123, 191, 205, 219, 237, 257, 272
Lichtenstein, Aharon, 223
Lieberman, Simche Bunim, 233, 300
Lithuania, xviii
Liturgical reform, 66
Liverpool, 15, 82, 148
Livingstone, Isaac, 129, 184
Loewe, Louis, 267
London Beth Din, xvi-xvii, xix, 70, 115-116, 127, 130, 132, 135, 141, 146, 171, 177, 183, 198, 201, 203-205, 217, 220, 226, 244, 287
London Board of Jewish Religious Education, 139
London School of Jewish Studies (Jews' College), 299
London, xii, 3, 27
Longley, Clifford, 237
Lousada, Herbert G., 50
Lubavitch (Chabad), xvi, 223, 261

Lucas, Henry, 56-57
Lucas, Victor, 223, 229, 242-244, 298
Lyons, Frank I., 89-90

Machzike Hadath, 45, 257, 268
Magnus, Philip, 47, 270
Maiden Lane Synagogue, 15
Maimonides, 106, 209
Mainstream Judaism, xxi
Manchester, 15, 51, 77, 82, 85, 110, 124
Manchester Central Synagogue, 284
Manchester Yeshivah, 284
Mandela, Nelson, 243
Manna (Reform journal), 235
Marble Arch Synagogue, 299
Marburg, 17
Margolies, Raphael, 284
Margulies, I.L., 133
Marks, David Woolf, 50
Marmur, Dow, 221
Masorti, xxi, 221
Maybaum, Ignaz, 284
Meir, Golda, 172, 290
Melbourne, 292
Melbourne Hebrew Congregation, 81, 121, 125, 278
Meldola, David, 3, 263
Meldola, Raphael, 11, 263
Melinek, Abraham, 290
Menasseh ben Israel, 106-107
Mendes, Abraham Pereira, 43
Mikve Israel Synagogue (Philadelphia), 273
Mill Hill Synagogue, xx
Milner, Lord (Alfred), 275
Ministry, xviii, 31 seq., 45, 60 seq., 66, 68 seq., 86-87, 95, 106, 108, 112, 125-126, 129 seq., 133, 135 seq., 140-141, 149, 153-154, 157, 171, 174, 180-181, 183-184, 191, 195-196, 209, 214, 217, 220, 225, 244, 248, 254, 269, 280, 292
Mintz, Louis, 301
Mir Yeshivah, 123, 125
Mirvis, Ephraim, xvii, xxi, 222, 261, 297
Mishnah Berurah, 240
Mizrachi, 285
Modes of election, xiii, xv-xvi, 8-10, 14-15, 18-20, 42, 49, 52 seq., 69, 72 seq., 81, 85 seq., 90, 94, 110, 114, 125 seq., 137, 139, 142, 148-149, 162-163, 171-172, 175, 181-182, 198, 221 seq., 231, 243-245, 261, 263, 280, 282
Montagu, Ewen, 112, 117, 123 seq., 161, 182, 272
Montagu, Lily (Lilian), 107, 272
Montagu, Louis Samuel (2nd Lord Swaythling), 73-75, 78, 84, 270, 272
Montagu, Marian, 272
Montagu, Samuel (1st Lord Swaythling), 46-49, 51-52, 54-56, 67, 269, 272
Montefiore, I.M., 265
Montefiore, Moses, 3, 27, 106-107, 265
Morais, Sabato, 79, 111, 273
Moravia, 20
Moses, R.L., 25
Moss, Abraham, 124, 137, 147-148, 283
Munk, Elie, 165, 288
Munk, Eliyahu, 284
Muskin, Elazar, 223

New London Synagogue, 301

New Synagogue, 15, 55, 153
New West End Synagogue, 56, 82, 162, 231, 279, 286
New York, 78, 80, 85, 94, 96, 121, 160-161, 167, 197, 199
Newcastle, 15, 20, 148
Newman, Aubrey, 223-225, 299
Northern Ireland, 148

Observer, The, 162-163, 205
Oheb Zedek Congregation (New York), 80
Old Hebrew Congregation (Witwatersrand), 77
Old Paths, xxi, 286
Oppenheim, Simon, 17
Orach Chayim Congregation (New York), 77-78, 96, 276
Oral Law, 3, 216
Ornstein, Philip, 67, 77, 81, 271-272
Ottawa, 222, 302
Oxford University, 120, 270

Pack, Stephen, xv, 260
Palestine, 116-118, 127, 156, 257
Paneth, Philip, 258
Panim el Panim, 182
Paris, 12, 119, 288
Peace mission (Jakobovits), 184, 189
Penzance, 15
Philpot Street Synagogue, 79, 132
Piron, Mordechai, 223
Pluralism, xx, 239-241, 262
Plymouth, 15
Poets' Road Synagogue, 82
Poland, 45, 268
Poplar, 60
Portsmouth, 15
Porush, Israel, 116, 121, 163, 278, 279

Posen, 12
Prague, 12, 43
Prenzlow, 1
Priesthood, 30-31, 33, 60-61, 110, 209-210, 265, 277
Progressive Judaism, 220-221, 225, 235, 238, 297
Provincial Rabbinical Council, 226

Rabbinical Council of America, 222
Rabinovitch, Nachum, 248
Rabinow, S. 133
Rabinowitz, Louis Isaac, 163, 169, 180 seq., 186, 292
Rackman, Emanuel, 163-164
Radicalism, 88, 273
Ramsgate, 51
Ranke, Leopold von, xi
Rapoport, Abraham, 131, 184
Rapoport, Solomon Loeb, 43
Rav Rashi (Chief Rabbi, Federation of Synagogues), 199-200, 203-205, 219, 296
Recall to the Synagogue, 109, 276
Reform Judaism, xvii, xx, 1, 4, 44, 48, 66, 70, 78, 83, 219, 221, 226, 231-232, 237, 264
Reith Lectures (Sacks), 259
Riskin, Shlomo, 223
Rivkin, Moshe, 284
Rodrigues-Pereira, Robert, 223, 299
Rogosnitzky, B., 131
Romania, 91, 268, 270
Rose, Maurice, 201-202, 205, 291
Rosen, Bella, 124, 279
Rosen, Kopul, 110, 116, 123 seq., 129 seq., 146, 279, 281, 283
Rosenberg, Rosita, 238-239, 300
Rothschild, Lord (Nathaniel Mayer

de), xviii, 42, 46 seq., 67, 72 seq., 78, 84, 88 seq., 266, 269
Rothschild, Baron (Anthony Nathan de), 109, 265-266
Rothschild, Baron (Lionel de), 265-266
Rothschild, Edmund de, 170, 289
Rothschild, Evelyn de, 93
Rothschild, Leopold de, 266
Rothschild, Nathan Mayer, 266
Royal Air Force chaplaincy, 121
Rubin, S., 131
Russia, 45, 91, 101, 213, 251, 268, 294
Rutherford College, 120

Saadiah Gaon, 106
Sabbath Observance Organisation, 281
Sabbath-afternoon services, 66
Sacks, Dina, 248
Sacks, Elaine, 224, 244, 248
Sacks, Gila, 248
Sacks, Jonathan, xiii, xv-xvii, 222-223, 226 seq., 231 seq., 238 seq., 243, 261, 300
Sacks, Joshua, 248
Salaman, Redcliffe, N., 89
Salmon, J., 265
Samuel, Frank, 112, 117, 140
Samuel, Stuart M., 89-90
Sanderson, Harold, 238, 300
Schapp, Mrs Marcus, 267
Schechter, Solomon, 87, 273-275
Schiff, David Tevele, 1
Schiff, Otto, 89, 122, 279
Schism, xvii, xix, 2, 6, 27, 65, 190, 221, 253
Schleswig-Holstein, 269
Schloss, L., 49
Schochet, Yitzchak, xv-xvi

Scotland, 148
Secession, 4-5, 8, 13-14, 44, 50, 201
Second World War, xx
Segal, Moshe Yitzchak, 284
Selinger, Oscar, 89
Sephardi Beth Din, 44, 204-205, 269, 296
Shaftesley, John, 290
Shalom Hartman Institute, 298
Shashar, Michael, 300
Shazar, Shneur Zalman, 294
Shechitah, 10, 41, 46, 66, 143, 196, 201, 203-204, 219
Shulchan Aruch, xix, 71-72, 81, 116, 297
Shulman, Nisson, 223
Silverman, Alfred, 141-142, 172, 201-202, 282, 291, 295
Singer, A., 133
Six-Day War, 257
Solomon, Mrs Henry, 267
Soloveitchik, Joseph, 116, 121-123, 130-131, 162-163, 187, 279, 286, 288
Soloveitchik, Moshe, 121
South Africa, 78, 121, 162, 169, 229, 241-242, 275, 301
Southampton, 15
Southsea, 148
Spanish and Portuguese Jews' Congregation, 1-2, 47-49, 204, 269, 270, 273
Spital Square Synagogue, 46
St George's Settlement, 107
St John's Wood Synagogue, 82-83, 178, 181, 207, 228, 230, 247, 256, 298-299, 301-302
Stamford Hill, 107
Stamler, David, 283
Stanmore Synagogue, 227
Steinberg, Baruch, 284

Steinberg, Meyer, 184
Stepney, 60
Stepney Boys' Club, 279
Stepney Synagogue, 82
Stern, J.F., 71, 86
Stern, Samuel M., 283
Sternberg Centre for Judaism, 235
Sunday Times,The 181, 187, 221
Sunderland, 148
Super, Arthur Saul, 278
Swansea, 15
Swift, Harris, 298
Swift, Lionel, 228, 242, 298
Swift, Morris, 115, 132, 184
Switzerland, 179, 293
Sydney, Algernon, 90, 92
Sydney Beth Din, 292
Synagogue Council of Great Britain, 138
Szold, Henrietta, 102

Taylor, J.H., 140
Teck, Duchess of, 264
Tel Aviv, 154, 179
Temkin, Sefton D., 119, 278, 284, 297
Templeton Prize, 247
Tessler, Gloria, 288
Thatcher, Margaret, 242
Times,The, 85, 87, 179, 235-236, 237-238, 301
Traditional Alternatives conference, 226, 228, 240, 243, 259
Traditional Judaism, 106-107, 112, 153, 286-287
Treptow, 267
Trier, 124
Tuck, Adolph, 89-90
Turkey, xvi, 91
Twersky, J.H., 131

Union of Anglo-Jewish Preachers, 125-126, 129, 137, 140, 149, 171, 180, 183
Union of Jewish Students, 229
Union of Liberal and Progressive Synagogues, 176, 236, 297, 300
Union of Orthodox Hebrew Congregations, 201
United Synagogue, xiii, xv-xvi, xviii, xx, 40, 45-46, 55 seq., 66 seq., 69, 73 seq., 89, 91, 112, 123, 125, 144 seq., 153, 227
United Synagogue Rabbinical Council (Council of United Synagogue Ministers), xv, 171, 180, 183, 226, 231, 244, 261
University College London, 43, 120, 283
Unterman, Issar Yehudah, 187
Unterman, Maurice, 290

Vatican, 119
Vienna, 12
Vilna, 81
Voice of Jacob, xviii, 4, 11-12, 14-15, 17, 19, 22

Wagner, Leslie, 223-224, 244, 297, 299
Wales, 148
Waley Cohen, Robert, xix, xxiii, 108, 111 seq., 118 seq., 125 seq., 129 seq., 170, 282
War Office, 151
Warsaw, 121
Warzburg, 17
Washington, 172
Weber, I., 269
Weiss, Abner, 223, 231, 235, 299
Weiss, Isaac Jacob, 289
Wellhausen, Julius, 103

Werner, Abraham Aba, 46
West End (of London), 6, 266
West London Synagogue, 1, 8, 43, 47, 49-51
Western Jewish Girls Free School, 23
Western Synagogue, 8, 15, 129, 177, 263
Whitechapel, 46, 107
Wilson, Woodrow, 102
Wolf, Lucien, 89
Wolfson, Charles, 197
Wolfson, Isaac, 161 seq., 177 seq., 185 seq., 197, 202, 285-286, 293, 295
Wollstein, 7, 17
Woolf, Albert, 93
Woolf, Alfred, 163, 172
World Union of Progressive Judaism, 107
Worms, Henrietta, 266
Worms, Henry de, 42, 266
Wright, Aaron, 111, 123-124, 137 seq., 147, 283
Wurzheim, 269
Wyzanski, Charles E., 121-122, 279

Yeshiva University, 121, 288
Yiddish, xviii, 72, 84, 120
Yom Kippur War, 257
Yom Tob (Rabbenu) of York, 62

Zelig, Simcha, 125
Zichron Ephraim Congregation (New York), 80
Zionism, 106, 112, 232, 272
Zivotofsky, Ari Z., 281
Zondek, Hermann, 178, 291

Also by Meir Persoff

The Running Stag:
The Stamps and Postal History of Israel
(1973)

Immanuel Jakobovits:
a Prophet in Israel
(2002)

Faith Against Reason:
Religious Reform and the British Chief Rabbinate, 1840–1990
(2008)

Another Way, Another Time:
Religious Inclusivism and the Sacks Chief Rabbinate
(2010)

www.ingramcontent.com/pod-product-compliance
Lightning Source LLC
Chambersburg PA
CBHW021149230426
43667CB00006B/311